# BEHAVIOR MANAGEMENT

# BEHAVIOR MANAGEMENT

## THE NEW SCIENCE OF
## MANAGING PEOPLE AT WORK

LAWRENCE M. MILLER
**Behavioral Systems, Inc.**
**Atlanta, Georgia**

A WILEY-INTERSCIENCE PUBLICATION

**JOHN WILEY & SONS**, New York • Chichester • Brisbane • Toronto

**Library of Congress Cataloging in Publication Data**

Miller, Lawrence M., 1945–
  Behavior management.

  "A Wiley-Interscience publication."
  Includes index.
    1.  Personnel management.  2.  Psychology,
Industrial.  I.  Title.
HF5549.M476      658.3      77-28602
ISBN 0-471-02947-5

Printed in the United States of America

10  9  8  7  6  5  4  3  2  1

# FOREWORD

Quarterbacking a professional football team and managing an organization have a great deal in common. Both the quarterback and the manager are concerned with measurable results. Results are obtained through the performance of people, the members of the team. That performance is best defined in terms of behavior: who does what, when, and how often. To achieve the results for which he or she is accountable, the manager must be able to manage the behavior of the people who make up the team.

Since 1970 I have been involved in what I consider to be the most exciting development in management in many years: the application of a data-based, empirical approach to the management of people in the workplace. In more than 200 industrial and sales organizations our managers have established systems of behavior management that have demonstrated measurable economic benefits as well as improved job satisfaction. Behavior management identifies the conditions that the manager can control which produce both high motivation and high job satisfaction. It explodes the myth of the motivating manager as a cheerleader. Rather, it identifies the sure, systematic, and positive methods that produce behavior change and continued performance whether in organizations or in athletics.

Most of the 20,000 managers with whom we have worked continue to practice behavior management as a way of life, not because it is logical or sounds good, but because of their ability to measure the improved performance. It is rewarding to know the score. The ability to successfully manage behavior not only produces economic results but also makes the manager's job more enjoyable. Every manager enjoys the ability to obtain the desired performance and results from employees. Behavior management helps the manager achieve objectives by improving his or her management of human performance.

This book provides a thorough guide to the basic principles, research, and applications of behavior management. I am sure that you will find these as helpful as I have in both of my careers.

Fran Tarkenton

# PREFACE

The tools managers are given to manage the performance of their employees are inadequate. Widespread employee dissatisfaction, mounting concern among managers for increased productivity, and the worsening problems of turnover and absenteeism are evidence of the need for improved management of human performance. The tools managers need are not those requiring capital investment. Rather, they are the tools of knowledge—knowledge of why people perform.

During the last several decades managers have been fed a steady diet of theoretical, humanistic psychology that has not been well digested. This has not been well accepted for two reasons: first, managers know that they are accountable for performance, not for satisfying the inner needs of their employees; second, the tools provided by humanistic psychology have not produced results that justify the effort required for continued implementation of these theories.

Over the past few years the nontheoretical, empirically based approach to human behavior has been applied in more than 200 separate business and industrial settings and has produced both the performance demanded by the manager and the enhanced job satisfaction demanded by the employee.

There has been a need for a comprehensive description of the principles of behavior management applied to the work setting. This volume attempts this explanation, a description of basic techniques of

vii

application, and a report of a number of cases illustrating both the successes and failures of behavior management.

It is intended that this book will prove useful to the manager who may try to gain greater ability to manage the performance of his employees, the student of management, and the student of organizational psychology. The books that present the manager and student with an overview of psychological tools that may be applied to the workplace are predominantly based on the "soft approaches" to human behavior, those of Maslow, Herzberg, and McGregor. This is ironic, since business and management are generally concerned with hard measures of performance. For more than 20,000 managers trained in behavior management during the past few years, almost entirely by corporate consultants, the "hard approach" of behavior management has proved to be highly consistent with their well-founded insistence on measurable results and performance. It is hoped that this book will make these techniques available to more managers and students so that they may at least be given full appraisal.

This book could not have been written if it were not for the patience of my wife Carole, whose tolerance of my behavior borders on defying the very laws of behavior I have attempted to describe. I hope that I have not excessively deprived my two daughters Layli and Natasha. Many of the staff of Behavioral Systems, Inc., have contributed to this volume, either by the preparation of case studies or simply through the successful work they have performed for clients. None of this work would have come about if it had not been for the pioneering of Francis A. Tarkenton and Aubrey C. Daniels. But the greatest credit of all is undoubtedly due the many managers of client firms who have demonstrated not only that they have the ability to apply behavior management but also that, given powerful tools of control, they will use them for the betterment of employee and manager alike.

LAWRENCE M. MILLER

*Atlanta, Georgia*
*February 1978*

# CONTENTS

# BEHAVIOR MANAGEMENT

# INTRODUCTION

It is the task of management to make people and material resources productive. Management has become increasingly technological and sophisticated. Most of the technology and the sophistication have, however, been in material resources and in the management of finances, products, and other things. The management of people is still in the dark ages. Worse yet, management has been kept in the dark ages by unscientific, impractical, and academic theories of motivation. While producing precious little in measurable, documented improvements in either employee performance or job satisfaction, these theories and their gurus have consumed tens of thousands of valuable hours of management training.

The management community has virtually ignored the findings of empirical psychology, which has been built on the same technological methods that have produced the greatest gains in productivity in the material area. The findings of behavior modification or behavior management and the results of carefully measured empirical research not only contradict much of what is preached by the motivation theorists but also make practical sense. Empirical psychology has demonstrated what managers have known for a thousand years. People work for a payoff. Productive behavior is a function of the consequences following the behavior. If performance "matters" to the individual, the individual will perform. The job of the manager is to *make performance matter*. Call it the *payoff principle*, rewards and punishment, or the principle of reinforcement. The findings of behavior modification and behavior management have produced a system of applying the consequences of behavior in a way that produces maximum performance. This book is devoted to the proposition that both productivity and job satisfaction can simultaneously be increased through the application of a results-oriented, empirical, data-based system of management.

During the past several years the behavior management technology has been implemented in more than 200 organizational settings. Consistently, the results have demonstrated increases in both human performance and the satisfaction the individuals have derived from their work. The author is not a psychologist offering his theory of psychology to the manager. Rather, the author is a manager who has sought out principles of psychology that have demonstrated their value *to the organization* and its managers. This is a *manager's psychology*, not a psychology of management proposed by a psychologist hoping to change the direction and philosophy of the organization.

2

Do we need another theory of motivation and performance in organizations? Managers are currently trying to sort out the competing claims of Theory X and Theory Y, job enrichment, participative management, the management grid, organizational development, and numerous other theories and practices of management. Does behavior management simply add one more theory to the already overcrowded supermarket shelf of management psychology? No. It is a set of procedures, not a theory. The study of the effect of the environment on behavior has been well researched over the past thirty years. The conclusions regarding the effects of reinforcement and other procedures on behavior are no longer theories but are established bodies of science. The theories of motivation, such as Theory X and Theory Y, present broad and general assumptions about motivational states. Research that would establish these as a science does not exist.

Behavior management is distinguished from these other approaches to human performance by another characteristic. It is concerned with discrete relationships between specific events and behavior. To use a behavior management effort to change performance does not require an entire corporate commitment to years of job restructuring, alteration of decision-making patterns, or changes in the basic relationships between managers and employees. Whereas many of these changes may prove valuable, behavior management procedures, and resulting benefits in increased outputs, may be initiated on the level of one line supervisor and one line employee. On the other hand entire corporate commitments and systems of behavior management have been instituted and have affected the relationships throughout the organization.

Behavior management is, in large measure, a response to the needs of the manager. Other theories of behavior have failed to influence the manager because they have asked him to adhere to a philosophy of human nature often apparently inconsistent with his own experiences. These theories of management and behavior tell the manager how he should perform his job on the basis of what those theories believe to be a correct assumption about human nature. Behavior management asks the manager what performance of his employees, or himself, he would like to see improved. What change will be of benefit to him in the achievement of his objectives? Behavior management procedures then provide a method of achieving that change in behavior.

Although behavior management techniques may be applied on

an individual basis, the greatest benefits to the organization are derived from a total organizational effort, fully supported by a participating chief executive. The most successful programs have included the active participation of top management. The principle that behavior is maintained by reinforcement must be applied to all the behaviors at each level of management.

The behavior management approach to managing human performance attempts to be more scientific than many other procedures, both in the investigation and refinement of techniques and in their practical application. This emphasis on the measurement of effectiveness should not be alien to today's manager. It may appear alien because of its application to people. Today's manager is very aware of the value of measurements of performance, particularly in finances. Managers are more scientific in the management of money than in any other area of their job. Every well-run business carefully observes the financial data on investments, marketing procedures, new products, inventory, interests, and dozens of other variables. Decisions for future action are largely based on past performance in similar circumstances. The techniques of behavior management apply this same concern with measurable performance to human behavior.

Virtually all major corporations are investing heavily in the development of their human resources. Because of the importance of human performance to the economic success of the enterprise, chief executives are beginning to insist on some form of accountability in the human resource and management areas of their firms. This desire for economic accountability, as well as the increasing reports of measureable improvements in performance resulting from behavior management, is resulting in a dramatic increase in interest and activity in organizational behavior management.

The techniques and case studies described in this volume provide a guide to the manager and human resource specialist who is seeking to implement management procedures that at once measurably increase performance and job satisfaction.

**CHAPTER ONE**

**A NEW LOOK AT WORK
AND PRODUCTIVITY**

The management profession is changing. The manager of one hundred years ago would be lost in the management world today, as a pedestrian of a hundred years past would be lost on any city street today. Management has changed in many ways. A manager today has a vast source of information that was unthinkable in the past. Management is confronted with enormous technical innovations and competing social demands inconceivable a century ago. But perhaps an even greater change for management has been the changing perception of the worker. Today's work force is no mere tool of production. The worker has become a liberated person, demanding rights, job satisfaction, and input into the decision-making process (Terkel, 1972). On top of this, the manager has had to develop an increased awareness of human performance as a critical factor in the equation of the balance sheet. Profit or loss, survival or extinction, may be determined by the manager's skill at managing his "human resource."

Both the greater sensitivity of the work force and the increasing demands for performance necessitate new approaches to the management of people. This book represents one approach: behavior management. What is behavior management? It is the application of the empirical approach to psychology, behavior modification, to the performance of people in organizations. Behavior management is a new and developing science. As behavior modification has done in other settings such as mental health, schools, prisons, and child rearing (Kazdin, 1975; Hilts, 1974), behavior management applies the demands for empirical analysis of cause-and-effect relationships and reliance on measurable results to the organizational setting. Because of this insistence on hard evidence the techniques of behavior management are undergoing constant evalution and refinement. Moreover, because of this insistence on data, behavior management is having greater appeal to the manager who must justify his expenditures for training, management developments, and efforts to improve performance (Odiorne, 1970). The measurable results that must accompany every behavior management effort provide the means for economic evaluation by the manager with financial responsibility.

Given the number of books written on managing people in organizations, it might be concluded that there is a wealth of knowledge on the subject. This, unfortunately, is not the case. There does not yet exist a true science of managing people in organizations. There are literally dozens of theories, inadequately tested, that attempt to organize knowledge of human motivation and behavior. The large number of such theories is, in itself, testimony to the fact that a true science has not yet emerged (Kelly, 1969). This is, however, a period in which tremendous advances are being made. We are moving rapidly toward a science of human performance in organizations. The contributions to this development are coming from many directions: from academic investigations, from industrial efforts to maximize performance and to meet increasing demands of workers, and from increasing awareness of the work design, performance, and management/employee relations in other countries.

## BEHAVIOR MANAGEMENT AND SCIENTIFIC INQUIRY

The process of science is fundamental to the practice of behavior management. The methods of science not only are used to evaluate or research the results of behavior management techniques but also are basic ingredients in the routine application of efforts to improve human performance. During the past six years more than 20,000 supervisors have been trained in the techniques of behavior management. Each supervisor, as an element of his training, has initiated projects that include the collection of baseline data, the recording and graphing of that data, the use of an intervention procedure, and the evaluation of postintervention data. Few of these supervisors had a profound understanding of scientific methods. They were, however, taught and understood a fundamental method of scientific inquiry and were able to apply that method to their daily job performance.

It is a popular and unfortunate trend in contemporary society to be skeptical of science and even to deride its value as a source of solutions to current social problems. Increasingly, people are involving themselves in nonscientific or superstitious phenomena, such as astrology and certain healing practices that not only lack scientific support but also have been demonstrated to lack validity. This reaction against science may be due to the unfulfilled expectation that science would, in a short time, provide the solution to all man's sufferings. The failure has been in the unrealistic expectation rather than in the science. Where science has been applied diligently to problems that rightfully fall into areas in which the scientific method is applicable, such as the control of major diseases, and the physical sciences such as physics and

astronomy, the results have been impressive. The basic methods of scientific inquiry have produced the majority of the significant advances
in man's well-being during the past century.

Perhaps where science has been least efficacious is in the area
that concerns us most: human behavior and performance. We have not
begun to solve the problems of criminal or antisocial behavior. Our
mental hospitals are still overflowing with patients, and the anxieties
and distress experienced by a majority of our population still remain
areas for future progress.

Psychology today is not just one field of study. It is divided into
dozens of fields of inquiry, theories, competing schools of interest,
and divergent techniques. Psychologists run the gamut from those involved in highly methodical investigations with computer programming of pigeons pecking away at colored keys in cages to the intuitive
therapist encouraging his patient to engage in a primal scream. Somewhere in between these extremes of method there are beginning to
emerge some well-recognized and uniformly accepted principles. We
owe these principles largely to the empirical investigation of human
behavior conducted in many settings with a wide range of subjects.
Behavior management draws heavily from the reasearch with human
subjects in schools, mental hospitals, families, and other settings.

Because behavior management asks the manager to practice science in its basic form, it is important to understand the essential elements of science. Ernest Nagel (1967), a leading philosopher of science,
summed it up this way:

> The major impulse which generates science is the desire for ex-
> planations that are at once systematic and controllable by factual
> evidence. The distinctive aim of science is therefore the discovery
> and the formulation in general terms of the conditions under
> which events of various kinds occur, the generalized statements
> of such determining conditions serving as explanations of the cor-
> responding happenings. This goal can be achieved only by dis-
> tinguishing or isolating certain properties in the subject matters
> studied, and by ascertaining the repeatable patterns of depend-
> ence in which those properties stand to one another.

What is the subject matter being studied in behavior management? It is the behavior of people in their work settings. The aim of
behavior management is to discover "the conditions under which
events of various kinds occur," the conditions under which certain

types of behavior occur. Behavior management seeks to define those circumstances in which people are more likely to arrive to work on time, to continue to work on a given job, or to work more efficiently. Behavior management also seeks to determine the situations in which people enjoy working. The enjoyment of work is also a behavior. Perhaps most importantly, behavior management seeks to "ascertain the repeatable patterns of dependence" so that the conditions that influence behavior can be systematically managed to produce constant levels of performance.

This ability to produce repeatable patterns of behavior is of critical interest to the manager. The manager must be able to predict and control. He cannot be in the position of guessing how people will behave, any more than he can be in the situation of guessing how equipment will operate or what interest rates will be charged for his capital requirements. Yet the current position that most managers find themselves in is exactly that: guessing how the human behavior element of the production and profit equation will perform. Application of the methods of science produces data to indicate how people will behave in certain circumstances in the future. Because of the research already conducted on human behavior in the workplace, we know considerably more and we can predict and control to a much greater degree than we could just ten years ago.

Given the tools of behavior management, the manager is able to institute those conditions in his setting that more nearly approximate the ideal working situations in which people perform. Applying behavior management techniques regularly, the manager becomes precisely aware, by observation of the data, how his employees perform in certain environments. He is then able to alter conditions to improve performance in predictable ways and to predict how human performance will affect his enterprise in the future.

## FREEDOM, CONTROL, AND THE FUNCTION OF MANAGEMENT

Throughout this book I discuss methods of predicting, controlling, and managing human behavior. For many, there is an automatic negative response to such talk. B. F. Skinner (1972), in his book *Beyond Freedom and Dignity*, addressed this very issue at length. He attributes this response to the literature of freedom that has prepared us to respond positively to anything with the label "freedom" or "liberty" attached and to respond negatively to anything labeled "control." Skinner argues that we are rightfully opposed to negative forms of "control" such as dictatorship, mandatory requirements of various sorts, or even group or peer insistence on certain forms of behavior. On the other hand there are positive forms of control that go largely unnoticed and that affect the behavior of each of us. These forms arouse considerably less opposition.

Behavior management techniques focus on the positive forms of control of behavior in organizations. This focus is determined not only by the humanistic wishes of those who practice and advocate behavior management techniques but also by the empirical evidence indicating the desirability of positive forms of control. Positive control pays off for the controller and the controlee. An employee may be encouraged to improve his attendance by a supervisor who comments favorably on his attendance at the end of a week during which he was at work every day. This employee is now more likely to complete a second week with perfect attendance. This is beneficial to the manager and to the employee. The employee is more comfortable, satisfied, and happy with his job and himself. On the other hand, if the supervisor had chosen to exert negative control, punishing the employee after being absent from work, the results would have been very different. The employee may now avoid the work situation more often simply because of the punitive environment. This would have been the opposite of the manager's objective. The results of this approach would also have been less advantageous to the employee, who would have greater anxiety and negative emotions about his work and himself and would be less comfortable in the work setting. In addition to these effects of positive and negative control there are many generalizing effects. The worker who is more comfortable in his work environment is more likely to perform high-quality work, to make creative contributions, and to remain at his current job. Each of these results is of obvious benefit to the manager.

Through this discussion of behavior management techniques the advantages of conscious, planned, and positive forms of behavior control in the workplace will become evident, for worker and manager alike. The commonly perceived adversary relationship that exists between manager and employee is largely a function of the insistence on negative control. Under positive control many of the condtions that result in this adversary relationship break down. Everyone benefits— employee, manager, and owner.

Moreover, under the conditions of positive control, the objections to the "controlling" nature of behavior management become insignificant. Few people object to the controlling nature of a salary. The salary for which most of us work is a reasonably effective and stringent form of control. But because it is mutually agreed to, socially accepted, and positive, there are no objections. All behavior management procedures addressed in this volume and recommended for organizational application are aboveboard. There are no secretive or manipulative techniques. All the techniques are admittedly ones of influencing, managing, or controlling human performance. Control should not, however, be an objection if these techniques are implemented, as will be recommended, in a forthright, overt, and in many cases negotiated or participatory manner. After implementing behavior management procedures in more than 200 separate organizational settings, I can state that opposition to the techniques of control by those whom I have sought to influence, the employees, is extremely rare.

On a few occasions employees have reacted negatively to the use of behavior management procedures because, for the first time, they were being held accountable for results. But this is rare. The institution of behavior management programs almost always involves increased feedback to and reinforcement of employees. Feedback and reinforcement are probably the two elements that contribute most to a satisfying job. Some employees and managers have worked for years in an environment in which their performance was evaluated subjectively with no measurement of outcome, no stated levels of expected performance, and no consequence to the achievement of measured levels of performance. When systems that provide accountability are implemented, the employee or manager may react out of a fear that the new procedure will unjustly result in a negative evaluation of his performance.

Experience has shown that, once the system is in operation, and the individual has experienced the behavior management system, his fear is alleviated. In most cases these same employees become advocates of the system. I have often heard employees express the wish that these systems had been introduced years earlier, or I have received requests from employees in departments not included in a program to extend it to their work areas. In one unusual case of opposition an employee quit his job because he felt that "managers aren't supposed to go around praising workers, they're supposed to be tough." You can't please all of the people all of the time.

In several cases I have received more serious opposition to behavior management procedures from managers, owing to the issue of behavioral control. These managers were generally versed in the humanistic notion that efforts at control or "manipulation" are intrinsically "evil." However, the overwhelming majority of managers, after a period of training, have understood that the techniques of behavior management are simply more effective ways of performing the functions of control that they were already attempting in a less effective and less positive form.

The issue of control must also be viewed in terms of the selection of behavior to be changed. What behaviors may the manager rightfully attempt to manage? The answer to this lies in the implications of the employment contract itself. The employment contract, whether written or implied, generally states that the employee will behave in a certain manner, a manner that will produce some valuable result for the employer, and in return the employer will provide the payment of a certain amount of money and other benefits. The employer has a legitimate concern with those behaviors implied in this contract. All the behaviors that contribute to the productive aspects of the job, the speed at which the job is performed, the regularity with which the employee is in attendance at work, and the thoroughness or quality of the work performed are relevant to the contribution for which the employer has contracted.

Many behaviors do not fall into the legitimate purview of the manager. These are behaviors that do not relate directly to the productive contribution of the employee. Many managers, in attempting to follow fashionable trends in popular psychology, and in particular the "sensitivity" movement, have strayed beyond their sphere of legitimate concern. While it is valuable to be sensitive to the needs of his employees and to empathize with personal problems, the manager must not confuse his responsibility for performance with an irrelevant concern for private affairs. In group sensitivity or "laboratory training" the boundary between job-related behavior and medling in one's personal life becomes very hard to distinguish. The current theories of

management psychology have led to considerable confusion and misunderstanding about the skills required of the manager. Drucker re-
flects on this in his statement that,

> Managers show sound instincts in being leery. . . . The manager,
> if one listens to the psychologists, will have to have insight into
> all kinds of people. He will have to be in command of all kinds of
> psychological techniques. He will have to understand an infinity
> of individual personality structures, individual psychological
> needs, and individual psychological problems. He will, in other
> words, have to be omniscient. But most managers find it hard
> enough to know all they need to know about their own immedi-
> ate area of expertise, be it heat treating or cost accounting or
> scheduling (Drucker, 1974).

Although the techniques of behavior management are based on
psychological research, in no way is it intended that the manager
applying these techniques is to act as a psychologist. The psychologist
is primarily concerned with the personal interests of the individual, the
behavior and inner emotions that may be inhibiting the functioning of
that individual. The manager is concerned with the functioning of his
organization and with the behavior of the individuals within that
organization, only as those behaviors relate directly to the work
function.

The theory of behavior or personality that forms the basis of one's
approach to improving functioning of the people within an organization has an influence on the ability to distinguish between private
affairs and affairs of legitimate management concern. Theories of personality have become an interwoven element of our culture. We have
learned to label individuals according to our understanding of the
types of personalities and our interpretation of observed behavior.
We consider certain employees "neurotic," others "passive-aggressive,"
others to be speaking from their "child ego state," and we apply other
labels to individuals such as emotionally disturbed, lazy, or self-actu-
alized. If one adopts a "personality approach" to improving human
performance, the manager is confronted with the Sisyphean task of
altering the individual's personality before hoping to improve job performance. Entering into an attempt to alter the individual's personality
inevitably leads one into the private affairs of the employee.

The manager who believes that the path to improvement in human performance lies through the murky channels of personality change may soon recognize that a simpler solution is to drop efforts to change performance and simply replace the troublesome individual. That is, perhaps, the most prevelant response among industrial supervisors. It is easier to "get rid of 'em" than to "change 'em."

The behavior management approach to improving human performance provides far more distinct guidelines to the areas of legitimate management concern and private affairs. Behavior is discrete and distinguishable. The question "Does this behavior relate to the individual's productivity and therefore, that for which I am paying him, or is this none of my business?" can be easily answered. The time that an employee arrives to work is a legitimate concern. So, too, are the number of units of work produced, the number of specific objectives achieved, the amount of time spent in various productive and non-productive activities, and in certain jobs such as that of a sales clerk, the manner in which the clerk speaks to the customer, the facial expressions and tone of voice. All these behaviors and thousands more pertain to job performance. Behavior management procedures address these activities directly without attempting to alter underlying personality traits. Because the behavior manager addresses overt behavior directly, it may be argued that these techniques are less manipulative and controlling than those efforts that address the more generalized personality characteristics or motivation of the individual.

## REFERENCES

Drucker, Peter. *Management: Tasks, Responsibilities and Practices.* New York: Harper & Row, 1974.

Hilts, Philip J. *Behavior Mod.* New York: Harper Magazine Press, 1974.

Kazdin, Alan. *Behavior Modification in Applied Settings.* Homewood, Illinois: The Dorsey Press, 1975.

Kelly, Joe. *Organizational Behavior.* Homewood, Illinois: The Dorsey Press, 1969.

Nagel, Ernest. "The Nature and Aim of Science," in Sidney Morgenbesser (Ed.), *Philosophy of Science Today.* New York: Basic Books, Inc., 1967.

Odiorne, George. *Training by Objectives.* New York: The Macmillan Company, 1970.

Skinner, B. F. *Beyond Freedom and Dignity.* New York: Alfred A. Knopf, 1972.

Terkel, Studs. *Working: People Talk about What They Do All Day and How They Feel about What They Do.* New York: Pantheon Books, 1972.

# CASE STUDY NUMBER ONE
# IMPROVING ATTENDANCE

Parkdale Mills, Inc., in Lexington, North Carolina, was experiencing a rate of absenteeism that it considered unacceptable. Behavior manager Ed Fowler began a program to improve the declining rate of attendance. The problem was focused on the second shift in the carding department.

## BACKGROUND CONDITIONS

Baseline data on attendance were compiled averaging eighty-six-percent for a fifteen-week period. The shift could not operate efficiently at this level of attendance. Carding machines were sitting idle owing to the absence of operators. There were twenty-five employees and one supervisor in this department, and relations between them were satisfactory. The relationships among employees were satisfactory, except for minor, isolated incidents. It was, however, felt that there was a lack of teamwork and shift enthusiasm. Management generally worked toward molding the employees of a shift into a team with accepted goals. It was felt that this had not yet been accomplished on this shift.

During the baseline period, individual absentees were being reprimanded and workers who had good attendance records were not receiving any recognition for their attendance.

A goal was established to reach an average level of ninety-three percent attendance for three weeks.

## PROCEDURE

A visual feedback system and social reinforcement were identified as consequences that could be delivered contingent upon improved

15

attendance. A daily attendance chart was placed in the work area. Every employee's name was entered on the chart, and a blue dot was placed on the chart for each day that the employee was present and a red dot for each day that the employee was absent. A weekly attendance graph was also posted in the work area to indicate the percent of employees attending each day. The goal of ninety-three percent was indicated on the graph with a horizontal colored line.

Each worker reporting for work was verbally reinforced by the shift supervisor each day. When a worker was absent, he was welcomed back the next day and no reprimand was administered. The supervisor also encouraged each employee to look at the attendance chart and help the department reach its goal of ninety-three percent. The shift supervisor maintained the graph daily.

## RESULTS

From the baseline average of eighty-six percent, attendance began to rise immediately after the implementation of the program procedures.

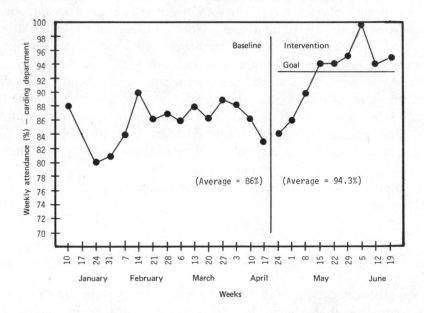

**Figure 1**   Attendance, carding department; Case Study 1.

For the following nine-week period attendance averaged 94.3 percent and attained one hundred percent for one week, a record never before attained. The supervisor reported that, in addition to the improvement in the measurable data, the employees were demonstrating a greatly improved enthusiasm and teamwork previously lacking. All the employees had expressed pride in their accomplishment and verbalized their commitment to continue this level of attendance.

The costs of this program were less than ten dollars. This cost was for graph paper and dots for the chart. Parkdale Mills, Inc., estimates that the absence of an employee costs them at least ten dollars per day. The program saved thirty dollars per day using this figure. This would result in an annual savings of approximately $9,000. Additional savings were realized but not computed in operating efficiency and reduced turnover, occurring as a result of the more positive atmosphere and behavior on this shift.

## DISCUSSION

This project is typical of hunderds that have been used in plants in which behavior management programs have been conducted. This program was relatively simple, straightforward, inexpensive, and effective. It demonstrated the impact of the supervisor's behavior on the behavior of his employees. The supervisor's behavior of graphing and charting the attendance levels, and more importantly, his social reinforcement of his employees improved their performance. This performance also produced a generalization effect to other behaviors such as turnover, enthusiasm, and departmental efficiency. The behavior manager who assisted the shift supervisor in designing and implementing this project reported that "The reaction of the people to improve their shift has been the most gratifying of all."

## QUESTIONS FOR DISCUSSION

1. Describe the manner in which data were used in this project. What was the effect of these data? What might have been the result if the data had not been put to use in this manner?

2.  Discuss the effect of this program on the "job satisfaction" of both the employees on the shift and the shift supervisor. Who benefitted from this program? How did they benefit?

3.  This procedure provided the shift supervisor with increased "control." How did this control affect the workers? Was this control increased at the "expense" of the workers or did they also benefit? Explain.

# CHAPTER TWO

# THEORIES OF BEHAVIOR:
# A MANAGER'S PERSPECTIVE

The actions a manager takes to affect the performance of employees is determined by his view of behavioral causation. Why do people behave the way they do? There is no period of human history, in which efforts were not made to answer this question. We can be sure that, long after our passing, our descendents will ask this same question and will undoubtedly view our answers as laughably primitive. Clear disagreements about the cause of human behavior can be traced to Plato, Aristotle, Socrates, and the Hebrew traditions. Some of the same sources of disagreement 2000 years past are to this day the subject of heated debate in academic circles.

Undoubtedly the greatest single source of debate in the search for principles or laws of behavior is the issue of internal (cognitive or mental) versus external (environmental) causation. Is behavior a direct result of environmental influence, or is it primarily under the control of internal forces of personality and motivation? Plato believed that behavior was the result of how people were taught by their educators and their social system. Plato set out therefore, to design the ideal social system, his Republic, in which optimum learning might occur. Aristotle viewed society as a result of the instinctive and unchanging nature of man. Behavior was the result of this inherited nature. These two views of the determinants of behavior, while somewhat modified and certainly decorated with dozens of supplemental theories, remain the essential distinctions between current theories of psychology. (Krasner and Ullman, 1973)

This book is not intended to serve as a review of previous psychological theories or management theories and practices. Rather, the intent is to present one theory and method that the author regards as most useful to the practicing manager. However, for perspective, a brief evaluation of these two approaches and their current application to management and organizations will prove useful.

## THEORIES OF INTERNAL CAUSATION

The internal approach is distinguished by the description of behavioral causes in terms of a state, motivation, process, or other explanation within the individual's mind or consciousness. Circumstances or events in the environment are not discounted. These external events have caused changes in the states of mind or consciousness that in turn affect behavior. The explanation is stated, not in terms of a direct relationship between the environmental event and the resulting behavior, but rather as a result of an internal state influenced by the environment. The question must be asked, "Do these internal mental states or conditions in fact exist?" and "Are explanations that rely on the use of these internal states more or less productive than those that describe behavior in terms of a direct relationship between the environment and the resulting behavior?"

The methods used by the manager to motivate and manage the performance of employees are influenced by the answer to this question. For example, if the manager feels that the performance of the salespeople is determined primarily by their internal state of motivation, he examines ways to improve that internal state. Sales managers for many years have conducted meetings to strengthen the internal motivation of their salespeople. At the end of these meetings the salespeople do appear to be more "motivated." They are visibly excited about the possibilities of their making more sales and are prepared to "charge out and sell that product!" The sales manager is satisfied that he has succeeded in creating an internal state of motivation. The degree to which this apparent internal state results in increased sales performance may go unevaluated. On the other hand the manager who believes there is a direct relationship between external environmental events and behavior focuses attention on those environmental events and the specific behavior to be influenced.

Until the past two decades views of behavior were concentrated on the cause and treatment of abnormal behavior. Normal behavior has been a subject of significant concern only recently. The early approaches to abnormal behavior were heavily influenced by religious conceptions. The idea of evil spirits within, possessing control over the individual, has been the basis of treatment in many cultures throughout human history. Cultures as diverse as the African tribal villager, the American Plains Indian, and the Western European of the Middle Ages contrived methods of warding off the evil spirits that might take hold of mankind. Many forms of exorcism have existed throughout the ages, and it is certainly one of the great contradictions of human progress that today, in the twentieth century, exorcism and the belief in possession by evil spirits have gained a relatively wide and active following. Fortunately, managers have not yet resorted to excorcising the evil spirits from their poor performers.

### The Medical Model

The most popular of the major influences in current psychological thought that may be viewed among the indirect approaches to behavior are the personality theories, derived primarily from the work of Sigmund Freud. Our entire culture has been strongly influenced by Freudian psychology. We have evolved a system of labels to describe the internal workings of the individual as we perceive them. It is even common to hear industrial supervisors discussing the ego states of an employee or the mental condition, the neurosis, of a manager. These views of the personality as an entity, with a distinct characteristic, have become an accepted part of our cultural foundation.

If the view is accepted that the cause of behavior lies "within" the personality, then abnormal behavior may be viewed as deriving from a diseased or unhealthy personality, while normal or healthy behavior may be viewed as a function of a healthy or well-constructed personality. This view is often referred to as the "medical model" of psychology because of its application of the analogy of physical health and illness.

In medicine an external symptom, such as a skin rash, a fever, or an uncomfortable feeling, is the result of some internal malfunction such as a bacterial or viral infection or a disease. The illness is not healed by treating the symptom. An aspirin that may reduce a fever does not cure the illness of cholera. The medical doctor must go beyond the symptom, the observable event that calls attention to the illness, to the underlying cause.

Freud and others of his period, trained in medicine, were quick to assume that the same model could be applied to human behavior. An undesirable behavior, such as feelings of intense anxiety, must be caused by some underlying circumstances, an illness. Freud argued that treating the symptom, the behavior, directly would only result in another symptom's appearing and would not result in a resolution of the underlying cause. Freud attributed the underlying cause to the individual's personality. A troublesome behavior was not to be treated directly but was merely a distressing symptom of an underlying defect in the personality.

Without ever witnessing any element of the sick personality in a microscope (although Freud did draw a picture of the ego; it looks peculiarly like an Idaho potato) Freud developed a system of diagnosis and treatment, attributing all overt behavior to some unconscious personality process.

Whereas this model of symptom and disease has proved effective in the medical field, its results in the field of human behavior have been disappointing. Treatment derived from the Freudian perception of human behavior has not proved successful in solving the problems of abnormal behavior (Stuart, 1970), and there is no reason to believe that in the more complex world of organizational behavior the confusing and uncertain applications of the medical model hold any greater promise.

A current and popular reformulation of Freudian psychology is found in Transactional Analysis. Transactional Analysis asserts that each individual is characterized by three "ego states." These three ego states are the Parent, Adult, and Child. Our behavior, particularly our interpersonal behavior, may be explained in terms of the ego state "from which we are speaking." Thomas A. Harris, in his popular *I'm OK–You're OK*, tells us that

> continual observation has supported the assumption that these three states exist in all people. It is as if in each person there is the same little person he was when he was three years old. There is also within him his own parents. These are recordings in the brain of actual experiences of internal and external events, the most significant of which happened during the first five years of life. The first two are called Parent and Child, and the third, Adult (Harris, 1967).

Eric Berne, the originator of the theory of Parent–Adult–Child Ego States, goes even further in proclaiming the material reality of these interpretations of behavior: "Parent, Adult and Child are not concepts like Superego, Ego, and Id . . . but phenomenological realities" (Berne, 1961). So we are asked to believe that these states exist, in reality, somewhere within our being, recording and playing back previous experiences as a tape player would play back an audio recording.

Transactional Analysis (TA) has been popular in communication or interpersonal relations training. TA has been applied increasingly to sales training to help salespersons communicate more effectively with their clients. It is asserted "that TA is a theory of personality and a system of communication . . . that can help you become more open in your dealings with your clients and other people in your life, help

you read reactions accurately, and give you increased self-confidence"
(Corporan, 1975). The advocates of TA further claim that this training
will help you "know where a client is; that is, learning to read him or
her more intelligently, and then responding to that reading, improves
closing ratios, lowers complaints, and raises renewals" (Corporan,
1975).

It is entirely possible that being able to categorize a statement
made by another person as "coming from his Parent" may help in
formulating a response that will lead to improved interactions, although
there is little research to indicate that this is in fact the case. Most
evaluations of the application of TA in industry are characterized by
anecdotal reports such as "Since the implementation of this type of
sales development program in our organization, we recieve almost
daily calls during which a salesperson will reveal with considerable
excitement: 'Hey, this P-A-C stuff really works'" (Mandia, 1974). For
any training, development, or performance improvement programs,
there will be reports of its "working." It feels good to be able to explain
why someone is behaving the way he is. The individual salesperson,
for example, may feel that he has benefitted from TA training because
he is now able to apply the label of Parent, Adult, or Child to the
behavior of his client. Whether or not this ability actually results in
improved closing ratios is another matter entirely. Only the empirical
analysis of data on closing ratios, before and after training, given
necessary controls and replication, can demonstrate that this training had an economic benefit to the organization.

I was once told by a trainer that he was very impressed by TA
because it had a lasting effect. This aroused my interest because I was
aware of very little evidence that TA had any effect at all on measurable performance in an organization. I asked him why he thought this.
He reported that a year ago his organization had undergone a group
TA training program. Just last week in a meeting one of his department
managers had become upset and somewhat aggressive toward another
member of the group concerning some decision that had been made.
The manager, toward whom the frustration was directed, coolly pointed
out to the first manager that he was addressing him from his Parent
Ego State. This impressed the trainer as the "lasting effect." While this
may be a lasting effect, it is not the effect in which the organization
has an investment. The behavior of pointing out which ego state someone is speaking from is not the goal of any training program, even a

training program in TA. The goal of an industrial training program must be to change behaviors that result in some improved functioning of the organization. The trainer had no idea at all what functions of the organization might be improved by TA and whether or not that had occurred to begin with, or whether it had a lasting effect on that functioning.

One of the problems with training programs directed at internal processes such as ego states, emotions, or motivation is that they lead to evaluations equally indirect. The ability to identify ego states becomes the goal and the subject of evaluation, rather than actual improvements in performance. Unless a direct relationship can be established between a training procedure and improved output, the intelligent manager will do well to steer clear of that training procedure.

This inability to evaluate procedures properly stems from the formulation of the theory itself. Thomas A. Harris reported that "continual observation has supported the assumption that these three states exist in all people." Laypeople may be impressed by the authoritative sound of this statement. However, the statement could similarly be made that "continual observation of voodoo rituals has supported the assumption that voodoo effects a profound change in the personalities of those participating." This statement is equally true. In fact, it is probably more true than the first statement. Contrary to Harris's statement, there is no evidence at all that these three states exist within the individual. Both Harris's statement and the statement about voodoo are based on speculations about the relationship of environment to internal process to behavior. Neither statement provides any evidence that a specific procedure will effect any specific change in performance. And the question must be asked, "Is that change in performance one that you desire for your organization?"

Although TA may improve the ability of some individuals to communicate more effectively, the reference to ego states is merely a convenient method of categorizing patterns of behavior. The individual is not, in fact, "speaking from his Child Ego State." There is absolutely no evidence that any such state exists. There is also a well-demonstrated danger in labeling individuals. Application of a label to a pattern of behavior, whether it is a personality label such as neurotic, or an ego state label, has potentially negative effects that may create more problems than may be solved by the convenience of labeling (Stuart, 1970).

### Trait Theory

A second set of internal explanations for behavior embraces the theories of "traits." Traits are used to describe observed patterns or sets of behavior. We may refer to an individual as lazy, another as ambitious, and another as aggressive. The traits are useful if they are understood to refer to a pattern of overt behavior, rather than an internal state that may explain the external behavior. We infer a state of aggressiveness following our observation of behavior that we consider to be aggressive. We have evidence only for the aggressive behavior itself. We have no support for the presence of a "state of aggressiveness" within the individual that may be used as an explanation for the overt behavior.

Skinner describes how we initiate trait names as adjectives and evolve them to become nouns. He uses the example of "narcissism." We began by observing a preoccupation with a mirror, which recalled the legend of Narcissus. We invented the adjective "narcissistic" to describe the behaviors indicating admiration for oneself. We then evolved the noun "narcissism" to describe this state of self-admiration. We then finally assert that the thing referred to by the noun is the cause of the behavior with which we began. Narcissism becomes the cause of narcissistic behavior. At no point is there any demonstration of a causal relationship between the "narcissism," the internal state, and the behavior of self-admiration (Skinner, 1953).

The acceptance of trait explanations for human behavior is extremely popular among managers and supervisors, particularly when referring to individual performance. There is a certain comfort in the acceptance of traits as a causal explanation. If an employee is "lazy," you need not look further for an explanation for his poor performance. You may then assert that the "blame" for the poor performance lies within the individual, freeing the manager from responsibility for that performance. We have often heard supervisors assert that there was nothing wrong with their supervision and that their only problem was that their employees "didn't have any motivation." What can a good supervisor do with employees who lack the trait of motivation? Similarly, if we can argue that an employee possesses an "aggressive trait" we need not look any further for the cause of his aggressive behavior. We are freed from the responsibility that would be present if we accepted that some element in the environment, over which we might have control, was the cause of the aggressive behavior.

Kazdin (1975) argues that there are three reasons why traits present an inadequate explanation of behavior. First, traits are inferred from the behavior. The trait that has been inferred from the behavior is used to account for the behavior. This is circular reasoning and an inadequate explanation for the presence of traits. Second, the evidence suggests that people do not perform consistently across situations, as would be expected if the trait were an internal condition. Much behavior occurs only under specific situations; as the situation changes, so does the behavior. Third, there are no antecedent conditions to explain traits. If traits explain behavior, what explains traits (Kazdin, 1975)?

## Theories of Motivation

Most popular among managers, trainers, and human resource specialists are the motivation theories based on the work of Abraham Maslow, Frederick Herzberg, and Douglas McGregor. Whereas motivation theories are based on a perception of the interaction between the individual and the external environment, they are considered an internal motivational state, need, or drive. Rather than attempt to explain the behavior as a direct function of an environmental event, they assert that, somewhere between the occurrence of an event or circumstance in the environment and the behavior, there is an arousal or change in a state of motivation. This state is presumably within the individual.

The works of Herzberg and McGregor are built on the foundation laid by Maslow. Maslow summarized his theory in the following points:

> (1) There are at least five sets of goals which we may call basic needs. These are briefly, physiological, safety, love, esteem, and self-actualization. (2) These basic goals are related to one another, being arranged in a hierarchy of prepotency. This means that the most prepotent goal will monopolize consciousness and will tend of itself to organize the recruitment of the various capacities of the organism. The less prepotent needs are minimized, even forgotten or denied. But when a need is fairly well satisfied, the next prepotent ("higher") need emerges to dominate in turn the conscious life and to serve as the center of organization of behavior, since gratified needs are not active motivators (Maslow, 1943).

What's wrong with postulating the existence of "needs"? A more useful question would be "Why postulate the existence of needs?" In science there is a principle often referred to as the "Law of Parsimony," which states that the simplest, most direct explanation for a phenomenon is the best explanation. No process, matter, activity, or presence should be presumed if there is a more simple explanation for an event and if there is no evidence to support the existence of that process, matter, activity, or presence. Not that this law has not been routinely violated throughout history. It has been particularly violated in the explanation of human behavior. As recently as 1911, Dr. Charles Williams, a London physician, vigorously defended the idea that mental illness was caused by demons who possessed the body of the patient (Whaley and Surratt, 1968).

The need for parsimony and the difficulties that may arise when intervening explanations for events are unjustifiably presented may best be understood if we leave the difficult world of human behavior.

Imagine that an individual takes an apple off an apple tree, eats that apple, and becomes deathly ill. Let us assume that several individuals eat other apples from this tree and also become ill. How may we explain this phenomenon? We may explain it by stating that the eating of apples from this tree produces the result of illness. Or we may explain it by stating that the apples from this tree possess a spirit that when entered within the body produces the reaction of illness. The spirit is an intervening explanation for the observed interaction between the eating of the apple and the illness. It provides an explanation for "why" the illness occurs from eating the apple; however, there is no support for the existence of such a spirit. This explanation is not parsimonious. It is parsimonious simply to state that the eating of the apples from this tree, the observed cause, produces the observed reaction, the illness.

This is not to deny that a further explanation may exist, such as the presence of a bacterium or virus within the apple. This explanation must, however, be demonstrated by some evidence beyond the mere observation of the eating and the resulting illness.

No evidence for the existence of any motivational state or need has ever been presented that cannot more parsimoniously be explained as the simple outcome of a direct cause. Specifically, Maslow asserts that there are five needs: physiological, safety, love, esteem, and self-actualization and that man's action (or consciousness, another unnecessary intervening explanation) are dominated by a lower need until that need is satisfied. It is undoubtedly true, and research substantiates the fact that, given the deprivation of hunger, for example, a physiological need, and love, one of the higher needs, a person is more likely to respond to satisfy his hunger, or need for eating, than to satisfy his need for love. Maslow explains this by stating that the lower need is "the most prepotent goal that will monopolize consciousness and will tend to organize the recruitment of various capacities of the organism" (Maslow, 1943). This can, however, be explained more parsimoniously simply by stating that, given a set of circumstances in which a person has been deprived of food and of personal attention, he is more likely to behave in a manner to obtain food than personal attention. An external cause, the enviornmental set of events, is present and a behavior results. There is no reason to assert the presence of an internal need.

Maslow's hierarchy of needs may be useful in understanding that, given various states of deprivation, a person responds in different ways and that it is useful to consider the nature of deprivation in understanding human behavior. However, the imposition of a need not only results in a great deal of unnecessary academic hypothesizing but also leads one to attempt to identify solutions to problems of behavior that may be less than effective. How many industrial supervisors, when instructed in Maslow's hierarchy of needs, have reacted with a silent "so what?" What is the supervisor supposed to do with this information? Provide food, safety, love, esteem, or self-actualization to his employees? These concepts are of far more value to the academic, who has the luxury of floundering in ineffective hypotheses. The manager wants to know what he should *do* to produce a *result* directly and immediately. The difficulty with the theories of work motivation based on Maslow's need hierarchy is that they have built theory on top of theory, attempting to come back to a point of understandable action. Many well-intentioned managers have been lost in the process.

Frederick Herzberg developed the Motivation–Hygiene Theory to explain the relationship between Maslow's needs hierarchy and the job situation (Herzberg, 1966). Herzberg proposed that there were essentially two types of needs relating to the work situation, each of which functioned in a different manner. The first set of needs he called hygiene factors. The presence or absence of these hygiene factors operates to prevent or remove obstacles in the work environment rather than motivate or improve performance. He related these hygiene factors to the lower needs: physiological needs, safety, and love. The conditions that fall within Herzberg's hygiene category include company policy and administrative practice, supervision, interpersonal relationships, working conditions, salary, status, and security. According to Herzberg, these conditions all create dissatisfactions. The second set of conditions he referred to as the motivator factors. These needs concern the higher level needs of esteem and self-actualization. Herzberg maintained that it was these higher level needs, the motivator factors, that would lead to high levels of performance. Application of this theory to the work environment has been based on the idea that the satisfaction of higher level needs is far more likely to lead to high performance than the satisfaction of lower level needs. The efforts to satisfy these higher level needs of esteem and self-actualization have led to the development of the procedures referred to as "job enrichment."

Research has been conducted to substantiate the claim that workers are more likely to respond to the satisfaction of the higher level than the lower level needs. But the research demonstrates that the types of rewards that motivate workers differ greatly between highly skilled and lower skilled workers. The higher skilled workers are more motivated by the intrinsic rewards of their jobs (related to the higher level needs of esteem and self-actualization), while the lower skilled workers are more motivated by the external rewards of the job: pay, security, and so forth (Centers and Bugental, 1966).

Human beings behave in a manner to obtain what they lack. Depriving a person of any pleasurable stimulus, such as food or warmth, results in behaviors attempting to remove that state of deprivation. In our society a person is generally not deprived of the physiological needs of hunger, warmth, and so forth. Therefore, he will emit little behavior to obtain what he already possesses. The hygiene factors that Herzberg identified and claimed do not result in high levels of performance are those categories of environmental events that a person is not deprived of in our culture. If a person is not deprived of safety, he will not perform at high levels to obtain safety. Herzberg was correct in his assertion that these hygiene factors, or the sets of environmental events that meet these needs, do not result in high levels of performance. This is true simply because the individual is not deprived of these factors. The importance of deprivation is demonstrated in the studies that show the varying degrees to which workers are motivated by different motivational forces. Workers are consistently motivated to achieve what they lack.

The motivator factors that Herzberg described, the needs of esteem and self-actualization, describe events of which man is commonly deprived. What is esteem? Esteem is a good feeling that results when someone else makes a positive comment about your work, when your work results in a set of general reactions to you because of your "status," or when others demonstrate their respect for you. Esteem is not a mysterious inner need. It is an internal response resulting from the behaviors of others toward you. You may be said to "have esteem" when others behave in this manner and when you experience the resulting emotional responses.

What is self-actualization? Self-actualization is the individual's response to obtaining rewards identified with the individual's own development. For example, an engineer may experience a "sense of self-actualization" when he is assigned the first project for which he is to be in charge and over which he may have the decision-making responsibility. Self-actualization may also be experienced when a woman, previously in a clerical position, experiences the rewards following a promotion to office manager. These rewards have the effect of increasing performance. They increase performance because there has been deprivation of this reward. However, once the engineer has been in charge of ten projects, he will no longer experience the same "sense of self-actualization" upon being assigned a project. This is now a reward that does not occur in a state of deprivation. The hygiene factors, those that satisfy the lower level needs, rarely occur when the individual is deprived of hunger, safety, or love. All factors that may at some time result in increased performance must be viewed in terms of the degree of their deprivation. If there is no state of deprivation, no behavior or performance results to obtain the reward, regardless of whether it falls into the category of motivation or hygiene factors. Rather than attempt to identify which factors are motivators and which are hygiene, which needs are satisfied and which are not, the manager might ask the more parsimonious question: "For what consequence will this individual work?" The answer provides the basis for direct, simple, and workable performance improvement programs.

Job enrichment techniques have sought to change the structure and definition of jobs to provide more satisfaction, or rewards from the job itself, rather than from external rewards. Some of the advocates of job enrichment have clearly seen this effort in light of man's deprivations and efforts to obtain the rewards for which he is still deprived. M. Scott Meyers (1970) states that

Primeval man's efforts were directed primarily toward survival needs—safety, food and shelter—leaving little time or energy for preoccupation with his latent higher order needs. As his survival needs were satisfied, he became sensitized to social and status needs. Finally, in the affluence of recent decades, these lower order or maintenance needs are being satisfied to the point that he is ready to realize other potential, to experience self-actualization in terms of intellectual, emotional, and aesthetic growth, or to satisfy his motivation needs (Meyers, 1970).

While this analysis relates the changing nature of the goals of mankind's behavior to the internal needs, it nevertheless correctly points out the understanding that mankind is not, generally, deprived of those factors that previously created what Maslow termed the lower order needs. Today, to increase motivation, efforts must be made to make available rewards that satisfy a need that exists or to overcome a state of deprivation. Lack of satisfaction from the job is one such state of deprivation, and job enrichment efforts are designed to increase this satisfaction.

Job enrichment efforts have resulted in increases in performance (Maher, 1971). Job enrichment is, however, suffering from the inadequacies of the theory on which it is built. Because it has been built on a theory of indirect causation, that a person responds when his needs are being satisfied, the efforts at job enrichment have not adequately analyzed which specific circumstances in the environment, when changed, results in which specific changes in performance. Most descriptions of job enrichment portray complex changes in the environment. For example, supervisors may be trained to understand the various needs to which their employees may be responding: The jobs may be changed to increase the variety of tasks performed and the decision-making processes may be changed to provide for greater employee input. These changes involve many complex modifications in the human interactions, as well as the person/job interactions. It is very difficult, if not impossible, in most of these experiments to identify what change caused what effect on performance.

A study reported by Earl D. Week, Jr., from Texas Instruments, Incorporated, provides a fine example of the multitude of interventions that make up a job enrichment effort (Weeks, 1971). This report deals with the "enrichment" of the cleaning service jobs at Texas Instruments. The data reported resulting from these changes clearly show an improvement in performance relative to the data before the job enrichment program. But the factors changed included the following: (1) The service was changed from an outside contractor to an internally managed service; (2) wages were increased for performance of the same jobs; (3) supervisors were carefully selected and trained in the techniques of developing teamwork; (4) jobs were redesigned so that individuals would have a role in the planning and control of their work; (5) a new employee orientation and training program was instituted; (6) a quarterly orientation program was initiated; (7) weekly team meetings were begun; and (8) a cleaning services recruiting program was undertaken to ensure a reservoir of "good people to fill vacancies."

The results of this effort were a reduction in the number of people required to perform the job, reduced quarterly turnover rate, and improved cleanliness ratings. But what changes caused what result? Does this case, or the many others like it, demonstrate that "job enrichment" results in the satisfaction of needs, which in turn results in improved performance? Frankly, this study does not demonstrate anything beyond the fact that a similar change in all eight of the variables altered is likely to result in a similar change in the three outcome variables affected. And the evidence for this assumption is weak because there is no demonstrated control or replication, essential elements of any empirical investigation of behavior. [The author of this study views the matter quite differently: "It is becoming increasingly obvious that the need to experiment to test the theories of McGregor [and others] should come to an end. All excuses and rationalizations for not implementing these concepts have been surfaced and worn thin. . . . It is time for all managers to gain insight into these behavioral concepts, to creatively implement them and to be measured on their success with the same degree of discipline as that demanded by a profit and loss statement" (Weeks, 1971).]

Another difficulty with current job enrichment efforts is that they seek to create an environment in which the employee's needs are being met, rather than one in which the employee can work to earn the satisfaction of his needs. If the environment created is one in which the employee's needs are met, regardless of his own efforts to meet those needs, there is little motivation for him to work harder, faster, or better. Improved performance may result from efforts to obtain a reward, or if you prefer, to satisfy a need. There is, however, little evidence that any individual works harder when rewards are delivered without regard to performance. On the contrary, much evidence exists that people work to obtain rewards, and once the reward has been delivered, a reduced rate of work may be expected until the individual is again working in anticipation of a reward.

The job of the manager is to achieve the objectives of his business or organizational unit. The manager is responsible for performance, not for satisfying needs. If the manager embarks on a job enrichment program, he should carefully assess his own motivation. Is he implementing such a program to improve performance? Or is he simply doing so because it is the "right" thing to do? The philosophy of job enrichment and the functions of the manager in relation to his employees are an important consideration. Robert N. Ford, one of the first and most nearly comprehensive researchers in job enrichment, has stated:

> The "right reason" for trying to improve the work itself for every human being in the business is simply because he is a human. The fact that this program appears to be cost free does not alter the fundamental assumption. A business owes the employee the most satisfying work it can give him within the limits of staying in business (Ford, 1969).

Efforts to provide satisfying work have often proved ineffective because they have assumed that, if a state of satisfaction exists, employees perform well. This places satisfaction first and performance second. Systems that have succeeded in improving performance and satisfaction have placed performance first, with satisfaction or rewards following and contingent upon the desired performance.

The implications of the concept that a "business owes the employee the most satisfying work it can give him within the limits of staying in business" are profound. The manager who does accept this premise had best think this through to its logical conclusions, namely, that the business exists to provide satisfaction to the employee. If job enrichment is founded on this assumption, then increases in performance are only interesting, not essential. This is not to argue against providing a satisfying job. It is, however, a good policy because it is more desirable to have employees who enjoy their work than employees who do not, both because it is humanitarian and because it is good business. It must be demonstrated that more satisfying jobs contribute to the organization's achieving its objectives. A manager must pursue a management policy because it makes "business sense," because of its economic implications, both in the short and long range, not because he owes such a policy to his employees. It is one of the more popular myths that there is a contradiction between systems that demand performance and those that provide satisfaction. The system that provides satisfaction or reward contingent on performance can fulfill the interests of both.

If the manager, management, development expert, trainer, or whoever is attempting to implement organizational change approaches the task from the standpoint of helping the organization achieve its objective, the successful performance of its mission, then the effort can and will be measured in terms of its contribution to the purpose of the organization. If, however, the individual attempting to initiate organizational change approaches the task from the standpoint that the organization owes a certain type of job or satisfaction to anyone, worker or manager, then the effort is likely to fail.

There is much that is valuable and productive in the job enrichment movement. Any procedure or set of procedures that succeed at increasing productivity or job satisfaction to any degree should be examined carefully to identify which elements result in which changes. These elements should then be carefully adopted elsewhere, while continuous emipirical evaluation is conducted.

It is only logical that everyone benefits from work that is more intrinsically rewarding. No manager or employer would choose to make work dull. M. Scott Meyer makes an interesting analogy between work and play (Meyer, 1970). He asks why bowling (or any game) is fun. His answer is the following seven characteristics of bowling: (1) The bowler has a visible goal; (2) he has a challenging but attainable goal; (3) he is working according to his own personally accepted standards; (4) he receives immediate feedback; (5) he has opportunity to satisfy social needs; (6) he is an accepted member of a group; (7) he can earn recognition. These characteristics fairly well describe the conditions that job enrichment seeks to create. But to do so and to cause the resulting improvements in performance, there is no reason to muddy the waters with theories about needs, motivators, hygiene factors, and so on. These explanations merely create confusion, obstacles to understanding, evaluation, and acceptance.

During the late 1950s Douglas McGregor proposed an additional set of theories about human motivation and management. He argued that there were two general approaches to management based on two views of human nature. He called them Theory X and Theory Y (McGregor, 1960).

McGregor argued that Theory X, the management practice most common, was characterized by the following assumptions: (1) Management is responsible for organizing the elements of production; (2) with respect to people, management must motivate, control, and generally manage their behavior to fit the needs of the organization; (3) without this intervention by management, people would be passive, or resistant, to organizational needs. They must therefore be persuaded, rewarded, punished, controlled—their activities must be directed. These three assumptions are reasonably accurate. Managers have operated on these assumptions for centuries, contrary to the popular view, and continue to operate on them, *correctly*.

McGregor went a step further. He added to these assumptions, which the overwhelming majority of managers have found effective, his value-loaded interpretation. He claimed that the first three assumptions implied several others: (4) The average man is by nature indolent and works as little as possible; (5) he lacks ambition; (6) he is inherently self-centered, indifferent to organization needs; (7) he is resistant to change; (8) he is gullible, not very bright, the ready dupe of the charletan and the demagogue.

In defense of McGregor it must be said that he made his assumptions at a time when it was in vogue, particularly in academia, to assume all good things about anonymous individuals, workers in particular, and to assume all negative things about "the system," business and management. It is hard to imagine that many managers, who did accept the first three assumptions, would have recognized the following five assumptions. McGregor referred to this set of assumptions as Theory X.

McGregor's analysis of the effectiveness of these Theory X assumptions and his view of their consequence are grim, indeed:

> Management by direction and control—whether implemented with the hard, the soft, or the firm but fair approach—fails under today's conditions to provide effective motivation of human effort towards organizational objectives. It fails because direction and control are useless methods of motivating people whose physiological and safety needs are reasonably satisfied and whose social,

egoistic and self-fulfillment needs are predominant (McGregor, 1970).

By McGregor's own analysis most managers were (are) operating on Theory X. With that amount of failure, and useless methods of motivating people, it is a miracle that business and organizations in our society have remained productive at all. By McGregor's analysis chaos and anarchy should have prevailed. They have not, and McGregor's analysis of Theory X and its implications was incorrect.

McGregor proposed an alternative to Theory X, Theory Y. Of course, if the assumptions about Theory X are incorrect, then the need for a Theory Y is questionable at the outset. Theory Y is based on the following assumptions: (1) Management is responsible for organizing the elements of production; (2) people are not by nature passive or resistant to organization needs but become so as a result of experience; (3) the motivation, the potential for development, the readiness to direct behavior toward the fulfillment of organizational goals are present in people and it is the responsibility of management to make it possible for people to recognize and develop these human characteristics for themselves; (4) the essential task of management is to arrange organizational conditions and methods of operation so that people can achieve their own goals best by directing their own efforts toward organizational efforts. McGregor states that this is a process of "creating opportunities, releasing potential, removing obstacles, encouraging growth, providing guidance" (McGregor, 1970).

The burdens and responsibilities that McGregor attempted to place on the shoulders of the manager are unrealistic, and the manager will recoil against them. Perhaps it is for this reason that McGregor's theories have not stood up to empirical investigation (Luthans and Kreitner, 1975).

Theories that demand heroics on the part of the manager are doomed to failure. The manager is busy. His primary function is to achieve the objectives of his organization, and human needs must be satisfied in the process of fulfilling the manager's primary responsibilities. How many managers will "conceive of their job as helping each of his subordinates to achieve their mutual goals in the subordinate's own way" (Gellerman, 1963)? This would be an enormous task for a trained psychologist in a controlled setting, never mind a manager, with little training in psychology and little time or motivation to conceive of his job in this manner.

Saul W. Gellerman calls the managers to heroism:

> This is where heroism comes in: To effectively implement Theory
> Y the manager must learn what impressions he actually makes on
> others, why he affects them in this way, and what some of his
> own motives are for dealing with them as he does. Before he can
> deal sensitively with others, he must become a lot more sensitive
> to himself. He must grow personally to a considerably greater
> stature, in terms of self-awareness and self-acceptance, than most
> people ever have to. Unless he does this, he will constitute a
> bottleneck in the whole process of releasing suppressed motiva-
> tion that Theory Y prescribes (Gellerman, 1963).

Is a manager hired and paid to perform such heroics? Better to be a
successful manager, who achieves his own goals and the goals of his
organization, than a heroic one who attempts to fulfill McGregor's
utopian vision, but who may fail to achieve the goals of his organization in the process.

How does one become a Theory Y manager, if it is accepted that
the theoretical basis for Theory Y is valid and that behaving in the
manner that McGregor described will result in some increase in performance? The method of becoming a Theory Y manager has most
often focused on the development of the personal qualities of sensitivity, self-awareness, and self-acceptance that Gellerman has prescribed. Sensitivity training, T-Groups, or encounter groups have been
attended by thousands of managers desiring to develop in the direction of Theory Y. Unfortunately, there is little or no evidence for
believing that participation in such sensitivity training sessions results
in any improvement in management performance.

George Odiorne launched a frontal assault on these group training
techniques and ably pointed out that between 1948 and 1961 there
was not one single research report that demonstrated improved performance on the job following sensitivity training (Odiorne, 1970). A
more recent review of the literature by Patten, while reporting changes
in attitudes, reports no change in job-related behavior (Patten, 1971).

The sensitivity training controversy indicates the basic problem
with the indirect approach to improving performance. Sensitivity training attempts to change attitudes, emotions, or feelings, which in turn,
it is hoped, will result in some change in productive behavior on the
job. Most evaluations of sensitivity training are based on questionnaires
and self-ratings designed to measure changes in internal states, not

behavior. The connection between these internal states and external behavior on the job has not been made.

In addition to ineffectiveness in improving managerial performance, group training has violated an essential concern that every manager should have when considering organization change strategies: The only legitimate concern of the manager in relation to his employees is those behaviors that contribute to or detract from the productivity of his organization. Peter Drucker more articulately stated this principle in his encyclopedic *Management: Tasks–Responsibilities–Practices:*

> An employer has no business with a man's personality. Employment is a specific contract calling for specific performance, and for nothing else. Any attempt of an employer to go beyond this is usurpation. It is immoral as well as illegal intrusion of privacy. It is abuse of power. An employee owes no "loyalty," he owes no "love," and no "attitudes"—he owes performance and nothing else. . . . Management and manager development . . . should concern themselves with changes in behavior likely to make a man more effective. They do not deal with who a man is—that is, with his personality or his emotional dynamics (Drucker, 1973).

## Expectancy Theory

Expectancy theory presents an explanation of motivation that has re-received a great deal of attention recently among academic investigators (Vroom, 1964; Lawler, 1971) and little, if any, attention from those applying performance improvement strategies in industry. Expectancy theory is a cognitive theory. Cognition is the thought process. It is, therefore, an internal approach to motivation and behavioral causation. Expectancy theory comes closer, however, to the external or reinforcement view of performance than any of the other current internal theories of behavior and motivation. Petrock and Gamboa (1976) have examined the similarities between expectancy theory and reinforcement theory in some detail. A brief comparison will be sufficient for our purposes.

Expectancy theory presents an explanation of the causes of motivation, which in turn influence the behavior of the individual. For this reason it is consistent with other internal theories of motivation and distinct from the external approach of behaviorism, which concerns itself with the direct relationship between frequencies of behavior and environmental conditions. Expectancy theory is an "incentive theory"

of motivation. Incentive theories describe behavior as being consciously purposeful and goal directed (Lawler, 1971, 1973). Expectancy
theorists assume that man consciously anticipates desirable outcomes
and rewards and that this results in behavior following the rational,
deliberate decision to behave in a manner to obtain the reward. This is
similar to reinforcement theory in the recognition that consequences
that may follow behavior influence the occurrence of that behavior.
Expectancy theory is, however, based on the mediating factors of motivation and cognition, where reinforcement theory or the external
approach does not concern itself with the internal processes but
merely analyzes the relationship between frequency of behavior and
external events.

Petrock and Gamboa (1976) identified four statements by Lawler
(1973) that summarize the expectancy theory propositions:

**1.** *People have expectations about the likelihood that certain outcomes will follow their behavior.* Expectancy theorists refer to this as
the *performance outcome expectancies*, the perceived relationship between performance and desirable outcome. This is a subjective internal
relationship rather than a factual one. The individual has a belief or
thought regarding the likelihood of a reward's following performance,
and this belief is a determinant of his performance. If a person believes
that a desirable outcome will follow performance, the motivation to
perform will be high. This is similar to reinforcement theory in its
statement of the effect of consequence; however, reinforcement theory
does not concern itself with the *belief* regarding the consequence.
It studies the relationship between the frequency or probability of
performance before and after the presentation of a consequence without attempting to explain any internal effect.

**2.** *People have a preference about the various outcomes potentially
available to them.* It is fairly self-evident that individuals have varying
preferences for rewards. Expectancy theory describes the preference
for a reward as a valence, which may be positive, negative, or neutral.
Valence is similar to the concept of value or worth of an outcome.
This valence is another factor that affects the level of motivation and
subsequent performance. Reinforcement theory similarly considers the
differential effect of consequences. But, rather than describe the
valence or preference for a reward, it examines the differential effects
that various consequences have on behavior. The expectancy theorist
would state that a particular reward has a high valence and therefore

results in high motivation, which then results in high performance. The reinforcement theorist would simply ask what the effect of this conse- quence is on the frequency of the behavior. Some reinforcers have greater effect on behavior than others. Some reinforcers are more reinforcing than others, as evidenced by the difference in their effects on measurable performance. These two views are not so much con- tradictory as they are merely different views of a similar or identical process.

**3.** *People have expectancies about the likelihood that an action on their part will lead to the behavior or performance needed to produce the outcomes.* This statement is perhaps the most cognitive of the four elements of Lawler's version of expectancy theory. A person may not believe that his effort will result in the level of performance required to obtain the reward. He may, therefore, fail to act. Reinforcement theory would simply state that the individual, from prior experience with similar requirements and consequences, will either act or not act, depending on the history of reinforcement. History has either demon- strated or failed to demonstrate that under similar conditions the behavior required either leads or fails to lead to the desired reinforce- ment.

**4.** *"In any situation, the actions a person chooses to take are deter- mined by the expectancies and the preferences that the person has at the time."* An individual's preferences and valences are not constant; they change, and the individual's motivation is a function of his expec- tancies at that moment. Reinforcement theory also recognizes that performance is not constant. But it describes the events that alter per- formance as a function of environmental events. Both discriminative stimuli and recent consequences affect the frequency or probability of response at any given moment. A stimulus in the environment may signal that the occasion is not one that, if the behavior is emitted, will be followed by reinforcement. Both theories, therefore, account for differences in performance by the same individual at different times.

It can be seen that expectancy theory and reinforcement theory have a great deal in common in their respective explanations for performance. But they differ primarily in the use of a mediating causal process, cognition or motivation, on the part of expectancy theory and the absence of such a process in the explanation of rein- forcement theory. Although recent work by reinforcement theorists is bringing these two views even more closely together (Mahoney, 1977), they still present major differences in their utility and application by the manager. The manager, in the case of expectancy theory, is faced with attempting to understand a relatively complex formula and identifying the elements of that formula in his situation. He must then alter these elements and infer the effect on beliefs and motivation and then anticipate a change in performance. On the other hand, following reinforcement theory, the manager may alter some condition in the work environment such as the frequency of pay or personal praise and observe and measure the direct effect on performance. The latter view is more functional for the manager because of its simplicity and directness of application, regardless of theoretical arguments.

In summary I may say the following about the internal approach to improving work performance: (1) Most current efforts to improve job performance or satisfaction are based on the assumption that internal states or motivational needs must be influenced to affect performance. The existence of such internal states is in doubt and is not relevant to improving performance. (2) Efforts to improve job performance or satisfaction by altering internal states or motivation are often ineffective, poorly evaluated, and sometimes damaging to the individuals involved. (3) Many efforts based on the indirect or internal approach ask the manager to live up to a utopian ideal of what the manager should be, an ideal that the manager is unlikely to obtain, and there is little evidence that if he does obtain this ideal any benefit will follow to the organization or himself. Holding this ideal up to the manager is likely to produce a response of frustration, failure, and antagonism. (4) While many of the efforts to improve performance based on the internal approach have resulted in increased performance, these increases can be explained more parsimoniously by a direct analysis of the conditions changed and their effect on behavior. This direct analysis is more consistent both with principles of science and principles of business management.

### REFERENCES

Berne, Eric. *Transactional Analysis in Psychotherapy.* New York: Grove Press, 1961, p. 24.

Centers, Richard, and Bugental, Daphne, E. "Intrinsic and extrinsic job motivation among different segments of the working population." *Journal of Applied Psychology,* **3,** 1966, pp. 193–197.

Corporan, Chuck. "What do you say after you say 'good morning'?" *Training and Development Journal,* November 1975.

Drucker, Peter. *Management: Tasks, Responsibilities, and Practices.* New York: Harper & Row, 1973, pp. 424–425.

Ford, Robert N. *Motivation through the Work Itself.* New York: American Management Association, Inc., 1969.

Gellerman, Saul W. *Motivation and Productivity.* New York: American Management Association, Inc., 1963, pp. 90 and 92.

Harris, Thomas A. *I'm OK–You're OK.* New York: Avon Books, 1967, pp. 39–40.

Herzberg, Frederick. *Work and the Nature of Man.* World Publishing Company, 1966.

Kazdin, Alan E. *Behavior Modification in Applied Settings.* Homewood, Illinois: The Dorsey Press, 1975, pp. 4–5.

Krasner, Leonard, and Ullman, Leonard P. *Behavior Influence and Personality.* New York: Holt, Rinehart & Winston, Inc., 1973, pp. 24–109.

Lawler, E. E. *Pay and Organizational Effectiveness: A Psychological View.* New York: McGraw-Hill Book Company, 1971.

Lawler, E. E. *Motivation in Work Organizations.* Monterey, California: Brooks/Cole Publishing Co., 1973.

Luthans, Fred, and Kreitner, Robert. *Organizational Behavior Modification.* Chicago: Scott, Foresman & Company, 1975, p. 8.

McGregor, Douglas M. *The Human Side of Enterprise.* New York: McGraw-Hill Book Company, Inc., 1960.

McGregor, Douglas M. "The human side of enterprise," in *Management and Motivation,* edited by Vroom, V. H., and Deci, E. Baltimore: Penguin Books, 1970, pp. 314–315.

Maher, John R. *New Perspectives in Job Enrichment.* New York: Van Nostrand Reinhold Company, 1971a.

Mandia, Richard J. "Sales training: As simple as P-A-C." *Training and Development Journal,* November 1974.

Maslow, A. H. "A theory of motivation." *Psychological Review,* **50,** 1943, pp. 370–396.

Meyer, M. Scott. *Every Employee a Manager.* New York: McGraw Hill Book Company, 1970, pp. 66 and pp. 47–48.

Odiorne, George. *Training by Objectives.* New York: The Macmillan Company, 1970, pp. 34–70.

Patten, Thomas H., Jr. *Manpower Planning and the Development of Human Resources.* New York: John Wiley and Sons, Inc., 1971, pp. 175–183.

Petrock, Frank, and Gamboa, Victor. "Expectancy theory and operant conditioning: A conceptual comparison," in Walter R. Nord (Ed.). *Concepts and Controversy in Organizational Behavior.* Pacifica Palisades, California: Goodyear Publishing Company, Inc., 1976.

Skinner, B. F. *Science and Human Behavior.* New York: The Free Press, 1953, p. 202.

Stuart, Richard B. *Trick or Treatment: How and When Psychotherapy Fails.* Champaign, Ill.: Research Press, 1970, pp. 103–120.

Vroom, V. H. *Work and Motivation.* New York: John Wiley and Sons, Inc., 1964.

Weeks, Earl D., Jr. "Job Enrichment cleans up at Texas Instruments," in John Z. Maher (Ed.). *New Perspectives in Job Enrichment.* New York: Van Nostrand Reinhold Company, 1971.

Whaley, Donald L., and Surratt, Sharon L. *Attitudes of Science.* Kalamazoo, Mich.: Behaviordelia, 1968.

## CASE STUDY NUMBER TWO

## IMPROVING SAFETY BEHAVIOR

This case demonstrates the use of both social and tangible reinforcement to improve behaviors of mutual interest to the employee and management. In a textile carding department the wearing of ear plugs was increased from 14.5 percent to between ninety percent and one hundred percent.

### BACKGROUND CONDITIONS

Behavior manager Don Longest, at a textile spinning plant of the Beaunit Corporation in North Carolina, was asked by the department manager of the carding department to assist in increasing the wearing of ear protection devices by employees. Wearing ear protection in a high-noise-level area is a Federal requirement as stated in the *Federal Register*—OSHA Rules and Regulations. Under OSHA regulations and regulations of the Beaunit Corporation, an employee failing to wear ear protection devices as required may be terminated. The management involved decided that it would be more desirable to attempt to solve the problem of employees' failing to wear ear protection in a positive manner, rather than resort to terminations. All employees are provided ear protection devices at no cost.

In the carding department, employees are subject to noise levels of approximately 92 dbh for a period of seven hours per day for five days a week. The working relationships in this department were very satisfactory. All twenty-three employees enjoyed friendly relations and competition within the department.

Some employees came to work without their ear protection and some appeared to lack an awareness of the need to wear ear plugs. On a number of occasions employees have been asked to wear their ear protection. Even with this, employees did not seem to be aware of the seriousness of this requirement. No one had been formally reprimanded for this violation.

A program goal was established to have one hundred percent of the employees wear their ear protection devices while in their work areas.


## PROCEDURE

Baseline data were collected to determine the preprogram level of ear plug usage. Each morning and each afternoon the manager made a tour of the department and counted the number of employees wearing their ear plugs. Of the twenty-three employees, an average of 14.5 percent wore their ear plugs during the baseline period. These data were collected for six days before the behavior management procedure was implemented. Employees were not aware that the manager was counting the number of employees wearing ear plugs during this period.

The change procedure began on January 27, 1975, when the department manager called all the employees into his office and explained the importance of wearing the protection devices, the possible damage to their hearing that might result from excessive noise, and the importance of following the OSHA regulations. An effort was made to demonstrate a concern for the health of the employees and the benefit of this regulation to them. At this time the employees were also shown a graph of the baseline data indicating low usage of the protection devices. Employees were told that checks would be made on an intermittent schedule throughout the day beginning on January 28th. They were told that those employees who were wearing ear protection would be served coffee. It was also explained that a feedback graph would be posted on the department bulletin board that would indicate the number of employees per day wearing ear plugs. Two of the employees stated that they had lost their ear protection, and new ones were provided.

The data for the first phase of the program are indicated as phase I on the accompanying graph. During phase I the department manager handed each employee a cup of coffee and told him what the coffee was for and gave the employee a hearty thanks for his effort.

During phase II of the program, doughnuts were added as an additional reinforcer for those wearing ear plugs. This was done to offset any satiation* effect that might have been occurring.

In phase III, employees who were wearing ear plugs were given an opportunity to draw from the grab bag. The grab bag consisted of the following reinforcers: silver dollars, 50 cents, 15 cents, quart-size cokes, large bag of potato chips, sandwiches and cokes from the canteen, and a pack of cigarettes or forty cents for nonsmokers. Throughout all phases of the program, the department manager continued his social praise and calling attention to the feedback graph.

During phases I, II, and III the feedback and reinforcement were delivered each day during the last hour of the workday. During the last phase, phase IV, the schedule was changed so that the reinforcement was delivered on a group basis. During this phase, a goal of 22

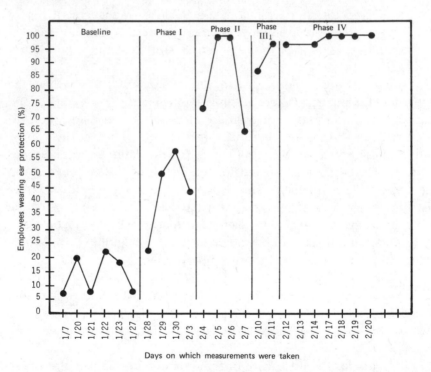

**Figure 2**  Percent of employees wearing ear protection; Case Study 2.

* See Glossary for definition.

out of 23 employees checked wearing protection devices was set for three consecutive days. Only if this goal was met would reinforcement be delivered. It was then delivered for the entire group. This goal was met the first three days of phase IV. The goal was then set at one hundred percent, and that goal was met the following three consecutive days.

## RESULTS

During the baseline period the average level of protection device usage was 14.5 percent. During phase I the level of usage rose to an average of forty-three percent with a range of from twenty-two percent to fifty-seven percent. Phase II caused a use to an average of 84.7 percent with a range of from sixty-five percent to one hundred percent. During this phase employees reached a level of one hundred percent for two days and then fell to sixty-five percent. During phase III employees averaged 91.5 percent, with a range for the two days of eighty-seven percent and ninety-six percent. Phase IV averaged 98.3 percent; however, phase IV actually consisted of two periods during which the goal was set for the group, first at ninety-six percent and then at one hundred percent. During both of these periods the goal was met.

This program was considered by the department and plant management to be a tremendous success. The wearing of ear plugs continued to remain at or near one hundred percent for several months following the termination of the program. This program produced numerous benefits. The benefit to the employees is evident in terms of health and safety by preventing hearing loss that can result from the noise levels in this department. This program was also beneficial to the Beaunit Corporation in that it ensured that the company was operating within OSHA guidlines. Direct financial savings cannot be computed for this program, but substantial fines are levied by OSHA, and employees may file for hearing loss compensation as a consequence of loss of hearing resulting from the *absence of protection devices.*

The program also served as an excellent means by which the department manager established himself as a social reinforcer to the employees. The tangible reinforcers were considered to be beneficial only in that they provided the opportunity for the department manager to pair himself with the dispensing of reinforcement and thereby establish himself as a social reinforcer.

The cost of this program was $15.14: $9.24 for grab bag prizes, $5.00 for doughnuts, and ninety cents for two pairs of ear plugs. The price of the coffee cannot be computed, because it is bought in bulk by the company.

Following the implementation of this program in the carding department, employees on other shifts and in other departments began asking, "What do we have to do to get this program in our department?"

## DISCUSSION

This is a good example of the type of program that can be implemented at little cost, without a great change in management style or theory, and yet provide a significant change for the better from both the management and employee viewpoint. Contrary to the common feelings that, when management benefits from a change the employee somehow pays the cost, it was demonstrated that common management problems, such as this one, can be solved in a manner that is of benefit to all concerned.

This program also demonstrates the importance of "watching the data." Note that during the first two phases of the program the data began to decline immediately before the procedure was changed. This may be explained by "satiation." The reinforcer of coffee, after numerous presentations, may have begun to lose its effect; then the addition of doughnuts again boosted the behavior, but this also began to lose its effect. By watching the data, the behavior manager, Don Longest, observed these changes and was able to make intelligent recommendations for altering the procedure to maintain performance. The last phase, using a group procedure and a fixed-ratio reinforcement schedule, maintained the performance consistently over a long period of time.

## QUESTIONS FOR DISCUSSION

1. The perception that a manager has of the causes of behavior affects how that manager responds to problems. How did this manager view the causes of his employees' failure to wear ear protection devices? Explain how this affected his course of action. Selecting one other theory of behavioral causation, explain how this performance problem might be explained by that theory and what actions to improve this situation might be expected to follow from acceptance of that theory.

2. The theory of Abraham Maslow asserts that there is a needs hierarchy, which places safety needs in a lower category than needs of love, esteem, or self-actualization. Discuss how this theory relates to the situation described in this case. Does this case support or contradict Maslow's theory?

3. The "Law of Parsimony" states that the simplest explanation is the best. Describe how this law was applied in this case. How might this law have been violated if the manager had pursued some other course of action?

# CHAPTER THREE

# BEHAVIOR MANAGEMENT: A BUSINESSLIKE APPROACH TO BEHAVIOR CHANGE

The advantage of the behavior management approach to changing performance is well illustrated by an incident that occurred on an airplane a few years back. One of our consultants sat next to the president of a medium-sized corporation. They began talking, and the consultant described the type of service he performed. The president responded by noting that he could really use some help with his senior vice president. He described this vice president as having a very bad attitude, which had persisted for several months. Our consultant asked "What does this vice president do that causes you to feel that he has a bad attitude?" The president thought for a while and then responded, "Well, whenever I give him a report to read, I never hear back from him. And when I do, he's always so critical." It was agreed that there was nothing else that this vice president did to manifest his bad attitude and that if these behaviors were to change it would indicate an improvement in attitude. Our consultant then made some specific recommendations involving measurement and techniques of feedback that would be likely to alter the rates of the problem behaviors.

The president was able to understand and implement a few relatively quick and simple procedures to alter these specific behaviors. The problem of his vice president's "bad attitude" had become a simple and relatively easy matter to improve. This is the essence of the direct approach to behavior change in the workplace.

## DIRECT, EXTERNAL APPROACH TO BEHAVIOR

The direct or external approach to changing behavior has gained increasing acceptance and adherence over the past ten to twenty years. This direct approach is also referred to as the behavioral model, behaviorism, behavior modification, or behavior management. All these terms refer to the behavior change techniques based on the effects of environmental events, stimuli, without reference to explanations of mental conditions, states, motivations, needs, or drives. Behavior management does not deny that internal states exist. Whether internal states exist or not is irrelevant. The question is can behavior be changed and predicted from changes in the external environment? The research overwhelmingly demonstrates that the answer is affirmative (*Journal of Applied Behavior Analysis*, 1967–1977).

The differences between the direct and indirect approaches to improving human performance in organizations can be summarized in the following four points:

**1.** The *change in behavior is explained as a direct function of the changes* in the environment, rather than as a change in an internal motivation or need that in turn causes a change in behavior. Behavior management studies the specific conditions that exist in the individual's environment, alters those conditions, and measures the subsequent change in behavior.

**2.** *Evaluation of the effort to improve performance is based on the direct measurement of behavior and its results.* The indirect approaches have relied heavily on measures of attitude and satisfaction.

These internal conditions are generally assessed by the use of attitude questionnaires. Behavior management does not consider the responses to questionnaires significant when the goal behaviors of concern, such as rates of work, attendance, and on-time arrivals to work, can be measured directly.

Goals for behavior management are stated in terms of increasing or decreasing rates of behavior or the product of behavior. The ongoing measurement of behavior is an essential element of every behavior management effort. Because of this direct measurement and because goals are stated in terms of increasing or decreasing behavior, the evaluation mechanism is built into every project. Economic evaluation of these projects becomes relatively simple and direct.

**3.** *Behavior management is a technique of management.* Behavior management is not a theory to which managers should attempt to conform because it is a correct theory of human nature. It is a technique designed to assist the manager in achieving his goals and should be applied to aid the organization in accomplishing the specific goals that define its productivity. It may be applied to improve the quality of products, reduce absenteeism or turnover and increase output measures, sales, new business development, and increase other specific contributions of managers and employees. The manager should have specific, measurable objectives in mind before implementing a behavior change effort.

**4.** *The direct approach is more acceptable and receives a more favorable response from the manager because it is focused on his objec-*

*tives*, for it provides him with a procedure for directly affecting the achievement of his objectives and demonstrates observable results in a relatively short period of time. Because of these factors and the compatibility of the direct approach with the "business of managing," the manager is more favorably disposed toward performance improvement efforts.

Behavior management is a nontheory of behavior (Skinner, 1950). It is the study and application of what works. Its development is based on empirical research. It did not start with a grand theory of human nature. Simple questions were asked and tested. Why does one specific behavior increase or decrease? How is a behavior acquired, or why does a behavior decrease? Highly controlled laboratory studies were conducted to answer these questions. As these questions have been answered through data collection and analysis, a set of principles has developed. The goal of behavior management is to discover lawful relationships. Investigation has determined that some lawful relationships between environmental events and behavior do exist, much as the study of physics has determined that larger bodies tend to attract smaller bodies.

Whereas the historical evolution of behavior management is undoubtedly of secondary interest to most managers, a brief review of its development may help in understanding its principles.

The development of the science of behavior involved dozens of individual researchers; however, the work of the following men represents the most essential contributions: John B. Watson, Edward L. Thorndike, and B. F. Skinner.

### John B. Watson

John B. Watson, more than any other single individual, is responsible for the initiation of behaviorism and for its first applications to business. Watson believed that all behavior was explainable as a function of stimuli that preceded the behavior. The so-called Stimulus-Response (S-R) model is the result of Watson's work. Watson described the purpose of his work in the following passage:

Behaviorism, as I tried to develop it in my lectures at Columbia in 1912 and in my earliest writings, was an attempt to do one thing—apply to the experimental study of man the same kind of procedure and the same language of description that many research men had found useful for so many years in the study of animals lower than man. We believed then, as we do now, that man is an animal different from other animals only in the types of behavior he displays (Watson, 1920).

Before Watson psychology had been dominated by the internal approach, and he challenged its advocates to demonstrate the effects of their work and to apply the methods of empirical science. Watson demonstrated that human behavior could be studied scientifically and that it occurred in predictable patterns relative to conditions in the environment.

Perhaps Watson's most famous experiment, the one that led him to some of his conclusions, involved Little Albert, an eleven-month-old boy who had become friendly with a white rate (Watson, 1920). Although this experiment was highly questionable from an ethical point of view, it did demonstrate some important principles of behavior. Watson decided that he would try to condition the response of fear in poor Little Albert. He attempted to pair a number of different stimuli with the white rat to condition a fear of the rat. He tried scaring Little Albert with a mask, a dog, a monkey, burning newspapers, and other stimuli that might elicit the fear response. Albert was not impressed by any of these. Finally, Watson created a loud noise by hitting an iron bar with a hammer behind Little Albert's head. This succeeded in sending Albert into a screaming fit. Watson then paired the frightening stimulus of the loud noise with the white rat. Every time Albert was permitted to see his little white friend, he was startled by the loud noise. Eventually the sight of the white rat, by itself, created the fear and caused poor Little Albert to cry.

In addition to showing that fears may be caused by conditions of the environment, this experiment demonstrated the principle of generalization. The newly acquired fear of the white rat generalized to other furry objects. Albert was now afraid of a dog, a rabbit, and even a Santa Claus mask. At Albert's expense some of the most basic forms of emotional learning had been demonstrated. (In Watson's defense it must be reported that he demonstrated that Albert could be deconditioned or unlearn these same fears.)

Watson limited his investigation to the relationship between preceding stimuli and subsequent behavior. For this reason the relationship he described is referred to as the Stimulus–Response (S–R) model. He believed that all behavior could be explained in terms of eliciting stimuli that occurred some time before the behavior. Although this explanation is no longer considered sufficient to explain all forms of learning, it did lay the foundation for the empirical investigation of human learning.

Watson defined the "behaviorists' platform":

> The behaviorist asks why don't we make what we can observe the real field of psychology? Let us limit ourselves to things that can be observed, and formulate laws concerning only those things. Now what can we observe? We can observe behavior— what the organism does or says. And let us point out at once: that saying is doing—that is behaving. Speaking overtly or to ourselves (thinking) is just as objective a type of behavior as baseball (Watson, 1924).

### Edward L. Thorndike

While Watson was pursuing the study of the effect of preceding stimuli on behavior, E. L. Thorndike was developing his Law of Effect (Thorndike, 1913). He placed small animals such as cats, dogs, and chickens in "puzzle boxes" from which they learned to escape. There was an exit door to the box that could be opened by manipulating a lever. The animals were deprived of food until they managed to open the door. They obtained food, their reinforcer, after they managed to manipulate the lever and open the door. Thorndike found that the animal's speed of opening the door increased following experience. The animals were learning. From these experiments Thorndike formulated his Law of Effect:

> When a modifiable connection between a situation and a response is made and is accompanied or followed by a satisfying state of affairs, that connection's strength is increased: when made and accompanied or followed by an annoying state of affairs, its strength is decreased.

Thorndike accepted Watson's stimulus–response relationship but added that these relationships are strengthened as a function of the consequences that follow the behavior. Thorndike also argued that the effects or consequences of a behavior are direct and do not need to be explained in terms of mediating processes such as thought. The behavior is increased or decreased as a direct effect of the consequence.

## B. F. Skinner

B. F. Skinner has been acclaimed by the American Psychological Association as the most influential living psychologist, and he is without a doubt the most controversial. Skinner's contributions to the development of psychology as a science and as a means of improving human behavior are tremendous but difficult to categorize. Many cannot be as clearly defined as his own science would require. Four of the more significant are (1) his development and articulation of a technology of empirical investigation of behavior, (2) his distinction between operant and respondent behavior, (3) his development of the concept of "contingencies of reinforcement", and (4) his advocacy of behavior change and cultural design based on the empirical analysis of behavior.

### Empirical Investigation

Skinner is the antitheorist. Whereas the results of his research may be termed a theory of behavior, he opposed the formulation of theories of human behavior. Skinner (1950) argues that the empirical data from the direct observation of behavior and its environment are a sufficient source of knowledge and that no interpretative theories are necessary. Skinner defined terms empirically. For example, reinforcement is defined as the presentation or removal of a stimulus, resulting in an increase in the rate of a response. It is defined by its effect on the behavior; reinforcement increases the rate of behavior. It is impossible, therefore, to say that an event is reinforcing unless an increase in the rate of a behavior can be demonstrated.

Skinner developed the language of the empirical investigation of behavior. All sciences require clear definition of terms to enable investigation to proceed in an orderly fashion. The definition of the language of behaviorism is one of Skinner's most significant contributions.

Skinner also provided a framework for behavioral research. He divided his observations into those concerned with independent variables (factors that affect a behavior and that can be managed in such a way as to cause a change in behavior) and the dependent variables (the behaviors affected by the independent variable). Skinner is concerned with discovering the specific relationships or "functional relationships" between the dependent and independent variables.

The essential elements of Skinner's system are summarized in the following table:

*Independent Variables*

Type of reinforcement or punishment
Schedule of reinforcement or punishment

*Dependent Variables*

Rate of responding
Rate of acquiring a new response
Rate of extinction

At least as great as any technical innovations Skinner may have contributed is the general approach toward his subject that he promoted. This "attitude of science" is the single most distinguishing feature of the direct approach to behavior change.

> Science is first of all a set of attitudes. It is a disposition to deal with the facts rather than with what someone has said about them. . . . Science is a willingness to accept facts even when they are opposed to wishes. . . . The opposite of wishful thinking is intellectual honesty. . . . Scientists have simply found that being honest—with oneself as much as with others—is essential to progress. Experiments do not always come out as one expects, but the facts must stand and the expectations fall. The subject matter, not the scientist, knows best (Skinner, 1953).

## Operant and Respondent Behavior

Skinner defined types of behavior according to the manner in which they are acquired and maintained. Respondent behaviors are those *elicited* by a stimulus and are acquired through the procedures of "classical conditioning," the pairing of an unconditioned stimulus with a conditioned stimulus. Operant behaviors are those that are *emitted* by the organism and that act on the environment. They result in reinforcement. In other words, in respondent behavior, the organism reacts to the environment, while in operant behavior the response acts on the environment.

Skinner defined and studied operant behavior. He argued that most of the behaviors performed by any organism, human or animal, are operant behaviors and may be explained by an analysis of the reinforcements that have resulted from the operant behavior's acting on the environment. For example, the behavior of coming to work results in social approval, payment of money, and other reinforcers that maintain the performance of this behavior. If the behavior of coming to work did not act on the environment, if there were no consequences resulting from it, the operant of coming to work would extinguish; that is, it would cease to occur.

### The "Contingencies of Reinforcement"

The relationships between the behavior of an individual and the environment are described by Skinner as the contingencies of reinforcement:

> An adequate formulation of the interaction between an organism and its environment must always specify three things: (1) the occasion upon which a response occurs, (2) the response itself, and (3) the reinforcing consequences. The interrelationships among them are the "contingencies of reinforcement" (Skinner, 1969).

The contingencies between behavior and environment are often stated in terms of an if–then relationship. If *A* occurs, then *B* will follow. If I finish this chapter on time, I can go to the beach this weekend. If you increase the number of customers on whom you call, then you will increase your commissions. If Johnny finishes his homework by eight o'clock, he may watch television for one hour.

Our world is composed of our behavior and the reaction of the environment to our behavior. These contingencies of reinforcement are the structure within which we live, the relationships that may explain our slow rate of learning, our feelings of depression, or our overeating. Skinner laid the foundation for the analysis of the contingencies of reinforcement.

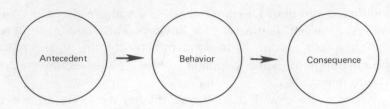

**Figure 3**   The contingencies of reinforcement.

## Advocacy of Behavior Change and Cultural Design

Many of Skinner's writings are not scientific. Most notably his well-known novel *Walden II* and his more recent *Beyond Freedom and Dignity* have gone beyond his data to propose applications of the science of behavior to social problems. Unfortunately, this advocacy has led to serious misunderstandings of the science of behavior and of his own positions in regard to this science. Skinner has devoted the greatest portion of his most recent book *About Behaviorism* to answering these criticisms and misunderstandings.

Skinner desired to create public debate on the social and cultural application of behavior change, and he has undoubtedly succeeded. If, however, the degree to which his recent writings have been misunderstood is an indication of his success at communicating his ideas, he has not been entirely successful. Perhaps the greatest controversy followed his publication of *Beyond Freedom and Dignity*. Contrary to the misinterpretation of many, Skinner does not argue against freedom. He is very much in favor of freedom and increasing individual freedom. He does, however, argue that the popular comprehension and the literature of freedom have hindered the progress of our culture. Skinner argues that mankind is not free in the sense of being autonomous and free from influence. On the contrary, Skinner argues that mankind's behavior is controlled by his environmental conditioning, and freedom must, therefore, be viewed in the context of this environmental control. He believes that mankind reacts negatively to aversive or negative control such as would be imposed by a dictator. These forms of control characterized by the threat of punishment are the ones we fear. Forms of control based on positive reinforcement are the ones that we least notice and that are most desirable. Skinner argues that these forms, already present in our environment, should be carefully studied and used to create a society that results in the greatest benefit.

Skinner's outspoken advocacy of the application of his techniques to cultural design has created considerable debate because these techniques contradict the popular view and require a reexamination of accepted beliefs and habits. As has been the case at previous periods in human history, positions that contradict popular understandings of the human condition and that are supported by empirically gathered data have resulted in significant changes in the course of human history. The work of Galileo and Darwin resulted in similar controversy, change of traditional views, and eventual progress. Only future generations will be able to assess Skinner's final contribution to the understanding of the human condition.

## DOES BEHAVIOR MANAGEMENT WORK IN ORGANIZATIONS?

Behavior management is the result of the trial-and-error applications of operant conditioning principles in the work setting. Does it work? This is the question that Skinner would hope we would ask. Behavior management has been systematically applied in the business and industrial settings only during the past few years. The contingencies of reinforcement have, however, been operating since the first person began working. All work behavior, regardless of the system or philosophy of management in effect, is explainable by analyzing the contingencies of reinforcement and may be changed by altering these contingencies.

The argument is often made that changing behavior in the work setting is not as simple as in the laboratory, classroom, or mental hospital. This is certainly true, and the complexity of the contingencies operating in the workplace is one of the primary reasons why application to organizations has not been more extensive. But behavior management has demonstrated its ability to change behavior, both in the workplace and other settings. It is the task of this book to present some of the results, as well as the principles and techniques of behavior management.

Behavior management systems are currently in use in more than fifty major corporations that I know of, and probably many more. Among the corporations now using these programs are the 3M Corporation, Western Electric, Westinghouse, Airco Alloys, Inc., Milliken & Company, General Mills, AT & T, Dart Industries, Inc., Pennwalt Corporation, Emery Air Freight, Questor Corporation, Ford Motor Company, American Can, Connecticut General Life Insurance Company, General Electric, Weyerhaeuser Company, and numerous others.

The application of behavior management to industrial organizations may be the best kept secret in management today. Most companies have no desire to advertise the techniques they are using or the results they have received. Nonetheless, a sampling of results leaves one wondering why there is not more discussion of these techniques in management publications and why more systematic research has not been conducted. The following are a few of the documented results witnessed during the past few years:

- One of the largest textile firms in the country has reported savings or earnings of approximately $20 million that can be directly attributed to behavior management programs.
- A midwestern plant of one of the major corporations listed in the preceding paragraph has reported that their cost accountants have attributed $600,000 in annual cost reductions to a behavior management effort that cost approximately $70,000 to implement.
- A textile-finishing plant that had been having a number of serious personnel problems implemented a six-month behavior management training program, and a year later the plant set a record for attendance—down to 0.9 percent absenteeism for eight weeks running. This same plant boosted quality, savings to $25,000 per week over the same eight-week period.
- The City of Detroit Garbage Collectors instituted a behavior management program in which efficiency was reinforced with bonuses to the garbage collectors. The city saved $1,654,000 during the first year, after bonuses of $307,000 were paid to the collectors.
- ACDC Electronics Division of Emerson Electronics, instituting a program to improve attendance, met engineering specifications and production objectives. Profits increased twenty-five percent over forecast; costs were reduced by $550,000, and they received a return on investment, including consultant fees, of 1900 percent.
- B. F. Goodrich Chemical Company started a program to meet production schedules and increased production by 300 percent.
- Emery Air Freight has instituted numerous programs since 1969 and attributes direct savings of more than $3 million to behavior management.
- Waste in the spinning department of a carpet mill was identified

as an area in need of improvement. By posting feedback data and providing verbal reinforcement and small tangible reinforcements, waste variance was reduced from $1,153 per week to $437 per week—an annualized savings of $37,232.

- A thorough analysis of the cost benefit of one behavior management program in one textile plant demonstrated improvements in plant turnover ($102,000 savings); finishing department efficiency ($32,895 savings); attendance ($26,457 savings); quality ($29,725 savings); sewing department efficiency ($15,158 savings); attendance in the sewing department ($27,333 savings); for a total plant-wide annual savings of $233,369.

- A major textile firm began several programs with their trucking operations. One involved reducing the average time that loaded trailers wait for a tractor. The time was reduced from an average sixty-seven minutes to between thirty-five to forty minutes. This program is in operation in forty-two plants and has reported savings in excess of $1 million.

The results listed here are only a small sample of those obtained. Each of these programs specified behaviors to be changed, altered specific environmental contingencies, and measured the changes in behavior and corresponding outcomes in terms of productivity, and so forth. In each of these programs environmental contingencies were complex, though the ones changed were relatively simple. While there may be a dozen consequences to our behavior (such as quitting a job or remaining on a job), one consequence may change the course of our actions (such as a raise or a compliment by our boss). It is not necessary to understand all the complexities of environmental influence to put the technology of behavior management to work. It is necessary only to identify clearly the behavior to be changed, the consequence to be altered, and measure the rate of the behavior before and after the consequence is changed. The result, in terms of an increase or decrease in the rate of behavior, indicates whether or not the procedure is working.

More than 20,000 managers and supervisors have been trained in the application of behavior management during the past five years by just one consulting firm specializing in it. All of these managers or supervisors have used behavior change projects as a routine part of their job. Most of these projects have followed a four-step process that has become known as the "cookbook" method of behavior management. This method, while deceptively simple, contains the basic ingredients of operant conditioning as applied to the work situation. These four steps are *pinpoint, record, consequate, evaluate* (Miller, 1974) and include the following:

- *Pinpoint*: The manager must identify and define the specific behavior or behaviors he wishes to change. A behavior is pinpointed when it may be accurately and reliably observed and recorded. For example, "working slowly" is not pinpointed. Completing "forty-three work units per eight-hour day" is. Similarly, "having a good attitude" is not pinpointed; "smiling at least once during each conversation with another person" is. The ability to specify behavior in pinpointed terms is both a necessary first skill for the manager who wishes to increase his ability to manage his employee's (or his own) behavior and a skill that requires a major change in the behavior pattern of most industrial supervisors.

- *Record*: The manager is asked to count the occurrence of the pinpointed behavior or some result of it. The frequency is to be recorded before any effort is made to change the behavior. This is for establishing baseline data. These data serve as the means of evaluating the behavior change strategy to be implemented after their establishment. The manager generally graphs these data to determine whether the frequency of the behavior is increasing, decreasing, or remaining the same. The establishment of baseline data before the initiation of a change procedure is a fundamental practice of the scientist that has been adopted with no great difficulty by the line manager and supervisor, who often have less than a high school education. The value of knowing where you have been, where you want to get to, and when you have arrived is understood by most individuals of good sense. /

- *Consequate*: To consequate a behavior is to arrange for a consequence to follow it. The manager is encouraged to arrange a "reinforcing consequence," one that results in an increase in the rate of the desired performance. The reinforcing consequence most commonly used in behavior management is visualized feedback or knowledge of results. Managers often use the graph of the baseline data they have plotted to illustrate a goal level of performance and either post the graph in a visible location in the work area or personally show it to the worker whose performance is being recorded. The supervisor pairs verbal praise and approval with the visual feedback. This simple procedure has been used literally thousands of times to increase individual workers' productivity. Other reinforcers are raffle tickets, time off, job changes, letters of recognition, or anything else that may prove meaningful to the employee. A consequence may also include a "punisher," an event that results in the decreased rate of behavior. Managers have been taught the empirical meaning and effective use of punishment as a management procedure. Punishment, which is used only when reinforcement does not work, usually involves the least drastic punishing consequence available. A consequence may also involve the removal of a reinforcer that may be maintaining the performance of an undesirable behavior.

The emphasis in most behavior management programs is on the use of "social" reinforcement. This includes the recognition by the manager of a job well done. When social reinforcement can be instituted in an organization on an ongoing basis, the organization is most likely to maintain high levels of performance. The use of tangible reinforcement, unless it becomes an institutionalized part of the compensation system, is not likely to be maintained over a long time, and performance is likely to drop as the procedure is discontinued.

*Evaluate*: Every behavior management project, whether conducted by a consulting psychologist, an inhouse change agent, or the line manager, must include an evaluation procedure if it is to qualify as behavior management. The evaluation of most behavior management projects simply involves the continuation of the counting and recording initiated before the change procedure. Most managers continue to graph the data on the performance with which they are concerned. Behavior management teaches the manager to measure performance on an ongoing basis, even when it is good, so that the conditions affecting it can be studied and managed. One of the primary effects of this evaluation is to provide built-in, or intrinsic, reinforcement for the manager. The manager or supervisor can obtain a great deal of satisfaction from observing the line on a graph go upward or downward as he alters the conditions that he believes affects that performance.

Behavior management is much more than these four simple steps. These steps are one method used to initiate behavior management at the level of the individual supervisor. Behavior management may also involve the alteration of a company-wide system of compensation, objective setting, or information flow. When the principles of behavior management are fully understood by the manager, they become, not a technique to be called upon on difficult occasions, but a "way of life."

## REFERENCES

Miller, Lawrence M. *Behavior Management: New Skills for Business and Industry.* Atlanta: Behavioral Systems, Inc., 1974.

Skinner, B. F. "Are theories of learning necessary?" *Psychological Review,* **57,** 1950, 193–216.

Skinner, B. F. *Science and Human Behavior.* New York: The Free Press, 1953, pp. 12–13.

Skinner, B. F. *Contingencies of Reinforcement: A Theoretical Analysis.* New York: Appleton-Century-Crofts, 1969, p. 7.

Thorndike, E. L. *The Psychology of Learning.* New York: Columbia University Teachers College, 1913.

Watson, John B. *Behaviorism.* New York: W. W. Norton & Company, Inc., 1924, p. ix.

Watson, J. B., and Raynor, R. "Conditioning emotional reactions." *Journal of Experimental Psychology,* **3,** February 1920, 1–14.

# CASE STUDY NUMBER THREE

## REDUCING THE TIME REQUIRED TO COMPLETE A QUALITY CONTROL REPORT

This project reports the effort to improve the behavior of one individual employee working on one task. A combination of changing antecedent stimuli and increasing feedback and reinforcement was used to improve the speed at which one female employee in a textile mill was able to complete a statistical report. The manager in this case gradually increased the goal level of performance and the requirement for reinforcement. By reinforcing gradual improvements he achieved an increase in performance from an average of approximately one hundred minutes to approximately fifteen minutes.

### BACKGROUND CONDITIONS

The department manager of the finishing department in an apparel manufacturing plant in a small Georgia town reported that a sampler, who completes a daily report called the statistical quality control report, was having trouble learning to prepare it in the required amount of time. It was taking the new sampler an average of one hour and forty minutes to complete the report that normally required only fifteen or twenty minutes per day. The manager reported that he had given her the necessary instructions, but she did not seem to be able to complete the report on time.

The sampler completed the report in the canteen area of the plant, away from the noise and heat of the finishing plant's operations. She appeared glad to get away from her job into the canteen area. She had also reported that she felt "like a scab" completing this report. It was also noticed that this employee, an attractive young woman, was being visited by several young men while in the canteen working on her report.

The department manager, with the assistance of a trained behavior manager assigned to this plant, began a procedure to measure the performance of this sampler before any effort to improve her performance. A baseline count of the time required was obtained by measuring the elapsed time from her leaving the department to work on the report to the time she returned. Over a period of eight days she averaged one hundred minutes per report, a range of ninety to one hundred and twenty minutes.

## PROCEDURE

The department manager's goal was to reduce the time required to complete the quality control report to within the standard fifteen minutes.

The manager began his improvement program by changing the location of the work to remove competing activities and distractions. He asked the sampler to work on the report in his office. This change is reflected on the accompanying graph as phase I. On the third day the manager realized that the sampler was having difficulty using a slide rule required in some of the calculations and so replaced it with a calculator. This is phase II on the graph.

On the fifth day of the program the manager implemented a goal setting, feedback, and reinforcement program. Each day he would agree with her on a goal for time required for completion. After completion they would calculate the time required. The manager would praise the sampler each time that progress was made. This plant had a plantwide behavior management program, and a "reinforcer menu" was available from which an employee could choose those reinforcers that were most meaningful. The sampler was asked to select a reinforcer, and she selected trading stamps. Each time she met the established goal she was reinforced by the manager with trading stamps. This procedure is indicated as phase III on the graph.

After three weeks the reinforcement program involving trading stamps was terminated. Intermittent praise was continued for performance within the standard. One month after the end of the formal part of the program, this sampler continued to complete the report in less than the standard time. She was given a salary review, which had been postponed during the program, and was given a merit increase.

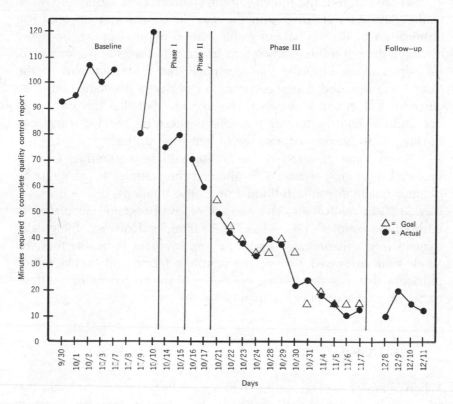

**Figure 4**   Time required to complete a quality control report; Case Study 3.

The manager made clear that the increase was due to her improvement in completing the quality control reports.

### RESULTS

During the first phase of the program the removal of interfering conditions produced a reduction in time required to complete the report by twenty-two minutes from the baseline. Phase II, during which the calculator was supplied, resulted in an additional reduction of ten minutes, to an average of sixty-five minutes. Phase III, during which goals were set and feedback and reinforcement delivered, resulted in a gradual reduction to the fifteen-minute standard time required. Of the twelve days during this period the goal level was met on ten. The termination of the formal program, with continued praise from the manager, did not result in any return to previous levels of performance.

The sampler reported that she now "felt more like part of the team." She reported that she was proud of her performance and discussed it with other employees. The manager felt that this change in her attitude contributed to the effectiveness of her reporting off-quality goods during performance of her other duties.

This program resulted in a reduction in time required by approximately one hour per day. This allowed the sampler to continue to monitor quality for this additional time. The total cost of the program was $3.80 in reinforcers. The savings of the program, calculated in terms of the sampler's time was $822.50 annually. However, the greater benefits from this program are in the improvement in quality that will result from increased time spent sampling fabric and the increased efficiency that may result from the desire of the employee to continue to be considered an effective member of the team.


## DISCUSSION

When behavior management programs are begun within an industrial plant, each manager and supervisor is trained to identify areas of potential improvement in human performance. This case illustrates one project conducted by one supervisor in such a plant. Each supervisor generally conducts several such projects. A total of fifty to one hundred individual projects may be undertaken in a plant during a six-month period.

This project illustrates the effectiveness of specifying the desired performance in measurable terms, of obtaining data on the performance, and of using positive procedure of feedback and verbal and tangible reinforcement. It also illustrates the value of setting goals for gradual improvement based on the previous measured performance. If this employee had been given an initial goal of fifteen minutes per report, she probably would have failed. The value of this employee to the company was increased as a result of her improved performance, and she is now obtaining greater satisfaction from her job.

## QUESTIONS FOR DISCUSSION

1. The manager in this case applied a direct approach to behavior change. Discuss why the actions taken by this manager may be considered direct. How did these actions differ from an indirect approach?

2. During the baseline conditions the sampler's behavior was being influenced by her environment. What were some of the stimuli in this environment that were influencing her behavior? What were the changes made in her environment that caused a change in her performance?

3. Douglas McGregor said that management by direction and control fails under today's conditions to provide effective motivation of human effort. Discuss this statement in relation to the case study. Does this case study support or refute McGregor's statement?

4. Discuss the concept of self-actualization as it related to this case. Did this employee achieve a greater or lesser degree of self-actualization? How do the methods used in this case compare to those generally associated with increasing employee self-actualization?

5. During phase III on two separate occasions the goal was not met. Which days were they? Describe what is meant by "testing the contingencies" and why you might expect this to occur in a program of this nature.

6. On both occasions when the goal was not met the behavior manager raised the goal for the following day. Describe why this is *not* a wise practice.

# CHAPTER FOUR

# BEHAVIOR AND RESULTS

A sk a manager what he manages and he will tell you he manages a sales organization, a retail store, or a manufacturing plant. While it may be true that the manager is *responsible* for the management of an organization, he does not directly *manage* it. Responsibility for the management of an organization implies supervision of all the component management activities that must be performed and resources that must be used if the organization is to achieve its goals. Among these activities is the management of people, human performance.

An organization achieves its goals only as the people who make it up behave in a manner that contributes to its achievement. During the past twenty years a great deal has been written on management by objectives or management for results (Raia, 1974; Odiorne, 1965; Mali, 1972). Thousands of managers have been trained to identify the measurable results toward which their organizations are working and to measure their performance and that of their subordinates by the achievement of these results. This emphasis has proved effective because measurable objectives provide a source of feedback, accountability, and evaluation (Ivancevich, 1976). Formally or informally, consequences are delivered contingent upon the completion of agreed-upon objectives. For this reason well-stated, measurable objectives are effective in improving performance of people in organizations (Kim and Hammer, 1976).

In management by objectives the desired measurable outcomes are identified through backward analysis. For example, the manager is aware he is responsible for the management of a retail store. He knows he will be held accountable for the economic success of the store. This success is the final result in a chain. The manager then asks the question, "What are the component results that comprise 'success' for this organization?" He may draw up a list of general results that would indicate success. On this list might be outcomes such as gross dollar volume per month, net profit per month, total costs per month, losses, depreciation, and others that indicate the economic success of the organization. The manager may also identify outcomes that are not economic but that contribute to the economic outcomes, such as employee turnover and absenteeism, turnover of inventory, reductions in customer complaints, and items returned to the store.

The manager then obtains data reflecting current levels of performance for each of these variables and sets objectives for improvement by a certain date. The manager may set an objective "to reduce

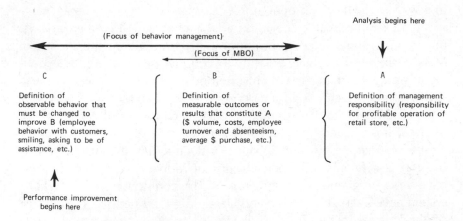

(Focus of behavior management)

(Focus of MBO)

Analysis begins here

C

Definition of observable behavior that must be changed to improve B (employee behavior with customers, smiling, asking to be of assistance, etc.)

B

Definition of measurable outcomes or results that constitute A ($ volume, costs, employee turnover and absenteeism, average $ purchase, etc.)

A

Definition of management responsibility (responsibility for profitable operation of retail store, etc.)

Performance improvement begins here

**Figure 5** Backward analysis.

customer complaints from the current level of an average eight per week to four or less per week within the next two months." An objective such as this contains the three generally accepted elements of a well-written objective: (1) the action verb (to reduce), (2) the measurable results (four or less per week), and (3) the date by which this result will be accomplished (within the next two months) (Morrissey, 1970).

The statement of a series of such objectives for the manager of an organization provides a basis for *directed activity*. The manager now knows what he hopes to accomplish during the next month, quarter, or year. But what the manager may not know is *what he has to do to cause the result to be achieved*. What does the manager have to do to reduce customer complaints, employee turnover or absenteeism, or waste, loss, or damages? Management by objectives generally leaves the manager knowing where he wants to go but only occasionally knowing how to get there.

The answers to the question "What do I have to do to cause the result to be achieved?" are often complex. The answer always contains, however, one crucial element: The manager must change someone's behavior. Someone will have to *do* something differently, behave in a different way, behave more or less often, if a different result is to be achieved. The behavior of the manager himself often needs to change. Results are a function of the behavior of people. This apparently simple fact holds true regardless of the degree of mechanization or technological complexity of an operation.

An example of this is evident as this chapter is being written. At this moment the Viking I is performing experiments on the surface of Mars. Sending this vehicle to Mars to conduct highly complex experiments on the Martian surface must be one of the most, if not the most, highly complex technological tasks ever undertaken by man. The Viking I lander virtually "thinks" through problems and solves those problems by itself. It is assisted by the most advanced computers and technology yet developed. Despite this reliance on technology the success of the mission is a function of the behavior of individuals. The computers have been programmed by individuals. The components of the Viking system have been constructed and checked out by people. The success of the mission depends on individuals' behaving in a manner that brings about the desired result.

It is a myth that the importance of human performance is reduced in a highly technological operation. The opposite is true. Human performance is more critical than ever. The costs of human error in the Viking mission may be assessed in the billions of dollars, rather than in the millions, thousands, or other figures with which we are more comfortable. This high cost of human error became clear during discussions with managers in a division of the Honeywell Corporation that assembled communication satellites. The assembly was conducted by people. Each tiny component was assembled, tested, and retested by people. Errors did occur and resulted in tens and often hundreds of thousands of dollars in time and materials lost.

In a highly technological or knowledge industry forms of human performance other than errors are also more critical than in less technological industries. For example, absenteeism and turnover in knowledge industries result in far greater costs and reduced earnings than they do among less skilled workers. Dissatisfaction and low levels of performance can deprive the organization of contributions that go unmeasured because of the absence of a method of measuring creativity or the initiating of projects or activities that may result in a new product or additional use of a product. In the highly technological organization, as well as the manufacturing operation or the sales organization, managing by objectives is not sufficient. The manager must analyze his function one more step backward to the behavior of his employees and himself. After his objectives are established, he must ask the question, "Whose behavior must be changed?" or, "Who must behave in what manner to achieve these objectives?" Once the manager has asked this question, he begins to manage behavior. Behavior is the one definable unit of activity that results in performance.

Few managers are aware that they must change behavior if they are to achieve their objectives. Most have been trained to think in terms of larger concepts such as systems, organizations, motivation, and operations. While these concepts also serve their purpose, they are too nebulous to maximize the probability of effective action. *Skills that enable the manager to cause his employees to behave in ways consistent with the achievement of his objectives provide a basis for effective action.* The manager of the future will be able to identify the specific behaviors an employee needs to perform and the conditions that will cause him to perform in that manner. This is the process of behavior management.

### PINPOINTING BEHAVIOR

The ability to manage behavior implies a series of skills that should be clearly distinguished from *knowledge*. The distinction between skill and knowledge is that between knowing and doing. For example, a manager may know that he should reinforce an employee for improved performance. He may know that the employee would be reinforced if he were told, in a sincere manner, that his improved performance was appreciated. But the manager may truly lack the social skills that would enable him to perform this task successfully. An unfortunately high percentage of managers lack this simple skill.

Behavior management involves a number of such skills that imply successful action in addition to knowledge. The first such skill a manager must acquire is that of *pinpointing behavior*. Pinpointing behavior is simple, but not easy. It's too simple. We have learned to think in highly complex operations, and pinpointing behavior asks us to think simply.

A pinpointed behavior is one that may be observed and counted. You can observe the behavior of arriving to work on or before 8:30 in the morning, of writing three letters per day, or of making a derogatory comment. You cannot observe the behavior of having a good attitude or a poor attitude, or of being lazy, or of having a high level of motivation.

Pinpointed behaviors are exactly what you see, what you know has occurred. Poor motivation cannot be observed and is an interpretation of observable behavior. You may observe the behavior of coming to work late and interpret it as indicative of a poor attitude or poor motivation. You may observe the behavior of arriving to work early, walking rapidly in the hallway, and speaking rapidly and interpret these behaviors to be indicative of high motivation. You do not observe motivation, attitudes, or qualities such as ambitious, lazy, self-disciplined, neurotic, or assertive. You only observe and can measure the behaviors that cause you to believe that the individual is characterized by these general traits.

It is often surprising to discover how difficult it is for the manager to pinpoint behavior of his employees or himself that he would like to change. Interpreting behavior is a strong element in our culture. Every child grows up making interpretations about his playmate's behavior: "Johnny is naughty, silly, or kind." Rarely is the child called upon to specify the behaviors that Johnny is performing to determine if these interpretations are well founded. Through our entire learning process this interpretation habit is strengthened by the commonly accepted interpretations of behavior that have entered our culture as a result of Freudian psychology. You are considered to be cultured if you can identify, with the most remote sort of reliability, who is neurotic, passive-aggressive, or defensive. Most managers will have to practice the new-found skill of pinpointing behaviors, a skill essentially more simple than the habit of interpretation.

It is important to be able to pinpoint behavior because it is behavior, observable and measurable, that may be changed. It is behavior that contributes to productivity. Motivation as traditionally defined never contributed anything to productivity. Fran Tarkenton, record-setting quarterback of the Minnesota Vikings and chairman of the board of Behavioral Systems, Inc., is fond of explaining the importance of behavior rather than interpretations of behavior by talking about one of his linemen. Alan Paige, Fran explains, can have any attitude he wants. If he wants to have a poor attitude or rotten motivation, that's his business, as long as he makes tackles.

The same holds true for improving performance in organizations. Employees or executives can have any attitude they want, so long as they perform. The question is "What specific behaviors constitute performance?"

*The skill of pinpointing behavior must be developed through practice.* The best way to do this is to attempt to define a performance you would like to see improved in specific, pinpointed ways. Then begin to count the occurrences of this behavior. If you can reliably observe and count it, it is probably pinpointed. The true test of a pinpointed behavior is whether two persons can observe and count the behavior and obtain the same count. For example, you may pinpoint a behavior of "completing letters to customers." You may count five letters one day, two the next day, and three the next. The individual may then write one letter that he asks his secretary to mail to all his customers. This may account for twenty letters in one day. Has he written twenty letters that day? One individual may count this as one letter, another may consider it twenty. If this difference in observation arises, then the behavior is not sufficiently pinpointed. The definition of this pinpointed behavior may then be modified to "the number of original letters written and mailed to a customer during the day," the confusion thereby being eliminated.

The ability to clearly pinpoint behavior becomes increasingly important as behavior change projects are implemented. This ability eliminates or reduces many problems as an immediate result of defining them clearly. An employee may feel that he is not performing well but may not know what to do differently. A manager may feel that he could improve his own performance but may have only general feelings about the need to improve performance and may have identified no behaviors to increase or decrease. And many managers are unsatisfied with their employees' performance but have not analyzed their own dissatisfaction to the point of identifying the specific behaviors they would like to see changed. By his pinpointing these behaviors, feedback regarding their performance may account for rapid changes in behavior. General feelings of dissatisfaction are not as likely to result in improved performance as knowledge that " I made sales to five new clients last quarter while the average for the district was eleven."

## PROBLEMS OF SKILL AND RATE

All performance problems fall into one of two categories: problems
of skill and problems of rate. Problems of skill involve the ability to
perform. Problems of rate involve the number of times a person does
perform. If someone lacks the skill of typing, for example, all the
motivation, desire, reinforcement or other influence will have little
effect except to create frustration and anxiety. *Problems of skill demand
training as a solution.* New behaviors must be acquired if a performance
deficiency is a problem of skill. One way to determine if a problem is
one requiring the acquisition of a new skill or is one of rate is to ask
yourself the question "If I offered him/her a million dollars to perform
the task I want, would he/she be able to successfully perform the
task?" In other words, given maximum motivation, will the behavior be
performed? If you offer someone who sings like a frog a million dollars
to perform an operatic aria, that individual despite tremendous motivation will not be able to sing that aria. Similarly, if you ask the individual
to conduct a sales presentation in a manner that will result in an order
from one of your most difficult customers, the individual may fail owing
to lack of selling skills, despite a high level of motivation.

*Problems that we traditionally consider to be ones of motivation
are more usefully described as problems of rate or frequency.* All motivation can be described in terms of frequency of performance. The
salesperson who is highly motivated performs certain behaviors at a
higher rate than the one who is not. The executive who is highly motivated performs certain behaviors at a higher rate than one who is not.
For example, the salesperson who may be described as highly motivated may make more sales calls per week, arrive to work at an earlier
hour, make more telephone calls per day, complete reports more
quickly, ask customers for more leads, or walk and talk at a higher
rate. Rate or frequency, the number of times a behavior is performed
within a period of time, is a more useful concept than motivation
because it provides for precise measurement and hence an accurate
evaluation of behavior change efforts. The ability to measure motivation accurately has been a stumbling block in performance improvement efforts for years. You will be well advised to forget about motivation as an entity and, in the future, consider it only in terms of rate
of performance. All future references to motivation in this book will
be explicitly defined as the rate or frequency of performance of a

specific behavior, the number of times that behavior may be observed to have occurred within a given period of time.

It could be argued that the best thing that might happen to management practice would be the elimination of the two words most commonly used in discussing performance deficiencies: motivation and attitude. These two words hang over the world of organizational management like big black clouds, fogging the view and blocking the sun. If these words were eliminated from the vocabulary of the manager, performance deficiencies would be described in more meaningful terms. Managers often use these terms as a scapegoat: "My employees have a bad attitude," "What we have here is a motivational problem." These terms are used to assign repsonsibility elsewhere. When the problem has been defined as one of motivation, the feeling of personal responsibility is dissipated. No one feels that he can improve someone else's attitude or motivation. So no action need be taken to improve the situation. But how about increasing the number of times reports are handed in on time, the percent of first-quality production, or the number of fifteen-minute intervals spent working on priority A tasks? Yes, these can be changed. Responsibility for measurable variables is not so easily assigned elsewhere. These are manageable.

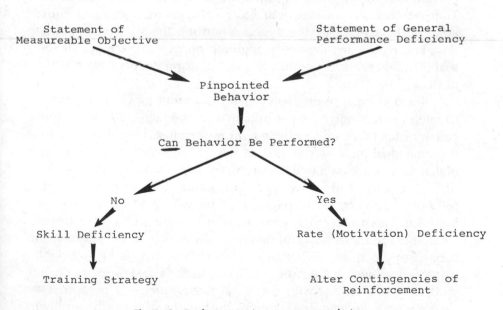

**Figure 6** Performance improvement analysis.

When the performance in need of improvement is a skill deficiency, training is required. That does not mean that the training department is called upon. Most training is accomplished on the job under the supervision of the line manager. Whereas most training in the formal sense is conducted by trainers, this should in no way be confused with the acquisition of new skills. Most new skills are acquired on the job. Without any formal preparation a large number of managers accomplish their training tasks suprisingly well.

Training is conducted whenever an individual engages in an activity that results in the ability to exercise a skill that he did not previously have. This training may be as simple as instruction in the completion of sales reports, or it may be as complex as learning to manage a sales organization. The manager, in addition to the day-to-day operations and the long-range planning and direction of his organization, must assume responsibility for the development of the people under him who will perform the tasks that will result in organizational effectiveness. The best managers are often those who are most concerned with this task of developing subordinates in the organization.

Behavior management provides a basis for skill acquisition, learning new behavior, in addition to increasing or decreasing the rate of performance of behavior currently within the individual's repertoire. Training generally involves four basic components: acquiring knowledge of the skill, observing a model perform the skill, practicing the skill, and reinforcing the newly acquired behavior. These are all steps that the manager does perform and can perform with greater effectiveness.

If a performance deficiency is a motivation problem, a problem of rate of peformance, the performance can be increased by the application of feedback and reinforcement procedures. The environment of the individual must be changed so that it "pays off" to perform at a higher rate. In addition to pinpointing the behavior, measuring the rate of that behavior, and following the procedures that are outlined in the following chapters, the manager must be willing to change his own behavior. The manager must realize who has the problem. In training supervisors the techniques of behavior management, I often hear the supervisor moan that the employee "oughta wanna do his job right," or "the employee has a problem." The truth is that workers do not work harder, faster, or with greater accuracy, precisely because they *do not have a problem*. The supervisor is the one who has the problem, not the employee. Ask the employee who is working at sixty percent efficiency if he has a problem. He doesn't have a problem. He is getting paid each week, his job is comfortable, and he has lots of energy left when the day is over. What problem does he have? The supervisor who is held accountable for the total performance of his work unit has the problem. The manager responsible for the productivity of the organization has the problem. *And it is the person to whom the problem belongs who must assume responsibility for change.* It is in the best interest, it will pay off, for the supervisor or manager to initiate change. That change must be directed at making it matter, making it a problem for the employee.

Whether or not performance matters to the employee is a function of "the contingencies of reinforcement," the consequences that the environment delivers to the individual following his performance. Behavior management is a method of altering the events in the environment that affect the performance of the individual employee. Behavior management makes performance matter to the employee, supervisor, manager, or executive whose behavior needs to be changed.

## INTERNAL AND EXTERNAL BEHAVIOR

Behavior is of two types: internal and external. Behavior management is concerned with changing both types of behavior. Internal behavior includes all those responses that occur within and may not be observed. External behaviors are, of course, all those responses that may be observed by someone else. Internal behavior includes all those feelings, emotions, thoughts, or other reactions to events in our lives that remain as private events. These internal activities are not commonly thought of as behavior. Behavior, to most individuals, refers to external behaviors, visible responses. But internal behavior is more similar to external behavior than most people imagine. Emotions and thoughts are also learned and are subject to many of the same laws of learning and control as external behavior.

The manager is concerned with internal responses only to the degree that they are related to external responses. Managers often feel they are responding to an employee according to that employee's emotions, when in reality they are responding to external behavior. The employee who appears depressed has a "drawn-out" facial expression and a reduced rate of smiling, does not converse in the same spontaneous manner as normal, may tend to stare into space, and is likely to be relatively unproductive. All these behaviors are external. They are, however, closely associated with the internal response of depression. The manager is correctly concerned about this set of responses, because while it may result from an unhappy family situation or other personal experience, it does affect work performance. It is not, however, the internal response, the depression, that is the cause of the manager's concern. It is all the corresponding external behaviors. If the manager can cause this employee to smile more often, react in an enthusiastic and spontaneous manner, and concentrate on productive activities, the employee will be more satisfied and the other workers who associate with the troubled worker will be more comfortable and productive.

Internal and external behavior occur concurrently and interact. Feeling sad affects the probability of talking with friends, an external behavior. Talking with friends has an effect on the internal behavior of feeling sad. When concerned about the emotions or attitude of an employee, should the manager attempt to change the internal behavior directly or indirectly by changing the corresponding external behavior? If the external behavior can be changed, then the corresponding internal behavior will also be affected. The manager will find, as much psychological research has found, that it is more effective to focus one's efforts on the external behaviors that are observable, measurable, and more easily modified (Bandura, 1959).

Advocates of behavior management are sometimes accused of ignoring thoughts and emotions or of being unconcerned about these obviously important factors in the employee's well-being. Behavior managers are concerned about thoughts and emotions but usually

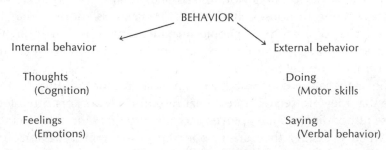

Figure 7   Types of behavior.

focus on the external behavior as the subject of change simply because this approach is more direct. The result of their focusing change efforts on the observable behavior is usually a more nearly satisfied manager and employee. Changes in external behavior usually produce a corresponding change in internal behavior.

## FACTORS IN TARGET SELECTION

The behavior manager begins his effort to improve performance by identifying specific measurable results (i.e., production, quality, absenteeism) to be changed and specific pinpointed behaviors that cause the result to be achieved. In addition to selecting observable and measurable behaviors and results, there are several other considerations when one is deciding where to focus one's behavior change effort. Three are as follows: *first, the reinforcing value of the change; second, the shaping consideration; and third, the economic consideration.*

*It is important to begin a behavior change effort by influencing a behavior or outcome that will be pleasing to all of those involved.* The initial effort must be reinforcing to those whose participation and cooperation will be necessary for later efforts. If the manager or behavior manager begins by successfully influencing a behavior that is of no concern to those of influence in the organization, he will have difficulty acquiring support for future efforts. The manager should begin by asking "What change in performance will be most reinforcing to those whose support will be required for further change efforts?" A manager may be invited by a plant manager to try to improve performance. The manager may begin by identifying the behavior of arriving to work on time as his initial target. He may have selected this target because it is easily measured and can generally be influenced by simple feedback. After establishing a feedback system and causing a significant improvement in this behavior, the manager may find greater cooperation in the future cooperation. If this program had been used among knowledge workers, rather than production workers, it might have been of little consequence to the managers and it might have produced a negative reaction on the part of workers and managers alike. The change agent must do his homework in determining which changes in performance will be most rewarding to the management team and the highest manager within the organization involved in the effort. This needs identification is best accomplished by interviewing managers at various levels. This questioning may not reveal the improvement that will be most productive in economic terms or the change that may have the most long-lasting or the broadest effect. It simply reveals the change "of greatest concern," the change that will be most reinforcing or pleasing to the managers. This selection of initial targets for improvement is critical to the success of behavior management within an organization.

*Second is the "shaping" consideration.* Shaping, as is discussed in greater detail in Chapter 6, is the procedure of reinforcing successive approximations to a goal behavior—in other words, reinforcing bits and pieces of improvement in performance. The initial target for improved performance should be one that can be easily achieved. It should not require mammoth changes in the behavior of many persons. It is far better to begin small, succeed, and gradually progress to more difficult and more nearly comprehensive changes in performance. Entire behavior management programs involving many individuals, six to twelve months of work, and tens of thousands of dollars have been lost because the changes expected were unrealistic. In a case that occurred in a sales organization of a nationally known corporation a comprehensive system of behavior measurement, feedback, and reinforcement was established and months of baseline data were computed, but the program was not successful. The task of operating this system, which would ultimately have saved the manager's time, appeared overwhelming to them. They had not experienced any previous success with the positive approach they were asked to implement. They had managed their salespersons through fear and threats for many years. They were now asked to focus their attention on desirable behavior and reinforce salespersons who improved their performance. This was too difficult a task and required too great a change on their part. They were not able to use the management system designed for them. They needed to be shaped gradually, into the use of positive and systematic techniques of management. Small, simple, and easily operated behavior change procedures would have been more valuable than the comprehensive system designed for them.

The principle of shaping is also critical in focusing performance improvement efforts on one individual. For the employee operating at sixty percent efficiency an intial target of seventy percent efficiency is reasonable. After seventy percent efficiency is achieved for several weeks, a new target of increasing efficiency to eighty percent becomes reasonable.

Shaping is simply directed at the well-recognized principle of beginning where you can succeed. It is likely that a simple improvement will be followed by future efforts to enhance improvement. Achieving desired improvement reinforces the behaviors required for change. An initial failure to achieve a major change may witness the end of behavior management efforts within the organization. Failure is punishing, and the behavior that led to the failure will be avoided.

*The third consideration in identifying initial targets for improvement is economic.* The economic concern is tied closely to the first concern, that of the reinforcing value of one's change effort. Every performance improvement effort is an investment by the organization. The manager proposing or using behavior management should view his role as that of investing other people's money. He must plan his program to produce maximum return on investment and minimize risk, and he must be accountable to the investor. Whenever a behavior management effort is begun, there are costs and economic benefits. Among the costs are the time of the manager and other personnel concerned, the costs of any tangible reinforcers used, and costs associated with delaying other efforts to improve performance. Among the economic benefits are those that result directly from improving performance and avoiding the potential for economic losses from deteriorating performance.

The behavior manager should assess the potential economic impact of behavior change before beginning that change effort. He should clearly spell out the current costs of the performance problem and estimate the improvement that may be expected and its economic result. These estimates should be checked out and agreed upon with the next higher level of management before the program is started. This agreement provides the basis for mutual and objective evaluation of the program's effectiveness. Obtaining agreement on the potential economic benefit also helps to ensure management support.

By estimating the costs and benefits of behavior management, one can determine the priority or value of various potential changes. For example the department manager of a manufacturing plant may have several areas of potential improvement in performance such as increased production and reduction of waste, of second-quality goods, of absenteeism, of equipment downtime, and of turnover. This department manager should attempt to identify the current costs of each of these performance deficiencies. To do this there must be some standard against which current performance may be measured. Industrial engineers have established such standards in most facilities. While improvements in performance can often be made well beyond the standards set by industrial engineers, these are often the best estimates of a reasonable target for performance. If the manager can compare the costs of second-quality goods, during a one-month or three-month or six-month period, against the standard, he can then estimate the potential savings that may result from a behavior change effort to reduce second-quality goods.

Managers most often select a target for improvement based on the emotional reaction, "What's bothering me most?" The greatest bother at the moment may not be the most costly problem. It may simply be the problem that has come to the manager's attention most recently, or it may be the one that has undergone the greatest change during a recent period. *A careful analysis of the various components of total organizational* performance and the potential economic benefits that may be derived may indicate a priority change very different from that of greatest emotional concern.

If the change that would be of greatest economic benefit and the change most emotionally desirable are different, the behavior manager has to consider carefully which factor is more important. While he may be most reinforced by a demonstration of significant dollar savings, the plant manager or corporate executive may be more reinforced by the elimination of his greatest nuisance. In this circumstance the behavior manager is well advised to consult with the higher level manager, present the facts as he understands them, and let the higher level manager decide the priority. It is very often the case that a manager is more pleased by the removal of a thorn than by an economic savings. If the thorn is removed, progress toward the other change effort will probably be facilitated.

### SUMMARY

In this chapter we have examined the focus of behavior change efforts in organizations. Management by objectives (MBO) is currently one of the most widely practiced and successful methods of providing a format for behavior change. These MBO programs are compatible with behavior management and provide an excellent takeoff point for its methodology. Behavior management begins where MBO leaves off, with the question, "What do I have to do to cause the result to be achieved?" Managing someone's behavior is always a crucial element in the achievement of objectives.

The first step in the process is to pinpoint behavior. Pinpointed behaviors are those that may be observed and counted. We have developed the habit of interpreting behavior and labeling individuals on the basis of our interpretation of their behavior. *The manager must develop the habit of describing behavior* in terms that avoid interpretation and state what is observable.

A performance deficiency may be a deficiency of either skill or rate. Deficiencies of skill are operations that the individual cannot perform, regardless of the level of motivation or desire. Deficiencies of rate involve how often the behavior occurs. Motivation problems are more usefully described in terms of rate of performance. Problems of skill require a solution that will provide for the acquisition of the behavior. These are training tasks. Problems of motivation or rate require the change of the environmental conditions that "make performance matter." This is a management task.

Behavior management addresses both internal and external behavior. Internal behaviors are those traditionally described as thoughts and feelings. External behaviors are those that may be observed, what someone says or does. Both internal and external behavior are influenced by environmental circumstances controlled by the manager. Internal and external behavior interact and affect one another. A change in internal behavior corresponds to a change in external behavior. The manager is advised to focus his efforts on external behavior that may be observed and measured. This focus is most productive, not because he is unconcerned with the thoughts and feelings of the individual, but because this focus produces more satisfactory results in improving both internal and external behavior.

When selecting initial target behaviors or results for improvement one should take three factors into consideration. These are the degree to which a change in performance is reinforcing to the management whose support is required; the shaping consideration, rewarding improvements in bits and pieces; and the economic considerations of performance improvement.

Behaviors and results are the dependent variables, the outcome of a change effort. The next chapter examines the independent variables, those conditions that may be changed to cause a change in behavior and results.

### REFERENCES

Bandura, Albert. *Principles of Behavior Modification.* New York: Holt, Rinehart & Winston, Inc., 1969.

Ivancevich, John M. "Effects of goal setting on performance and job satisfaction." *Journal of Applied Psychology,* **61** (5), 1976, 605–612.

Kim, Jay S., and Hamner, W. Clay. "Effect of performance feedback and goal setting on productivity and satisfaction in an organizational setting." *Journal of Applied Psychology,* **61** (1), 1976, 48–57.

Mali, Paul. *Managing by Objectives.* New York: Wiley-Interscience, 1972.

Morrissey, George L. *Management by Objectives and Results.* Reading, Mass.: Addison-Wesley, 1970.

Odiorne, George S. *Management by Objectives.* New York: Pittman Publishing Company, 1965.

Raia, Anthony P. *Managing by Objectives.* Glenview, Ill.: Scott Foresman & Company, 1974.

# CASE STUDY NUMBER FOUR

## DECREASING
## HIGH BOBBINS

This case reports the management of spinning doffer behavior's resulting in high bobbins on spinning frames. If a bobbin is not pushed all the way down on a spindle by the doffer, it is called a high bobbin. This causes tangles, resulting in waste, lower winder efficiency, and lost man-hours clearing tangles. After collecting baseline on incidence of high bobbins, a feedback graph was posted in the department, showing the number on each of four shifts. The department manager posted these data daily and brought it to the attention of his shift supervisors and their doffers. Subsequently, high bobbins decreased dramatically. Later, suspension of feedback resulted in an increase in high bobbins and thus established a functional relationship between the feedback and the number of high bobbins.

### BACKGROUND CONDITIONS

The department manager of spinning in a yarn mill wanted to decrease the number of high bobbins found in the spinning frames. The feedback intervention was planned by the department manager as a result of behavior management training conducted by an outside consultant. As part of the training, each manager was assisted in setting up a behavioral project.

### PROCEDURE

First, the department manager began counting the number of high bobbins on each shift. He counted five days a week, once a day on

---

Appreciation is expressed to Michael McCarthy for the use of this case study.

each shift, without announcing what he was doing. This provided a baseline of eight days, averaging 55.9 high bobbins.

Next, this baseline was posted on a graph showing the numbers for each shift and the department total. A goal was drawn on the graph to gradually reduce to twenty high bobbins (five per shift) within two weeks. All shift supervisors were told of this goal, and they in turn announced it to their doffers. The shift supervisors were instructed to reinforce their doffers verbally with praise whenever an improvement was made (close to or below the goal line). The department manager verbally reinforced both shift supervisors and doffers.

## RESULTS

In the total department high bobbins decreased to the first goal of twenty. At no time during the two weeks did they exceed the goal level drawn on the feedback graph. The department manager reinforced the entire department with coffee and doughnuts, pairing this with praise as he personally distributed them to each doffer. As a coincidence the spinners and fixers in the department were similarly reinforced for improvements they had made in another project on bids out of production.

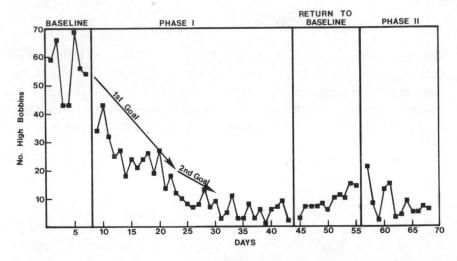

**Figure 8**   Number of high bobbins; Case Study 4.

A second goal of twelve was set over a week's time. When this goal was met, a third goal was set at zero. Before this was reached, the department manager, in consultation with the consultant, decided to suspend feedback to test the effectiveness of his procedure. He stopped posting the data (although continuing his counts) and then removed the feedback graph. The total department average from intervention until this point was 14.2 high bobbins.

With feedback removed the data rose from a low of three to a high of fifteen, averaging 8.7 high bobbins. Then, after eleven days without feedback, it was restored. Again the data decreased, from high of twenty-one to a low of two, averaging 8.1. At this point the department manager was promoted into another department and the project ended.

### DISCUSSION

During this project the consultant received anecdotal reports from employees and supervisors about "getting more positive comments" from their department manager. Self-reports from the department manager indicated he believed that he was "being more positive." Further anecdotal reports indicated that the employees accepted the goals as a challenge and responded good-naturedly about "wanting to beat that goal." The plant manager publicly commended the department manager for his success in this project.

The consultant believes that in large measure the success of this project was due to the high indicidence of fact-to-face verbal feedback and verbal reinforcement. Future research would be helpful in isolating the differential effects of consistent verbal feedback paired with graphed visual feedback, as opposed to posted graphed feedback alone.

### QUESTIONS FOR DISCUSSION

1. Describe the pinpointed behavior in this case. Also describe how a manager might interpret this behavior in terms commonly used to describe motivational states.

2.  Describe the antecedents that were changed or added to improve performance.

3.  Describe how changes in external reinforcers may have influenced internal reinforcers of the employees.

4.  The return-to-baseline phase illustrated on the graph is a component of research methodology. Describe both the advantages and disadvantages of using such a method in an industrial setting.

# CHAPTER FIVE

# MOTIVATION
# BY REINFORCEMENT

Any analysis of the determinants of individual or organizational performance necessitates a formulation that will simplify the reality. Performance is the function of so many complex conditions, current, past, and future, that a complete understanding of these determinants is virtually impossible (Cummings and Schwab, 1973). All we may hope for in an arrangement of some of our knowledge about these determinants in a manner that will facilitate application by the manager. Behavior management has contributed a model of behavior change that has proved effective in a wide variety of settings in which human behavior is the direct or primary concern (Luthans and Kreitner, 1975; Kazdin, 1975).

This chapter presents a model of the determinants of human performance within an organization based on the formulations of behavioral psychology. This formulation focuses on current behavior and current conditions in the environment, which are the factors over which the manager may hope to exert some control. The manager may be able to rearrange some of the conditions in the work environment, such as statements of objectives and rewards for performance, but has little hope of arranging conditions for the performance of behavior five years from now. And the manager obviously has no control over past conditions that affect an individual's behavior.

The manager should be aware that a major factor in determining today's performance is the previous experience, the learning history of the individual. The selection procedures that most corporations employ are designed to choose those individuals who have the ability and motivation that will enable them to function successfully in the job for which they are being screened. Selection must be concerned with the past behavior of the individual and the conditions under which it occurred. These previous conditions and behavior, if properly studied, are the best predictors of performance.

### ENTERING CHARACTERISTICS

Each individual brings to his job two general characteristics that determine his response to conditions in the work environment. They are, *first, his ability to learn; second, his current repertoire of behavior, learned from prior experience.* The successful selection matches the employee to the work environment in a manner that enables the worker to succeed there. The manager must structure the work environment to maximize the probability that those employees being hired can perform successfully at their work. The function of the personnel specialist is to analyze the job and the work environment to determine which learning abilities and behavioral repertoires are compatible with the existing conditions.

Although there is little the manager can do to change either the capacity to learn or prior learning, their recognition may help him understand the limitations and possible reasons for success or failure of his own efforts. A clear recognition of these factors and consideration of the relationship of each of these factors to his own work situation may also help the manager present valuable input to the personnel specialist.

### Ability to Learn

Individuals differ greatly in their ability to learn. This ability may vary according to the complexity of the tasks, the rate at which learning may occur, and the nature of the tasks to be learned. Variance in task complexity is most obvious between production line workers and knowledge workers such as engineers. The complexity of the assembly line task may be characterized by ten or twenty basic functions, that of the engineering task, by thousands of separate functions. The ability to perform tasks is acquired at different rates. Whether the behavior is the recall of information, the performance of abstract logic, or the matching of a screw to a hole, the acquisition of these behaviors is what we commonly refer to as learning. The manager or personnel specialist may analyze the amount and speed of learning required for a given job. He may then assess the learning ability of a job applicant to determine that the individual may learn the task within an acceptable time. Individual ability to learn also varies across types of tasks. For example, some individuals are said to have a "talent" for music. Having this talent simply means that the individual may learn behaviors associated with performing music at a faster rate than another individual. The same individual who has this talent or learning ability may be slow to learn mechanical tasks or tasks involving abstract reasoning. Once the type of learning required for a job is assessed, matching that type of learning with individual ability is a selection criterion.

### Behavioral Repertoire

In addition to the ability to learn, the individual brings with him prior learning. The previous history of the individual, the environmental conditions during his childhood, schooling, and prior work experience have conditioned a range of behaviors that are present when he enters the new job. The selection procedure should determine the behaviors currently within the individual's repertoire that may be required before he enters the job. It is a decision of considerable economic importance to determine which behaviors may be taught on the job and which are required before selection. For example, the manager of a sales organization is concerned both with the sales applicant's ability to learn the product knowledge required to sell successfully and with a broad range of interpersonal or social behaviors. The salesperson must have the ability to communicate with and persuade clients. The salesperson may decide he can afford to expend time and money required to teach a salesperson the necessary product knowledge, but he cannot afford to teach the salesperson the interpersonal skills required to perform the job successfully. Interpersonal skills are both difficult and time consuming to teach. Instead of deciding not to teach interpersonal skills at all, he may decide he can afford to teach certain refinements of communication skills, if a predetermined base of social skill is present before selection. The sales organization that decides it can teach communication, interpersonal, or selling skills to the applicant, regardless of entering behaviors, is going to find itself with enormous training costs, high turnover, and an unsuccessful sales program.

The manager and the selection specialist should perform a task analysis of each job for which applicants are selected. This analysis should determine the behavior required for a given job. They should then determine which behaviors are required and which may be learned on the job or in formal training. They may then establish a selection procedure to determine, through demonstration of performance, that the applicant has the required behaviors within his repertoire. Most often this determination is made by contacting references to ask whether or not the applicant was able to perform the required tasks on his previous job. Too often that is inadequate and provides misleading data. Former employers are much too likely to relay the positive aspects of the applicant's behavior and less likely to relate performance deficiencies. The best determination of existing skills is a test of their performance. This is usually possible with mechanical skills or social skills such as selling but becomes increasingly difficult with more complex jobs such as general management positions.

Motivation, the rate at which an individual performs those tasks he is able to perform, is a function of previous experience and of contingencies in the current environment. Because previous experiences vary, individuals respond differently to environmental contingencies (Mischel, 1958). For example, after years of receiving weekly paychecks, an individual becomes conditioned to this set of expectations and may have great difficulty delaying gratification for a monthly paycheck. Another individual may have worked on a bonus system or commission for many years and may be used to performing at a high rate to earn this contingency. Hired or transferred to a job in which a higher salary is paid but no bonus or commission is available, this same individual who performed at a high rate previously may experience a deterioration in performance although he may be receiving the same net pay. A third individual may have worked previously on a job in which he received daily feedback on his performance from a manager. The new job, requiring the same tasks, paying the same compensation, but providing only intermittent, perhaps monthly, feedback, may result in a serious deterioration in performance.

Each individual has been conditioned by prior work experience to respond, to be motivated, by a particular set of contingencies of reinforcement. When the contingencies are significantly altered, a change in performance may be expected, either for better or worse. Again the selection specialist or the manager should examine the previous contingencies under which the individual applicant was motivated to perform and compare these to the ones provided by the new job. To do this successfully, the manager or personnel specialist must understand the effects of various types of reinforcement procedures.

## MANAGEMENT RESPONSIBILITY/ENVIRONMENTAL CONTROL

The job of the manager is to achieve results through his organization. To accomplish this effectively, the manager must determine measurable results to be achieved by given dates and then change or maintain the behavior of his employees in a manner that will produce the desired results. *The manager must manage behavior. He must manage what people do that will cause the results he desires.* The manager may affect the behavior of his subordinates by the control of environmental conditions. If the manager can exert no control over the environment of the employees, he cannot manage. The greater the control over the environment and the greater the manager's ability to use this control in an effective manner, the greater his ability to achieve results.

The concept of managing the circumstances in the environment that affect behavior is not new. Managers have always been engaged in this effort. There is, simply stated, no other means of obtaining results. H. L. Garret (1908) discussed how managers must train "workmen in habits of industry and organizations." Garrett provided an analysis of training and environmental conditions that is still, for the most part, valid. What has been lacking is an empirical analysis of how the change in environmental circumstances affects behavior, which in turn affects results (Figure 9).

*All practices of managers involve the manipulation of the environment to achieve results.* The manager who threatens his employees with termination if they do not produce a certain rate is manipulating an environmental variable, the potential dismissal. The manager who restructures the work to provide greater variety of tasks, increased participation in decision making and greater self-management is manipulating environmental variables to achieve results. The manager who communicates with the employees frequently and in an empathetic and reinforcing manner is manipulating another environmental vari-

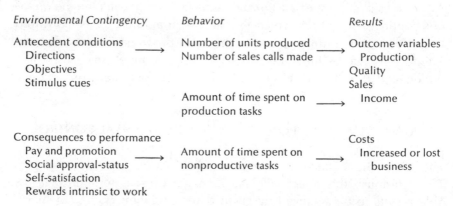

| Environmental Contingency | Behavior | Results |
|---|---|---|
| Antecedent conditions <br>   Directions <br>   Objectives <br>   Stimulus cues | Number of units produced <br> Number of sales calls made | Outcome variables <br>   Production <br>   Quality <br>   Sales |
| | Amount of time spent on <br> production tasks |   Income |
| Consequences to performance <br>   Pay and promotion <br>   Social approval-status <br>   Self-satisfaction <br>   Rewards intrinsic to work | Amount of time spent on <br> nonproductive tasks | Costs <br>   Increased or lost <br>   business |

**Figure 9**   Environmental contingencies, behavior and results.

able. Any of the circumstances in the environment of the worker may affect the worker's performance.

At the outset of an investigation into the effective use of environmental influence to manage performance it is important to understand that whether or not to manipulate, control, or manage the circumstances in the environment is not at issue. Whereas other writers may choose to view the practice of environmental change from other theoretical perspectives, the practice is much the same. All schools of management thought or practice prescribe some type of environmental change to manage performance.

Imagine that a manager determined not to control environmental influences on performance. This manager would choose to provide no direction or objectives for performance. He would choose to provide no feedback, positive or negative. He would provide no rewards, either tangible or intangible. Each of these are elements of environmental control that influence performance. Without them, there can be no management of human performance. The question the manager must ask is not whether arrangements of environmental contingencies affect performance, but which types of contingencies, delivered in what manner, on which schedule, and to which individuals, result in which types and rates of performance.

The control of environmental contingencies determines not only performance but also learning that will result in future performance. Current and future behaviors are a function of the influence of environmental variables on them. The behavior rewarded today is the behavior performed tomorrow. The manager is the primary trainer in any organization, whether deliberate and acknowledged or unwitting. Few managers recognize their training responsibility and fewer still recognize how they can maximize their training effectiveness by using their influence over environmental contingencies.

Too often managers unwittingly train their employees to perform behavior that they would rather see eliminated. The line manager who complains to his employees about upper management policies is training that employee to complain about policies that the manager may have determined. The manager who frequently makes derogatory statements about customers is training his employees to think, feel, and act in a derogatory manner toward those customers. Similarly the manager who presents a model of dedication, working for long periods without break, arriving to work early and leaving late, and speaking enthusiastically about the organization's future plans, is training the employees to engage in similar behaviors.

Although it is unpopular to allegorize the role of the manager in terms of parenthood, there are some similarities worth consideration. The inescapable nature of the training role is similar to that of parent and manager. Children and employees tend to model or imitate the behavior of parents and managers. The force of example is one of the most powerful educational forces in any environment. Employees, particularly those who are ambitious and seeking advancement, select models who exemplify those characteristics they believe are necessary to obtain advancement. Unfortunately, like the child, the employee imitates not only desirable behaviors, but also those the manager may later wish he had never observed.

The manager must recognize that he manages not only the forces in the environment external to himself, such as pay and direction, but also those that include his own conduct. The ability to manage one's own conduct in a manner that presents the most desirable model is a critical element of successful management.

## CONTROLLING CONDITIONS

All conditions in the work environment that exert control over behavior may be divided into two categories: *first, those stimuli that act on the individual before the occurrence of a behavior; second, those stimuli that act on the individual after the occurrence of the behavior, and are consequences to the behavior.* These, the antecedent stimuli and the consequences, are all-inclusive categories. There are no events influencing the behavior of individuals that do not fit within either.

These three categories—antecedent, behavior, consequences—are Skinner's contingencies of reinforcement (Skinner, 1969). Maintaining and changing behavior are a function of the relationships among these three operations. By identifying the pinpointed behavior he wishes to change, the antecedents that set the occasion for the behavior, and the consequences that follow the behavior, the manager has identified the elements of environmental control.

Figure 10 illustrates the relationships among these factors and examples of each.

While all the forces that influence behavior may be divided into antecedents and consequences, within each of these categories are

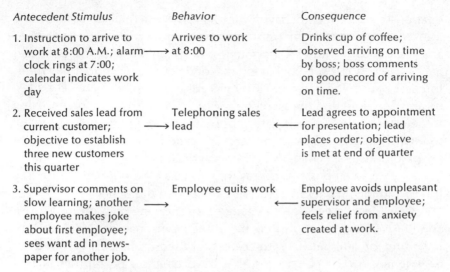

**Figure 10**   Sample antecedents, behavior, and consequences.

several different types of antecedents and consequences and many patterns of relationship. The next several chapters expand the explanation of these relationships, and later chapters discuss specific methods of application for obtaining efficient use of the contingencies available to the manager.

On first exposure to this formulation of behavior management most individuals feel that something has been left out. This can't be all there is that influences behavior. Surely this is too simple. This initial feeling is largely based on the misunderstanding that these categories of antecedents, behavior, and consequences include only those that are external or observable. Behavior management, while emphasizing the importance of observable events, includes an analysis of those contingencies that occur entirely or partially within the individual. Each person is a system providing his/her own antecedents, behavior, and consequences to that behavior. A good example of this occurs when one tries to gain control of an undesirable habit. You may speak to yourself, reprimanding (consequence) yourself for smoking (behavior) the cigarette you promised (antecedent) yourself you wouldn't smoke. Another example is the internal pat on the back (consequence) that you may experience after having completed a full day without eating sweets (behavior).

Another complicating factor in the analysis of the "functional relationship" between behavior and its environmental determinants is the concurrent nature of causal processes. The manager attempts to analyze one behavior at a time, trying to identify one antecedent that may serve as a cue for a behavior and one consequence that may reinforce or punish the behavior. But the causal process is highly complex. At any one time, for any given behavior, there are many forces acting to determine the type and nature of behavior. If an attempt was made to identify all the forces acting on any single behavior, the task would become hopelessly complex and impractical. It is most often possible, however, to identify a few events that serve as the primary controlling forces and that, if altered, result in a change in the behavior.

Consider the decision to change jobs. Leaving one job in favor of another is the behavior. Among the antecedents may be (1) discussions regarding job alternatives with co-workers and friends, (2) hundreds of experiences on the current job that have taught a perception of that job's current and future value, and (3) recent interactions with managers who have indicated the possibility or lack of possibility of promotion. Among the consequences that may occur after the decision to change jobs are (1) increased income resulting in improved living standard, (2) altered status among co-workers, and (3) increased satisfaction or dissatisfaction resulting from the nature of the job itself. The list of antecedents and consequences may be expanded to include hundreds of events. There is generally, however, some balance of experiences that weigh in both directions. A behavior is either performed or not because the balance is tipped in one direction or the other. This balance may be altered by slight changes in the antecedents or consequences. Despite hundreds of influencing variables an employee may make the decision to leave a job because of one statement by his supervisor such as "John, I don't know what I'm going to do with you." Or the employee may decide not to leave because of experiencing reinforcement such as: "John, I've noticed that you've been working pretty hard lately. Yesterday, I was discussing with the department chief how valuable you are."

The manager must not expect to understand all the influences on behavior in the organization. He must be concerned with understanding how best to use the influences that he can control and that are most likely to tip the balance of forces in the direction that will produce the behavior in the best interest of the organization and the individual.

## THE INFLUENCE OF CONSEQUENCES

Although antecedents occur before the behavior and consequences after, I have chosen to discuss consequences first. Without first understanding the process of reinforcement an adequate understanding of antecedents is virtually impossible. I am, therefore, working backward, first exploring the effect of consequences on behavior.

Behavior management relies heavily on the use of consequences to effect change in performance. Skinner's theory of operant behavior states the *voluntary behavior that is emitted by the individual is controlled primarily by its consequences* (Skinner, 1954). These behaviors are said to be *operant* because they operate on the environment and generate consequences. All behavior that is voluntary is operant behavior. The choice the individual makes to perform in a given manner is conditioned by the consequences to previous performance. Most behaviors performed in everyday life are operant. Coming to work, working at a fast or slow rate, saying positive things about the company, or going out on strike are all voluntary or operant behaviors conditioned by the consequences that have previously followed the same or similar behavior.

Both desirable and undesirable events influence behavior when there is a *contingent* relationship between the behavior and consequence. A relationship is contingent when the behavior results in the consequence. This relationship between the behavior and the contingent consequence may be described as a *contingency*. There is a contingency between making innovative contributions to the company for which an individual works and the probability of receiving a promotion. There is also a contingency between "laying out" from work and the probability of receiving the consequence of being fired. *An examination of these contingencies in the work place provides the basis for understanding the motivation, the rate of behavior, of the employees in an organization.*

## REINFORCEMENT

*Reinforcement refers to a procedure that produces an increase in the frequency of behavior followed by a consequence.* Reinforcement may be said to have occurred any time the frequency of a response has increased as the result of the contingency between a behavior and its consequences. Reinforcement is distinguished from reward in that a reward is something that is perceived to be desirable and is delivered to an individual after performance. An increase in pay, a promotion, and a comment on good work performance may all be rewards. But rewards are not necessarily reinforcers. Reinforcers are defined by the increase in the rate of behavior. A reward may be delivered and may be followed by no increase in behavior. In this case a reward may have been given but no reinforcement has occurred. In other cases reinforcement may have occurred but the reward may be unidentifiable.

The distinction between rewards and reinforcers is a critical one. At the heart of this distinction is the difference between the behavior management approach and other theories of management. Whereas other theories have postulated what should be rewards for various people, and therefore what should motivate individuals, behavior management relies on an empirical analysis to determine which conditions are motivational for an individual or group of individuals. The behavior manager must approach the process of motivation by measuring what works. What objects, events, activities, or jobs are reinforcing may be determined by the observation and measurement of behavior. If the presentation of a stimulus following a behavior results in an increase in the rate of behavior, it may be concluded that the stimulus is a reinforcer for that individual.

It is also important to reinforcement theory that the "presence of rewards" does *not* motivate. Rather, the contingent delivery of reinforcers results in motivation. Other writers exploring motivation have examined the rewards or satisfaction in the environment and have attempted to correlate those rewards with levels of motivation, without careful analysis of the contingent relationship between behavior and consequent reward (Herzberg, 1966). Behavior management examines the manner in which rewards are delivered and their effect to determine which rewards result in reinforcement and may therefore be said to be motivating. Only a reward that does result in an increased response rate is reinforcing or motivating.

Reinforcement is defined from the perspective of the recipient of reinforcement rather than of the provider. The manager views his actions in terms of the reactions of the employee. Traditionally managers have rewarded employees and assumed that the reward had the effect of motivating the employee. Too often this assumption has proved inaccurate. Managing the motivation of employees from the behavior management approach requires that the manager be more empathetic. The manager must carefully consider the response of the worker. He must understand the relationship between rewards and the response of the employee to those rewards. If, through observation, the manager determines that a reward does not result in increased performance, it is not a reinforcer and another reward or reward procedure must be attempted and examined for its influencing effect.

Much of the work of motivation theorists has focused on employee satisfaction. The assumption has been made that satisfaction results in motivation. McGregor (1957), Herzberg (1966), and their followers have sought to devise ways of increasing levels of employee satisfaction in the workplace. According to these job enrichment theories, when higher levels of employee satisfaction are present, higher levels of performance are likely to be achieved. This hypothesis has not stood up to empirical investigation (Umstot, Bell, and Mitchell, 1976). The research in operant behavior provides a basis for understanding why increasing levels of satisfaction do not necessarily result in increased levels of motivation (Ferster and Perrott, 1968). Motivation, rate of behavior, increases as effort is extended to obtain reinforcement. If an event, such as an interesting job, is present, there is no reason to work for it. An individual performs in anticipation of receiving reinforcement. An individual does not work to receive what he already has. Therefore, the presence of a more rewarding workplace, intrinsic job satisfaction, pay, or employee benefits do not result in improved performance. *If a contingent relationship, an if–then statement, is established between the desired level of performance and the receipt of the desired consequence, then improved performance results.*

There are many examples of high levels of motivation, high rate behavior, performed voluntarily, for tedious and boring tasks. Bingo is a good example. What could be more boring than the task of sitting at a table for hours on end, listening to numbers being called out, and placing small squares over the numbers on a board? This task would rival the most tedious production line work for lack of intrinsic satisfaction. However, millions of people not only are willing to perform this task but also actually pay money to do so. The explanation for this high level of motivation may be found in the schedule of reinforcement. All gambling is arranged to provide reinforcement on a variable-ratio schedule of reinforcement, a schedule of reinforcement that has proved in the laboratory and in the workplace to produce high rates of behavior.

Another example of high levels of motivation that may be produced despite the lack of intrinsic job satisfaction was clearly pointed out by the description of one worker.

> I have the most boring job in the world. When I go to work I have virtually no choice in my assignments. I go to my machine and have to sit in the same seat for up to twelve hours at a time. When I first arrive, I make a few adjustments on some switches and dials. I make sure all of the dials read the way they are supposed to and then I sit there, hour after hour, watching the dials, only occasionally making a few adjustments. At the end of my work day I make a few more adjustments and turn off my machine. After eight hours of rest, I go back to my machine and go through the same procedure.

Surely this is a good description of an "unenriched" job, one that might result in high rates of turnover, absenteeism, and poor work quality. But the workers who do this job have virtually no turnover and no absenteeism and are well known for their very low rate of errors or mistakes. The worker who described this job was a pilot of a Boeing 747 who made two trips a week to Brazil. The excellent performance of pilots can be explained, not by the intrinsic rewards of the job, but by the consequences, monetary and social, delivered contingent on good performance.

Research on pay and performance has demonstrated that pay is motivating to the degree that it is contingent on performance. High pay does not produce high performance. The availability of high pay as a reinforcer for good performance does produce high performance. Lawler (1976), who has conducted extensive research on pay and performance, has concluded that "There are two conditions that must exist for pay to be a motivator—it has to be important to the individual and the individual has to see a connection between his or her behavior and pay." Unfortunately, most firms do a poor job of creating the necessary contingency between pay and performance. To establish this relationship, there must be accurate measurement of performance, statement of desired performance (objectives), and demonstration by the organization that it will pay off when the individual does perform. If these conditions exist, pay will serve as a reinforcer.

For reinforcement to occur, there must be another condition present in addition to the contingent relationship between behavior and consequence. The subject of the reinforcement, the worker, must experience deprivation of the reinforcer. *There must be some level of dissatisfaction if reinforcement, increased rate of performance, is going to occur following the delivery of a reward.* In other words the individual who has as much money as he wants is not motivated by money. The individual who has just eaten a three-course meal may not be reinforced by food. Fortunately, or unfortunately, depending on your perspective, virtually all of us are experiencing deprivation of a number of conditions that are adequate to establish rewards as reinforcers if properly presented. Money is a particularly useful reinforcer because of its generality. It is a token that may be cashed in for a wide variety of items. Money may be exchanged for food, vacation, a home, schooling for children, and thousands of other objects and activities. This generality of money permits the use of money as a reinforcer for a wide diversity of individuals.

The use of rewards for which deprivation does not exist fails to reinforce. This is often the case in sales incentive or motivational contests. An item such as a television, vacation in the Bahamas, or some other specific event may be offered as a reward for high levels of performance. This is likely to result in high levels of performance among some individuals and not among others. In such incentive programs a wide choice of rewards must be made available if reinforcement is to occur for a large percent of the individuals.

## POSITIVE AND NEGATIVE REINFORCEMENT

Reinforcement may be either positive or negative. *Positive reinforcement* refers to the presentation of a desired stimulus following a behavior, resulting in an increased frequency of response. *Negative reinforcement* refers to the *removal* of an aversive or unpleasant stimulus, resulting in an increased frequency of a response. *Both positive and negative reinforcement are procedures resulting in the increased rate of responding.* Negative reinforcement should not be confused with punishment, which is discussed later.

*Positive reinforcement* includes most of the examples of reinforcement generally used in the organizational setting. A promotion is *presented* following the desired performance, resulting in increased response. A certificate of achievement is awarded (presented) following a period of perfect attendance. Social status and approval are attained (presented) following the earning of an academic degree. In all cases of positive reinforcement a reward has been presented and an increase in frequency of behavior has followed.

Positive reinforcement often occurs when it is not planned or desirable. Many forms of misbehavior or poor performance are maintained or increased by positive reinforcement. A group of employees may engage in organized work slowdowns or disruption, followed by the presentation of improved working conditions, benefits, or pay. This is likely to result in an increased probability of this behavior's occurring in the future. Positive reinforcement may be said to have occurred in this case. Supervisors, often inadvertently, positively reinforce poor performance of workers. The employee is expected to perform at an acceptable level and is not provided much attention or recognition when doing so. When an employee is performing below the accepted standard of performance, the supervisor may call that employee into his office for a discussion. This attention may be desirable to the employee. Most workers desire to be noticed, to receive attention from their supervisors. If this attention is withheld when performance is high and delivered when performance is low, it is likely that the low performance is being positively reinforced.

The stimulus that may serve as a positive reinforcer may be of many types. The reinforcer may be a social consequence such as praise, approval, and status among fellow workers, in the community, or at home. The reinforcer may also be tangible, an object such as a gift, award, or even something as simple as a cup of coffee. A reinforcer may also be a token or negotiable reinforcer such as money or some type of certificate that may be exchanged for a choice of things or activities. Reinforcers may also occur within the individual (internal) or outside of the individual (external). Internal reinforcers include all the emotions of self-satisfaction, pride, and a feeling of achievement. These are positive reinforcers when they are presented following the behavior, even though they occur from within. Reinforcers may also be intrinsic to the task itself, such as observing a finished piece of woodwork after many hours have been devoted to its construction.

Or positive reinforcers may be extrinsic, delivered deliberately to provide reinforcement and not naturally occurring as a result of the task. All of these are positive reinforcers if they are delivered or presented following the behavior and result in increased rates of performance.

*Negative reinforcement* refers to increasing the frequency of a behavior by removing an aversive event after the behavior is performed. Although negative reinforcement is less noticeable in the work environment, much of the behavior that occurs in the organizational setting is motivated by it. Negative reinforcement essentially involves avoidance. A behavior is performed to avoid an unpleasant situation. When an employee quits his job (unless he is motivated by the opportunity to obtain a better job), he is probably avoiding an unpleasant situation. His behavior of quitting has been negatively reinforced. After he performs the behavior of quitting, his world feels better than it did while he was working. He has gone from an unpleasant environment to a somewhat more pleasant one. This experience is reinforcing and results in an increased rate of behavior. An employee may learn that he can avoid work by taking extended breaks or by causing a mechanical breakdown. These situations result in the change of stimulus from one that is aversive to one that is less aversive. This change is desirable and causes an increase in the rate of the behavior that resulted in the change.

In the industrial setting there are many work situations that are unpleasant for the employee. The unpleasant situation may involve all of the five senses, but most often may be noise, odors, heat and physical exertion. In any industrial setting where this is the case it is likely that a close examination will reveal examples of negatively reinforced behavior.

Rarely should negative reinforcement be employed by a manager to improve performance. Positive reinforcement may be delivered contingent on performance to increase desired performance. Negative reinforcement can be planned only by structuring a situation from which an employee would want to escape. Obviously, it is not desirable to construct unpleasant situations simply to provide an opportunity to increase avoidance behavior. The avoidance behavior most likely may be avoidance of the job itself. However, awareness of negative reinforcement that is already occurring in many jobs may help the manager remove the aversive stimuli that occasion the avoidance behavior. Or the manager may choose to structure the contingencies so that the employee may avoid the unpleasant stimulus contingent upon predetermined amount, quality, or duration of performance. For example, if the manager is in charge of a painting and heat enameling operation, in which high temperatures and fumes are unavoidable, he may make changes in job assignments or arrange breaks that provide escape from the noxious stimuli contingent upon specified performance. This would be preferable to an unstructured situation in which employees sought to cause breakdowns, do a poor job to avoid those assignments, or quit working if they perceived that this was the only response that could result in the desired avoidance.

### Intrinsic and Extrinsic Reinforcement

Reinforcement may be either intrinsic or extrinsic. *Extrinsic reinforcers* include pay, fringe benefits, and promotions because they are controlled by someone other than the employee. *Intrinsic reinforcers*, on the other hand, are those over which the employee exerts a high degree of control and that are a naturally occurring function of the work itself. Intrinsic versus extrinsic reinforcement has become a controversial and important issue (Notz, 1975) in the recent management literature. Intrinsic reinforcement is extremely important, because of the potential for both increasing performance and for improving the general level of personal satisfaction of millions of workers.

The subject of intrinsic and extrinsic reinforcement evokes strong opinions and is charged with personal value considerations. Intrinsic reinforcement involves all the satisfactions an individual may obtain from the work itself. Extrinsic reinforcers include all those controlled by the employer. There is a tendency for both the worker and the student of the workplace to desire to create environments in which the individual is relatively free of extrinsic reinforcers and more under the control of task-related intrinsic reinforcers. Extrinsic reinforcement is by definition controlled by the organization, while intrinsic reinforcement occurs more naturally as a consequence of the tasks associated with the job. However, intrinsic and extrinsic reinforcement may not be as easily separated as might at first appear. Extrinsic reinforcement increases intrinsic reinforcement. The employee handed a one-hundred-dollar bonus check for submitting an innovative suggestion to the company has been extrinsically reinforced. But he feels better about his innovative idea than he would have if he had not been handed the check. While he may have achieved some degree of intrinsic reinforcement simply from seeing his suggestion accepted and acted on, knowing that he made a worthwhile contribution to his company, the extrinsic reinforcer has added to the value of the intrinsic reinforcer.

The evidence to suggest that intrinsic and extrinsic reinforcements are incompatible or in any way interfere with each other is subject to debate (Miller, 1976; Pinder, 1976; Foster and Hamner, 1974). There is good reason to believe that intrinsic reinforcement is conditioned by extrinsic reinforcement (Bandura, 1969). This conditioning explains why some people find certain tasks enjoyable, such as art forms, handicrafts, or writing, while others would find these same tasks lacking in intrinsic reinforcement and would perform them only in the presence of an extrinsic contingency. The individual who receives intrinsic satisfaction from writing does so because his writing has been reinforced by others. He does not write, a behavior that is tedious and very much like work (believe me), because he enjoys reading what he has written. He derives satisfaction from completing a work because he has received approval as a consequence of his writing behavior in the past. Because he has received this extrinsic reinforcement, he now receives intrinsic reinforcement from his work itself, independent of the external consequences.

Intrinsic and extrinsic reinforcement are closely tied and there are many opportunities for increasing job satisfaction and the rewards from the job itself by planning the contingencies of reinforcement related to the work in a manner that increases positive reinforcement.

### Internal and External Reinforcement

Another view of reinforcement is based on the occurrence of the reinforcement from within or from outside the individual. *Internal reinforcement refers to those thoughts or feelings that occur within the individual in response to some other behavior of the individual and that reinforce that behavior.* An example of internal reinforcement would be any feeling of satisfaction at one's own performance. A pleasant thought, perhaps about the vacation being planned, may reinforce the behaviors that result in the vacation. Internal reinforcement may reinforce behavior that is either internal or external. The internal feelings of satisfaction at achieving some result considered worthwhile may occur in response to an external action, such as hitting a hole-in-one on the golf course, or arise from a cognitive activity, such as thinking of a solution to a problem.

Internal reinforcement maintains a great percentage of our daily activities. We think of something we should do (internal behavior) and think of the satisfaction that will result from having accomplished that task (internal reinforcer). We then engage in the task (external behavior). While performing the task we think of how well we are performing it (internal reinforcer), and when we finish the task (external behavior), we feel satisfied that we have finished it and won't need to worry about it in the future (internal reinforcer). Internal reinforcement is a major element of self-control. If internal reinforcement did not occur, then we would truly be dependent on others for our reinforcers. We would be entirely under the control of others. We have, however, learned that certain outcomes, behaviors, and events are desirable, and the thoughts and feelings about these events produce the internal reinforcement that allows the individual to perform without the statement of a contingency by someone else. We are capable of independent action and of what has been classically considered "self-motivation" to the degree that we are capable of internal reinforcement.

Internal reinforcement is often confused with intrinsic reinforcement, and the distinction is often cloudy upon first introduction. Intrinsic reinforcement is intrinsic to the task being performed. For example, cooking a meal involes many behaviors, such as assembling the proper utensils, chopping the onions, mixing the salad, and mixing the ingredients of a sauce. As a result of all of this activity a meal results that one can see spread out on a table and may taste. Intrinsic reinforcers occur as a natural result of performing the task of cooking. Nevertheless, many of these intrinsic reinforcers, such as tasting the meal, are external. Although a natural result of the job, they occur outside of the individual. Intrinsic reinforcement may also produce internal reinforcement. After tasting the casserole, which the cook has just spent three hours preparing, he may say to himself, "This is the best Persian rice I've ever prepared." The taste of the Persian rice is an external reinforcer and the thought that "this is the best Persian rice I've ever prepared" is an internal reinforcer. Both of these events are intrinsic to the task of preparing the meal.

While the manager can do little to manage the internal reinforcement of the employee, he may benefit by the realization that this process is maintaining much of the behavior of that individual. The manager can arrange the work situation and the consequences to the work to produce external reinforcement, both intrinsic and extrinsic. As a result of this external reinforcement the employee also experiences internal satisfactions. External reinforcement teaches the employee that certain performances are desirable. This increases the probability that similar performance in the future will result in internal reinforcement.

### Tangible and Intangible Reinforcement

I have discussed a number of types of reinforcement: positive and negative, intrinsic and extrinsic, internal and external. One more distinction, and perhaps the one that receives the most attention by managers implementing behavior management and by consultants and trainers serving as change agents, is that between tangible and intangible reinforcement.

*Tangible reinforcement involves the presentation of an object* such as a selection from a gift catolog. Money is also generally considered to be a tangible reinforcer. *Intangible reinforcers include any reinforcing activity in which an individual may participate and any behavior of another person, social reinforcement.* Both tangible and intangible reinforcers are widely used in behavior change strategies in organizations. Intangible reinforcement, particularly social reinforcement, is a virtual requirement of any successful program. Tangible reinforcers are optional and may be effective and appropriate in some situations and highly ineffective and inappropriate in others. Social reinforcement is important because the social interaction between supervisor and employee is a powerful stimulus and one that has lasting effects on the work behavior of the employee. A primary goal of behavior management programs is to increase the frequency and quality of social reinforcement. The improvement of social reinforcement in organizations is often an area in which great improvement in performance can be obtained. It is one of the most neglected, taken for granted, and poorly performed management functions.

Tangible reinforcement is often a source of controversy in behavior management programs. The consultant or manager making behavior change efforts must ascertain the effect of using tangible reinforcers. In many organizations the mere suggestion of tangible reinforcement produces a very negative reaction toward the change agent. Many programs have been implemented in large, complex organizations with the use of tangible reinforcers, including money, and have resulted in significant behavior change. This is an area of concern that requires great sensitivity on the part of the consultant or manager and should be well planned at the beginning of any program. In Chapter 10 a procedure is suggested for determining reinforcers to be used in a behavior management program.

### Feedback as a Class of Reinforcers

Feedback has been used as a management tool for many decades. The reason feedback has been recognized as important in the work setting is that it influences behavior. *When feedback results in an increase in the frequency of behavior, it is, by definition, a reinforcer.*

Feedback is generally defined as *information about past performance presented to the individual who has performed.* Feedback may also be defined as *knowledge of results.* Management systems, in general, include a complex of feedback systems. Virtually every modern business includes computerized data processing of information to provide quick, complete, and reliable feedback data. Much of these data does influence the behavior of members of the organization. Often, however, this feedback is not delivered to the individuals most responsible for achieving the result. Feedback serves as a reinforcer if it is delivered to the people who control the result. Sales organizations often have a complex of data systems that generate excessive data on sales performance. But the salesperson often goes with little or no feedback on his performance. The same is true, perhaps to a greater extent, in most industrial manufacturing organizations. The data are collected, processed, and fed back but often do not reach the individuals who must perform. In such cases the information fails to serve as a reinforcer.

As can be seen by reading the case studies persented in this volume, feedback is one of the two most common reinforcers used in the organization setting (the other being social approval) during behavior management programs. Feedback is particularly advantageous as a reinforcer because it increases both performance and job satisfaction. Many job enrichment programs have included the use of feedback to increase job satisfaction. One of the most clear and consistent characteristics of sports or other forms of competition is the feedback the participants receive. Much of the satisfaction of athletics may be explained by the feedback effect. Who would enjoy watching a basketball game if there was no scoreboard? The knowledge of the result is what makes basketball, or any other sport, enjoyable for the participant and the observer.

Feedback is also advantageous for two other reasons: first the cost factor and second the ability to create ongoing systems of reinforcement. The consideration of costs is one of the realities of applying behavior management in work settings to which every manager is well accustomed. Many reinforcers cost money. Information on performance is often available to the manager at no additional cost. He just has to deliver it to the person whose behavior he wishes to change.

One of the most important practical considerations in the initiating of behavior management is that of implementing procedures that are efficient in terms of the management time required. For this reason systems that can be counted on to provide reinforcement with little required management time present an advantage. Feedback is the reinforcer best suited to systematic presentation. On the assumption that the information on performance is being collected, as it is in most business organizations, a system may be designed to present the individuals with that information frequently and regularly with little or no management time involved.

## REFERENCES

Bandura, Albert. *Principles Of Behavior Modification.* New York: Holt, Rinehart & Winston, Inc., 1969, pp. 238–239.

Cummings, L. L., and Schwab, Donald P. *Performance in Organizations: Determinants and Appraisal.* Glenview, Ill.: Scott, Foresman & Company, 1973.

Ferster, C. B., and Perrott, Mary Carol. *Behavior Principlese.* New York: New Century, Meredith Corporation, 1968, pp. 192–194.

Foster, L. W., and Hamner, W. C. "Are intrinsic and extrinsic additives a test of Deci's cognitive theory and task motivators?" Paper presented to the Academy of Management Conference at Seattle, 1974.

Gantt, Henry Laurence. "Training workmen in habits of industry and cooperation," in Harwood F. Merrill's *Classics in Management.* New York: The American Management Association, Inc., 1970.

Herzberg, Frederick. *Work and the Nature of Man.* New York: World Publishing Company, 1966.

Kazdin, Alan. *Behavior Modification in Applied Settings.* Homewood, Ill.: The Dorsey Press, 1975.

Lawler, Edward E., III. "Effective pay programs—An interview with Edward E. Lawler, III." *Compensation Review,* **8,** (3), Third Quarter, 1976.

Luthans, Fred, and Kreitner, Robert. *Organizational Behavior Modification.* Glenview, Ill.: Scott, Foresman & Company, 1975.

McGregor, Douglas. *The Human Side of Enterprise.* New York: McGraw-Hill Book Company, 1960.

Miller, Lawrence M. "Does paying people always increase work performance?" *Work Performance Magazine,* **2** (4), February 1976.

Mischel, Walter. "Preference for delayed reinforcement: An experimental study of a cultural observation." *Journal of Abnormal and Social Psychology,* **56,** 1958, 57–61.

Notz, William W. "Work motivation and the negative effects of extrinsic rewards." *American Psychologist,* September 1975.

Pinder, Craig C. "Additivity versus Nonadditivity of intrinsic and extrinsic incentives: Implications for work motivation, performance, and attitudes." *Journal of Applied Psychology,* **61** (6), 1976, 693–700.

Skinner, B. F. *Science and Human Behavior.* New York: The Free Press, 1954.

Skinner, B. F. *Contingencies of Reinforcement: A Theoretical Analysis.* New York: Appleton-Century-Crofts, 1969.

Umstot, Denis D., Bell, Cecil H., and Mitchell, Terence R. "Effects of job enrichment and task goals on satisfaction and productivity: Implications for job design." *Journal of Applied Psychology,* **61** (4), 1976, 379–394.

# CASE STUDY NUMBER FIVE

## INCREASING EFFICIENCY AND ATTENDANCE AND REDUCING LABOR TURNOVER

Through the systematic application of visual feedback and social reinforcement a behavior manager in a weave mill gradually increased the production efficiency of a weave department from a baseline average of sixty-nine percent to a goal level of ninety-five percent. By reinforcing employees individually and as a group, the behavior manager was able to form social interactions between employees generally associated with "team spirit" and improved the satisfaction derived from the work, as indicated by a reduction in both absenteeism and turnover. The increased cooperative behavior was also demonstrated by increased car pooling and other nonwork activities.

### BACKGROUND CONDITIONS

A behavior manager completed a two-week behavior management training course and was assigned to a weave mill in Georgia. He began to work with one weaving department on the "C" shift. There were fifteen employees on this shift. During the past few months, five of them had been threatened with dismissal and several others had been reprimanded for poor performance. There had been no follow-up to the dismissal threats by the previous supervisor on this shift.

The previous supervisor had not developed a close supervisor/employee relationship. He did not communicate with employees often, and his communications tended to be formal and centered only on necessary business. The employees themselves were not socially involved with each other and kept to themselves before the shift began and during breaks and had few interactions during the work shift.

**119**

Many rumors circulated among the employees concerning the supervisor and the reprimands handed out.

The previous supervisor had posted production graphs but did not keep them up to date and had not discussed them with the employees. There did not appear to be any sense of competition among the employees and there was little discussion among them of the levels of production.

## PROCEDURE

The behavior manager decided to focus his efforts on standard production efficiency because the baseline level of efficiency, at sixty-nine percent, represented a financial loss for the company. Efficiency in a weave room is a function of the number of "picks" per hour. A pick is the passing of the shuttle back and forth across the loom. The number of "picks" is recorded by an automatic counter on each loom. Industrial engineers have established a standard efficiency for picks per hour for looms in this weave department. This is represented as one hundred percent standard efficiency. The weaver may influence the number of average picks during his shift by his maintenance of the equipment and supply of yarn. While mechanical failures may influence the efficiency during any one period, the average standard efficiency for any period other than a very short one represents the behavior required of the weaver to maintain the operation of the looms.

The supervisor initiated the project by altering several variables related to feedback and social reinforcement. At the end of each shift each weaver received a sheet reporting the number of picks from the previous day and a goal number of picks for the next day. When a weaver had achieved the goal number of picks during the previous day, the supervisor wrote what he termed "words of encouragement" at the top of the sheet. These comments would include "great job, keep it up," "job well done," "we appreciate your efforts," and other, similar comments. The supervisor posted a graph reporting the performance in standard efficiency for each weaver. The graph was updated daily. A graph was also posted that reported "team effort," the average standard operating efficiency for all weavers in the department. The supervisor visited with each weaver on the job, an average of once daily, to talk about performance and ask if he had seen his production recorded on the graph. During this talk subjects of interests to the employee would also be discussed.

No employee meetings were held to discuss production, set goals or for any other purpose with one exception. During the ninth week of the program, efficiency and quality declined. The supervisor held a meeting to "read the riot act to them." This is the only occasion on which any group meetings were held.

One additional reinforcement procedure was used. A surprise hamburger cookout was held during the fifteenth or sixteenth week of the project. The supervisor bought hamburgers and placed the hamburger grill outside the weave room door. This cookout was held on a Saturday, when absenteeism is often high. The supervisor explained to the employees that this was to reinforce them for achieving eighty percent efficiency, which they had done during the previous week. The supervisor explained that he used this as a surprise rather than as a prearranged consequence because he did not want them to expect this or any similar reinforcer every time they met the eighty percent level of standard efficiency.

The supervisor placed the hamburger grill outside the weave room door so that the smell of the hamburgers drifted through the weave room during the shift. He had a "stand-in" relieve each individual weaver, one at a time, so that the weaver could go outside and eat his hamburger. The supervisor cooked and served the hamburgers and socialized with the weavers as they enjoyed their break.

## RESULTS

During the baseline period standard efficiency averaged sixty-nine percent over a three-month period. During the program period the standard efficiency rose over a twenty-seven-week period. During the last eight weeks for which data are available the average standard operating efficiency was eighty-seven percent. The supervisor reports that the efficiency remained over ninety percent for several months following that for which data are available. Labor attendance during the baseline period averaged 95.2 percent. During the last three months of the program attendance averaged ninety-nine percent. The percent of annualized labor turnover decreased from 142 percent during the baseline period to one hundred percent during the last three months

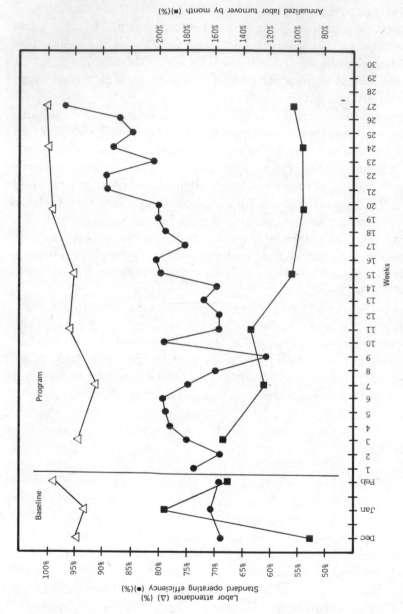

**Figure 11** Attendance, efficiency, and labor turnover; Case Study 5.

122

of the program. This represented no turnovers during the last three months of the program. Also reported during this period is a reduction in the number of defects per yard of yarn.

Although economic savings as a result of this program are not reported, they represent several thousands of dollars as a result of the increased yardage produced by the same number of people, the reduced training costs associated with turnover, and increased earnings as a result of reductions in the number of defects per yard of fabric. Employee satisfaction is also considered to have greatly improved, as evidenced by the reductions in absenteeism and turnover and by a number of anecdotal reports. The supervisor reports that the employees, who previously had little social contact, began to interact more often, began car pools, and made more favorable comments about their work. The supervisor also reports that the weavers would remind him to update their production graphs any day on which he either failed to record the previous day's data or was late doing so. Employees were evidently more interested in their levels of production as a result of the social reinforcement that had been paired with the data.

## DISCUSSION

This case demonstrates the influence an individual first-line supervisor can have on the production and satisfaction of his employees. The supervisor in this case engaged in a number of activities that established the conditions under which the employee was more likely to perform at a high rate. The supervisor set goals on a daily basis for the employee, gave feedback at a very high frequency, graphed performance to provide visual feedback, and socially reinforced the employees for increased performance. The combination of these specific procedures enhanced the general human environment in this department. The weavers undoubtedly felt that this supervisor "cared" about them and their performance. The supervisor was involved with the employees in that he expressed his appreciation to them and demonstrated by word and deed his concern about their productivity. This resulted in both increased performance and increased satisfaction among the employees.

## QUESTIONS FOR DISCUSSION

1. Discuss the relationship between intrinsic and extrinsic reinforcement that may be inferred from this case. What intrinsic and extrinsic reinforcers were present before and after the procedure was implemented? How do you know that either intrinsic or extrinsic reinforcement was increased?

2. List each of the events in this case that may be defined as reinforcing. Indicate whether these events are positive or negative reinforcers, intrinsic or extrinsic, internal or external, and tangible or intangible.

# CHAPTER SIX

# APPLYING POSITIVE
# REINFORCEMENT

The procedures that should be used most often by the manager to motivate employees are those of positive reinforcement. These are most commonly used by the practitioners of behavior management because these are primarily concerned with increasing or maintaining frequencies of behavior. Positive reinforcement has the fewest negative side effects and is the most manageable of the procedures of behavior change. The practitioner of behavior management uses it most often because it produces results that are reinforcing to the manager.

Because reinforcement is defined empirically, there can be no condition under which it may properly be stated that reinforcement "does not work." A procedure may be implemented and reinforcement may not occur. However, reinforcement either does or doesn't occur. If a procedure is one of reinforcement, it has, by definition, produced an increase in the frequency of a response (Skinner, 1953). Managers attempting to reinforce behavior and finding that no change has occurred, tend thereby, to conclude that reinforcement does not work. These failures, which do occur, may be explained by a failure to consider all the conditions necessary for reinforcement. In designing procedures of reinforcement a number of things must be considered in addition to the identification of the pinpointed behavior one wishes to change. This chapter discusses a number of these considerations in the application of reinforcement procedures, as follows: (1) *individuality, as affected by deprivation and satiation, expectations, and multiple schedules of reinforcement;* (2) *shaping behavior;* (3) *immediacy of reinforcement;* and (4) *the magnitude and quality of reinforcement.*

Individuality is the consideration of variance of response among individuals to procedures of reinforcement. Neither the behavioral scientist nor the manager expects all members of any group to respond identically to a single reinforcement. There are a number of methods for adapting reinforcement and management procedures to take these individual differences into account and maximize the effectiveness of reinforcement by the recognition of and adaptation to these differences. Shaping considers the current behavior of an individual, the goal behavior, and the steps necessary to maximize the probability of moving from existing to goal behavior. Reinforcement is also affected by immediacy, the proximity of the consequence to the behavior. Immediacy of reinforcement considers the influence of delay of reinforcement. The effectiveness of reinforcement is also a function of the magnitude, the amount of reinforcement, and the quality the individual preference for the reinforcing consequence.

## INDIVIDUALITY AND REINFORCEMENT

The experimental analysis of behavior has led to both an identification of uniformity in human behavior and a consideration of individual differences (Nord, 1976). The consideration of uniformity and diversity in human behavior is of concern to the manager as he seeks both to establish organization-wide systems for managing performance and to change specific behavior of individuals. It would certainly make life less complicated if the behavior of one individual could be entirely predicted on the basis of the pattern of behavior of another individual. This is obviously not the case, and no theory of behavior or management that proposed such uniformity would serve much purpose. On the other hand, if no prediction about the behavior of one person can be drawn from the behavior of other persons, the manager is left with an equally hopeless task. He would have to consider the best method of management or behavior change for each individual as though he had no previous experience and would have to devise an entirely unique approach for each individual. *Clearly, some generalizations about human performance must be made and also some considerations of individual variance must be recognized by the manager.*

The consideration of uniformity and diversity may be thought of along two dimensions: the process and the substance of the management procedure. Individuals tend to respond uniformly to various processes and differently to their substance. An example outside the realm of human behavior may help clarify the distinction. The science of physics provides some examples more apparent than the science of human behavior does. It is a "law of physics" that smaller bodies are attracted to larger bodies. Hence, the earth attracts the moon toward its center, the sun attracts the earth, and so on. The high school physics experiment in which a ball is spun around on a string, the centrifugal force of the ball being offset by the pull or attraction of the string, illustrates the manner in which these two forces offset each other. The law of physics stating that smaller bodies are attracted to larger bodies describes a universal process. If it is true for one relationship between a larger and smaller body, it is true for all relationships between bodies. When, however, the application of this uniform law to the relationship between the moon and the earth is considered, for instance, there is another dimension that describes the uniqueness of this relationship. Let's call this the "substance" dimension. The earth is a particular size or mass, as is the moon. There is a particular and unique distance between the earth and the moon. These relationships are unique to them and are probably not duplicated in any other relationship between two bodies in this universe. The substance of the application of this law of physics to the relationship between earth and moon is unique.

A similar analogy can be made in the science of biology. There is a series of processes, consistent across all human beings, to which individuals respond in uniform ways. On the other hand, the substance of a process results in unique responses by the individual. All human beings must breathe, consume energy-producing foods, and exercise to maintain muscle constitution, and organs within the body must process inputs into the body with some uniformity. To take one process as an example, all human beings must consume some level of carbohydrates to obtain the energy necessary for activity. Every human body transforms carbohydrates into energy, though the substance of the process varies from individual to individual. One individual requires a certain level of carbohydrate consumption for daily activity and another requires a different level. Although the substance of the process is unique, the process itself is universal to all members of our species.

In human behavior and management there are similar distinctions between process and the substance of a process. In the next chapter the process known as extinction is discussed. Extinction occurs when a reinforcer, which was maintaining the frequency of a behavior, is withdrawn and the behavior reduces in frequency or "extinguishes." This process is uniform across all individuals. Every human being may suffer from extinction. If the reinforcers for which an individual comes to work are withdrawn, that individual ceases coming to work. The process of extinction is universal among all individuals. On the other hand the substance of the application of extinction is unique for every individual. Imagine that a company decided to stop paying its employees for coming to work. Unquestionably, this would have an effect on every employee's behavior. The effect would, however, be diverse among the individuals in the organization. Some might stop coming to work immediately. Others might continue for a few days and then stop. Some would be very depressed, would have certain patterns of internal response different from those of other individuals. Some members would be out looking for another job the next day, while others might sit home for a month before they gathered the energy to look. The process of extinction would have occurred among all the individual members of the organization, but the specific response to the process, the substance, would be unique to each individual.

It is important that the manager understand this distinction between the application of the processes of behavior management and the specific substance of the application. The manager who attempts to apply a principle or process of behavior management without regard to the varying effect of the substance of that application to different individuals is likely to meet with failure and frustration. On the other hand, the manager who does not recognize the consistent process by which behavior is influenced in the organizational setting fails to capitalize on techniques that would enable him to maximize organizational effectiveness.

The processes representing uniformity among individuals are those of reinforcement, punishment, extinction, shaping, schedules of reinforcement, stimulus control, and other principles or procedures. These describe general patterns of relationship between conditions of performance, the independent variables, and the behavior or results, the dependent variables. While these general principles apply, the specifics of the application vary from individual to individual. The manager will know which principles he must apply to a case by identifying the general change in behavior he would like to effect (increase or decrease the rate) and the current level of performance and current environmental conditions (currently low frequency of behavior and very delayed reinforcement or currently too high a rate of behavior and very frequent and immediate reinforcement). From an analysis of these conditions he knows that he must increase reinforcement for the behavior, or withdraw a reinforcer, or reinforce an incompatible behavior, and so forth. The individuality factors enter when he is determining which is the target behavior, what level of performance may be expected, and what consequence effectively serves as a reinforcer for this particular individual.

## BASIS FOR INDIVIDUAL PERFORMANCE

The previous chapter discussed a number of entering characteristics that influence the appropriateness of a given procedure. The ability of the individual and prior learning were discussed as factors influencing the effect of the contingencies of reinforcement. Each factor has been determined before an individual enters an organization. The manager has no control over the inherited abilities of the individual or the prior acquisition of a repertoire of behaviors. The manager should understand these conditions, although he cannot do much about them.

Other conditions may be actively or currently influencing the individual's behavior. Among these are the levels of deprivation or satiation of the individual toward a given reinforcer, the expectations established for reinforcement, and the multiple schedules of reinforcement acting to influence the individual's behavior. The following three considerations are part of the contingencies of reinforcement. They are conditions that often go undetected or overlooked when behavior change or management procedures are planned in the organizational setting and may explain why two individuals with similar entering characteristics may respond differently in the work setting.

### Deprivation and Satiation

*Deprivation and satiation are the denial of access to a reinforcing event.* An individual deprived of a reinforcer works to obtain that reinforcer. Deprivation is similar to hunger in that it creates the condition in which an individual works to obtain that of which he is deprived. The individual who badly needs money is more likely to work to obtain money than the individual who is not deprived of it. For an individual to respond to obtain a reinforcing consequence there must be some level of deprivation. *If an individual performs in anticipation of a consequence, there must be, by definition, some level of deprivation for that consequence.*

Deprivation must be considered in the light of extinction. An individual may be deprived of a reinforcer, such as social approval from his supervisor, and may work to achieve that social approval. However, after a number of trials in which the individual performs the behavior he believes to be necessary to achieve that social approval, and in the absence of delivery of the approval, the behavior extinguishes. While there must be deprivation for behavior to occur, there must also be reinforcement. Behavior increases and is maintained when, first, there is a state of deprivation, second, the behavior is performed, and third, reinforcement follows. If only the first two conditions occur, they are eventually followed by extinction. This is the danger the manager runs when he fails to reinforce performance.

Theories of motivation and organizational behavior that have received the most attention during recent years have given considerable attention to individual needs. Maslow's (1943) needs hierarchy and the theories of Herzberg and McGregor, who applied Maslow's concepts to management, have viewed motivation as stemming from man's response to fulfill a need. They have theorized that an individual is dominated by a particular need, and performance results from its satisfaction. *Needs are more usefully viewed as states of* deprivation. When an individual is deprived of something, such as recognition, he may be said to "need" recognition. He then works to obtain that recognition. But these needs or state of deprivation are constantly changing. An individual deprived of recognition today may be satisfied in his receipt of recognition tomorrow. Performance results from the effort to achieve the fulfillment of the need, rather than from the fulfillment of the need itself. An individual performs for a reinforcer in anticipation of the delivery of that reinforcer. An immediate reduction in the rate of behavior may result following the delivery of the reinforcer (the satisfaction of the need). The point here is that performance does not result from conditions that *are* satisfying needs but from efforts to obtain reinforcement that will relieve a state of deprivation. Maslow recognized that a satisfied need (Cummings and Schwab, 1973) does not motivate. Other motivation theorists have also recognized the importance of deprivations (March and Simon, 1958).

Satiation is, in many respects, a condition opposite of deprivation. *Satiation is the condition in which the individual is not deprived of a given reinforcing stimulus; rather the individual has been satisfied with that stimulus.* The word *satiate* is related to the word *satisfied.* In a condition of satiation, responses are not made to obtain the reinforcer. Satiation does not commonly occur in the organizational setting. Most of the reinforcers that maintain performance in organizations would require very high levels of delivery to satiate. Among the most common reinforcers, such as money, social status, and recognition, and intrinsic reinforcement deriving from task fulfillment, the levels of reinforcement that would be required for satiation are almost beyond possibility. Satiation may, however, occur in the structuring of specific behavior change programs. A behavior change procedure may be devised in which a reinforcer such as free lunches, coffee, doughnuts, time-off privileges, or a limited range of gift items may be used. Each reinforcer has the disadvantage of presenting a narrow appeal that may be satisfied after a relatively few presentations. Many behavior change programs have resulted in immediate improvements in behavior only to be followed by the return of poor performance present before the program was begun. When the choice of reinforcers is narrow, and when the potential recipients of the reinforcer have experienced the consequence a number of times, satiation is likely to occur.

Satiation and deprivation explain why responses may vary among individuals. Because each individual has unique prior experience and a unique degree of deprivation or satiation, each may respond differently to opportunities for reinforcement. The manager planning behavior change must observe the behavior of those he is trying to motivate. He must observe the satiation effect and remedy that by varying the reinforcers available. He should be aware that the individual must possess some level of deprivation for a given reinforcer, and if one reinforcer is presented continuously, he must expect a decrease in performance.

To avoid the satiation effect the manager may use the token or point system of generalized reinforcement which provides for a variety of reinforcers while having the advantages of a uniform system of administration. Money, the tokens of our real world economy, serves the same function of providing not only a uniform system of administering reinforcement but also a sufficient variety of items for which the tokens may be exchanged so that satiation on money is unlikely.

### Expectations

The expectation of reinforcement affects individual performance in the work setting. *The employee will perform to achieve a reward if he believes, first, that he is capable of performing the behaviors required, and second, that the reward will be delivered.* Those beliefs are the result of prior learning. Expectations are internal beliefes, thoughts, and feelings about the probable consequences of one's behavior.

The concern with expectations or expectancy in motivation has been the province of the cognitive theories of psychology, which have attempted to explain the mental processes that precede performance. The expectancy theories of Vroom (1974) and Lawler (1973) have defined expectancy as "the belief concerning the likelihood that a particular act will be followed by a particular outcome." Expectancy theory attributes motivation to the expectancy that an act will be followed by a reward and to the value (valence) that reward holds for the individual. This is a close interpretation of the behavioral process of reinforcement.

The internal responses we refer to as expectations have received little study by empirical psychologists. Expectation may be explained as a *mental rehearsal of the behavior and the consequence anticipated.* The individual who is "expecting" an outcome may have observed another individual perform and experience the reinforcing outcome. Or he may have been told by his manager that he may expect the reinforcing outcome if he performs. This vicarious exposure to the consequence is similar to actually experiencing the consequence following actual behavior (Bandura, 1969). Internally the individual practices the response and experiences the desired outcome. This internal series of behavior and reinforcement strengthens the actual behavior.

Traditional sales motivation books and courses provide abundant examples of vicarious conditioning. The books of Napoleon Hill and W. Clement Stone (1962) are filled with anecdotes that present actions or behavior the individual may engage in and examples of highly reinforcing consequences that may follow. Select any page in *Success through a Positive Mental Attitude* and you will find stories such as this:

> So George completed his Social Time Recorder daily. The officials of his company were amazed. For the records indicated that after inventing his Social Time Recorder, George accomplished the following. He wrote four million dollars' worth of life insurance in a single year. He established a company record by submitting over a million dollars' worth of new business in one day. He consistently sold enough life insurance to become a life member of the Million Dollar Round Table—an achievement every life insurance man seeks, but relatively few attain. With justifiable pride, George said, "I began to pay off my debts, and eventually, when these were paid, I started a savings account. Finally, I had saved $6,000. A friend of mine and I each invested $6,000 in an enterprise that our bank helped us finance. Within a year, we each received $50,000 out of this project. This was a big step forward in acquiring wealth."

After reading this passage how can one not be motivated to start immediately completing a Social Time Recorder each day? Didn't this small step lead George down the road to acquiring wealth? Surely it will do the same for you! Unfortunately, it is very unlikely to result in anything approximating the success of our model George. But the effect of reading such stories is very strong. The reader internally rehearses the behavior of filling out the Social Time Recorder and vicariously experiencing the reinforcing events experienced by George. The probability that the reader will perform these behaviors after reading this passage is certainly higher than if the reader had simply been instructed to "complete each day the Social Time Recorder and it will increase your selling behavior, which in turn will increase your sales commissions." This is not nearly as reinforcing as the passage just quoted.

This type of model provides the basis for the internal rehearsal of the behavior and the consequence that established what other theorists have termed expectancy. While expectancy is undoubtedly related to performance, the effect is highly temporal. In the absence of actually receiving the expected reinforcer the behavior extinguishes. When a reinforcer has been experienced only one time, extinction occurs rapidly. This is a common occurrence following a motivational talk. The listeners may jump out of their chairs and shout slogans about their product or company, but within a short time back on the job their performance reverts to the pattern present before the motivation talk.

One advantage of mental rehearsal or expectancy is that the individual is able to rehearse the behavior and the consequence over and over again, providing a number of occasions of reinforcement. Nevertheless the ability to perform this internal rehearsal also extinguishes if the actual behavior is not followed by the anticipated consequence.

Another effect of expectation flows from the nature of the anticipated consequence versus the actual consequence. If a salesperson knows that an annual bonus will be awarded based on a measure of individual performance, although he has not been told specifically how the bonus will be computed, he develops certain expectations. He may have heard that another salesperson received one-quarter of his salary as a bonus the previous year. The salesperson may develop the expectation that he will earn a five thousand-dollar bonus; that is, he rehearses internally the behaviors required to achieve the bonus and the anticipated receipt of the bonus. During the year he experiences this rehearsal dozens or hundreds of times. The internal experience of this five thousand-dollar bonus has maintained considerable behavior throughout the year. When the time comes to receive the actual bonus, he may find that he receives only three thousand dollars. Because he has already experienced internally the five thousand-dollar bonus, the three thousand dollars actually received has the effect of denying a two thousand-dollar bonus. The reinforcing effect of the three thousand dollars, the degree to which that bonus actually strengthens future behavior, will be severely reduced by the discrepancy between the anticipated and the actual bonus.

This salesperson would have been much more reinforced if he had anticipated a one or two thousand-dollar bonus and actually received the same three thousand-dollar bonus. In this case the final delivery of the bonus would have been more reinforcing then the internal rehearsals the salesperson had been experiencing throughout the year. This would have resulted in strengthening future behavior more than in the first case.

The manager must manage expectations. When bonus, incentive, or profit-sharing programs are instituted managers often make the mistake of overstating the potential rewards. This results in unrealistic expectations, which in turn, result in punishing experiences when the actual bonus is received. This arrangement is then likely to result in reduced performance. The manager will get much more performance for his money if he understates the potential gain and overdelivers when the reinforcement is finally determined.

Each individual has a different set of expectations. These expectations influence performance in a number of ways. If there is no expectation for reinforcement, there is little performance. If expectations are unrealistically high, the individual may perform at a high level until he experiences the actual reinforcement and may then experience extinction. It is part of the manager's job to consider and plan the expectations of the employees. He presents to the employees the information on which their expectations are based. He must assume responsibility for their lack of expectations or overexpectations. By communicating with them he can monitor and modify their expectations to fall somewhere near or below the probable reinforcer he will finally deliver.

## Multiple Reinforcement Schedules

The multiple schedules of reinforcement describe which or how many responses will be followed by a reinforcer. For example, the delivery of a paycheck once a week is a schedule of reinforcement, and so is the payment of a commission for every automobile sold. The specific effects of various types of reinforcement are discussed in Chapter 7. Schedules of reinforcement are important to understanding the variance in individual response to a reinforcement procedure (Ferster and Skinner, 1957). *At any one time each individual is influenced by a variety of schedules of reinforcement, and these schedules may be either competing or supportive.* In other words there may be relationships between behavior and consequences that reinforce the same response or competing responses.

The manager may have control over a number of schedules of reinforcement that may act on the same behavior. For example, a manager may supervise a group of engineers. One schedule affecting the behavior of these engineers may be the monthly salary received by each engineer. A second may be the relationship between behavior and the receipt of a salary increase that may come once or twice a year. A third may be a bonus delivered upon the successful completion of an engineering project. A fourth may be a profit-sharing check delivered quarterly contingent upon the profitability of the company. A fifth schedule may be the social comments made by the manager and other members of the organization regarding the work being performed by the engineer. The manager would hope that these multiple schedules all reinforce desirable behavior, in some cases in an additive fashion; in other cases they may be reinforcing different but compatible behaviors.

Multiple schedules do not always back up each other or reinforce the same behavior. Schedules of reinforcement may compete in two ways: by reinforcing different behaviors or by punishing and reinforcing the same behavior. One of our engineers, for example, while benefitting from all five schedules of reinforcement indicated above, may be influenced by another schedule outside the work setting. His wife or friends may be dissatisfied with his current position. They may ignore any positive comment he may make about his work and become very enthusiastic any time he mentions changing jobs. This social approval at home is a schedule of reinforcement that is strengthening a competing behavior, that of leaving his present job.

A multiple schedule may also compete with another schedule by presenting the opposite influence, punishment. Our engineer, while being reinforced, perhaps by the first four schedules discussed above, may hear negative remarks about the quality of his work. This has the effect of punishing, reducing the frequency, of his work behavior. This schedule of punishment may be more powerful than the other four schedules of reinforcement combined. The net effect may be to maintain current levels of behavior, strengthen behavior, or reduce the strength of the behavior, depending on the degree to which the various schedules have control over performance.

Behavior management is sometimes accused of simplicity because it approaches behavior change by focusing on a specific behavior and on specific, often single, reinforcing events. Behavior management may apply the principles of behavior simply. This is its advantage. This does not, however, deny the complexity of the forces acting to determine the behavioral outcome. The manager should be aware that at any one time there are any number of multiple schedules of reinforcement or punishment acting to determine behavior. The manager can consider the behavior he desires to increase and examine the various schedules of reinforcement over which he has some control. He should be certain to remove any competing schedules that may be either reinforcing competing behavior or punishing the behavior he desires. He may also plan multiple schedules to enhance the probability of the desired increase.

Planned multiple schedules have the advantage of reducing the potential for satiation. If a single arrangement between behavior and reinforcement is planned and relied on to control behavior, the risk of the individual's becoming satiated on that reinforcer is high. If, however, the behavioral program is designed to include a number of different schedules supporting each other, the likelihood of achieving and maintaining the desired change is greatly increased. This may be accomplished by the use of feedback graphs, one schedule of reinforcement; the establishment of a point system that awards points based on the achievement of certain levels of performance, another schedule; the delivery of a backup reinforcer for which the points may be exchanged once a week, a third schedule; by the positive verbal comments made by the supervisor when the data on performance show any improvement, a fourth schedule; and by periodic letters from a higher level of management, a plant manager for example, to the employee who performs exceptionally well, a fifth schedule. These multiple schedules support each other and reduce the possibility of satiation on one single reinforcing event and the possibility of periodic decreases in performance during intervals between reinforcement.

Whereas the behavior manager is most concerned with the steps he must take to create the desired change in behavior, he should also be aware that individuals react to that system in unique ways. While all human beings may react to behavioral processes in similar fashion, the substance of that process and reaction is always, to some degree, unique. In this chapter I have discussed conditions that may determine an individual reaction to environmental conditions. These conditions are as follows:

1.   The entering characteristics: those characteristics of the individual present before he entered the current environment, which  include
    a.   inherited abilities, the potential to learn,
    b.   prior learning, the existing repertoire of behavior.
2.   Current contingencies affecting individual behavior, which include
    a.   deprivation or satiation of the available reinforcer,
    b.   expectations or internal rehearsal of contingencies,
    c.   multiple schedules of reinforcement.


### SHAPING

The principle of behavior shaping is one that must be considered in every behavior change program. The failure to do so is the cause of many performance deficiencies in management and training. *Shaping is the reinforcement of successive approximations to a goal performance or behavior.* When behavior is shaped, reinforcement is delivered contingent upon small improvements in performance. Shaping allows the individual to experience success immediately. When behavior is not shaped, a criterion for reinforcement may be too demanding and the potential for failure high.

Through application of shaping, progressive improvement is reinforced and the individual's willingness to attempt changes in performance is increased by the reinforcement for the prior success. Behavior shaping has resulted in dramatic changes both in the organizational setting and in school (Martin, Burkholder, Rosenthal, Tharp, and Thorne, 1968), mental institutions (Isaacs, Thomas, and Goldiamond, 1960), and other settings. Shaping has virtually revolutionized the treatment of retarded individuals. By the reinforcing of small improvements in performance retardates have learned skills that have previously been considered beyond their capability (Sulzbacher and Kidder, 1975). Retarded children have, for example, been taught to eat, walk, care for themselves, and communicate verbally when they would otherwise have existed in a vegetative state for the remainder of their lives. Children who appeared to have severe learning or discipline problems have undergone dramatic changes in behavior through the application of shaping in the school setting.

In the industrial setting equally dramatic changes in employee performance have been achieved through the application of the shaping principle. One case reported an increase in an individual's performance of sixty-five percent (Miller, 1974). In this case a woman had been employed in a textile mill, despite poor performance, for a number of years because of her good attendance record. This mill had experienced considerable turnover and absenteeism until a plantwide behavior management program was begun. As the absenteeism and attendance improved throughout the mill, her contribution to production, operating at a thirty-five percent efficiency level, became less acceptable. Her behavior was shaped by breaking down her job, that of a doffer in a textile mill, into very specific and discrete units. The rate at which she performed each of these units was measured, and she was reinforced for slight improvements in each of the component behaviors. Within two months her production had increased to more than one hundred percent efficiency and remained there for at least the following six months during which data are available.

*For shaping to occur, two basic conditions must be present: First, there must be a variability in the response pattern, and second, there must be selective reinforcement of responses* (Keller, 1969). Figure 12 illustrates the shaping procedure. During any given period, the performance of a behavior is illustrated by the xs appearing during that period. The scale from zero to one hundred may represent skill levels of a performance or the number of times a behavior is performed within a period of time. Zero would represent no performance at all, one hundred, the maximum possible performance. Let us assume that this scale represents the number of units a worker produces on a production task. We shall assume that it has been demonstrated that a worker is able to produce one hundred units per hour. The employee represented in this diagram has been producing between ten and forty-five units per hour. Each x represents the measured performance during one hour of a day. Each period represents one day's performance.

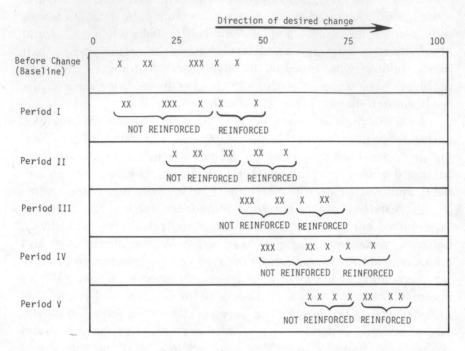

**Figure 12**   Shaping procedure.

Shaping is defined as the reinforcement of successive approximations to a goal behavior or performance. Performance to the right of the diagram is the goal direction toward which we want the employee to progress. The responses that most closely approximate the desired performance are reinforced. During period one, the first day of our intervention strategy, the three performances that are furthest toward the right are reinforced. The remaining responses to the left are ignored, not reinforced, and tend, therefore, to extinguish. In the case of a production worker the performance of producing greater numbers of products during the hour may be reinforced by verbal praise by the supervisor. Verbal attention and approval for improved performance by supervisors has been demonstrated repeatedly to be an effective reinforcement strategy in this type of situation. The verbal approval may be supplemented with small, tangible reinforcements such as sodas or cups of coffee. This behavior may also be reinforced by graphing the number of times the worker produces more than fifty units per hour or fulfills some other criterion performance.

Each day the performances representing further approximations toward the goal performance are reinforced. This reinforcement of approximations strengthens the behavior represented by that performance while the behavior represented by the nonreinforced periods weakens. In this manner the behavior gradually moves in the goal direction. By the shaping or reinforcing of improvements in performance the individual immediately experiences success. In this example, by the end of the fifth day, the worker has increased the average performance from twenty-five to seventy-five units. For each stage of improvement the worker has been reinforced. The desired behavior is strengthened through reinforcement.

Traditional approaches to performance improvement would place the emphasis on setting higher level goals for performance and reinforcing only the completion of the desired goal. In the same situation a goal might have been set for averaging seventy-five units per day. To the employee currently averaging twenty-five units this goal would appear unattainable. The statement of a goal would, in itself, be unlikely to provide a sufficient stimulus to evoke the desired performance. The employee would not experience reinforcement until reaching the seventy-five unit average, behavior would extinguish, and the employee would probably never reach the goal.

*Reinforcement must be sampled to have control over behavior.* Sampling reinforcement is an important element of the shaping procedure. An employee may be told that, if he achieves certain levels of performance, he may be eligible for transfer to another job or department in a plant. The manager who presents this offer may consider this transfer highly desirable and hence expect the employee to feel the same way. But the employee may never have sampled working on this other job. It is an unknown and has, therefore, no reinforcing value. The child who has never tasted ice cream has no desire to eat ice cream and will not perform any task to earn the privilege of doing so. But once the child has sampled ice cream and finds it pleasurable, it may be used as a reinforcer for which the child will work (as most parents well know).

In the work setting the shaping procedure provides for reinforcer sampling after behavior currently in the individual's repertoire. Rather than tell the employee that he may be transferred to the more desirable job if some level of performance is achieved, the supervisor might "catch" the employee at a relatively high level of performance and take the employee to the more desirable job for some period of time as a reinforcer for the behavior exhibited. The employee may then return to his regular job and be told that for improvements in performance he will gradually be transferred to this new work, which he may now consider, following his sampling, more desirable. The supervisor may then permit the employee additional samples of the new work as he demonstrates additional approximations to the goal level of performance.

The shaping procedure avoids the errors that commonly result in the failure of behavior change efforts. First, the goal is not set beyond the reach of the individual whose behavior is to be changed. Current behavior approximating the goal is reinforced. Reaching any goal involves the strengthening of some behavior. Shaping begins the strengthening procedure at the current level of performance. Secondly, the individual has an opportunity to sample the reinforcer because it is delivered at a level currently performed. This ensures that the reinforcer is "real" to the employee, and there is no doubt that the reinforcer will be delivered as promised.

The manager wishing to shape behavior should consider the following five components of the shaping process:

**1.** *The behavior or performance must be defined in specific terms* (pinpointed). This is absolutely necessary if the manager is to follow the remaining steps in the shaping procedure. The definition of a pinpointed behavior is one that may be accurately observed and recorded. Two persons should be able to observe the behavior and obtain the same measurement independently.

**2.** *Performance should be measured to obtain a baseline of average performance and a measurement of the variability of response.* This variability provides the information needed to establish the criteria for reinforcement. The responses that approximate the desired goal should be reinforced.

**3.** *The manager must have the ability to reinforce behavior selectively. Only those behaviors that do represent approximations toward the goal should be selected for reinforcement.* Reinforcement must be immediate. To reinforce selectively, the manager must have control over an event that is truly a reinforcer. The individual employee must be willing to work for that reinforcer. This can be true only if the individual has sampled the event. The manager must be able to withhold the reinforcer when criterion levels of performance are not met and to deliver contingent upon the criterion levels.

**4.** *The manager should continue to measure the performance after the initiation of shaping.* Only by having a baseline measurement of the performance and a measurement following the procedure does the manager know whether or not progress is being made. The measurement lets the manager know which responses he should now be reinforcing. Without the measurement he may continue to reinforce the performance that appropriately represented improvement at the outset of the procedure but that now may represent the average performance. If the average performance is reinforced, this is the performance that is strengthened, and progress is not made in the direction of the goal. The other error risked in the absence of measurement is that of setting the criterion level too high. If this is done, the individual may fail to achieve reinforcement and experience extinction.

**5.** *After the achievement of the goal performance the manager must make some provision for maintaining the new level.* There is no reason to believe that reinforcement may be terminated after the shaping toward the goal criterion. If reinforcement is terminated, the behavior is likely to revert to the previous level of performance. The behavior will remain at its new level only if that new level provides reinforcement on a continuing basis. That reinforcement may be derived from some intrinsic aspect of the new level of performance or from an extrinsic source. In most cases the manager will find it necessary to provide continuing reinforcement for the new level of performance for some time. Reinforcement may he "thinned out" gradually, as discussed in Chapter 7, to maintain the performance and reduce the requirement on the manager for continual delivery of the reinforcer.

Shaping has numerous applications in the organizational setting. Any effort to improve performance should consider and apply the shaping principle. Shaping is, however, particularly relevant to training the new employee, who is faced with the challenge of mastering a number of new skills and establishing a level of performance not currently in his repertoire. The manager or trainer, although unaware of the shaping principle, may already employ this principle. The effective and sensitive manager is aware that the new employee needs to receive signs of approval, acceptance, and success during the early stages of his efforts to learn his new job. The application of shaping can greatly reduce new employee turnover, and this generally accounts for a great majority of an organization's cost of training and recruitment. The greatest probability of turnover has been demonstrated to occur during the first ninety days of employment. During this period the manager should be particularly sensitive to the employee's need for reinforcement. The new employee placed on the job and expected to reach standard levels of performance without shaping is a turnover case waiting to occur.

## IMMEDIACY OF REINFORCEMENT

*Reinforcement has the greatest effect on behavior when delivered immediately after the performance.* The greater the delay between the performance and the delivery of reinforcement, the less effect on the behavior.

Delay of reinforcement, in addition to weakening the effect of the reinforcement, may also result in the inadvertent reinforcement of another behavior (Kazdin, 1975). All individuals behave constantly. If the behavior you wish to reinforce is performed today, such as completing a report on time, and you delay reinforcing the individual until next week, numerous other behaviors will have occurred between the response and the reinforcer. The delivery of the reinforcer may occur immediately after the employee has been procrastinating on the fulfillment of some other task. This reinforcement, delivered while the procrastination is occurring, may result in the strengthening of that behavior.

Managers often feel that by stating the "reason" why the reinforcement is delivered the desired effect will be achieved. In other words a secretary may have worked extremely hard on reorganizing a filing system. This task may have required several days' work, and the secretary may have worked overtime to accomplish this task in addition to her other duties. The attentive manager may express his appreciation for this by taking her out to lunch. If he takes the secretary out to lunch the day she completes the task and informs her that he is doing so to express his appreciation for the hard work she has put in on the filing system, she is likely to be reinforced for her effort. Another manager may do the same things but delay taking the secretary out to lunch for several days or a week. Although he may explain his motive for taking her out to lunch in the same manner as the first manager, the effect is not the same. In the second case the secretary will have undergone one week of extinction before reinforcement. The one-week delay in the delivery of reinforcement significantly weakens the impact of that reinforcer on future behavior.

There may be several different incidences of reinforcement related to a case such as the one described above. The approving comments of persons in the office, the manager's informing the secretary that he will take her out to eat, and the actual event of going out to lunch may all strengthen the secretary's behavior. If one or two of these events occur immediately, the delay of the third is not as critical as it might be if it were the only reinforcing event.

The effect of delay of reinforcement is also influenced by the individual's awareness of the contingencies. If a worker "knows" that he will receive a certain consequence for the performance of a behavior, his internal thoughts provide immediate reinforcement after performance. For this reason *contingencies clearly specified in advance of the behavior have the advantage of enabling internally mediated immediate reinforcement (Bandura, 1969b)*. This internal self-reinforcement for performance both provides the enhancing effect of immediacy of reinforcement and eliminates the potential of reinforcing irrelevant behavior that may occur between the desired performance and delivery of external reinforcement. A person paid on a piecework basis is likely to maintain performance and link the consequence that may be delivered at the end of the week to the behavior being paid on piece rate because of the individual's ability to reinforce himself internally as he completes units of work. Similarly the absence of knowledge of the contingencies has been shown to detract from performance (Georgopolous, Mahoney, and Jones, 1957). Much of the reinforcing effect of feedback systems may be explained by the enhanced ability of the individual to reinforce himself internally owing to the increased knowledge of performance provided by the feedback.

When behavior does not have a long history of prior performance and reinforcement, the effect of immediacy or delay is most critical. This is an important factor in the shaping of the new employee's behavior. This behavior is not well established, and a short delay in reinforcement may have a significant weakening effect. The longer the employee has been at the job, performing as desired and experiencing the consequences, the stronger that behavior's resistance to extinction and the less the effect of delay of reinforcement. After the employee has been performing his tasks and has experienced the desired consequences, the intervals between behavior and reinforcement may be gradually extended. If this extension is gradual, and if the intervals vary in length, the performance is maintained. This gradual extension has the advantage of reducing the requirement on the manager to deliver reinforcement immediately and reduces the employee's dependence on immediate reinforcement.

It is often impractical to provide immediate reinforcement in the organizational setting. When this is the case, a number of different types of systems may be established to provide substitute or token reinforcers that may, at a later date, be exchanged for the reinforcing object or event. Numerous programs have been established in industrial facilities by behavior management consultants using token reinforcement procedures. These programs have consistently resulted in reduced absenteeism and improved operating efficiency. Various types of raffle tickets may be given out immediately after a desired performance. The raffle may then be held weekly or monthly. The handing out of the ticket is a significant reinforcing event for the employee. Raffle tickets or other token awards, which may be exchanged at some later date for the reinforcing event or object, can provide the advantages of immediate reinforcement and of convenient and planned scheduling.

Token rewards have been found to reduce tardiness significantly among industrial workers (Herman et al., 1973). Herman established a procedure in a Mexican industrial plant that immediately reinforced arriving to work on time. Workers were handed a card indicating that they had arrived to work on time. At the end of the week the cards were exchanged for pesos.

Traffic tickets are one common example of a token system, although for punishment rather than reinforcement. The principle works very much the same. The effective punishing event is the occasion on which the red light appears in your rearview mirror and the policeman writes out that ticket. In a sense there is no "real" immediate consequence to the speeding or other violation. The fine for the illegal driving may not be experienced for weeks or, in some cases, months. But the punishment occurs when the ticket is given. Similarly the pleasure is experienced when a positive ticket is given in the workplace.

Very often long-range reinforcers are established for behavior but the delay in reinforcement is such that the effective control is lost. When this is the case, some other reinforcer may have to be established to provide the effective reinforcement required. The following quote from *Newsweek* (July 7, 1975) is an excellent example of such a case:

> For two full terms of the North Carolina Senate, Dallas Alford has been Chairman of the Education Committee. But it hardly ever met. There was trouble getting a quorum at the usual time, Wednesday at noon. "Right at the lunch hour," one of Alford's colleagues explained, "it was kind of hard to get some of the boys away from the table." So Alford tried an incentive system that filled the house and now has other Senators asking for honorary memberships: he gives door prizes.
>
> Actually, that's what the local press calls them. "I prefer something more cultured," says Alford. "I call them literary awards." Alford says he buys small gifts for $8 to $10 each from his own funds and holds a drawing at each committee meeting. One lucky Senator, Pleas Lackey, has won five times: an electric clock, a box of candy, a carving set, a book on revolutionary weapons, and a first aid kit. "They're coming to meetings like Grant took Richmond," Alford says. Not everybody is happy. "I think there was something crooked," says Senator Jack Childers. "I was present and on time at every meeting and they never pulled my name a single time."

## MAGNITUDE AND QUALITY OF REINFORCEMENT

The effectiveness of a reinforcement is also determined by the potency or strength of the reinforcer delivered. The potency may be determined by its quantity or magnitude and by its quality or the individual's preference for that reinforcer.

*The greater the magnitude of the reinforcer the greater the strengthening effect.* According to expectancy theory of motivation this magnitude and quality of reinforcement are referred to as "valence" and similarly describe the potency of the consequence in terms of behavior change (Campbell, Dunnette, Lawler, and Weick, 1970). Other conditions being equal, we will take the job that provides the greatest amount of compensation. Or, compensation being equal, we will take the job that provides the greatest amount of responsibility, recognition, or other quality we find reinforcing. The effect of the magnitude of the reinforcer is exhibited every time we go to the supermarket and are willing to pay more money for larger amounts of cereal, meat, or drink. The mere volume of a reinforcer causes us to emit a stronger response.

There is a limit to the effect of magnitude on behavior, and that is the limit of satiation. One can receive too much of a reinforcer. When this happens, the object no longer becomes a reinforcer.

The quality of a reinforcer is an important consideration for the manager or behavior manager. Quality refers to the preference of the individual for a reinforcer. Preferences vary greatly among employees, and the manager may too easily assume that he can predict an individual's preferences. The only certain way to know this is to observe behavior in response to reinforcement. We prefer what we are willing to work for. If an employee is not willing to perform to achieve a reward, it is not a reinforcer.

Because preferences vary, managers should try to stay away from limited selections of reinforcers. For example, sales managers commonly make the mistake of establishing incentive programs with one, two, or three selections of prizes such as televisions, appliances, or vacation trips as incentive awards. These objects will probably not be reinforcing for many of the salespersons. For this reason a number of incentive suppliers provide catalogs of gifts from which salespersons may choose. Green stamps or other trading stamps are also widely used in sales incentive programs and plant reinforcement programs. These have the advantage of immediate delivery plus the ability to be exchanged for items of individual preference.

If the manager is effective, he establishes a degree of communication with his employees that allows him to have some understanding of individual preferences. The manager should know how the employee will respond to verbal praise or recognition in some public forum. The manager should know whether the individual would prefer an extra day off, the opportunity to learn a new job, or a letter of appreciation from the plant manager or president of the company. These preferences can be known only if the manager is effective in his communication with his employees.

One way to increase the manager's knowledge of his employees' individual preferences is to have them complete an annual reinforcer survey. Figure 13 presents a sample reinforcer survey form that may be used to ascertain individual preferences (Miller, 1976). It is recommended that this be completed once a year, along with other evaluations of management that the employee may complete to provide management feedback. The reinforcer survey should be filed in the employee's personnel file and reviewed by the immediate supervisor, who should refer to this form when the employee performs in an exemplary fashion and select an item for delivery.

One of the great advantages of the reinforcer survey is the intrinsically reinforcing nature of receiving an individualized reinforcer. In

*REINFORCER SURVEY*

1. In my free time my favorite activity is _____
_____.

2. If I could take a weekend vaction, I would go to _____
_____.

3. If my wife (or girlfriend, etc.) and I have a day to spend together, we like to_____
_____

4. My favorite evening entertainment is _____
5. I would really like to visit _____
6. My favorite sports activity is _____
7. My favorite hobby is _____
8. Something that I really want to buy is _____
9. If I had ten dollars to spend on myself right now I would_____
_____

10. If I had fifty dollars to spend on myself right now I would_____
_____

11. If I had one hundred dollars to spend on myself right now I would_____
_____

12. If I had three hundred dollars to spend on myself right now I would_____
_____

13. If I had five hundred dollars to spend on myself right now I would_____
_____

14. The thing that I would most like to buy my wife (husband, girlfriend, etc.) is_____
_____

15. My job would be more rewarding if_____
_____

16. If my manager would _____
I would enjoy working here.
17. I would work harder if _____
18. The place that I most like to shop is_____
_____

**Figure 13** Reinforcer survey form.

addition to the direct effects of receiving an item selected from the survey, the fact that a manager is concerned enough with the individual's preferences to go to the trouble of individualizing reinforcement is in itself reinforcing. A survey similar to this was completed by the salespersons of a chemical company. The management of this company set aside five hundred dollars per month for individualized reinforcement. Each month they discussed the outstanding performances of the previous month and selected an item from the survey for the salesperson who had turned in an outstanding performance. When the survey was first sent out to the salespersons and they were asked to fill it out, a number of them failed to complete it. Others filled it out without any great thought. When the procedure was first put into effect, the person selected had indicated that he would like to have a load of wood to build an addition to his barn. One day the load of wood was delivered to his house. At first he was more startled than anything else. He hadn't believed that he would ever see any of the items indicated on his form. He wrote a glowing letter back to the managers expressing his appreciation for their concern about him and their recognition of his performance. Shortly after this had been made known to the entire sales organization, a significant number of the salespersons wrote to their managers requesting another copy of the reinforcer survey. They were not satisfied with the way they had filled it out, or had failed to fill it out, the first time.

It is common for managers to have difficulty identifying reinforcers in the organizational setting. One solution to this problem was established long ago by Dr. David Premack (Premack, 1959). He provided the work of behavioral psychology with what has become known as the "Premack Principle," which states that a *behavior of high likelihood of occurrence may be used to increase the performance of a behavior of low likelihood of occurrence by making the performance of the high-likelihood behavior contingent on the performance of the low-likelihood behavior.* In other words everyone is likely to engage in some behavior given a choice of activities. The activity that will be chosen, given the option, may be considered an activity or behavior of high likelihood of occurrence. The behavior of low likelihood of occurrence is the behavior you are concerned about increasing. For example, in the work setting an employee may prefer to spend time talking with his or her friends on the job. This is a high-likelihood behavior. The behavior you may wish to see increased may be a level of production, quality, or other performance that is not as intrinsically satisfying as socializing with friends. You may increase the behavior of concern by establishing a contingency, an if–then statement, between the two activities. "You may spend fifteen minutes in the snack bar together, if you complete 85 units during the hour."

Performance may be improved by making a more enjoyable work task contingent upon the completion of a less enjoyable one. Gupton and Lebow (1971) reported that they increased the frequency of low-probability sales by making the possibility of high-probability sales contingent on low-probability sales. They applied the Premack Principle to two male, part-time telephone solicitors in a large company. These solicitors were required to sell new appliance service contracts and renew old ones. Since renewal contracts calls and sales were performed at a higher rate than new service calls and sales, the opportunity to sell five renewal contract was made contingent upon one new service contract sale. The results indicated that the percentage of sales for both types of contracts increased when the contingency was in effect and decreased when this contingency was removed.

## REFERENCES

Bandura, Albert. *Principles of Behavior Modification.* New York: Holt, Rinehart & Winston, Inc., 1969a, pp. 231–232.

Bandura, Albert. *Principles of Behavior Modification.* New York: Holt, Rinehart & Winston, Inc., 1969b, pp. 30–32.

Campbell, John P., Dunnette, Marvin D., Lawler, Edward E., III, and Weick, Karl E., Jr. *Managerial Behavior, Performance, and Effectiveness.* New York: McGraw-Hill Book Company, 1970.

Cummings, L. L., and Schwab, Donald P. *Performance in Organizations.* Glenview, Ill.: Scott Foresman and Co., 1973, pp. 22–27.

Ferster, C. B., and Skinner, B. F. *Schedules of Reinforcement.* New York: Appleton-Century-Crofts, 1957.

Georgopolous, B. S., Mahoney, G. M., and Jones, M. W. A path-goal approach to productivity." *Journal of Applied Psychology,* **41,** 1957, 345–353.

Gupton, Ted, and LeBow, Michael D. "Behavior management in a large industrial firm." *Behavior Therapy,* **2,** 1971, 78–82.

Hermann, Jaime A., Montes, Ana Ide, Dominquiz, Benjamin, Montes, Francis, and Hopkines, B. L. "Effects of bonuses for punctuality on the tardiness of industrial workers." *Journal of Applied Behavior Analysis,* **6,** 1973, 563–570.

Hill, Napoleon, and Stone, W. Clement. *Success through a Positive Mental Attitude.* Englewood Cliffs, N.J.: Prentice-Hall, Inc., 1962.

Isaacs, W., Thomas, J., and Goldiamond, I. "Applications of operant conditioning to reinstate verbal behavior in psychotics." *Journal of Speech and Hearing Disorders*, **25**, 8–12.

Kazdin, Alan. *Behavior Modification in Applied Settings*. Homewood, Ill.: The Dorsey Press, 1975, pp. 106–107.

Keller, Fred S. *Learning: Reinforcement Therapy*. New York: Random House, 1969, pp. 39–46.

Lawler, E. E. *Motivation in Work Organizations*, Monterey: Brooks-Cole, 1973.

Martin, Marian, Burkholder, Rachel, Rosenthal, Ted, Tharp, Roland, and Thorne, Gaylord. "Programming behavior change and reintegration into school milieux of extreme adolescent deviants." *Behavior Research and Therapy*, **6**, 1968, 371–383.

Maslow, A. H. "A theory of human motivation." *Psychological Review*, 1943, **50**, 370–396.

March, J. G., and Simon, H. A. *Organizations*. New York: John Wiley, Inc., 1958.

Miller, Lawrence M. *Behavior Management: New Skills For Business and Industry*. Atlanta, Georgia: behavioral systems, Inc., 1974, pp. 86–92.

Miller, Lawrence M. *Self-Management Skills for the Sales Professional*. Atlanta, Georgia: Behavioral Systems, Inc., 1976.

Nord, Walter R. "Behavior modification perspectives for humanizing organizations," in *Humanizing Organizational Behavior*, Springfield, Ill.: 1976.

Premack, David. "Towards empirical behavior laws I: Positive reinforcement," *Psychological Review*, **66**, 1959, 218–233.

Skinner, B. F. *Science and Human Behavior*. New York: The Free Press, 1953.

Sulzbacher, Stephen, and Kidder, John. "Follow-up on the behavior analysis model: results after ten years of early intervention with institutionalized, mentally retarded children," in *Behavior Analysis: Areas of Research and Application* (Ramp and Semb, eds.) Englewood Cliffs, N.J.: Prentice-Hall, 1975, pp. 62–69.

Vroom, W. H. *Work and Motivation*. New York: John Wiley, Inc. 1964.

# REDUCING
# OFF QUALITY

This case documents the reduction of audited off-quality yarn packs being boxed by the packers of a textile preparation department. Two interventions were used. One was posting graphed feedback of percent off quality found. Another was the attachment of both positive and negative consequences for the shift supervisors involved. While the feedback had no effect, the intervention of contingent consequences markedly reduced the percentage of off-quality yarn packed. Whereas much research data deal with the behavior of employees, these results suggest fruitful results may also be obtained from the application of contingency management to the supervisor, who is a mediating influence on employee behavior and final results.

## BACKGROUND CONDITIONS

The manager of the preparation department in a yarn mill wanted to decrease the percentage of off-quality yarn packs reported by the weekly quality control audit. He planned an intervention of graphed feedback, in consultation with an outside consultant. The manager was participating in behavior management training being conducted by the consultant at his mill. Previous verbal instruction to "tighten up" on off quality had not been successful in reducing the problem.

## PROCEDURE

The department manager first graphed the weekly percentages reported by quality control for the previous five weeks. He then posted these

Appreciation is expressed to Michael McCarthy for the preparation of this case study.

data, the department totals plus totals for each of the four shifts, as a baseline, averaging 2.5 percent. Next he asked all four shift supervisors to bring the graph to the attention of their packers. The previously established goal was no more than 1.1 percent off quality. He further specified that this meant no more than three off-quality yarn packs in a box. He asked for improvement to this goal, using the graphs as a visual feedback.

Three weeks later a second intervention was added. The department manager specified that for each week that the quality goal was met they would award any supervisor meeting it with one hour off the scheduled work time. He further specified that any supervisor *not* meeting the goal would owe one hour of extra work time.

After the announcement of this consequence the department manager reported to the consultant that each supervisor was inspecting some boxes every day and giving feedback to the individual packer involved.

## RESULTS

After the first intervention, the percentage of off-quality yarns packed rose to an average of 2.8 percent during this three-week period (see Figure 14). After the second intervention the percentage dropped below the goal for the total department, averaging 0.8 percent for a four-week period.

## DISCUSSION

After the first intervention it was evident to the consultant that weekly feedback was not often enough. In addition, it did not isolate the amount of off quality attributable to an individual packer on a given shift. Thus the feedback was not specific enough. After discussing the possibility of instituting a daily audit with the department to provide daily, specific feedback, it was dismissed as too time consuming.

When the department manager proposed attaching reinforcing and punishing consequences to the supervisor's off-quality performance, the consultant encouraged him to do so. The only contingency discussed up until this point was verbal reinforcement. This was not

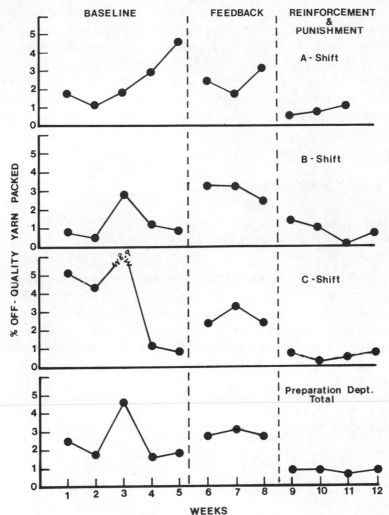

**Figure 14**    Percent of off-quality yarn packed; Case Study 6.

delivered, because of deteriorating performance after the first intervention.

The institution of consequences prompted the shift supervisors
to begin some random checking of their own each day and to give
feedback to the specific packers. This constituted, of course, an
informal "audit" that met the requirements of the consultants' initial
proposal. It succeeded.

While much research and practice of contingency management focuses on feedback and consequences for employees, a persistent but neglected problem remains in the *delivery* of the feedback and consequences by the immediate supervisor. Expansion of the contingency management approach to these and even higher organization levels should yield more consistent results. Research on the interface between self-management and management of others should yield some directions for practitioners.

## QUESTIONS FOR DISCUSSION

1. How does this study demonstrate the differential effects of reinforcers of differing magnitudes? How did the supervisor in this study utilize the principles of immediacy?

2. High performance may not provide sufficient intrinsic reinforcement to generate the necessary behavior to maintain that performance. This case illustrates that supervisors, who are generally expected to work for this intrinsic reinforcer, may require external contingencies. What implications does this study have for the implementation of behavior management programs in organizations?

# CHAPTER SEVEN

# SCHEDULES
# OF REINFORCEMENT

Schedules of reinforcement are directly related to the practical issues that arise in the implementation of behavior management or other management procedures in the organizational setting. How can a performance be increased in the most rapid manner? How can a limited quantity of tangible reinforcement be used to produce the maximum amount of behavior? How can behavior be maintained given limited resources or time on the part of a manager? How can satiation be avoided when a few reinforcers are available? The answer to all of these questions, and dozens of others that the manager must answer, are found in the study of schedules of reinforcement. No description, account, or explanation of behavior is complete unless the schedule of reinforcement is described. These schedules describe the major element of behavioral control.

A schedule of reinforcement describes when, how often, or which behaviors are followed by reinforcement. All occasions of reinforcement are presented according to some schedule. That schedule may be deliberately or accidentally established. All forms of compensation, bonus, commissions, social recognition, and other forms of reward in the organizational setting are delivered according to a schedule. Extensive research with animals (Ferster and Skinner, 1957), with children in school settings (Sulzer and Mayer, 1972), in mental hospitals (Hutchinson and Azrin, 1961), and in work settings (Yukl, Wexley, and Seymore, 1972) has demonstrated fairly predictable patterns of behavior in the presence of various schedules of reinforcement.

There are two general types of schedules of reinforcement: continuous and intermittent reinforcement. *Continuous schedule of reinforcement describes the presentation of reinforcement following every occurrence of a response. Intermittent schedules of reinforcement are those that provide for reinforcing some occurrences of a response but not others.* Intermittent schedules are generally divided into four types: ratio schedules, fixed and variable; and interval schedules, fixed and variable. These describe every possible arrangement or scheduling of reinforcement. Each is distinct in its characteristics and in the resulting pattern of response.

## CONTINUOUS REINFORCEMENT SCHEDULE

Continuous reinforcement (CRF) schedules are extremely rare in the organizational setting. Very few behaviors are likely to be followed by reinforcement every time they occur. A CRF schedule is usually not practical from the standpoint of the manager or the management system and is not the most effective one for maximizing productivity and maintaining performance over periods of time. In the work setting behavior generally occurs on a continuous basis. For a manager to reinforce on a CRF schedule he would have to be present when each behavior occurred and deliver reinforcement after each. This is impractical from the standpoint of the manager and in terms of maximum effectiveness. A CRF schedule is most likely to result in satiation. If the response is reinforced every time it occurs, the employee is likely to satiate on the available reinforcers after a short period.

The occasion on which CRF is the recommended procedure is when a new behavior is being initiated or a behavior that has been at a steady low rate is to be increased rapidly. Here CRF results in a relatively rapid increase in the rate of behavior. Training an employee on a new job or an additional task is an opportunity for applying CRF. Each correct response should be followed by reinforcement to establish the new behavior at a satisfactory rate.

If an employee has been performing a task at a low level for an extended period, this performance may be explained by the current schedule, which may reinforce the behavior only after a certain interval. For example, a production plant employee may have a low frequency of maintenance behaviors relative to the equipment the employee operates. Very often the behavior of cleaning equipment is not reinforced, but it results in punishment for failure to clean the equipment after some interval. The supervisor may notice the condition of the equipment after a period of one month's neglect. It may require one month for the equipment to acquire sufficient dirt and grime to elicit the supervisor's attention. The supervisor then makes a negative comment to the employee about the equipment, and the employee then cleans the equipment. This type of an interval schedule of reinforcement results in a low rate of cleaning behavior. The supervisor can alter this situation by placing the cleaning equipment behavior on CRF. Immediately after the behavior of cleaning the equipment the supervisor may reinforce the employee with positive verbal comments and some other available reinforcer such as a token, raffle ticket, or points toward bonus. The supervisor may let the employee know that he will be reinforced in a similar manner every time he cleans his equipment. He is likely to clean the equipment the next day. Reinforcement may then follow each occurrence of the behavior. This results in a rapid increase in performance.

While the effectiveness of achieving a rapid increase in response rate can be seen from this example, the difficulties with CRF are also obvious. What does the manager do after one or two weeks of CRF? The employee's behavior is also likely to suffer from satiation within a short time. Once the initial rate of behavior has been established, the manager should switch from a CRF to an intermittent schedule of reinforcement.

## INTERMITTENT REINFORCEMENT SCHEDULES

*Intermittent reinforcement (IRF) schedules provide for the reinforcement of some, but not all, emissions of a response.* There are three primary advantages to IRF schedules: first, their economic and practical efficiency; second, the avoidance of satiation; and third, the improved maintenance of performance under extinction conditions. These advantages dictate the use of IRF in most instances in the organizational setting. Most of the reinforcers common in organizations are one or another form of IRF schedule. Pay schedules, promotions, recognition, social reinforcement, bonuses, commissions, intrinsic reinforcement from task completion, and intrinsic satisfaction from the quality of performance all occur on an intermittent schedule.

The *economical and practical advantages* are self-evident to any manager in the organizational setting. Most managers are responsible for the performance of three to fifty individuals who may rely on reinforcement under his control. Most workers perform on a continual basis, and the delivery of reinforcement on the same continual basis is virtually impossible. It is common for managers receiving training in behavior management techniques to respond with concerns about the practical and economic application of reinforcement procedures. When the manager first comes to understand the importance of reinforcement the next thought that often occurs is, "How can I possibly find the time to go around reinforcing all of my employees?" There is an initial skepticism about behavior management for this very reason. On the contrary, an understanding of IRF results in a more economical use of the manager's time and resources. Greater reinforcement, and therefore performance, can be obtained from the same resources if the manager understands the effects of various schedules of reinforcement.

In the following discussion of interval and ratio schedules it will be seen that higher rates of performance may be obtained by using the same amount of reinforcement or the same number of occasions of delivery of reinforcement but delivering it according to a ratio schedule rather than an interval schedule. The same economy can be obtained in some cases by switching to a variable schedule from a fixed schedule. The economic benefit that can be gained by an alteration of schedules of reinforcement is staggering. A major portion of the amount of money spent by industry on bonus and commissions is misspent and results in a fraction of the potential performance that could be obtained from those same resources given a more effective schedule of reinforcement. Sales organizations, while the most aware of the benefits to be derived from performance-based incentives, are a major violator of many of the findings demonstrated in regard to scheduling reinforcement. It is not uncommon for sales organizations to spend hundreds of thousands of dollars on bonus or incentive programs that have little or no effect on performance.

The IRF schedules also help to avoid the problem of satiation, which may occur with verbal praise and approval, with awards that are primarily recognition, and with gifts or other tangible items. Satiation is less likely to occur in regard to generalized reinforcers, those backed by a wide range of potentially reinforcing items or events. Money is a generalized reinforcer, as are tokens, raffle tickets, green stamps, or other things that may be exchanged for a wide variety of items at the choice of the individual.

*An IRF schedule provides for avoiding satiation by delivering reinforcement after a number of responses rather than after each response.* Fewer reinforcers are delivered while maintaining the same high rate of response. The behavior continues to be emitted for a longer period of time before satiation occurs when reinforced on an intermittent schedule. The manager who requires a report from his employees once a week may begin reinforcing this behavior each week. After a couple of weeks' successful performance the manager may avoid expressing verbal approval for this performance and provide this reinforcement only after two successful week's performance. He may then continue to reinforce the behavior once every month, and after several months, may "thin out" the schedule to once every couple of months. In this manner the employees continue to perform the behavior as required but do not satiate on the verbal approval of the manager.

*The third advantage of intermittent schedules is the continuance of the behavior after the termination of reinforcement, or maintenance under extinction.* The ability to continue performing a response in the absence of reinforcement is critical to the success of any working individual. Organizations do not and cannot provide CRF. The individual must be trained to continue performing in the absence of reinforcement. The inability of many individuals in our society to succeed in the organizational setting may be explained by the failure of their prior training to prepare them for delayed or intermittent reinforcement.

A frequently used example to illustrate the different effects of CRF and IRF schedules on behavior during extinction concerns the behavior of the person who receives no reinforcement from a vending machine or a slot machine. Previous experience with candy, cigarette, or soft-drink vending machines has been that of a continuous schedule of reinforcement. We anticipate reinforcement following each response. We place a coin in the slot of the vending machine and a reinforcer is delivered each time. If the vending machine stops working, behavior extinguishes rapidly. The individual may attempt the behavior only once or twice after the initial nonreinforcement. A slot machine provides a very different response pattern. Gambling behavior is maintained on an intermittent schedule. Behavior is reinforced one out of a certain number of responses, and the occasion of reinforcement varies and cannot be predicted. This type of schedule produces behavior highly resistant to extinction. Any observation of a gambling casino will confirm this finding. Once an individual has been reinforced by the slot machine, behavior becomes very resistant to extinction. It continues for a high number of responses in the absence of reinforcement. This resistance to extinction is present, despite the knowledge that the machine is programmed to take more than it will give back. Ask the individual doggedly placing his money in the slot machine whether he is aware that the odds are against him, that the machine is programmed in a manner to ensure that it consumes more than it delivers, and the gambler lets you know he is well aware of that fact but continues to perform anyway. How many managers are able to instill the dedication and performance that the seemingly unintelligent slot machine evokes?

Much turnover in industry is caused by a failure to understand the relationship between schedules of reinforcement and performance. As many industries have moved into rural areas and employed persons with little industrial experience they have witnessed high levels of turnover and absenteeism. As industry has attempted to fulfill its social responsibilities by hiring those who for one reason or another may be classified as underprivileged they have also encountered difficulties in maintaining performance. This is also true among younger workers. These workers are often experiencing the effect of extinction owing to the variance between prior schedules of reinforcement and the new schedule in the industrial workplace. The rural workers may have worked for years on a fixed schedule, receiving pay for the number of pounds of a farm product picked in the field, or have received pay at the end of each day for the number of hours worked. While perhaps not CRF schedules, these may be said to be very "dense." The new schedule in the industrial setting may provide payment once a week or once every two weeks. This is too great a change in schedule for many workers. Even though their total pay may be greater, extinctions result. The rural or underprivileged workers may also be used to a high rate of social interaction on the job. They may have worked closely with other workers and derived reinforcement from the continuous social interaction. The new industrial setting it likely to result in diminished social interactions and reinforcement.

This situation could be altered by an intelligent assessment of the individual's prior schedules of reinforcement and an initial training or adaptation period during which the new employee is paid on a schedule similar to that with which he is familiar. The schedule could then be gradually thinned out to shift toward the more traditional weekly or biweekly paycheck.

A major difference in the response pattern of hourly workers and that of the manager results from the schedule of reinforcement. The hourly worker generally works under a more dense schedule of reinforcement, and the manager, under a thinner schedule. The manager's behavior is, therefore, more resistant to extinction. The manager may work for months on a project without seeing its completion or the resulting consequences. The hourly worker who has been conditioned by the more immediate and regular paycheck is less likely to perform under the delayed schedule that the manager may experience.

Management development programs generally focus on the skills required for managerial jobs. While managers must possess a wide range of skills, they must also possess the ability to perform at a high rate on a very delayed schedule of reinforcement. This ability must be learned by progressive experiences under delayed reinforcement schedules. This training does occur for many individuals as they rise through the organizational structure. They may initially be given projects that require several days' work and experience the consequences following completion. They may then engage in tasks that require weeks' worth of work. The probability for reinforcement may also change from virtual certainty to varying degrees of probability. As the prospective manager gains experience in the organizational setting he learns to perform under both delayed and variable schedules. This ability, though not articulated or measured by most organizations, is a primary prerequisite for success at the managerial level. An organization's ability to develop managers could be greatly enhanced by deliberate attention to IRF schedules.

Every manager who has supervised a new employee has been faced with the task of scheduling reinforcement in a manner to establish new behavior and maintain it over time. Although very few managers have ever recognized the task in which they were engaged, most have been able to succeed on their intuitive perception of the employee's need for attention. But many a new employee who is considered to have failed in adapting to the new job is, in reality, a casualty of the manager's inept scheduling of reinforcement.

The supervisor must schedule reinforcement to provide high density in the initial stages of the employee's learning and then gradually thin the schedule as appropriate response patterns become established. The manager can, by careful and sensitive observation of the employee's behavior, recognize signs of an excessively dense or excessively thick schedule. The employee on a schedule of reinforcement that may be too dense begins to show signs of satiation. His response to the reinforcer becomes "less appreciative," and he may actually become annoyed that he is being reinforced for so little behavior. On the other hand the employee on too thin a schedule shows signs of extinction. The behavior pattern of the employee on too thin a schedule is characterized by periods of termination of behavior or reduced rate of response. This employee may also demonstrate emotional responses that might be described as mild hostility toward the manager or other members of the organization. This apparent hostility is a result of the individual's frustration at not obtaining reinforcement needed to maintain the behavior that the individual knows is expected.

If an employee is experiencing satiation from a too dense schedule of reinforcement, the manager should, naturally, thin the schedule, requiring more responses or longer intervals between reinforcement. If the individual is experiencing the extinction effects of too thin a schedule, the manager should retreat to a more dense schedule providing reinforcement for fewer responses or for a shorter interval during which responses may occur.

The more gradual the thinning of the schedule the less likelihood of experiencing extinction. When a new employee is placed on a production task, the supervisor may attend to the employee once every two hours during the first day's work. The second day he may contact the employee and give him reinforcing feedback on his work every three hours or three times during the day. The next day he may contact him twice. He may continue to contact him twice a day for the remainder of the first week on the job. The second week he may give the new employee feedback once a day. By the third week the employee may receive feedback every other day. For most production workers this would represent a minimal schedule of reinforcement.

## RATIO SCHEDULES OF REINFORCEMENT

When *reinforcement occurs following the performance of a given number of responses the schedule is referred to as a ratio schedule.* The number of responses required may be fixed at a given number. In this case the schedule is a *fixed-ratio (FR) schedule.* If reinforcement is delivered, based on the number of responses but delivered after a varying number, the schedule is a *variable-ratio (VR) schedule.* A VR schedule is based on an average number of responses, and the person who's behavior is being reinforced is not able to predict which response will be followed by reinforcement.

The FR schedules are common in industry in the form of piece rate payment. Piece rate or piece work may be designed to reinforce the completion of every tenth, every twentieth, or every fiftieth task completed. When every twentieth response is followed by reinforcement, the schedule may be abbreviated FR20. The VR schedules are less common in the organizational setting but may occur in an unplanned fashion as in the case of the salesperson who may make a number of presentations to prospective buyers and experience reinforcement only after some presentations. The salesperson may average one sale for every ten presentations made. The salesperson does not know, of course, whether the buyer will be every tenth prospect or whether two prospects in a row will purchase. The average purchase to presentation may be one to ten. This is a VR10 schedule.

Ratio schedules produce certain predictable patterns of response, both while the person is under the experience of the schedule and during extinction. Whereas much of the study of performance under various schedules of reinforcement has been conducted in the laboratory with animals (Ferster and Skinner, 1957) other studies have duplicated many of the findings with human subjects (Hutchinsons and Azrin, 1961), and a few studies in the organizational setting (Yukl, Wexley, and Seymore, 1972) have tended to corroborate animal studies. Most managers who have experienced various types of reinforcement systems in the organization recognize the effects of most reinforcement schedules from their own observations.

Among the predictable patterns of behavior generated by ratio schedules of reinforcement are high and fairly consistent rates while the schedule is in effect and continued responding during at least the early stages of extinction (see Figure 15 and 17). Because reinforcement is delivered after a given number of responses, the individual exerts a great degree of control over the amount and occasion of reinforcement. Therefore, the faster the individual works the sooner he may receive reinforcement and the more reinforcement he may receive. Workers paid for the number of production units assembled, pages typed, or baskets of fruit picked can increase their earning by increasing their rate of behavior.

A number of factors determine the rate at which the individual will work under a ratio schedule. The ratio of reinforcement to nonreinforcement affects the performance. One study (Hutchinson and Azrin, 1961) showed that, to some maximal level, the larger the requirement, the more response required for reinforcement, the more rapid the rate of behavior. For example, it might be predicted that an individual paid fifty cents for each page of paper typed would work at the same rate as the individual paid five dollars for every ten pages typed. The total payout for performance is the same. But the individual paid for the larger task, the person on the FR10, rather than on the FR1, will work at a higher rate. It may be concluded that greater requirements are more effective than lesser requirements, given an equal total delivery of reinforcement. This should not, however, be assumed for all behavior of all individuals on all tasks. The individual may vary in his response to various schedules, and the nature of the tasks may mediate the most effective schedule. Given a specific job, the manager may test various schedules with his own workers and arrive at the most effective one for the workers on that task.

Although it may generally be true that the larger requirement produces higher rates of response, at some point the ratio requirement becomes too large and the individual begins to suffer from extinction. This is referred to as "ratio strain." Ratio strain refers to the extinction effect experienced when a schedule is thinned too much and the requirement for reinforcement becomes too great, resulting in reduced responding. When ratio strain develops, the individual begins to pause. The periods of pause lengthen until total extinction occurs. This can be delayed or prevented by gradually decreasing the requirement for reinforcement, carefully observing behavior and watching for ratio strain, and then slightly increasing the density of the schedule again.

The consistency of the response pattern varies between FR and VR schedules. The FR schedules may produce a pause following reinforcement (Figure 15). This "postreinforcement pause" is then followed by a resumption of behavior at the previous high rate. The greater the number of responses required on an FR schedule the greater the probability of a pause and the longer the pause is likely to be. But under the conditions of a VR schedule postreinforcement pause is unlikely. Salespersons generally work under a VR schedule and are often characterized by high rates of response and usually do not experience postreinforcement pause. This pause is not experienced, because the very next response might produce the reinforcing purchase by the customer, just as the previous customer purchased. If the salesperson knew that a purchase would result only from every fifth customer, a pause following each fifth customer could be expected.

Salespersons are often looked upon by salaried members of an organization as being somewhat odd. Salespersons are somewhat odd or behave in a somewhat different manner than straight salaried employees because of the schedule of reinforcement that controls their performance. Salespersons are often viewed as gamblers, betting on the big payoff, which they hope will follow the next presentation or the next customer uncovered. This gambling behavior is the type of behavior generated by VR schedules. The slot machine, roulette wheel, and all other forms of gambling are examples of VR schedules. They are highly effective for maintaining high levels of consistent performance.

Figure 15 illustrates the response pattern that may result from a VR10 schedule. An average of every ten responses is followed by reinforcement. You can see, however, that reinforcement follows the twelfth, fifteenth, twenty-sixth, thirty-fourth, forty-eighth, and fifty-third responses. Over the course of sixty responses an average of one of every ten responses has been followed by reinforcement. The exact response that will be followed by reinforcement cannot be predicted. Figure 15 also illustrates a typical response pattern of behavior under the control of an FR (FR10) schedule. The reinforcer follows every ten responses. This schedule produces postreinforcement pause and results in fewer cumulative responses then the VR10 schedule.

Once reinforcement is terminated, behavior previously maintained on ratio schedules has been shown to continue for relatively long periods of time. This continued performance depends on the type of ratio

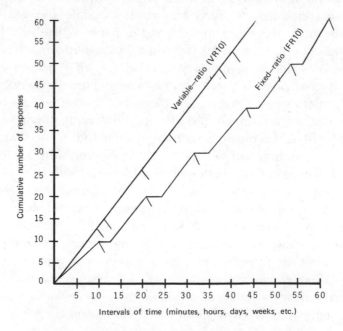

**Figure 15**   Performance characteristics on ratio schedules.

schedule and on the magnitude and quality of the reinforcer and the difficulty of the performance. Performance following the termination of an FR schedule is characterized by periods of high-rate behavior followed by pauses (see Figure 17). As the extinction period continues, the pauses become greater and the bursts of behavior are of shorter duration (Reynolds, 1968). Eventually the behavior ceases entirely. There is no schedule of reinforcement that ensures continued performance after the complete termination despite the absence of reinforcement.

The VR schedules provide the greatest reistance to extinction. The thinner the schedule on which the performance was previously maintained the more resistant to extinction the behavior. For example, the salesperson whose behavior was maintained by a schedule that provided for reinforcement on a VR30 schedule, closing only one deal of every thirty attempted, continues to perform longer than the salesperson who was maintained on a VR10, closing one of every ten deals attempted. The sales manager hiring salespersons might predict the behavior pattern of a prospective applicant by examining the previous performance and the prior schedules of reinforcement under which the applicant worked. Two applicants, both of whom had excellent records in previous sales positions, may behave quite differently given the new job. The sales manager should know the typical schedule of reinforcement under which his salespersons work. If the typical ratio of calls to sales is one to twenty for the new job and one applicant previously sold in a situation that delivered reinforcement on a VR5 schedule, and a second applicant previously worked under a VR30 schedule, it may be predicted that, all other conditions such as sales skills being equal, the second applicant will perform better on the new job.

Resistance to extinction can be developed by gradual thinning of the schedules of reinforcement. Our culture assigns value or admiration to the individual who can work for long periods without reinforcement. The artist, novelist, or athlete who can perform for long periods, in some cases many years, in the apparent absence of reinforcement is considered to have a great deal of "persistence." The athlete who trains for years to win the gold medal in the Olympics or the playwright who may work for years experiencing the rejection of his work is performing under the condition of a very thin VR schedule of reinforcement. Record-holding quarterback Fran Tarkenton of the Minnesota Vikings has been quoted (a quote that found its way to the office of President Gerald Ford, where it was placed on the office wall) as remarking that "it is not always the strongest, the quickest or the smartest who turn out to be the great ones. But it is those who keep getting up when they get knocked down. . . ." or, to state the case behaviorally, the person who can perform at a high rate on a thin VR schedule will eventually experience a high magnitude of reinforcement.

Schedules of reinforcement effect undesirable behavior just as they do desirable performance. Many undesired behaviors are maintained on VR schedules and are therefore extremely difficult to extinguish. The nagging wife (or husband, no chauvinism, please) is a good example. Nagging behavior occurs because it gets reinforced. The spouse may attempt to extinguish this annoying behavior by ignoring it. The spouse may, however, respond by taking out the garbage, doing the dishes, or performing whatever response is desired by the other partner on a variable schedule following the nagging behavior. This VR schedule is likely to be sufficient to maintain the behavior. As the naggee attempts to extinguish the behavior of the naggor, the reinforcement schedule is thinned out, increasing the nagging behavior required for reinforcement. If the naggee gives in occasionally and performs the behavior desired by the naggor, the behavior is strengthened and the resistance to extinction is enhanced. The point is to be sure not to reinforce *any* occurrences of the behavior once the decision is made to attempt to extinguish the nagging. The VR maintenance of undesirable behavior is also found in the organizational setting. Employees may complain about various conditions, compensation, rules, or work tasks and receive reinforcement occasionally. These behaviors can become very resistant to extinction, and the rate of these behaviors can be increased by the supervisor who provides the desired consequence on a VR schedule. By inadvertently maintaining undesirable behavior on a VR schedule the manager is increasing the eventual need to resort to punishment. This VR reinforcement thereby contributes to the total negative interaction in the organization.


## INTERVAL SCHEDULES OF REINFORCEMENT

Whereas ratio schedules of reinforcement provide for the delivery of a reinforcer after the performance of a number of responses, an interval schedule provides for the delivery of reinforcement after the passage

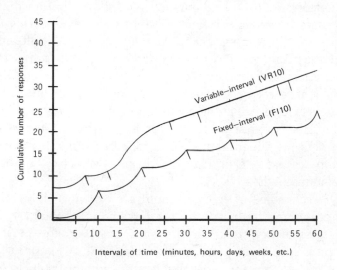

**Figure 16**   Performance characteristics on interval schedules.

of a specific period of time. When a response is reinforced *on an interval schedule, the first response that occurs after the time interval is followed by reinforcement.* If the interval specified is one hour, then the first response to occur after the end of the hour is reinforced. *When the time requirement is held constant, the schedule is a fixed-interval (FI) schedule. When the time requirement is not held constant but varies and is stated as an average time interval, the schedule is a variable-interval (VI) schedule of reinforcement.*

Many of the schedules of reinforcement in the work setting are FI schedules or similar to them. Most pay schedules that provide for the delivery of reinforcement at the end of a week, two weeks, or a month are delivered on a fixed interval. But they are not exactly FI schedules, because they do not require a specific response after the end of the interval. At the end of a week the paycheck is issued to the employee. The only response required is to show up at work and pick up the check. The check is not contingent upon any specific work performance. Many bonus plans are also delivered on a fixed interval. It is common for sales organizations to deliver a yearly or semiannual bonus. These are FI schedules. If, as is the case in many companies, the bonus is contingent upon a yearly performance review by the manager, the salesperson's performance may improve shortly before the end of the interval in anticipation of the performance review. This demonstrates one of the response characteristics of FI schedules that are discussed later. Annual salary reviews and increases are an FI schedule. Social reinforcement may also be delivered on an FI schedule. The supervisor who makes a practice of walking through his plant work area once or twice a day at the same time each day has established an FI schedule that is anticipated by the employees. If the supervisor walks through his department twice a day but varies the time of his observation so that it cannot be predicted, he has established a VI reinforcement schedule.

The FI schedules of reinforcement are, in most cases, the least effective of the four basic types of reinforcement schedules in producing high rates of performance. They are, however, the most widely used in the work setting. Interval schedules have a number of advantages that make them the most practical to administer. It is certainly easier to issue a paycheck once a month than to count the number of behaviors performed by an employee and reinforce the employee for a number of responses. Traditionally organizations have traded the high rates of performance that may be achieved by the use of ratio schedules for the administrative convenience of interval schedules.

Predicting response characteristics on interval schedules is somewhat more difficult than with ratio schedules. Performance may be influenced by a number of factors. It is possible to generate either high or low rates of responding on an interval schedule depending on the previous schedule of reinforcement. If a response was initiated on an FR or VR schedule, a high rate may have been established and may be maintained on the interval schedule. This may explain why there is great variability in the performance of workers reinforced on an FI schedule. Each of these employees has a history of reinforcement for performing similar work tasks. The effectiveness of those previous schedules is a major determinant of the current performance on the FI pay schedule.

There is only one requirement for reinforcement on an interval schedule: The behavior must occur one time following the completion of the specified time interval. If an employee is on an FI 30-minute schedule (FI30), the employee may sit without performing any work until the interval has been completed and perform one response following the completion of the interval and receive reinforcement. This fulfills the requirement of the FI30 schedule. A typical response pattern on an FI schedule demonstrates an increase in the frequency of response as the end of the interval approaches, a sudden pause following the completion of the interval, and again an increase in response frequency as the end of the next interval approaches (Mawhinney, 1971). On an interval schedule the individual cannot control the amount or frequency of reinforcement as he can on a ratio schedule. Regardless of the individual's performance only the prescribed amount of reinforcement is forthcoming. And the individual is not penalized for the pause in response following the delivery of reinforcement. For these reasons interval schedules generate lower response rates than ratio schedules of reinforcement. The FI schedules generally result in the lowest rates of response, given the same behavior and the same quantity of reinforcement.

The VI schedules generally result in higher response rates than the FI ones because the delivery of reinforcement is unpredictable. The variance in the delivery of reinforcement results in a more constant rate of behavior and therefore produces more cumulative responses during an interval than during the FI schedule. But high rates of performance are still unlikely on the VI schedule because the individual learns that he cannot increase the amount of reinforcement by performing at a high rate. High-rate performance does not pay off on either an FI or a VI schedule.

The size of the interval on either an FI or a VI schedule influences the rate of the response. The shorter the interval the higher the response rate. The shorter the interval the more frequent the response required to obtain the reinforcer and the less time during which pauses in behavior may be experienced. This is analogous to saying that the "closer" a worker is supervised the more consistent and productive his performance. A closely supervised worker is on a more dense schedule than a less closely supervised one. This assumes that the close supervision results in reinforcement and not in punishment for the employee.

Postreinforcement pause is common on FI schedules, and there are many examples of this in the work setting. The manager who has an annual report to complete increases his rate of performance greatly before completing the report. After the report's completion he may experience several days of low-rate responding as he pauses following the reinforcement that results from completing the report. The individual who has worked for a long period of time on a project such as a graduate degree may experience an initial elation at the receipt of the degree and then immediately experience a feeling of depression. This depression is a form of postreinforcement pause. The accomplishment of the graduate degree is achieved on an FI schedule. Obtaining the degree is a significant reinforcer. Because of the FI nature of the degree there is no possibility of immediately obtaining another reinforcer of this nature, and hence, the pause response occurs. This phenomenon is commonly known among doctoral students as postdoctoral blues. This postreinforcement pause resulting from FI schedules is also experienced after annual performance reviews, promotions that may be anticipated on an interval schedule, and exams that may be given on fixed intervals.

The VI schedules do not produce the inconsistency in response or the pauses experienced on FI schedules. Because the reinforcement is unpredictable the behavior is performed at a more steady pace. For this reason it is advisable to schedule reviews of performance on a VI schedule. Rather than have one annual performance review, performance might be reviewed an average of once every six months, without specifying when the review will occur. All reports, records, and data on performance would be examined at the time of the review and desirable performance reinforced. This procedure, accompanied by specific measurable objectives that establish an FR schedule (the accomplishment of the objective itself provides an occasion for reinforcement that may be controlled by the individual's behavior), produces higher and more consistent rates of performance than are experienced as a result of the traditional annual performance review.

One of the major advantages of providing intrinsic reinforcement that may be derived from the work itself is the establishment of a ratio schedule of reinforcement. If the major or only reinforcement schedule in the workplace is the salary, low rates of performance should be anticipated. If the individual derives intrinsic reinforcement from the work itself and can control the rate of performance, a higher rate is experienced. If, for example, the individual is producing furniture in a manufacturing plant, has no control over the flow of work, and is responsible for completing only one portion of the construction, little intrinsic reinforcement may be derived from the task. An individual may be responsible only for placing the springs in the bottom of a couch or chair as it passes by on an assembly line. The repetitive nature of the task produces quick satiation. If the job is redesigned so that the individual is responsible for the entire construction of the couch, satiation is delayed and the reinforcement derived from seeing the entire couch completed is added. This may be structured so that the individual can control the speed at which he works. He can therefore control the amount of reinforcement he obtains from seeing the completed couch by increasing his rate of performance. The redesign of the job has altered the schedule of reinforcement to delay satiation and to establish an FR schedule of reinforcement. Virtually any change in the design or structure of a job results in some change in the schedule of reinforcement and may, therefore, result in some change in performance. The careful examination of the schedules of reinforcement provided by the work structure and by the formal pay system and social reinforcement can result in identification of changes that may add no cost and produce increased performance. Many of these changes should focus on altering the schedules of reinforcement from relatively ineffective interval schedules to ratio schedules.

As with ratio schedules of reinforcement, interval schedules tend to maintain responding during extinction longer than a CRF schedule. Once reinforcement has been terminated, continued responding is determined by the history of reinforcement before the period of nonreinforcement. Similar to ratio schedules, the length of the interval on either an FI or VI schedule influences the length of the period during which behavior continues under extinction. The longer the interval between reinforcers that was maintaining performance the longer the period of responding after the termination of reinforcement. If an employee has been used to seeing his supervisor in his work area approximately once each hour, he may be said to be on a VI1 schedule. This is a fairly dense schedule. If the supervisor stops coming to this employee's work area, we may say that this reinforcer, that of observation and contact with the supervisor, has been terminated and the employee is on extinction relative to this reinforcer. If the schedule has been a VI1, it is likely that the behavior will extinguish rapidly. If, however, the supervisor had thinned this schedule gradually so that the employee observed the supervisor in his area only about twice a day, or approximately once every four hours, a VI4 schedule, the employee's behavior is more resistant to extinction and he continues to perform for a longer period than if he had been on the VI1 schedule.

The FI and VI schedules also produce different patterns of response after the termination of reinforcement. The FI schedules characterized by inconsistent performance, periods of pausing, continue to demonstrate this pattern during extinction. The period of pause gradually lengthens and the periods of responding gradually diminish until the behavior terminates completely. If the behavior was reinforced on a V1 schedule, the behavior continues to be performed more consistently during extinction as the rate of performance gradually diminishes.

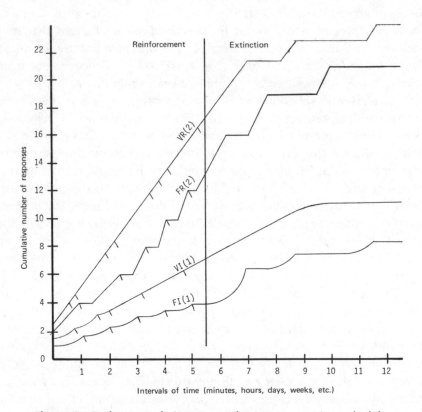

**Figure 17**   Performance during non-reinforcement on various schedules.

## VARIATIONS IN SCHEDULES OF REINFORCEMENT

In addition to the four types of intermittent schedules and continuous reinforcement a number of variations may be made in the manner of scheduling reinforcement. Three procedures have potential application in the organizational setting. These are the limited hold, differential reinforcement of high rates of responding (DRH), and differential reinforcement of low rates of responding (DRL).

### Limited Hold

A limited hold defines an additional restriction on an interval schedule. It requires that the behavior occur within a specified time period following the completion of a prescribed interval. If the behavior is not performed within the hold period following the completion of the interval, reinforcement is no longer available. For example, if there is an FI2 schedule that provides for the delivery of the reinforcer at the end of every two-hour interval, a limited hold of ten minutes may be placed on the performance. This would require that the desired behavior be performed within ten minutes after the end of the two-hour interval to receive reinforcement. If the behavior is performed fifteen minutes after the end of the interval, it is not reinforced.

A limited hold has the effect of increasing the rate of responding on interval schedules because of the potential for losing reinforcement if the behavior is not performed within the limited-hold period. This adds to the interval schedule one dimension of a ratio schedule: The individual has some control over the amount of reinforcement he may receive. Whereas he cannot increase his reinforcement beyond that defined by the interval schedule, he may be denied reinforcement if he fails to perform within the limited-hold period. A limited hold increases the rate of performance more on a VI schedule than an FI schedule. The reason for this is obvious. The individual may be losing reinforcement any time he is not performing because he does not know when the interval has occurred. On an FI, postreinforcement pause still occurs because there is no possibility of either gaining or losing reinforcement after the interval, and the limited hold has lapsed until the end of the next interval.

An example of a limited hold on an FI schedule may be a situation in which a monthly report is required. The report may be required at the end of each month, and points or merits toward bonus may be awarded contingent upon the completion of this report. This is an F11 (monthly) schedule. A limited hold of five days may be placed on this schedule, requiring the report to be turned in within five days after the end of the month in order for points to be received. Reports received on the sixth, seventh, or eight day of the month would receive no points. This has the effect of increasing the number of reports handed in within this five-day period. On a schedule of this type the consistency of the behavior may be intentionally reduced. The manager does not want reports coming in at all times of the month. He wants them at the beginning of the month. Therefore, the fixed interval with limited-hold contingency added produces the behavior he desires.

An example of a VI schedule with a limited hold may be illustrated by a sales organization of a major drug firm. The drug salespersons require a great deal of training and expertise in regard to the drugs they sell and the various effects of these drugs. The firm therefore requires an annual test to ensure that their sales staff's knowledge is up-to-date and adequate to properly represent the firm's drugs to medical doctors, hospitals, and pharmacists. Traditionally this test has been given once a year. This is an FI (FI1) schedule. Predictably this produces a high rate of studying behavior a few weeks before administration of the test. They have, under this FI schedule, imposed a limited hold requiring that the test be completed and mailed back to the corporate office within a one-month period. This sales organization could increase the preparedness of their sales force by making a number of changes in this schedule. They could change from an FI to a VI schedule. They could inform the sales staff that they would require the test twice a year and it would be mailed out without notice any time within the year. This would immediately have the effect of generating more consistent studying behavior because the time of the test requirement would be unknown. The limited-hold contingency could also be reduced to ten days. This would require that the test be completed immediately and would reduce the cramming for the test after it is received. The VI schedule with the ten-day limited hold would produce more consistent studying behavior and would ensure that the salespersons maintain a constant condition of preparedness and that the studying behavior has to occur before the test announcement, again necessitating a higher rate of consistent studying behavior.

## Differential Reinforcement High Rates (DRH)

Differential reinforcement of high rates of behavior is another method of increasing the rate of responding. A DRH schedule provides reinforcement only for high rates of performance. Athletics are full of examples of DRH schedules. Low rates of responding are generally not reinforced in athletic events. The football quarterback who is awarded a professional contract because he has a pass completion ratio of 55 percent is being reinforced for a high rate of pass completions. The quarterback with a low rate of this behavior is not reinforced. The same is true for basketball, foul shooting, hitting the ball in baseball, and running rapidly (under the four-minute mile) in track and field events. You can find examples of DRH schedules in any athletic contest. High rates of performance are differentially reinforced while low rates are ignored or, in some cases, punished.

These DRH schedules can be applied in the organizational setting by differentially reinforcing employees who exhibit high rates of the desired behavior and withholding reinforcement from individuals who do not perform at high rates or by reinforcing each individual only when he achieves a specific high rate of performance. In an organization in which innovation and creativity are important variables, such as high-technology electronics and data-processing corporations, DRH schedules may be used to reinforce creative contributions. When innovation is expected and is a routine function of an engineer's or scientist's job, a schedule may be established to reinforce particularly high rates of these behaviors. Individuals who have contributed five or more innovative applications of a specific technology may be reinforced with a monetary and social reward. This could and should be made available to any and all individuals who achieve this rate of innovative behavior. This eliminates the problem created when only one such award per year is offered and many persons give up; they consider the reinforcer beyond attainment and therefore do not perform for it. If a DRH is established, anyone who performs at the desired rate may be reinforced. This generates more productive behavior for the organization than a once-a-year offering.

A DRH may be used in a manufacturing setting to reinforce high rates of attendance. Every individual who has maintained a specified rate of attendance, such as above ninety-five percent, may be awarded a raffle ticket that may be drawn at the end of each month and result in a number of prizes. Individuals who do not achieve the 95 percent attendance rate are not punished or reinforced, but those who do attain it are reinforced by the raffle ticket and the chance to win the prizes available that month. This is a DRH schedule that differentially reinforces high rates of attendance behavior. Many of the behavior management projects that may be established in the organizational setting are based on the principle of DRH schedules.

### Differential Reinforcement of Low Rates (DRL)

The DRL schedules are the opposite of DRH schedules. *Reinforcement is delivered contingent upon specified low rates of responding.* These DRL schedules are employed when the manager wishes to reduce a rate of performance while not eliminating that performance entirely. These schedules may be useful when an employee on a production line is performing too rapidly and this results in defective products or an excess of output that the next worker on a line may be unable to process. The supervisor may specify a rate of performance and reinforce the employee for reducing his response rate. Employees may engage in other undesired behaviors such as excessive socializing, excessive breaks, or behaviors that may result in accidents such as running in work areas. Employing a DRL schedule may be used as an alternative to punishment in these situations. The supervisor may single out those employees who consistently do not run or engage in other accident-provoking behaviors and reinforce them for their low rates of behavior. An employee who has been disturbing other individuals with his or her excessive conversation may be reinforced on a day when the rate of that behavior has been somewhat lower than on other days. The supervisor may do this simply by thanking the employee for reducing this behavior. The supervisor may then shape the behavior downward as the rate reduces through differential reinforcement of progressively lower rates of responding.

### SUMMARY

Consideration of the schedules of reinforcement is a critical element in the design of any system or effort to change behavior or motivate high levels of performance. Every pay, bonus, commision, incentive, profit sharing, award, or reward system represents some schedule of reinforcement. Most of these systems are designed with little regard to the knowledge available concerning patterns of behavior under the influence of various schedules of reinforcement. It is foolish to continue to develop systems of reward intended to produce high levels of productive behavior without giving serious consideration to the wealth of research that has been conducted and the knowledge that is available to predict how individuals will behave given different schedules of reinforcement. Individual and organizational satisfaction and productivity can be enhanced by the effective scheduling of reinforcement.

We have seen that continuous reinforcement (CRF) may be effective in the initiation of a new behavior but results in rapid satiation and extinction following termination of reinforcement. The four types of intermittent schedules of reinforcement, fixed- and variable-ratio (FR and VR) schedules produce higher rates of performance than fixed- and variable-interval (FI and VI) schedules of reinforcement. Fixed-interval or ratio schedules tend to result in postreinforcement pause or inconsistent performance. Either VR or VI schedules result in more consistent responding. Variable schedules, particularly VR schedules, tend to result in greater resistance to extinction.

The effectiveness of interval schedules may be increased by adding the requirement of the limited hold, which defines a period within which the response must occur if it is to receive reinforcement. Additional variations of schedules may be used specifically to reinforce high rates of performance, DRH schedules, or low rates of performance, DRL schedules. These schedules are commonly used in the organizational setting to achieve specific performance goals.

## REFERENCES

Ferster, C. B., and Skinner, B. F. *Schedules of Reinforcement.* New York: Appleton-Century-Crofts, 1957.

Hutchinson, R. R., and Azrin, N. H. "Conditioning of mental hospital patients to fixed ratio schedules of reinforcement." *Journal of the Experimental Analysis of Behavior, 4,* 1961, 87–95.

Mawhinney, V. T., Bostow, D. E., Laws, D. R., Blumenfield, G. J., and Hopkins, B. L. "A comparison of students' studying behavior produced by daily, weekly and three-week testing schedules." *Journal of Applied Behavior Analysis, 4,* 1971, 257–264.

Reynolds, G. S. *A Primer of Operant Conditioning*. Glenview, Illinois: Scott Foresman & Company, 1968.

Sulzer, Beth, and Mayer, G. Roy. *Behavior Modification Procedures for School Personnel*. New York: Holt, Rinehart & Winston, 1972.

Yukl, Gary, Wesley, Kenneth, and Seymore, James D. "Effectiveness of pay incentives under variable ratio and continuous reinforcement schedules." *Journal of Applied Psychology*, **56**, (1), 1972, 19–23.

# CASE STUDY NUMBER SEVEN

## IMPROVING
## THE PERFORMANCE
## OF A SENIOR EMPLOYEE

A senior employee at an abrasives plant spent an excessive amount of time in nonproductive activities such as writing reports and leaving his machine to look for quality checkers. These behaviors resulted in low levels of production. The foreman implemented a program whereby he established his personal approval as a reinforcer and shaped improvements in performance. Operating efficiency rose from a baseline level of 81.3 percent to consistent performance over one hundred percent. The supervisor initiated reinforcement by differentially reinforcing high rates of operating behavior and gradually thinned reinforcement on a VI schedule.

### BACKGROUND CONDITIONS

This project was conducted during implementation of a plantwide behavior management program. Consultant John O'Connell was responsible for training this foreman and advised the foreman on procedures. This project was conducted as plantwide behavioral procedures were undertaken and all supervisors and foremen began similar individual behavior management projects.

The employee of concern had been with the company for thirty-five years and on his present job of operating a sandpaper-slitting machine for three years. The employee has worked steadily but has been operating at an 81.3 percent average efficiency. The standard efficiency level has been established by industrial engineers for this job and is being achieved by other employees performing similar jobs.

The plant is thirty-six years old and is located in east central Minnesota. The plant makes sandpaper and cuts the paper into various

Appreciation is expressed to Walt Wichser for providing this case study.

widths. The building has five floors, and the department in which the subject employee works is on the fourth floor, which is occupied by numerous sandpaper-slitting machines. Most of the machinery is quite old, and the standards for performance have been the same for many years, as have the training methods. The majority of the employees in this work area are cooperative and work well together. They generally meet production schedules. The foreman feels that he has a good relationship with most of the employees, although a few of them have recently developed a negative attitude because the company has been moving some of the machinery out of the department. The employee who is of concern in this project is described by the foreman as "being pretty set in his ways."

## PROCEDURE

The foreman observed the subject's behavior to attempt to determine the specific behavior that caused his low level of performance. The foreman was able to observe the following: (1) excessive time taken matching tickets accompanying material delivered to the employee with the material to be slit; (2) leaving the machine often to look for a "fabrication checker"; (3) too much time spent writing his report; (4) frequently stopping his machine to check his material. The foreman felt that if these behaviors, each of which was occurring at an excessively high level, were reduced, the employee would spend more time in the productive activity of operating his machine and thereby increase production.

The foreman had discussed the operator's poor performance with him. The foreman reported that, "I even told him that women could do better than that. His answer was that, 'I'm too old and I do quality work, not quantity.' He also said that the young guys made up for his performance."

The foreman began his procedure by establishing an interpersonal relationship that would serve as a reinforcing event. He did this by stopping by the employee's machine and talking to him about his locksmith business. Gradually they would get around to talking about his performance. The foreman asked him if he would take any advice on certain things he was doing. He said, "Sure," but he indicated that he didn't think anything would help, because he worked steadily all day.

The foreman suggested reducing one or two of the specific behaviors he had observed that detracted from performance. The foreman told the employee that it would take a while to improve his performance and he didn't expect him to make the one hundred percent standard operating efficiency immediately.

## RESULTS

After one week the employee began to improve his performance. Every day that there was any increase in performance the foreman stopped by the operator, engaged in a friendly discussion, and commented on the improvement in performance. Intermittently the foreman brought coffee and a sweet roll to the operator when improvements had been achieved. These were the only reinforcers available to the foreman in this plant. No bonus or other monetary system was available for use as reinforcers. Social approval, data-based feedback, and coffee and doughnuts, purchased by the foreman, were the only reinforcers available and were used successfully in this and many other individual projects being conducted simultaneously.

During phase I of the project (see graph) the foreman reinforced the employee every time that performance demonstrated any improvement over previous performance. The foreman differentially reinforced successively higher rates of performance. During phase I an average level of 100.1 percent operating efficiency was achieved. During phase II the foreman began thinning the schedule of reinforcement because the employee had achieved a rate of performance above the goal level of one hundred percent and appeared to be performing consistently at the new high rate. During phase II the foreman reinforced the employee three times per week, but only after the employee had achieved a high level of performance. During phase II the employee averaged 103.4 percent of standard performance. During phase III the foreman thinned the schedule of reinforcement further by reinforcing high levels of performance only once or twice a week. Again the operator was reinforced only after high levels of performance and the intervals between occasions of reinforcement were varied. During phase III performance continued at a high level, averaging 110.4 percent.

By the second or third month of the project the relationship

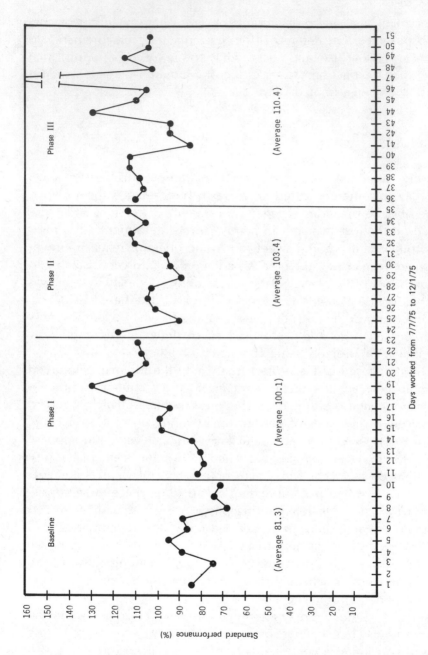

**Figure 18** Percent of standard performance; Case Study 7.

between the foreman and the operator had improved so much, and the relationship had been so clearly established between the operator's performance and the reinforcer of the foreman's social approval, that the operator would seek out the foreman to discuss his performance and point out the high levels of performance he had achieved.

Virtually no costs were associated with this program other than the time spent by the foreman. The operator raised his performance twenty-three percent and appeared to be more interested in his work and generally to be enjoying his job more. The foreman reported that the employee "is a lot more confident in his work now and is sharing stories about his high performance with other workers."

## DISCUSSION

This project is a good illustration of the improvement in performance that can be achieved by an individual supervisor who carefully considers the behavior and reinforcers of his employee. Typically this foreman had access to no powerful reinforcers such as job changes, salary increases, or bonuses, which are usually controlled by higher level managers. The foreman was, however, sensitive to the events in this worker's environment that made a difference and were reinforcing to him. A very large percentage of the determinants of individual performance are found, not in the larger managerial systems, philosophies, and theories, but in the pattern of daily interaction between the immediate supervisor and employee.

It is interesting that the foreman carefully observed the employee's behavior and was able to define those behaviors in which the employee engaged that contributed to his low level of performance. This was helpful to the foreman in first seeing the potential for improvement and then in advising the employee in changes that might improve his performance. The foreman chose, however, to measure for baseline and evaluation data the levels of standard operating efficiency. He did this because these data could be gathered without time-consuming observational procedures. These data are also meaningful to all management personnel within this plant. By use of these data for baseline and evaluation of the procedure the probability of the foreman's receiving reinforcement from his manager for his behavior change efforts was greater than if other, less traditional, data had been used.

An important element of this project was the foreman's ability to establish his interaction with the employee in a manner that proved to be reinforcing. If he had been unable to do this, it is likely that he would not have been able to achieve the increased performance. The foreman began his effort to establish this relationship by talking to the employee about his locksmith business, a topic that was reinforcing to him. This demonstrated the foreman's ability to participate in things of importance and pleasure to that individual. Advice was then more easily accepted and acted upon. It is important that the foreman had previously discussed the operator's poor performance with him and even ridiculed him with the comment that "even women could do better than that." This tactic merely resulted in excuse making by the operator and achieved no change in performance. After thirty-five years of service to the company the operator did not consider the possible punishing consequence of losing his job to be genuine. This operator was also not motivated by any desire to achieve promotions or other more traditional potential reinforcers. The foreman had, therefore, very few potential consequences that he could administer with this employee. He created the consequence of his reinforcing relationship.

The foreman in this project also successfully used schedules of reinforcement. He initiated the project with (DRH) and thinned the schedule on a (VI) schedule. The intelligent thinning of this schedule resulted in the maintenance of the new level of high performance. The pairing of the reinforcer of social approval with the data on high levels of performance also had the effect of establishing the data as a conditioned reinforcer. This is demonstrated by the fact that the operator began to seek out the foreman and show him high rates of performance and shared his data with other workers. The data began to reinforce the employee. It is clear that this was not the case before the project was begun. The operator had been previously quite satisfied to "let the young guys make up for my performance."

## QUESTIONS FOR DISCUSSION

1.  In this case two schedules of reinforcement were employed: DRH and VI schedules. Given the information presented in this case

discuss how the following schedules could have been employed to achieve the desired change in behavior:

a. (DRL);

b. FR schedules;

c. VR schedules; and

d. A limited-hold procedure.

2. The operator appeared to be deriving greater satisfaction from his job. Discuss the intrinsic reinforcers that the employee was now receiving and the schedules of reinforcement by which these reinforcers were received. Were these schedules ratio or interval schedules, fixed or variable? Explain these schedules and discuss why these intrinsic schedules, once established, are particularly effective schedules of reinforcement.

# CHAPTER EIGHT

# REDUCING
# POOR PERFORMANCE

In achieving the objectives of the organization, the manager must at times decrease the frequency of behavior. An employee may perform in a manner that results in excessive costs or that may block the productive performance of other individuals. An employee may spend too much time socializing in an office. A salesperson may incur excessive expenses resulting from unnecessary travel, entertainment, or luxury living while on the road. Or an employee may engage in behavior that presents a danger of accident and injury in the industrial setting. All these performance deficiencies requre a reduction in the frequency of a behavior.

The frequency of a performance may be reduced in one of three ways: *first, the undesirable behavior may be extinguished; second, an incompatible desirable behavior may be reinforced to take the place of the undesired behavior; and third, the undesirable behavior may be punished.* The manager must select the method of reducing the frequency of an undesirable behavior both to cause the desired change and produce as few undesirable side effects as possible. Managers most often employ punishment to eliminate or reduce undesirable behavior. Unfortunately, punishment, while it may cause the desired change in performance, may also produce undesired changes in other behaviors (Johnston, 1972). Punishment has a number of undesirable side effects and should be avoided whenever possible. Extinction and reinforcing incompatible behavior are two alternatives to punishment that may be equally successful and result in fewer damaging side effects.

## EXTINCTION

In the previous chapters reinforcement was discussed. In addition to motivating desired performance, reinforcement may also motivate undesirable performance. Some reinforcing consequence, such as social approval, may follow behaviors the manager would prefer to see reduced. By withdrawing reinforcement, the frequency of a behavior may be reduced. *The procedure of withdrawing reinforcement and the subsequent reduction in performance is known as extinction.* Behavior is extinguished in a manner similar to that of extinguishing a fire. Oxygen feeds fire. A fire extinguisher eliminates the fire by removing the source of the oxygen supply. Similarly reinforcement feeds behavior. The extinction procedure involves withdrawing the reinforcement maintaining behavior. Stated simply, when a reinforcer is discontinued the behavior previously reinforced no longer matters. It no longer produces a result desirable to the individual performing the behavior.

Extinction is often effective in reducing performances maintained by social consequences, for example, that of the office worker who spends too much time in social conversation, constantly pestering his manager with insignificant details and office gossip. Whenever someone is talking too much, someone else is listening too much. Listening and listeners reinforce talking and talkers. The manager may reduce the social conversation behavior of this individual by simply not paying attention. When the talker approaches the manager, the manager may simply continue to work at whatever task he has in front of him or may simply inform the talker that he does not have time to converse. The manager is withdrawing the reinforcement previously received for this behavior. The behavior will decrease in frequency.

The worker who spends too much time speaking with fellow workers is receiving reinforcement from them. The manager cannot reduce this behavior by withdrawing his own attention. This illustrates a condition necessary for the application of the extinction procedure: *The reinforcer maintaining the behavior must be identified and must be subjected to control.* Very often this condition is not present. If the employee who spends too much time conversing is reinforced by his peers, it may be very difficult or impossible to arrange for the elimination of reinforcement. On the other hand, in some cases, it may be possible to involve peers in the extinction of behavior.

Identifying the events reinforcing a target behavior may be difficult. In some cases the events may be very complex social circumstances controlled by many persons. In other cases the controlling conditions (for absenteeism and turnover) may exist entirely or partially outside the organization. The reinforcing event can be definitively determined only through empirical observation. By repeatedly observing which events consistently follow the target response, the consequence appearing responsible for maintaining the behavior can be examined. The consequences may then be removed while data on the frequency of the response are continuously monitored. It is recommended that the frequency of a behavior be recorded before any effort to extinguish the behavior. Recording the frequency after with-drawal of the reinforcement then reveals whether or not that removed event was the actual reinforcer.

It is also important to consider the extinction effect in the man-agement of desirable performance. Every manager has observed desir-able performance decrease in frequency. This decrease can often be explained by extinction. If desirable behavior, previously reinforced, ceases to result in reinforcement, it is reduced. The manager's job is to provide reinforcement for performance. If extinction of desirable behavior is occurring, the manager must evaluate his own practice of reinforcement. Has he been providing appropriate verbal praise and recognition for the accomplishment of objectives and target levels of performance? Has the employee received financial compensation for increases in productivity, skill level, or innovative contributions to the organization? If these conditions are consistently not met, the desired performance is extinguished.

A number of factors affect the manner in which a behavior re-sponds to the withdrawal of reinforcement (Kazdin, 1975). Among these are (1) the schedule of reinforcement that has maintained the behavior, (2) the magnitude of previous reinforcement, (3) the length of time the behavior has been reinforced, and (4) the number of times the behavior has previously undergone extinction.

A response reinforced every time (continuous reinforcement—CRF) rapidly extinguishes once the reinforcer is withdrawn. A response reinforced occasionally (intermittent) extinguishes much less rapidly. The more intermittent the schedule of reinforcement the greater the resistance to extinction. Behavior maintained on variable-ratio (VR) schedules is extremely resistant to extinction. Gambling is a good example of a VR schedule of reinforcement. Behavior is reinforced once in every ten, twenty, or possibly more, times. Gambling behaviors are extremely resistant to extinction because the gambler does not know when reinforcement will occur. He continues to gamble because his previous learning history has taught him that "possibly the next time" reinforcement will follow his behavior.

Many behaviors a supervisor may wish to reduce may be main-tained by this gambling principle. Any behavior that has a desired pay-off for the individual, one that occurs only sometimes when the be-havior is performed, is being reinforced on a schedule resistant to extinction. To extinguish behaviors that have been maintained on an intermittent reinforcement (IRF) schedule, the manager must be able to control the reinforcement in a manner ensuring that the reinforcer will not be delivered for a long period of time or over many occurrences. If the behavior is accidentally reinforced during the extinction period, it is strengthened and becomes more resistant to extinction.

Resistance to extinction is also affected by the magnitude or strength of previous reinforcement. The more powerful the reinforcement, the harder it is to extinguish the behavior. The employee or group of employees who receives a substantial increase in wages as the result of some concerted action, such as a strike, are more resistant to extinction than an employee or group of employees who receive a less substantial benefit from a similar action. The length of time over which reinforcement has occurred also affects resistance to extinction. The behavior of the employee who has been reinforced for complaining about his work, for complaining about fellow workers, or for changing jobs for many years, is very difficult to extinguish.

The more often the extinction procedure has been experienced the more quickly the behavior extinguishes. The individual learns that under certain conditions reinforcement is not going to occur and ceases to respond until the conditions change. As soon as the conditions change back to those under which reinforcement was previously delivered, the employee again begins to perform. Salespersons learn that, under certain conditions, reinforcement is not likely. If market conditions worsen, the new salesperson may continue to perform as he did under good market conditions. However, under poor market conditions, he may find it impossible to receive a bonus or commissions. The possibility of earning reinforcement has been removed and the behavior extinguishes. After a few market cycles the salesperson learns when the market conditions are such that he is not likely to earn commissions. He has learned to reduce his performance more quickly than he would have before previous extinction experiences.

When the reduction of a performance is required and when the reinforcer maintaining that performance can be identified and controlled, extinction is the first technique that should be employed. There are few negative side effects to extinction. If other methods are used to reduce the undesirable performance while reinforcement for the undesirable behavior continues, the likelihood of success of those other procedures is significantly thwarted.

## REINFORCING INCOMPATIBLE BEHAVIOR

Try to look at the positive alternatives to poor performance. Ask your-self: "If this person wasn't doing this thing I don't like, what would he be doing?" The answer is what should be reinforced.

Whenever one behavior is reduced in frequency, some other behavior must assume its place. The second method of reducing unde-sirable performance is to reinforce this other behavior. For example, if you wish to reduce the behavior of leaving the work task, you may reinforce the behavior of remaining on the work task for increased periods of time. If you wish to reduce the behavior of excessive spending on company travel, you may reinforce individuals who hold their expenses down. If you wish to reduce the behavior of arriving to work late, you may choose to strengthen the behavior of arriving to work on time. Each of the desirable performances in these pairs is incompatible with the undesirable performance. One cannot arrive to work late and arrive to work early at the same time. The strengthening of one behavior necessitates a weakening of the other. A number of articles have reported research demonstrating the reduction of unde-sirable behaviors such as absenteeism (Wallin and Johnson, 1976; Pedalino and Gamboa, 1974), tardiness (Herman et al., 1973) and safety-related behaviors (see Case Study 2).

Reinforcing incompatible behavior is a technique that may be used by itself or employed concurrently with extinction or punishment (McKelvey, Engen, and Pecht, 1973). Reinforcing incompatible behavior should be employed EVERY TIME a behavior requires reduction or elimination. For every behavior that must be reduced, some other behavior must take its place. If the manager does not select the behavior to take the place of the undesired response, the employee may select an alternative behavior equally undesired. If the salesperson who has been spending excessively on his travels is reprimanded (punishment) for his spending, he may reduce his expenses by reduc-ing his travel. This may have serious consequences for the sales mana-ger. If the sales manager chooses to reinforce the behavior of reducing travel expenses according to some ratio of travel to dollars spent, the reduction may be achieved without the negative side effect of reduced customer contact.

Reinforcing incompatible behavior is a relatively easy procedure to apply and should be used often to reduce undesired behavior. The manager or supervisor should ask himself the question: "What is the opposite of the behavior that is resulting in a problem?" The answer to this question identifies a beneficial and incompatible behavior that may be reinforced to substitute for the poor performance.

### PUNISHMENT

The third procedure for reducing undesired performance is punishment. Ask a manager if he uses punishment and he will deny it vigorously. Punishment is perceived as something reserved for children and pet animals. A manager will acknowledge that he may reprimand, correct, or warn employees to change negative behavior. Technically, each of these terms refers to punishment. Punishment, in behavior management terminology, is an empirical operation that reduces the frequency of a response. *Punishment is the presentation of an aversive event or removal of a positive reinforcer contingent upon a response, resulting in a decrease in the probability of that response.*

Punishment, while the least desirable method of reducing performance, is probably the procedure most commonly used in organizational settings. Warnings of possible aversive consequences, disapproval, written or verbal reprimands, reductions in income, and denial of privileges are forms of punishment if they result in a reduction in the rate of the behavior on which they are contingent. Often these aversive consequences do not result in a change in the behavior they were intended to change and are, therefore, not punishment in the technical sense. Often consequences intended to punish behavior result in reinforcement, and intended reinforcement sometimes results in punishment. The only way to be certain that either punishment or reinforcement has occurred is to measure the frequency of the behavior before and after the procedure.

Punishment, as reinforcement, may be of two types, either positive or negative. Positive punishment refers to the presentation of a stimulus following behavior and resulting in a reduced performance. Negative punishment refers to the removal of a stimulus event following a performance resulting in reduced performance. Positive punishment involves the presentation of an aversive event such as the reprimand, while negative punishment refers to the removal of a positive event such as a privilege or salary.

Positive punishment most often involves verbal statements. Managers use various forms of threats, warnings, reprimands, disapprovals, or even more subtle connotations such as tones of voice. Punishment may be delivered merely by the facial expression of a manager after observing an employee's behavior. Employees are very sensitive to the slightest change in the expressions and manner of their supervisors and are generally very quick to observe any expression of disapproval.

Verbal warnings and threats may be used only occasionally. The excessive use of verbal punishment results in a weakening of that punishment. Threats not backed by the threatened consequence lose their punishing value. The more frequent the threat the less effect it is likely to have. Managers commonly make the error of threatening consequences they either can't or won't employ. This not only weakens the likelihood that their threats will produce change in performance in the future but also reduces their general credibility in the eyes of the employee.

Termination may or may not be punishment. Termination is something like capital punishment; the behavior that was undesirable is not performed again, but then neither is any other behavior. Termination of an employee may reduce the probability of an undesirable behavior, such as repeated absences, in a future work setting. If other techniques of reducing the frequency of behavior, such as extinction or reinforcing incompatible behavior, are first attempted, and have proved unsuccessful, punishment and even termination may be the recommended action. In some cases the manager may be punishing the employee in that employee's own best interest. The employee who continues to engage in poor work behavior is reducing his own value to the organization and preventing his own advancement. While termination from the job may not benefit the employer, except in removing an annoyance, it may benefit that employee in that he may learn the relationship between his behavior and the consequences.

Negative punishment in the organizational setting, removing a stimulus resulting in a reduced response rate, may also be referred to as *response cost*. Negative punishment is a response cost because it involves removing something desirable as a consequence to the behavior. The response or behavior has cost the individual the item or privilege of value. Response cost items in an organization may involve the loss of privileges such as time off, desirable work assignments, merit points or achievement points that may be earned toward a raise or bonus, and outright salary reductions.

*A number of considerations determine the effectiveness of a punishment procedure. Among these are (1) the intensity of the punishment, (2) the relationship between a current punishing event and previous similar events, (3) the immediacy or delay of the consequence, and (4) the schedule of the punishment.*

Intensity of punishment is directly related to its effectiveness in suppressing behavior. The greater the intensity of the punishment the greater the probability of reduced frequency of response. This relationship may, however, be confounded by numerous other variables that may be influencing the punished behavior. The behavior may be simultaneously reinforced by a separate contingency. It must have been reinforced or it would not be present to begin with.

The effect of punishment is also determined by the second consideration, the relationship between the current punishment and previous punishment events. Research has demonstrated that the punishment is more effective when the aversive consequence is introduced at maximum strength immediately, rather than presented in gradual increases in intensity. When punishment intensity is gradually increased, the individual tends to adapt to the aversive event rather than change behavior. Managers often administer punishment in weak doses, intermittently. Rather than deliver a strong punishment on one occasion or every occasion of the behavior, they begin with weak and ineffective punishers, gradually increasing the intensity of the punishment and experiencing continual failure of the punishment procedure, and this finally results in the termination of the employee. It would be preferable and in the best interest of the manager and the employee to administer the reprimand or other punishment in sufficient dosage to have a significant impact on the behavior the first time. In this case the behavior is likely to undergo an immediate change. The manager may then provide immediate reinforcement for the improved performance and focus his energies on directing and reinforcing that desirable performance until it is well established.

All forms of consequences, punishment and reinforcement, are most effective when delivered immediately after the behavior. The greater the delay between the behavior and the consequence the less change in behavior to be expected from that consequence. Punishment

delayed for several days may not only result in no change in the undesired behavior but also punish desirable performance. If the manager
waits one or two days or a week after the behavior to deliver the
punishment, it may come immediately after the employee has been
performing well. This results in the punishing effect's influencing the
wrong behavior.

The schedule of delivery also affects the value of punishment, as it
does reinforcement (Schmitt, 1969). Punishment is most effective when
it follows every time the behavior occurs. The employee who is reprimanded for arguing with his peers should be reprimanded every time.
The individual who is punished by the loss of bonus pay as a consequence of equipment loss or damage should be punished every time
the behavior occurs. This principle should also be applied throughout
the organization. If one individual received punishment for a certain
action, then that same consequence should be administered to all
other individuals who have engaged in the same action. This assumes
other conditions are equal. This equity of punishment is a basic ingre-
dient in the employee's perception of the "justness" of the management of an organization. Equitable treatment is perceived as fair and
proper, whether punishment or reinforcement.

While punishment is often effective in reducing undesired behavior, there are a number of reasons why the *net effect* of punishment
within the organization may be negative. Punishment may result in a
solution to the immediate problem but may generate other and
possibly more serious problems in the process. Three side effects of
punishment are of particular concern to the manager: *(1) the emotional reactions resulting from punishment, (2) the response of escape
or avoidance from the source of punishment, and (3) the aggression
that may be elicited by the punishment.*

It is fairly obvious that punishment produces an emotional response on the part of the individual punished. In the workplace this
emotional response is heightened if the punishment occurs in the
presence of the employee's peers or becomes known to them. For this
reason any punishment should be a private affair between the individual and his manager. The immediate emotional reaction to punishment
may result in the inability to pay careful attention to the work task
and therefore may result in a temporary reduction in productivity and
work accuracy. An additional emotional reaction occurs as a result of
the pairing of the punishment with the stimulus of the person deliver-

ing the punishment and with any other stimulus present at the time of the punishment. These stimuli may become, either temporarily or permanently, paired with the punishment and may elicit a disruptive emotional reaction similar to that elicited by the punishment. This pairing of punishment with the manager is the opposite of the pairing that the manager hopes to achieve. The manager should work to develop his presence as a reinforcing stimulus that elicits favorable emotional responses. Punishment produces the opposite effect.

Organizations, particularly most industries and businesses, are competing for personnel. If the organization employs punishment frequently, that punishment generalizes to the organization as a whole. All people work to escape aversive conditions. Escape is negatively reinforced by the removal of the aversive condition. If an organization, company, supervisor, or manager has become an aversive stimulus to his employees, those employees tend to escape or avoid that organization or individual. Such a condition may be very costly in employee turnover and absenteeism costs. Many behavior management programs have demonstrated substantial impact in reducing absenteeism and turnover (Kempen and Hall, 1977). Many of these reductions may be explained by the substitution of punishment with reinforcement procedures.

Laboratory experiments have demonstrated that punishment results in an aggressive response against the source of the punishment (Azrin and Holtz, 1966). Individuals in the work setting may be induced to aggress against the organization or individual responsible for punishment. While the aggression toward the organization may not produce any desirable external consequence for the individual, an internal sense of satisfaction at "getting back" may be experienced. This satisfaction is reinforcing and results in increased future "getting back" behavior. Forms of aggression are increasing problems in the industrial setting, taking the form of assembly line defects, machine breakdowns, and other forms of disruption. Many of these instances of aggression may be a reaction to previous punishment experiences.

The high frequency of punishment on the part of managers can be explained by the immediate effects of punishment. The supervisor who punishes an employee is reinforced for his punishing behavior because the employee changes behavior immediately, if not for a long period of time, and because the manager immediately feels better because he has "done something" about the situation. These experiences on the part of the manager reinforce and increase the frequency of his use of punishment. This, in itself, is an undesirable side effect of punishment, compounding the previously stated problems.

When should punishment be used? It should be used when a behavior must be reduced in frequency and when the other two procedures, extinction and reinforcing incompatible behavior, have either been tried and failed or are impractical at the outset. Behavior should also be punished when it presents a danger to the well-being of other members of the organization or to the individual performing the behavior. Behavior that presents dangers cannot be experimented with and should be punished to provide immediate termination. Mild forms of punishment, such as instructive or corrective statements to an employee who has violated a company policy, performed a task improperly, or performed the wrong task, are often necessary to initiate the correct behavior that may be followed by reinforcement. Whenever such forms of mild punishment are used, the manager should make a deliberate effort to follow up that occasion with a positive response to the correct performance immediately after it is initiated.

It should be clear that punishment is less desirable than withdrawing the reinforcement maintaining the unwanted behavior and reinforcing the positive behavior. Whenever punishment is employed, the manager should also use reinforcement. This not only minimizes the negative side effects of punishment but also provides positive direction to the individual.

## REFERENCES

Azrin, Nathan, and Holz, W. C. "Punishment," in W. K. Honig (Ed.), *Operant Behavior*. New York: Appleton-Century-Crofts, 1966.

Johnston, James M. "Punishment of human behavior." *American Psychologist*, November 1972.

Kazdin, Alan. *Behavior Modification in Applied Settings*. Homewood, Ill.: The Dorsey Press, 1975, pp. 175–179.

Kempen, Robert W., and Hall, R. Vance. 'Reduction of industrial absenteeism: Results of a behavioral approach. *Journal of Organizational Behavior Management*, **1**, 1–21, 1977.

McKelvey Robert K., Engen, Trygg, and Peck, Marjorie B. "Performance Efficiency and injury avoidance as a Function of positive and negative incentives." *Journal of Safety Research*, June 1973.

Pedalino, E., and Gamboa, Victor U. "Behavior modification and absenteeism: Intervention in one industrial setting." *Journal of Applied Psychology,* **59,** (6), 1974, 694–698.

Schmitt, David R. "Punitive supervision and productivity: An experimental analog." *Journal of Applied Psychology,* **53,** (2), 1969, 118–123.

Wallin, Jerry A., and Johnson, Ronald D. "The positive reinforcement approach to controlling employee absenteeism." *Personnel Journal,* August 1976.

# CASE STUDY NUMBER EIGHT

# POOR SECRETARIAL PERFORMANCE

This case demonstrates the improvement in poor performance of a secretary by the use of behavior management procedures. In the absence of the procedures demonstrated, this employee would most likely have been terminated. The case demonstrates the varying effectiveness of several procedures, including performance reviews, praise, feedback, and specification of objectives. The effects of clearly specifying the contingency between behavior and consequences are illustrated by the changes in behavior during the various phases of this program.

## BACKGROUND CONDITIONS

Secretaries and other support personnel are often a critical factor in the efficient functioning of an office. However, the standards for their performance are seldom clearly articulated, and performance criteria and balanced measurement procedures and appraisals may inadvertently focus on highly visible (usually irritating) but peripheral office behavior. Subsequent efforts by the supervisor to improve performance tend to accentuate the negative and produce only surface changes in behavior. Recent studies suggest that important changes in performance of workers can be achieved by changing selective factors in the work environment, especially informational processes that communicate performance expectations and objective feedback of performance results.

Appreciation is expressed to Robert W. Kempen, of the Western Electric Company, for this case study, which was presented in a paper entitled "Applied Behavior Analysis in Organizations: Some Applications and Possibilities," American Society for Public Administration, Chicago, April 1975.

The subject of this study was Mrs. A., a twenty-five-year old, married, black woman who was performing at an unacceptable level in a staff office. She was hired under a special Affirmative Action Program that waived normal entrance skill criteria and provided "vestibule" training to bring job skills up to normal entrance standards. During her four years with the company, all in the same organization, she had seven different supervisors.

## PROCEDURE

The first step in the study was to specify performance in objectively measurable terms. Based on casual observation and job requirements, three performance measures were selected: (1) the percent of time Mrs. A. attended to her work tasks, (2) the number of errors she committed per page typed, and (3) the average turnaround time per typing job. Attending to task was selected to obtain a gross measure of Mrs. A's application. Intermittent observations of Mrs. A's office behavior suggested that she spent a significant amount of time in personal activities such as entertaining personal friends (other employees), talking on the telephone to relatives and friends, and taking rest breaks in the ladies' room. The other two measures were selected because approximately eighty-five percent of Mrs. A's workload was typing for about six staff personnel. The remaining work involved filing, record keeping, phone answering, and miscellaneous office services. There was a backlog of work for Mrs. A. throughout the period of the study.

Baseline measures were taken on two of the three performance dimensions, typing accuracy and percent of time attending to task. Initially all measurements were covert to avoid accidentally influencing the performance under study. Because staff personnel were frequently out of the office and therefore unable to observe work being returned, it was not possible to obtain a baseline measure of typing turnaround time (the elapsed time from submittal of a typing job to return of the typed product). Two people measured attending behavior, one as the principal observer and one as a reliability observer. All personnel serviced by Mrs. A, participated in the measurement of typing accuracy. During baseline Mrs. A. was observed to be attending to task less than fifty percent of the time, as shown in Figure 19. Her typing errors occurred at the rate of about one undetected, uncorrected error per

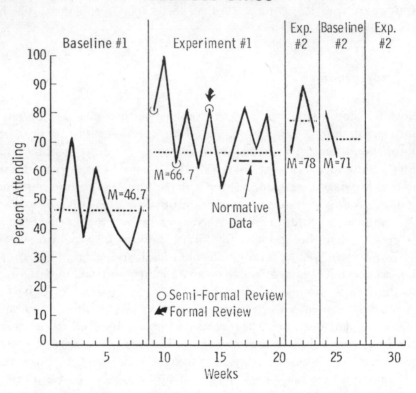

Baseline #1: Covert measurement.
Experiment #1: Covert measurement, periodic semi—formal
                performance reviews, intermittent praise for
                appropriate performance.
Experiment #2: Performance standards, overt measurement,
                weekly feedback,
                praise for improvements.
Baseline #2: Performance standards, overt measurement,
                no feedback.
Normative Data: Average of samples of five other
                secretaries.

**Figure 19**    Percent attending; Case Study 8.

two pages typed (Figure 20). Reliability of measurement throughout the study averaged eighty-eight percent and ninety-one percent respectively (percent of observer agreements divided by agreements plus disagreements).

Preanalysis of Mrs. A's performance suggested that error rate was affected by her attempts to type and carry on social activities simultaneously. Her low productivity appeared to be a direct function of low rates of application. The consequences to Mrs. A. for her performance seemed to be only intermittent negative comments from her supervisor. Although staff personnel frequently grumbled among themselves about her performance, few ever addressed these comments to Mrs. A.

Initial efforts to increase Mrs. A.'s productivity focused on her general office behavior, especially her application to work tasks. Office behavior rules were prescribed in an effort to reduce visitors and personal phone time and to increase application. Periodic semiformal performance reviews were conducted by her supervisor to communicate rules, provide general feedback on observed performance, and jointly diagnose performance difficulties. An organizationally prescribed formal annual performance review was conducted about midway through this period (arrow on Figures 19 and 20). Mrs. A. was formally rated as unsatisfactory and placed on six months' probation. The rules, "traditional" performance review, increased attention, and intermittent praise for improvements resulted in an increase in attending to about sixty-seven percent, comparable to the average for five other secretaries in the organization as determined by a one-month sample (dotted line in Figure 19). This rate of attending represented about forty-three percent improvement over baseline rates. However, aside from a brief improvement following the formal performance review, there was no appreciable change in typing error rate. The consensus of staff personnel was that no improvement in turnaround time was affected during this period either. Apparently Mrs. A. was spending more time on her tasks but without any real increase in productivity. The increased attention and generalized feedback appeared to affect general office behavior without improving work output.

The next experimental phase involved overt measurement of typing accuracy and turnaround time, Mrs. A's involvement in the measurement process, application of typing performance standards,

# Secretary
# Business Office

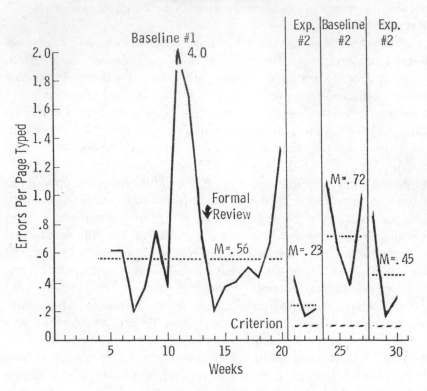

Baseline #1: Covert measurement.
Experiment #2: Performance standards, overt measurement,
             weekly feedback,
             praise for improvements.
Baseline #2: Performance standards, overt measurement,
             no feedback.
**Figure 20**   Errors per page typed; Case Study 8.


and formal weekly feedback and review of charted performance. During the weekly reviews Mrs. A.'s supervisor reviewed the individual measures and charts and restricted his comments to positive remarks about achievement of standard or improvements. During this three-week phase, Mrs. A.'s attending rose to an average of seventy-eight percent, an increase of sixteen percent over experimental phase one and sixty-six percent over baseline. Her typing error rate dropped from 0.56 to 0.23 error per page, more than a fifty percent improvement, although not achieving target level.

Mrs. A.'s turnaround time performance during the period averaged 2.3 hours per typing job (average of two pages per job). Although no prior measure of turnaround time had been obtained, office staff serviced by Mrs. A. commented profusely on the marked improvement. (see Figure 21).

After this experimental period the performance standards and measurement procedures remained in effect, but the weekly feedback

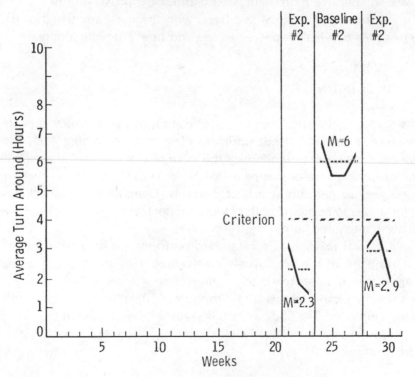

**Secretary
Business Office**

Experiment #2: Performance standards, overt measurement,
weekly feedback,
praise for improvements.
Baseline #2: Performance standards, overt measurement,
no feedback.
**Figure 21**   Average Turnaround Time; Case Study 8.

of data and formal reviews were discontinued. Attending dropped to seventy-one percent while typing errors increased to 0.72 per page, more than a 200 percent increase. Job turnaround time increased to 6.0 hours per job, a 160 percent increase. After this brief reversal phase, weekly feedback and review were reinstated. For the three weeks before Mrs. A. left on a personal leave of absence, her accuracy improved to 0.45 error per page and her turnaround time improved to 2.9 hours per job. It was in anticipation of her leave that the experimental and reversal phases were so brief.

Mrs. A.'s initial reactions to this whole process were negative. She viewed the procedures as somewhat embarrassing, especially since she was singled out among the office secretaries for this treatment. However, as her performance approached or exceeded criterion levels, she became more enthusiastic about the process. In her words, "This is the first time since I've been with the company that I've had a clear idea of what's expected of me and how I'm really doing."

## DISCUSSION

This study suggests that explicit specification of performance expectations is a necessary but not sufficient element in obtaining good performance from job incumbents. Objective measurement and feedback of performance results appear to be a critical factor in enabling employees to perform at expected levels. Generalized feedback and exhortations to perform "better" were ineffective in achieving improvements in measured output.

A typical reaction to substandard performance is to assume there is a problem in the employee's motivation. This study suggests that a more fruitful approach is to assume there is a problem in clarity of performance expectations and timely, objective feedback of results to the employee. The findings of this study are being used in the design of simple informational feedback systems for secretarial personnel in other staff functions.

## QUESTIONS FOR DISCUSSION

1. The frequency of feedback, reinforcement, or punishment is an important variable affecting behavior change. How was the importance of frequency demonstrated in this case?

2. Of the three procedures for reducing poor performance presented in Chapter 8 which procedures were employed in this case? How was each of these procedures used? Data-based feedback may be either punishment or reinforcement. Discuss this statement in your answer.

# CHAPTER NINE

## OBJECTIVES, INSTRUCTIONS, AND OTHER STIMULUS CONTROL PROCEDURES

**A**lthough most organizational behavior is determined by its consequences, management has devoted greater efforts to objectives, direction, and instruction, all of which take place before the performance. Stimulus events or circumstances that influence a performance beforehand are termed *antecedents*. *All forms of instruction, direction, example, objectives, and goal setting are antecedents.* They are presented before the performance, they are intended to influence subsequent behavior.

A great deal of research has been conducted in experimental psychology on the relationships among antecedent stimuli, behavior, and the consequences to the behavior (Terrace, 1966; Ferster and Perrott, 968). Some of the findings contribute greatly to an understanding of why management by objectives works well in some organizations and produces little change in others; why instructions and directions are explicitly followed by employees of some managers, while other managers have great difficulty obtaining compliance with instructions; and why an individual may perform well in one organization but fail to perform well in an apparently similar organization.

Laboratory experiments have demonstrated that, when an antecedent stimulus, such as a colored light, is presented, a behavior is performed, such as pecking a key, and the behavior is followed by reinforcement, the behavior is more likely to occur in the presence of the antecedent stimulus in the future. Similarly, if the laboratory animal is not reinforced after a performance preceded by a stimulus, the behavior is less likely to occur in the presence of that preceding stimulus. If a response that has been preceded by a stimulus, such as a colored light, is consistently reinforced only when the light is present, that stimulus gains controlling influence over the performance. *As the response is reinforced under the antecedent stimulus conditions, those conditions gain "stimulus control" over the performance. The behavior occurs when the antecedent stimulus is present. The antecedent stimulus may be said to set the occasion for the response.*

There are hundreds of examples of stimulus control in our everyday environment. For example, traffic lights exert stimulus control over the behavior of braking or pressing the gas pedal. We obediently continue the behavior of depressing the brake as long as the antecedent stimulus of the red light is present. As soon as the controlling stimulus is changed, we alter our behavior. Stimulus control is also present in social interactions. Various facial expressions of our manager may exert stimulus control over our behavior. When we observe a smile on the face of our manager, we may perform the behavior of initiating a discussion. When we observe the stimulus of a frown on the face of our manager, we are likely to avoid the initiation of a discussion. The stimulus of the facial expression of the manager may be said to exert stimulus control over our behavior.

These stimuli gained control over our behavior because specific behavior was differentially reinforced in the presence of these stimuli. *Differential reinforcement refers to reinforcing a response in the presence of one stimulus and consistently not reinforcing the same response in the presence of another stimulus.* When a response is consistently reinforced in the presence of a given stimulus and not reinforced in the presence of another stimulus, each stimulus signals the consequences that are likely to follow. The stimulus present when the response is reinforced comes to signal that the performance is likely to be reinforced. We are reinforced for initiating conversation with our boss when he has a smile on his face. In the presence of this stimulus our conversation is likely to be friendly, the boss is more likely to accept an idea presented and to make positive reinforcing comments to the employee. When the boss is not smiling or is frowning, the initiation of conversation is less likely to result in a friendly response from the boss, and he is less likely to accept the ideas presented and to make positive comments. The boss is differentially reinforcing the behavior of initiating conversation. In the presence of one stimulus (smiling) the boss reinforces the behavior of initiating conversation, and in the presence of a different stimulus (not smiling) the behavior is not reinforced or may be punished. The stimulus of smiling gains control over the behavior of initiating conversation.

*When the individual has learned to respond differently in the presence of different stimuli, he has learned a discrimination.* The individual discriminates between sets of circumstances and behaves in ways likely to result in reinforcement in those circumstances. Discriminations are made based on past histories of reinforcement or punishment in the presence of different stimulus conditions. For example, a speaker changes his language depending on the audience to which he is speaking. If he is speaking to the ladies' garden club, he uses one set of vocabulary, metaphors, and humor. If he is speaking to the local athletic club or the sales/marketing club, he uses a somewhat different vocabulary. This discrimination is based on the history of consequences to behavior in the presence of these different sets of stimuli. The stimulus of a group of women facing the speaker evokes the responses likely to be reinforced by them. The stimulus of a group of athletic coaches or sales managers facing the speaker evokes an entirely different response, one likely to be reinforced by that audience. The speaker has been differentially reinforced for his speaking behavior in the presence of these different stimulus conditions, which now occasion different responses.

The critically important factor for managers is that the influence of antecedent conditions, including all objectives, goals, directions, and instructions, is determined by the history of consequences that followed the response to those antecedents. The behavior following the presentation of an antecedent stimulus must be reinforced if it is to continue being performed when the stimulus is presented. When objectives are set, the behavior that results in their achievement must be reinforced if objectives are to serve as occasioning stimuli in the future. Similarly, when a manager gives his employees instructions, the performance following those instructions must receive some type of reinforcement, if similar instructions are going to continue to result in performance.

A number of research studies have pointed out the effects of antecedent stimuli and consequences on behavior. Ayllon and Azrin (1964) found that instructions not backed by actual consequences tend to lose their power, and the behavior quickly returns to that reinforced in the environment. Johnson (1975) recently performed a study in which he simulated a zero defects program common in the industrial setting. These programs attempt to improve quality and production through a campaign of publicity designed to influence the attitude and awareness of the employees regarding quality production and through a series of awards. Johnson tried to identify which elements of a zero defects program might be expected to exert influence over performance. He preconditioned workers to perform under contingencies that reinforced high levels of production. He then attempted to influence performance by (1) what he called persuasive influence, instructions to perform quality work; (2) announcement of a pay contingency for quality work; and (3) an actual pay contingency in which workers were paid according to the quality of their performance. Johnson found that (1) persuasive influence (instructions) for quality, following a series of trials in which speed had been reinforced, produced neither an attitude change nor a significant behavior change; (2) announcing new quality contingencies following the preconditioning period had no effect on the quality or quantity of performance; and (3) there were marked differences in performance depending on the pay contingency. The experimenter got what he paid for. When the subjects in Johnson's experiment were paid for quality production, they worked more accurately than when they were paid for quantity performance.

Johnson's study, as well as research by other investigators (Festinger, 1964; Greenwald, 1965; and Bandura, 1969), clearly demonstrates that instructions, objectives, or other antecedent stimuli intended to influence performance are likely to be ineffective in the absence of contingent reinforcement.

## WHY MANAGEMENT BY OBJECTIVES (MBO) WORKS, OR DOES NOT

The consequences that may reinforce the behavior under stimulus control may be as simple as feedback to the employees that the manager has observed the completion of the task. Or the consequence may be a system of salary increases, contingent bonus, or profit-sharing plans based on the fulfillment of objectives. Many companies using MBO programs have assumed that objectives, in and unto themselves, produce performance. The assumption is made that, if the company has an accurate, timely, comprehensive system of objectives, the employees and manager will pay attention to these objectives, perform to achieve them, and be rewarded by their achievement. In all the research conducted on human behavior there is not a shred of evidence to suggest that people will respond to antecedent stimuli without a history of reinforcement for responses under similar conditions.

Many MBO programs produce increases in performance immediately after they are begun although no provisions for consequences for completion of objectives have been provided. This may be explained by the fact that the manager or employees have been reinforced for the completion of objectives or punished for the noncompletion of objectives in their prior learning. For example, our educational system provides some stimulus control training for objective completion. While in college the student receives assignments from his professors. These assignments are similar to objectives in that they are antecedent conditions intended to evoke certain behavior. A date is generally set for assignments to be handed in. The handing in of an assignment in college is generally reinforced by the presentation of a grade or the simple feedback on how well the assignment was done. The failure to hand in the assignment may be punished by the professor's calling out the student's name in the classroom on a list of those who owe him assignments. In this manner the setting of assignments or objectives gains stimulus control over the behavior of fulfilling those assignments.

All managers have some history of reinforcement for completing objectives of some type. Therefore, upon the initiation of an MBO system, it is reasonable to expect that management will perform to achieve the objectives. But many organizations provide no consequences of any type for the fulfillment or nonfulfillment of the objectives. After a series of presentations of the stimulus (objectives) and responses (performance to achieve objectives) and the absence of reinforcing consequences to that behavior, the behavior extinguishes, just as that of an animal in a laboratory experiment who is presented with a stimulus that previously signaled that the performance of a behavior would result in reinforcement. When, after a series of trials, the reinforcement is removed, the animal's behavior extinguishes.

This absence of reinforcement following the completion of objectives, instructions, directions, and examples explains why these conditions often do not result in the desired performance. This is the most neglected aspect of most MBO programs. Most of the literature on MBO entirely ignores the relationship between the setting of the objective and the consequences following completion. Managers, and the consultants who have assisted managers in establishing MBO programs, have often operated on the assumption that the completion of objectives itself was sufficiently rewarding to maintain performance. The experience of many companies, who have begun MBO programs with a flurry of enthusiasm and increased performance, only to be followed in a few years by the total neglect of those same objectives, bears witness to the importance of providing consequences to the performance of setting objectives, working to achieve the objectives, and finally achieving them.

When an antecedent stimulus initiates behaviors that are reinforced, it becomes a discriminative stimulus for that behavior. This discriminative stimulus ($S^D$) sets the occasion for the response. The question with which the manager must be concerned is "What are the discriminative stimuli that will set the occasion for the responses I wish to see my employees perform?" The skillful manager is one who presents antecedent objectives, instructions, and examples in a manner that will cause those antecedents to become $S^D$s.

Management by objectives is based on a number of assumptions about our prior learning and the events likely to be $S^D$s for most managers' and employees' behavior. For example, Morrissey (1970) lists a number of criteria for well-written objectives. Among them are the following:

- It starts with the key word *to*, followed by an action verb.
- It specifies the key result to be achieved.
- It specifies a target date for its accomplishment.
- It is as specific and quantitative (and hence measurable and verifiable) as possible.
- It specifies the "what" and "when"; it avoids venturing into the "why" and "how."
- It is willingly agreed to by both superior and subordinate, without undue pressure or coercion.
- It is recorded in writing, with a copy kept and periodically referred to by both superior and subordinate.
- It is communicated not only in writing but also in face-to-face discussion between the accountable manager and those subordinates who will be contributing to its attainment.

According to Morrissey, a well-stated objective should contain three parts: the action verb, the result to be achieved, and the date by which the result is to be achieved. Such an objective might read: "To increase efficiency from eighty-four percent to eighty-eight percent by the end of the second quarter." It is assumed that these guidelines, such as the statement of a measurable result, have higher probability of serving as an $S^D$ for the desired behavior than a nonmeasurable result would. This is undoubtedly a correct assumption in most cases. Each of the guidelines presented by Morrissey and other writers is a statement of probability about the controlling properties of those stimuli. The statement of a result to be achieved by a specific date is undoubtedly more likely to be an $S^D$ than the statement "meet the objective as soon as possible."

The question may then be asked "Why are these guidelines, or objectives stated in the prescribed manner more likely to serve as $S^D$s than objectives stated in other ways?" The answer may be found in the learning history of the average manager or employee. Prior learning has taught that an objective or instruction accompanied by a suspension date is more likely to be followed by a consequence, either reinforcing for completion, or punishing for noncompletion, than a statement not accompanied by a suspension date. There is a high probability that for many managers this learning history will apply and the date will serve as an $S^D$. Similarly the statement of a measurable outcome is more likely to serve as an $S^D$ than a statement of a more general result.

Managers and employees may respond to objectives in somewhat different ways. This, too, is based on prior learning. The statement of specific and measurable objectives may serve as an $S^D$ for feelings of anxiety and result in no productive behavior. For another manager the objective may evoke no anxiety arousal and a high level of purposeful activity. These differential responses are based on the individual's prior experience of consequences following similar objectives. The first manager is likely to have experienced few reinforcing consequences and a high probability of punishment. Many organizations produce this by imposing objectives that are very unlikely to be met and that result in failure or condemnation, or both. The second manager is likely to have experienced an organization in which objectives were obtainable and were followed by reinforcement for completion, an outcome that thereby increased the likelihood of purposeful behavior to achieve future objectives.

Whereas the guidelines and instructions for managing by objectives outlined by Morrissey and other writers are statements based on assumptions likely to be valid within our culture, many organizations have structured learning experiences to cancel out these predictions. The young manager fresh out of the university may have a high probability of responding constructively to the well-stated objective. But that same manager, after a few years within the organization may be less likely to respond constructively to those same objectives. The reason for this extinction of response to objectives is the absence of reinforcement provided by the organization for objective completion. The young manager responds to the objectives because his recent learning history in the university has taught him that there

are consequences to the completion of objectives (course assignments). He has completed several years of very careful responding
to assignments and experiencing the predictable consequences to his
completion or noncompletion of those assignments. This has well
established the objective as an $S^D$. Now the organization engages him
in a similar process of objectives and yet often follows the completion
of those objectives with no effective consequence. I have seen several
organizations whose objectives are dutifully set and similarly forgotten
about a week or two later. The objective is remembered only when it
is time again, often a year later, to engage in the ritualistic process of
setting objectives. This arrangement of the contingencies of reinforcement soon teaches the manager that the objective may no longer be
followed by a consequence and is, therefore, no longer an $S^D$ for any
performance.

## SOURCES OF ANTECEDENTS

The $S^D$s may be categorized according to their source. *Antecedents
may derive from the physical setting, the social setting, the behaviors
of other persons, the individual's own thoughts and feelings, and the
individual's own previous behavior.* Each of these may generate
stimulus conditions that evoke particular behavior, owing to previous
reinforcement or punishment in the presence of those conditions. A
procedure has been described by Miller (1976) by which salespersons
may study the antecedents that occur before their behavior in each of
these five categories. The salesperson identifies the antecedents that
commonly occur before a specific behavior he would like to increase.
The behavior may be increased in frequency by increasing the frequency of the antecedent stimulus. For example, a salesperson may
wish to increase his behavior of asking clients for leads, which is an
activity that may generate a good deal of anxiety because it calls on
the client to issue an implied endorsement of the salesperson and his
product or service. Because of the anxiety associated with this task
many salespersons avoid asking for leads and therefore inhibit the
development of their business. By tracking the occurrence of the
desired behavior and identifying the stimulus conditions present immediately before or at the same time of the response (see Figure 22), the
salesperson may identify those conditions likely to serve as $S^D$s for this

# Antecedent Survey

Acting client

The behavior being analyzed is ___ for a lead ___    I want to (increase) (decrease) _increase_ this behavior.

| BEHAVIORAL EVENTS | PHYSICAL CIRCUMSTANCES | SOCIAL SETTING | BEHAVIOR OF OTHERS | YOUR THOUGHTS/FEELINGS | YOUR PREVIOUS BEHAVIOR | CONSE-QUENCE |
|---|---|---|---|---|---|---|
| EVENT #1:<br>DATE: 9/31<br>TIME: 9:40 | In Fred Herbert office sitting on his couch. | With client in office. | Fred was placing an order for additional paper. | I thought this was a good time to ask since he was positive about the new paper. | I showed him our new color line. I had just completed writing the order. | + |
| EVENT #2:<br>DATE: 9/31<br>TIME: 11:30 | In Sy Solomitz office. Standing, his office ready to leave. 3rd office. | With Sy and his chief pressman. 3rd Robert. | He told me he wasn't interested in our new colors. | I thought he was an S.O.B. | I had shown him our new color line, and was getting ready to leave. | − |
| EVENT #3:<br>DATE: 9/29<br>TIME: 2:15 | In the Central City Print Shop. | With Al Storey. | Told me our paper was running well. | I was thinking that they would shaten his a client then a lot of potential was getting ready to leave. | I had just shaten his hand and was getting ready to leave. | + |
| EVENT #4:<br>DATE: 9/14<br>TIME: 10:30 | In the Johnson Brothers Print Shop | Talking to Jim Johnson. | Jim had just given me an order and was thanking me for stopping by. | I was thinking that Jim would be a good source of leads. | I had just filled out the order on a customer order pad and was getting | + |
| RECURR-ING ANTEC. | Usually alone with client. | | Each time they had just placed an order and were positive about their business commitment. | I was thinking they were ready to place additional orders. | Was getting ready to place their orders. Writing out orders. | |

**Figure 22** Antecedent survey. Copyright Behavioral Systems, Inc. Atlanta, Georgia, 1976. Used by permission.

222

response. The salesperson may have identified antecedents such as positive and friendly comments on the part of the customer immediately before his asking for a lead. These comments may indicate a degree of trust and acceptance by the client, creating feelings of assurance on the part of the salesperson and thereby setting the occasion for the response of asking for leads. By his using the antecedent assessment survey these antecedent conditions may be identified.

Once the $S^D$s for the desired response are identified, steps may be taken to increase the probability of those $S^D$s' occurring more often. For example, the salesperson who has identified positive comments on the part of the client as occasioning the desired response of asking for leads may increase those positive comments by asking a question such as "Mr. Jones, how do you feel about the service we have been able to provide over the past six months?" Mr. Jones is then likely to make a positive comment about the service, and the occasion is set for the response of asking for leads.

Antecedent conditions in the *physical environment* may include factors such as noise levels, lighting, colors in work areas, the piles of paper that clutter one's desk. Some conditions, such as lighting, may influence behavior because of physical constraints. But other physical circumstances influence behavior because of the history of consequences associated with them. A manager may find that he feels more confident in a management meeting when he wears a particular suit. This may well be a superstition. His behavior of feeling confident is occasioned by the presence of his favorite suit. This suit has become an $S^D$ for "feeling comfortable or relaxed" because of experiences when he previously wore this suit. In previous management meetings when wearing the suit, the manager was reinforced for his contribution and participation by the other managers. He felt that he performed well in the meeting while wearing this suit. The suit is now associated with the comfort response and sets the occasion for feeling comfortable in management meetings.

The *social setting*, such as a bar or board room, athletic stadium, or academic classroom, occasions different sets of responses. We have learned that different types of behavior are likely to be reinforced or approved of in different social surroundings. The crowd watching a tennis match and the crowd watching a college football game are identified by very different sets of behavior. The individual quickly adapts to the behavior of the crowd simply because behaving as others are behaving is reinforced. Behaving in a manner significantly at variance with other persons in one's surroundings is likely to be punished. The individual who may cheer and scream at a tennis match as he would at a college football game is the subject of disapproving stares. If accompanied by someone else, that someone would be unlikely to accompany him again. Through the effect of these consequences different social settings become $S^D$s for different behavior. The crowd at the tennis club or the football stadium gains stimulus control over the behavior of cheering or clapping.

Often the most subtle *actions of other persons* may gain stimulus control over behavior. Movements of another person's eyebrows, glances toward or away from an individual, or a smile can serve as $S^D$s for a wide range of behavior. The subordinate with a proposal or request for his superior observes the behavior of his superior very closely to determine the best time to present the proposal. Behaviors such as the tone of voice, laughter, smiles, and head movements may indicate to the subordinate with the proposal that a particular superior is in the "right mood" or "wrong mood" to act favorably on the proposal. When an individual feels that someone else is "in the right mood," what he means is that "by my observation of his behavior and my previous experience in similar situations, I can predict that he is likely to behave in a particular fashion." Whereas this process may not be "thought through," the behavior of the subordinate is under the control of the behavior of the manager. These behaviors of the manager have stimulus control over the subordinate's behavior.

Most of our social interactions with any individual are influenced by similar discriminations. We are constantly responding to the cues we receive from the person to whom we are speaking. It is helpful to understand that the other person to whom we are speaking is similarly influenced by our behavior. Our behavior is serving as $S^D$s for their behavior. If other people do not feel comfortable speaking with us, it is because our behavior is serving as an $S^D$ for their uncomfortable feelings rather than for comfortable conversation. This can be changed by increasing the probability that the other person is reinforced when he speaks with us.

The behavior of other persons serves not only as $S^D$s for interpersonal behavior but also as a model for the learning of new behavior. Modeling, vicarious learning, or imitation has been the subject of a great deal of experimental investigation and explains a great deal of social learning (Bandura, 1969). From infancy through adulthood our behavior patterns are altered by our observation of models, other persons whom we imitate. Bandura (p. 120) has identified three separate effects of modeling influence: *observational learning, inhibitory* or *disinhibitory effects,* and *response facilitation effect.* Bandura argues that these three effects are distinctly different and the function of different sets of variables. Whether or not these are three distinct operations is of little interest to the manager, but the distinctions among them may further the understanding of the modeling influence.

Observational learning occurs when the observer of a model acquires a new response pattern that did not previously exist in his behavioral repertoire. For example, the child learning to speak imitates a model and acquires new vocal responses not present before the modeling and imitation. In the workplace observational learning is used to train employees in new mechanical operations with which they were not previously familiar. The operator of a lathe may learn the operation by observing a skilled operator and imitating his behavior. It has been demonstrated that observational learning is enhanced, learning occurs more rapidly, and the learned response is more likely to be maintained if the new response is followed by reinforcement. Observational learning may, however, occur without an external reinforcer evident. The imitated response is likely to result in the increased probability of reinforcement, particularly in the workplace, and is unlikely to be maintained unless reinforcement does follow.

The second effect of modeling, the inhibitory or disinhibitory effects, occurs when the observer witnesses another individual perform a behavior and experiences the reinforcing or punishing consequences following that behavior. Inhibitory responses are internal responses that counter or act to stop another response from occurring. The behavior of stealing from the company for which one works provides a good example of inhibitory responding and of the effects of modeling on inhibitory responses. Taking an item from the company, such as consumable supplies, is intrinsically reinforcing. It is intrinsically desirable to the individual to be able to take supplies home and use them. A benefit is gained at no cost. Employees stop themselves from performing this behavior by their inhibition or inhibitory response that "tells them no." By observing models, this inhibitory response may be strengthened or weakened. If the observer witnesses another employee continually taking company supplies home with no adverse consequence, the observation has a disinhibitory effect. The inhibitory response is weakened, and the observer's probability of engaging in the petty theft is increased. On the other hand, if the observer witnesses the behavior of taking home supplies and sees the offender being caught and punished, the inhibitory response is strengthened.

A more positive example of the inhibitory or disinhibitory effect of modeling may be found in the example provided by assertive behavior. Traditionally women have been characterized by certain inhibitions by which men have not. A woman of equal competence and experience would be less likely, more inhibited, to engage in the behavior of asking for or applying for a promotion to a managerial position. If one woman in a work area applies for or otherwise pursues a position as a manager or supervisor and obtains the position, other women who have observed her behavior and the reinforcing consequences of her behavior experience the disinhibitory effect of her modeling. "Role-play" training uses the disinhibitory effect of modeling by presenting a model performing behaviors that the trainees may be inhibited from performing. The trainees are then called upon to perform those behaviors and are more likely to do so after having observed a model. The observation of the role-play model causes the disinhibitory effect on the part of the observer.

The third effect of modeling, the response facilitation effect, occurs when the probability of a response already within the repertoire of the individual is increased and the behavior was not previously inhibited. The first effect, observational learning, explains the acquisition of a new pattern of response while the second effect explains the increased or decreased performance of a response by the modification of the inhibitory response. The third effect simply explains the increased rate of a modeled response that the observer is able to perform and that was never previously punished or inhibited. An example of response facilitation would be found in the case of observing another individual eat a particular food and express pleasure at the experience. The observer has vicariously experienced the reinforcement experienced by the model and may now engage in the behavior of eating this food. The observer did not eat the food previously simply because no reinforcing consequences had been associated with this behavior. The observer was able to perform the behavior and was not inhibited from performing but simply had "no reason" to perform this behavior. The observation of the model's receiving reinforcement for this behavior causes vicarious reinforcement on the part of the observer and thereby increases the observer's likelihood of performing the modeled behavior.

The behavior of other persons in the workplace exerts a powerful influence over the behavior of employees. The behavior of managers and the consequences to the manager's behavior exert an especially powerful control over the employees directly under the manager. The employee perceives the manager to be more highly reinforced than the employee. It is assumed that the behavior of the manager is behavior that receives reinforcement. The behavior patterns of the manager is, therefore, imitated by the employees. It is both folk wisdom and empirically based psychology that the manager must manage by example. The effective manager displays those behaviors he hopes to see performed by his employees. The manager who behaves in one way and expects his employees to behave in another is creating an incongruity that produces poor performance and job dissatisfaction.

An employee may engage in a behavior or change his performance, in the *apparent absence* of any change in antecedent conditions or consequences. An employee may be a consistent, hard, and reliable worker. All conditions in the environment may appear to be unchanging, and the employee may reduce his performance. There are two possible explanations for this change in performance in the absence of any apparent change in the employee's work environment: First, there may be a change in conditions outside the workplace, some family or home concern, or other job possibility, that has reduced the reinforcing effect of the current job. Secondly, there may be a change in internal responses that serve as antecedents for the external work behavior. The employee may not have received a promotion in two years, and he may experience the recurring thought that "I should have been given a raise. What's the matter with my supervisor? Doesn't he care about me? Why should I break my neck for him?" If the employee experiences these thoughts and feelings for a period of time, they are likely to set the occasion for reduced work performance. This employee may also be said to be suffering extinction. The absence of reinforcement produces its effect over time and sets the occasion for the internal dissatisfaction.

All individuals are constantly experiencing *thoughts and feelings* that affect their work performance. There is little the manager or the employee himself can do directly to alter thoughts and feelings to modify the behavior they may occasion. But each of these thoughts and feelings is occasioned by previous events in the environment. For example, the employee who is having the thoughts that his supervisor doesn't care about him has experienced a series of stimulus conditions that have set the occasion for these internal responses. The frequency of the supervisor's commenting on the quality of the employee's work, the observation of other employees receiving promotions or raises, and the observation of the rate or quality of the work performed by these other workers are all antecedent stimuli that have occasioned the internal responses, which in turn are now occasioning the external behavior of reducing the pace of work.

To avoid the "can of worms" that internal responses and their modification present, the manager will do well to recognize that changes in performance may be occasioned by internal responses that have themselves been occasioned by external conditions. The manager should seek to identify the external conditions that may be altered to affect both sets of responses. The manager may identify these antecedent events by asking the employee how he feels about his work. The manager may directly observe the event that preceded the reduced performance. This may or may not produce the information the manager needs to change the behavior of concern. The manager may, however, simply be aware that if performance is decreasing it is due to the absence of reinforcement for performance. Experiencing the reinforcing consequences to performance corrects the situation.

## CHAINING

Most of our daily behavior, particularly our work behavior, occurs in a sequence of responses that lead toward the receipt of a reinforcing consequence. Rarely do single or isolated responses achieve reinforcement. The employee who seeks to obtain a promotion engages in a series of behaviors that may require months or years to perform and that ultimately lead to the reinforcing consequence of the raise.

*Sequences of behavior that lead to reinforcing events are known as response chains.* The process of linking behavior together to develop these response sequences is referred to as *chaining*. When a response chain has been developed in the repertoire of an individual, each behavior in the chain appears to occur in the absence of reinforcement and is followed by another behavior, and another, eventually resulting in reinforcement. Almost any behavior that occurs commonly in the workplace occurs in a chain. Reading this book is unlikely to be followed by immediate reinforcement. But past behavior of reading books on management and psychology may have been followed by the application of some technique to one's own work situation, which then resulted in some desirable outcome, a positive comment by one's superior, an increase in productivity, or the reduction of some troublesome situation. The reading of this book need not be followed immediately by reinforcement, because it is one link in an established chain of behavior.

Because of the chaining effect an individual's own previous behavior may serve as an $S^D$ for further behavior. Each behavior in an established chain of behaviors sets the occasion for the next response in the chained sequence. The everyday activities of coming to work each morning comprise a chain of discrete responses. The first response in the chain is getting out of bed, the next showering and shaving, then dressing, eating, gathering together objects to be carried to work, finding the car keys, and so forth. Each response in the chain sets the occasion for the subsequent response.

Increased performance may be achieved if the entire chain of behaviors can be increased by increasing the frequency of one behavior in the chain. A salesperson performs a chain of behaviors that lead to the response of asking for the order. A salesperson cannot simply increase the terminal behavior of asking for orders without regard to the entire chain of events. If the behavior of asking for orders is to be increased significantly, it may be necessary to begin by increasing the initial performance of asking for leads, then telephoning leads for appointments, making presentations to prospects, and so on.

Undesirable behavior may also be decreased by interrupting a chain of behaviors. If a chain of behavior can be interrupted by stopping one behavior in the chain, the occasion is not set for the continuance of subsequent behaviors in the chain. An individual may wish to eliminate or reduce a habit such as smoking or drinking coffee excessively. These behaviors often occur in chains that may be interrupted. The chain of behaviors that lead up to the drinking of coffee, for example, may be identified and the weakest linking behavior selected for modification. Drinking coffee is often preceded by a chain that goes something like this: You are sitting at your desk working, you experience some minor frustration at your work, you would like immediately to avoid this work, you see your coffee cup in front of you, you then get up and take your coffee cup to the lounge, you get a cup of coffee and return to your desk. The behavior of getting a cup of coffee is occasioned by the frustration of work. Rather than try to reduce the amount of coffee you drink, you may attempt to alter the one behavior of leaving your desk with your coffee cup. You may instead leave your desk and simply walk around the office and get a piece of chewing gum or a drink of water instead of the coffee and then return to your desk. By altering the first behavior in the chain, leaving your desk with coffee cup in hand, you have altered the antecedent conditions that set the occasion for walking into the longue and pouring a cup of coffee.

### SUMMARY

The environment of the workplace presents a continual series of stimulus events that set the occasion and have stimulus control over work behavior. Whether the physical environment, social setting, other person's behavior, the individual's own thoughts and feelings, or the individual's own previous behavior, these antecedent conditions may be altered to produce increases or decreases in performance. Current management practice makes extensive use of antecedent events in the form of management objectives, directions, instructions, and other forms of communication. Unfortunately most current management practice does not take into account the way in which these events come to gain stimulus control over the behavior they seek to influence. This lack of awareness of the importance of reinforcing consequences that condition the response to the antecedents has resulted in grossly inefficient procedures. The manager aware of the nature of stimulus control has gained a set of procedures that may greatly enhance his ability to determine the performance of his employees.

### REFERENCES

Ayllon, T., and Azrin, N. H. "Reinforcement and instructions with mental patients." *Journal of the Experimental Analysis of Behavior, 7,* 1964, 321–331.

Bandura, Albert. *Principles of Behavior Modification.* New York: Holt Rinehart & Winston, 1969.

Ferster, C. B., and Perrot, Mary Carol. *Behavior Principles.* New Century, Meredith Corporation, 1968.

Festinger, L. "Behavioral Support for Opinion Change." *Public Opinion Quarterly,* **28,** 1964 404–417.

Greenwald, A. G. "Behavior Change following Persuasive Communication." *Journal of Personality,* **33,** 1965, 370–391.

Johnson, George A. "The Relative Efficacy of Stimulus versus Reinforcement Control for Obtaining Stable Performance Change." *Organizational Behavior and Human Performance,* **14,** 1975, 321–341.

Miller, Lawrence M. *Self-Management Skills for the Sales Professional.* Atlanta: Behavioral Systems, Inc., 1976.

Morrissey, George L. *Management by Objectives and Results.* Reading, Mass: Addison-Wesley Publishing Company, 1970.

Terrace, H. S. "Stimulus Control," in W. K. Honig, (Ed.). *Operant Behavior.* New York: Appleton-Century-Crofts, 1966.

# CASE STUDY NUMBER NINE

## AN ATTEMPT TO IMPROVE OBJECTIVE SETTING IN A SALES ORGANIZATION

This case reports the failure of an effort to improve the management of a New York apparel manufacturing sales organization. During the preliminary assessment of this organization it was found that the systems of management were not being used and managers were responding primarily to crises or immediate needs. Efforts were made to create management systems that would be more useful to the managers and would have a greater impact on performance. The consultant was unable, however, to get the managers to operate the management systems.

### BACKGROUND CONDITIONS

Marvel Sportswear is a medium-size apparel manufacturer whose sales organization is in midtown Manhattan. Marvel has approximately fifteen salespersons who make approximately ten calls per day on retail accounts. Marvel has approximately fifty lines of clothing. The business is highly seasonal, and the fashion trends add another complicating factor in the effort to manage the sales organization consistently. Certain lines of clothing may be consistent with the fashion trend that has "caught on," while other lines may have been poorly received by the fashion critics and retail buyers. Every season is, therefore, a gamble. Much of the success of the business is determined six to twelve months before the opening of the season when the lines of clothing are designed and fabrics selected.

The assessment of the organization's management was intended to identify what management systems were in place and the degree to which those systems were achieving their objectives. It was found that the managers had an objective-setting procedure they termed "target-ing." Each salesperson would target certain lines to retail accounts. The managers would then review the targets and almost always revise them upward to include more targets. Not every line of clothing manu-factured by Marvel would be an appropriate purchase for every buyer. Some buyers were very high-priced, high-fashion boutiques that sold blouses for seventy-five to one hundred dollars. These buyers would have no interest in blouses priced in the fifteen- to twenty-dollar range. Marvel made a range of sportswear, and the salesperson had to have sufficient knowledge of his client's price-range, specific market, fashion preferences, and decision-making dates to make effective presenta-tions. The targeting system set objectives for placing certain lines with each account.

One of the difficulties in managing the salespersons employed by Marvel was the variance in accounts from one salesperson to another. One might have fifteen of the high-fashion boutiques as accounts, while another might have five high-fashion boutiques, fifteen moder-ately priced stores, and responsibility for one chain store account; a third salesperson might devote all of his time to a single chain store account. Obviously the sales performance of the three salespersons could not be readily compared.

When the management assessment was conducted, the sales-persons were asked how many targets they had during the quarter just completed and how many of these targets they successfully ful-filled. Of the approximately ten salespersons interviewed, none knew exactly how many targets they had, and no one knew how many they had achieved. They were asked to estimate the percent of their targets completed. These estimates ranged from fifty to ninety percent, with an average of around seventy-five percent. These were estimates, but they did give an idea of the salesperson's knowledge of the results he was achieving compared to his objectives.

After the interviews with the sales staff, the assessor obtained copies of each salesperson's target lists and the computer printout that reported sales for the previous quarter. The data given on page 234 were obtained.

These data clearly point out that the sales staff was unaware of their performance against the targeted objectives. It was, therefore, concluded that these objectives were not functional in that the sales staff and managers did not pay attention to them and were not

| Salesperson | Number of Targets | Number of Targets Completed | Percent Completed |
|---|---|---|---|
| 1 | 70 | 15 | 21.4 |
| 2 | 287 | 11 | 3.8 |
| 3 | 199 | 12 | 6.0 |
| 4 | 213 | 14 | 6.5 |
| 5 | 155 | 20 | 12.9 |
| 6 | 160 | 21 | 13.0 |
| 7 | 303 | 27 | 8.9 |
| 8 | 154 | 2 | 1.3 |
| 9 | 219 | 15 | 6.9 |
| 10 | 103 | 30 | 29.1% |
| Average | 186.3 | 16.7 | 8.9% |

responding to them. This was further pointed out by another question asked of the sales staff and by the responses received. The assessor asked the key operating managers to list the product lines they considered highest priority. They were asked, "If a salesperson had the opportunity to present any line he or she wanted, which lines would be the highest priority?" The managers then listed in order of priority the lines they considered most important. When the salespersons were interviewed, they were asked this same question. The responses to this question are indicated in Figure 23.

It is clear from observing the relationship in the priorities of the salespersons and managers on two product lines that there is, if anything, a negative relationship between the priorities of managers and those of sales staff. The purpose of any objective-setting procedure is to communicate priorities and direct performance to achieve those outcomes that are most important to the organization. This is particularly important to Marvel Sportswear because it attempts to place its products in a manner to establish a position in the market. The marketing staff devotes a great deal of time and money to developing placement strategies. A product properly placed in the market can "take off" and produce sales for many months following.

Another observation made during the assessment was the degree to which the managers were involved in the actual selling. All the managers had been salespersons and were very proud of their knowl-

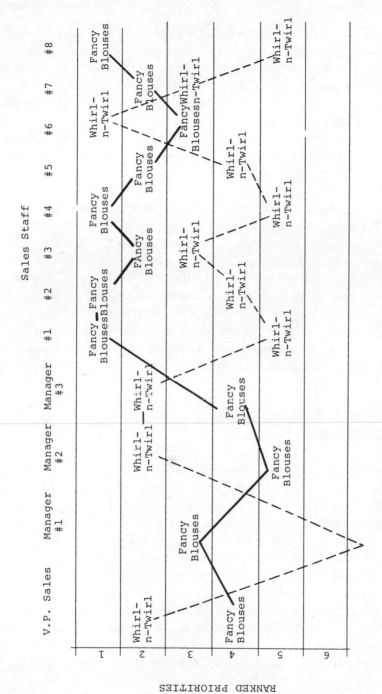

**Figure 23** Relative ranking of manager's and salesmen's priority objectives.

235

edge of the marketplace and their ability to close sales. They were emphatic in pointing out to the assessor how this business is fast moving and constantly shifting and requires quick reactions. The managers spent a great deal of time on the telephone or with clients. Some of the salespersons complained that the managers interfered too much in their work with the client.

Whenever one of the managers was asked about the functioning of a management system, such as how often he reviewed the data available to him, or how often he reviewed objectives, he would respond by pointing out how many hours a day he worked and how little time he had for additional activities. Every manager would explain that the assessor had to understand how unique this business is and how much attention the manager had to pay to the customers and what was going on in the marketplace. Managers would be observed literally running from one office to the other with some piece of news about a development in the marketplace. This type of behavior was also typical of the president of Marvel, who had previously been the vice president in charge of sales. The current vice president had worked directly under the president and exhibited very similar behavior, both in terms of his attention to the management systems and his verbal behavior.

## PROCEDURE

A procedure was proposed to develop a targeting system that would provide more realistic targets, provide high-frequency feedback to the salespersons, visual display of the feedback, and increased social consequences for meeting objectives.

A consultant spent several months gathering baseline data on various performances, gaining the input into the design of the system from all salespersons and managers. A point system was also proposed that would provide point earning for the fulfillment of each objective. The managers could provide more points for targets of lesser importance. The administrative assistants to the salespersons were trained to graph the number of points earned for target completion by each salesperson. This graph was posted in the sales office near each salesperson's desk. The graph was to be updated once each week.

The program was to be implemented with the beginning of the

June-ending quarter. A meeting was held with all the managers to explain the new system. A brief explanation of behavior management principles was given. Training of each manager in behavior management principles and techniques had been proposed. Training was highly resisted owing to the time pressures felt by the managers. They felt that they could not take off one or two hours per week for training. The vice president for marketing concurred with this. The consultant organizing the program felt that training was necessary. It was, however, agreed that the consultant would attempt to provide one-on-one training while consulting individually with each manager. It was hoped that the managers would observe some initial results from the new system and have their interest heightened by them. Training would then be offered, perhaps in the evening, if this was the only time available.

The system provided for the salesperson's initiating the selection of targets, followed by a negotiation session between the manager and the salesperson. At this time the point values for each objective would be discussed so that the salesperson could understand the manager's priorities. The manager was to discuss the objectives weekly with each salesperson and provide feedback on his performance. The managers were encouraged to go by the salesperson's desks and observe the graphs of their point earnings.

Initially the point earnings were not going to be backed up by any tangible reinforcer. The sales staff was very competitive and responsive to social reinforcement and feedback. The consultant felt that the points alone would be sufficiently powerful reinforcers if the managers discussed the point earning with them.

### RESULTS

The first negotiations of targets and points did take place, although several weeks late. The consultant found it necessary to ask the managers several times each week whether they had a chance to complete the targets. The graphs were posted, and the administrative assistants began to post the point earnings. This continued for a few weeks. After a few weeks the managers were paying no attention to the system. They made no comments on the point earnings. At the weekly sales meeting the vice president for sales ignored requests by the consultant to reinforce the salespersons who were doing well on their point earnings. Instead the vice president chose to "chew out" the sales staff for falling below where they should be. This berating of the sales staff at the sales meeting was the usual practice. The consultant attended ten to fifteen sales meetings before and after the program was begun, and they all included the vice president's tirade about how badly they were doing and how "the pressure was on."

After a couple of months of neglect on the part of the managers and frustration on the part of the consultant the managers of the consulting firm under contract insisted on terminating the program. It was pointed out that no system of management would produce results if the manager failed to use the system. The managers of the consulting firm were very concerned about the lack of results and sought the client manager's evaluation of the consultant. The client managers spoke highly of the consultant, commenting on how impressed they were with her knowledge and how much they enjoyed her presence and acknowledged that she had been very persistent in attempting to get them to implement the new targeting and feedback system.

Although extensive baseline data were compiled on a number of performance measures, the program was not in effect long enough to produce any change in outcome.

### DISCUSSION

This case points at a major problem in the use of behavior management programs. The purpose of these programs is to introduce procedures that will increase and maintain performance over an extended period of time. The program procedures must be incorporated into the routine management practice. They must, therefore, be used by the line managers, and not the consultant, trainer, or anyone other than the line manager. The first focus of behavior change must be a change in the managerial behaviors of the managers. If objectives are to serve as occasioning events that exert some control over the behavior of the sales staff, they cannot be ignored by managers. The managers' behavior must provide both the consequences following the achievement of the objectives and a model for attending to objectives.

The primary failure of this program was the failure to initiate change at the right level of the organization. The first behaviors that should have been changed were those of the president and vice president. They set the models for the managers, who in turn set the models for the sales staff. No one provided feedback or reinforcement after completion of objectives or completion of any behaviors associated with the maintenance of a management system. Hence, no management system, regardless of the design or nature of that system, could result in improved performance. The program should have been initiated with training for the top level of management so that they were aware of the importance of their behavior as it affected the other managers and sales staff.

It was pointed out to the managers, although this point was never accepted, that if they spent the time necessary to make the management system functional, they would reduce the amount of time they had to spend responding to crises or immediate situations.

### QUESTIONS FOR DISCUSSION

1. List the antecedents to performance that were present in this sales organization. List the consequences following performance that were present that established the antecedents as discriminative stimuli.

2. Discuss the modeling effect present in this organization.

3. Which behaviors were likely to be followed by reinforcement in this organization?

# CHAPTER TEN

## INDIVIDUAL
## BEHAVIOR CHANGE PROJECTS

This chapter presents a six-step strategy for implementing individual performance improvement projects in the work setting. Behavior management efforts in the organizational setting may include both organization-wide system changes to improve overall performance and individual projects initiated by managers. In addition to a discussion of the six major considerations in instituting individual behavior change projects, a simplified *short form*, which may be used in training managers to introduce behavior change strategies is also presented.

Strategies for changing individual performance by applying the behavior management model have been presented by a number of authors (Luthans and Kreitner, 1975; Hamner and Hamner, 1976; Sundel and Sundel, 1975). All of these strategies, in various forms, involve the following six steps: (1) specification of target performance, (2) measurement, (3) behavioral analysis, (4) design and implementations of change strategy, (5) evaluation, and (6) modification/maintenance. The supervisor or manager can apply this approach to improve the performance of a single employee or to improve the performance of a number of employees working as a team.

The individual project worksheet provides space for recording the behavior change strategy and the implementation of that strategy. It is useful for the manager to complete this form so that he makes a decision and considers all the factors that determine the success or failure of his effort.

## SPECIFICATION OF PERFORMANCE

Specification of the performance or behavior to be changed is not only a necessary first step but is often the most difficult for managers to perform. The type of specification required for an effective behavior change strategy is distinctly different from the type of performance descriptions the manager is accustomed to providing. The manager (as well as parents, teachers, and others concerned with changing behavior) has become accustomed to describing performance in interpretative terms. Typical descriptions provided by managers include "unmotivated," "lazy," "not interested in his work," and "a sloppy worker." None of these descriptions are useful in designing a behavior change strategy. *The manager must pinpoint the performance to be changed so that it may be observed and accurately counted and recorded.* This is the major criterion for a well-specified performance.

In addition to defining the performance in a pinpointed manner the manager should consider the performance he is planning to change from the standpoint of his priorities and those of the employee. Does this performance really matter? To whom does it matter? The improvement in the specified performance should make some significant difference to the organization, the employee, or both. Often a performance improvement for the organization may also increase the skill and value of the individual. There are times when a specified performance may be in the interest of the organization but serve no interest of the employee. For example, merely increasing productivity may result in no benefit to the employee. There are other occasions when the specified performance may serve no benefit to the organization but may be of benefit to the employee. This may be the case if there is a waiting pool of prospective employees capable of assuming a current employee's job. If the current employee is performing poorly it may be in the interest of the organization to replace the individual. But managers usually take steps to shape the employee's behavior in the desired direction so that the individual does not suffer the loss of his job. This may very well be counter to the best interests of the organization because of the training costs and production lost. Concern for the interests of the individual worker may, however, encourage the manager to engage in the behavior change efforts that are in the best interests of the employee.

When selecting target performances to improve, the manager is advised to select those that are in the best interest of the greater number of people. If the change is only in the best interest of the organization and not of the individual, there is a resistance to change that has to be overcome. The same is true if the change is only in the best interest of the employee. Changes that produce a benefit for an individual are usually (but not always) reinforcing to that individual. Improved performance may save a worker his job. It is hoped that this is reinforcing to him. This reinforcing element of the change increases the probability of success of any behavior change effort.

The specified performance may be either a *behavior* or the *result* of behavior. Production, waste, quality, efficiency, and other such measures of performance are results, not behavior. The assumption made when an individual is held accountable for a result is that his behavior determines that result. This is usually true only to some degree. In considering outcome performances there are usually factors involved that determine the outcome in addition to the individual's behavior. For example, quality of goods produced may be influenced by the care and accuracy of the individual, but it is also influenced by the quality of the input materials used to produce the output, the maintenance of the equipment or tools used in the production, and the behavior of any individuals involved in the production process. In using a result as a measure of performance, it must be realized that the individual whose performance one wishes to improve makes only a contribution to that result. For this reason it is necessary to establish more extensive baseline data on the outcome to determine in individual performance.

In selecting a pinpointed behavior as the performance to be changed, less baseline measurement is necessary than in selecting a result because the measure of behavior is direct. In many cases it is useful to compare the measure of actual behavior to that of an outcome performance. For example, you may be concerned with the number of pages typed by secretaries in a typing pool. You may have observed the secretaries and noticed that they spend a great deal of time socializing. You assume that if they reduce the amount of time socializing and increase the amount of time they spend at their typewriters, they will increase their output of number of pages typed per day. Which performance do you decide to change? The performance of producing a specified number of pages per day or the performance of sitting at a typewriter typing? If you measure the behavior directly by taking one random count per hour, you may find that an average of fifty percent of the typists are engaged in work behavior. After starting a program in which the behavior of typing receives feedback and reinforcement, you may find that you have increased this behavior to seventy-five percent of the typists engaged in work at the time of the counts. How does this change affect the change in the outcome measure, number of pages typed per day? To your surprise you may find that it doesn't affect this outcome at all. It is possible that other factors, such as the nature of the typing assignments, have influenced the outcome. Perhaps during the time when the typists spent only fifty percent of their time actually typing, they were typing fairly simple letters that required little time. Now they may be typing an audit report with extensive columns of figures that must be checked and double checked for accuracy. It is possible that the typists are working harder but producing fewer pages of output.

In this example, for which performance would you establish a contingency—the behavior or the outcome? The advantage of focusing on the behavior is that this is the performance most directly controlled by the individual. The advantage of focusing on the output is that this is the result with which you are concerned. The best answer in this case is to measure the result, the number of pages typed, but weight the value of those pages according to their difficulty. You might assign a number of points for the typing assignments that are straight typing and another value for those that require more careful and time-consuming work.

Whereas specifying the results of behavior is most desirable in this case, specifying behavior may be advantageous in other cases. When a change in the individual's behavior cannot be reliably correlated with changes in outcome or result, your behavior change effort will be more successful if it focuses directly on behavior.

## MEASUREMENT OF PERFORMANCE

All behavior management efforts include a measure of performance before the initiation of a behavior change program, during that change effort, and following the effort to improve performance. If this is not accomplished, the change agent should not consider his project a behavior management project. It is an absolutely essential element of any behavior management program that this before and after measurement be accomplished. Behavior management has progressed because of this measurement and the feedback provided to the change agent. Most human resource development efforts have not advanced, both because of the reliance on theory and because of the absence of useful measurement. The behavior manager's skills improve as a function of his measurement of his own efforts. Not all behavior management projects work. Many fail to produce the desired result for any one of a dozen reasons. Having a clear measure of results, the change agent can modify his tactics according to that feedback. This greatly increases his effectiveness and value to the organization. The behavior manager holds himself accountable for the results he achieves or fails to achieve. This accountability assumes that the behavior manager is willing to accept the negative outcome, that he is sufficiently mature and secure to recognize objectively and accept his own efforts that fall short of his goals. This objectivity not only increases the net effect of the behavior manager's efforts but also provides the basis for the one of the two critical foundations of science:

> . . . underlying every science is observation and measurement, providing a description of events and a way of quantifying them so that experimental manipulation may be achieved. It might be said that the two critical foundations of science are observation and experiment and that measurement provides a meaningful way in which events and their manipulation may be ordered. The ultimate goal in science is, of course, an ordering of facts into general, consistent laws from which predictions may be made, but it inevitably starts with observation (Bachrach, 1962).

### From Judgement to Measurement

It is often difficult for the manager who has been conditioned to *judge* the quality of performance subjectively to consider performance in terms of objectively measured behavior. The usual performance evaluation procedure in the industrial setting includes a series of dimensions on which the employee is rated. For example, a salesperson may be rated on his selling skills by his manager. The rating form lists indicators of his selling skills such as (1) sells to identified needs; (2) establishes sound working relationships with customers; (3) uses appropriate selling skills to obtain commitments; (4) ensures appropriate product utilization and/or implementation; (5) identifies new customers and new selling opportunities. Three columns may then be provided for indicating that the salesman is "below," "meets," or is "above" standards on each of these categories. This type of evaluation process asks the manager to make a judgment, once a year or each six months, regarding the salesperson's performance on each of these skills. The difficulty with this evaluation procedure is that it is not a measurement but a judgmental procedure. Behavior management does not ask the manager to make these types of judgments. Rather, the manager is asked to specify behavior or results and measure, not judge, performance on those behaviors or results.

How can the traditional evaluation procedure be converted to a behavioral measurement procedure? There are two possible ways. In the case of the sales skills evaluation procedure described above, the sales manager may directly measure performance by (1) direct observation and counting of behavior and (2) measurement of results. In addition the salespersons may be encouraged to measure their own performance directly. The items on the evaluation procedure should be converted to behavioral description. Item 1, sells to identified needs, can be converted to a behavioral description of "salesperson restates the need of the customer as he understands it and obtains agreement on that need before presenting the features or benefits of his product," or "salesperson states a benefit and relates that benefit to a need previously acknowledged by the client." Item 2, establishes a sound working relationship with customers, can be converted to a behavioral description of "customers initiate calls to salesperson when they have an order, customers and salesperson are on a first-name basis, and the customer has provided salesperson with one lead during the past year." To convert a judgmental statement to one that may be measured, ask the question, "How would I know if I saw one?" (Mager, 1970).

It may be that some evaluative statements cannot be redefined in measurable terms. These judgments are usually best dropped entirely. Those that can be converted to behavioral definitions should be the subject of observation and counting, both by the salesperson and the manager. Field trips by the manager with the salespersons should include measurements of some of the behaviors specified as important in their functioning. Some managers and salespersons initially react to this suggestion with some anxiety. They may feel that this creates a discomfort in their relationship and applies too much pressure during the field trip. When these procedures are implemented, the reverse turns out to be the case. Salespersons and managers and most employees and managers have an element of anxiety in their relationship. This anxiety is, to a large extent, related to the subjective nature of the evaluations that the manager must make about the employee. When the manager goes out on field trips with his salespersons, there is no question but that he is engaged in some type of evaluative process. The anxiety is heightened, not by the clarity of the measurement, but by its fuzziness. When the measures are well known to both salesperson and manager, and when the measurement is discussed openly, the anxiety is reduced and the relationship between the manager and salesperson may be more open, frank, and comfortable.

The difficulty with measurement of behavior is the practical problem of obtaining a meaningful sample of the behavior. The salesperson argues that his manager goes on field trips with him only once a month and has no idea what he is doing the rest of the month. This is a valid objection. The manager cannot count, directly, sufficient behavior of his employees to provide an adequate basis for determining reinforcement. This is the advantage of measuring results. The sales manager who can observe his salesperson only one day out of twenty should use that one day to observe and provide the salesperson with *feedback* on his behavior. He should rely heavily on the measurement of results for determining *reinforcement*. If the behaviors and results have both been selected intelligently, there is a correlation between them. If the salesperson behaves in the most desired way, identifying needs, establishing the appropriate relationship with the customer, and so forth, the results follow. If results do not follow from these behaviors, then the wrong behaviors have been selected and the salesperson should not be held accountable for performing those behaviors.

### Types of Measurement

Behavior may be measured according to the *frequency*, *duration*, or *intensity* of the behavior. Results may be measured according to the *frequency/quantity* produced or the *quality/type* produced (Figure 24). Frequency refers to the number of occurrences of a response within a given interval of time. Ten sales presentations per week, six breaks from work per day, and twenty pages typed per day are statements of frequency of behavior. Duration of behavior refers to the length of time that the behavior is ongoing. Duration is of concern in attempting to increase the period during which an individual may remain "on task." When working on a report, an individual may have a tendency to work for very short periods and take a large number of breaks. The breaks may very well last longer than the periods of time working. The individual may then record the duration of the work periods and record the duration of breaks and lengthen the duration of "on task" behavior. Kempen and Hall (1977) found in a study of absenteeism at a Western Electric plant that the greatest gain could be obtained by reducing the duration of absences, the number of days individuals stayed out, rather than the frequency of absences. Intensity of a response is a less common measure in the work setting but may be of concern in attempting to improve a skill, such as personal assertiveness. A manager may have difficulty asserting himself with troublesome workers and may tend to talk very softly and thereby give the impression of lacking strength. Through behavior rehearsals the intensity of a verbal response may be increased. This may also apply to public speaking, in which the tone of voice and amplitude are critical elements of the speaker's behavior.

In measuring results there are generally fewer alternatives and the nature of the measurement is likely to be determined by existing systems in the work setting. Either the *frequency/quantity* or the *quality/type* of results may be measured. Frequency and quantity are grouped because the result is measured in the number of units produced during some given time period. A quantity of production results from the frequency within the time period. Quality and type are grouped because quality is a judgment of the type of production. "Off-quality" goods are a type of unit produced during the time period. What is "first quality" or "second quality" is the judgment about the type of units produced.

Two procedures may be used to record the measurement of either behavior or results: *continuous recording* and *time sampling*. Continuous recording refers to the observation and recording of every occurrence of a behavior or result over a period of time. Continuous recording is often practical in measuring results but rarely practical

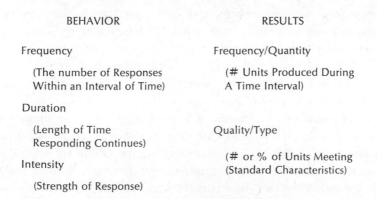

| BEHAVIOR | RESULTS |
|---|---|
| Frequency | Frequency/Quantity |
| (The number of Responses Within an Interval of Time) | (# Units Produced During A Time Interval) |
| Duration | |
| (Length of Time Responding Continues) | Quality/Type |
| Intensity | (# or % of Units Meeting (Standard Characteristics) |
| (Strength of Response) | |

**Figure 24**   Performance measurement options.

in measuring behavior. The results of behavior in most organizations are tabulated in some systematic fashion. Most industrial plants maintain continuous records on production, first- and second-quality goods, waste, efficiency, and other measures of the results produced by employee behavior. All the results are recorded over extended periods of time. We may, therefore, say that the results are recorded continuously. The same is true in sales organizations and most other organizations engaged in business. This is often not true in service or government institutions and represents one of the major areas of performance deficiency in service institutions. Continuous recording of the results of performance are the basis for effective feedback and reinforcement systems.

While organizations generally provide for continuous recording of the results representing measures of performance for the organization, there may not be a system for continuous recording of the results of an individual's performance. A secretary, manager, line production worker, or clerk may lack the feedback and evaluation that would be available if a method of continuous recording of results was present. The manager may begin by establishing a method of recording results on a continuous basis.

Continuous recording of behavior is usually much more difficult. To record the occurrence of behavior on a continuous basis, one must observe the behavior continuously. For the manager attempting to improve the efficiency of a single machine operator, this may be impossible. He does not have the time to observe the operator all day every day. Neither does almost any other manager for almost any other type of employee. In some cases it is possible to establish a self-recording system whereby the individual employee may record the occurrences of various behaviors. The manager may record the number of times he has contact with various employees on a continuous basis or the number of times he performs some other task. But for attempting to change someone else's behavior, continuous recording does not often prove practical.

The alternative to continuous recording is time sampling. This is a procedure in which intervals of time are specified for recording in an intermittent fashion. For example, an industrial supervisor may observe the behavior of an employee for four ten-minute intervals during the day. When a sales manager goes on field trips with his sales-

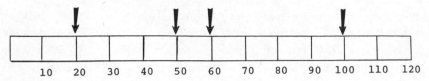

Figure 25   Time sampling: four of twelve ten-minute intervals.

persons he is observing behavior during the time sample of one day within a month, week, and so forth. Time sampling enables the manager to measure behavior over a period of time, while observing only during selected time intervals. In sampling intervals of behavior it is important that the intervals be distributed in a manner that provides a representative sample. Intervals might be spaced so as to provide data that would indicate a frequency different from what might be obtained for continuous recording. For example, a supervisor might be concerned about the amount of time two employees spend talking to each other and not working. Knowing he doesn't have the time to observe these two workers continuously, he might set up an interval schedule of recording their behavior once each hour, eight times each day, for one week. He may then establish his intervals so that he records their behavior each hour on the hour. It is possible that this fixed-interval schedule of recording may correspond with breaks. Every two hours, on the hour, the workers may take a five-minute break. This would obviously result in data that are not indicative of the behavior of the workers throughout the day. For this reason it is wise to vary the intervals in a random fashion. To obtain indicative and reliable data, one must also make certain that a sufficient number of intervals are recorded. Too few intervals, for example, only three or four counts of the behavior, do not provide enough of a sample on which to base a reliable frequency measure. Obtaining sufficient sample size is similar to obtaining enough samples to determine a probability. If a coin is flipped four times, heads might come up three of the four times. Does this mean that heads always come up three-fourths of the time? Of course not. The limited size of the sample has provided insufficient information. To obtain a sufficient sample of coin throws for a correct fifty-percent probability, one may have to flip the coin fifty, seventy-five, or a hundred times. Similarly an insufficient sample of behavior leads to the wrong conclusions about an individual's performance. This is a common mistake among managers. A sample of fifty or more counts of a behavior may be required to obtain a sample that may be relied on to provide a true indication of the individual's performance.

Time sampling may be conducted in one of two ways: during the time interval the manager may record the number of responses that occur during that time interval, or he may simply record whether or not the behavior occurs at all during the interval. If he is concerned with the rate of a behavior that would normally occur numerous times within the time sample, such as the number of questions a salesperson may ask of his customer during a presentation, he is likely to record the number of occurrences within the time period. If the behavior is less frequent, but perhaps of longer duration, he may record the simple presence or absence of the behavior during the selected intervals. If he is concerned with the number of breaks employees are taking and the duration of those breaks, he may walk through a work area eight times a day and record the working or nonworking behavior during each of these intervals.

Whenever measuring behavior, one should write down the count observed at once. No manager is so smart that he can remember the counts he has taken for more than a few minutes. A simple interval recording chart as illustrated in Figure 26 is helpful in measuring behavior observed during intervals.

When scheduling intervals during which to measure performance, one should take into account some of the same considerations as when scheduling reinforcement. The measurement of behavior, by itself, may serve as an occasion for feedback and reinforcement. If the employees whose behavior is being measured are aware of the measurement, they may assume that a contingency is associated with the measurement, and the observation procedure is likely to affect performance. For this reason either the frequency of the time sample should be very high or the intervals should be on a variable schedule. One project the author was associated with undertook to measure on- and off-task behavior in an industrial setting. The behavior manager walked through the work area to record the on- and off-task behavior eight times per day. Initially it appeared that his presence in the plant work area increased the on-task performance. After several days of recording, however, the employees began to ignore his presence and behaved as they would in his absence. For this

# Behavior Count Sheet

Behavior Pinpoint __Taking Coffee or Rest Breaks__

Count Schedule __8 times per day - Random Intervals__

Date __8/24/77__ Time _____

Location __Plant 2 - Shift C__ Recorder __Joe Thompson__

Code _____

| Interval #1 | 2 |
|---|---|
| 2 | 4 |
| 3 | 4 |
| 7 | 0 |
| 5 | 6 |
| 2 | 3 |
| 7 | 8 |
| 4 | 5 |
| 9 | 10 |

**Figure 26** Behavior count sheet.

reason the first few days of data were discarded. The observer continued to record his counts on a fixed-interval basis, at the same times each day. If there is less time to establish baseline data, the observer cannot wait until the employees extinguish on his presence as a discriminative stimulus for on-task performance; the same result can be achieved by varying the times of recording.

### Establishing Baselines

Performance is measured before initiating a behavior change project to establish the baseline data against which the effects of the procedure can be evaluated. In order for the baseline data to serve as a basis for evaluation, they must be of sufficient quantity to provide a stable measurement. There is no formula answer to the question "How much data do I need for a good baseline?" The amount of baseline data required depends entirely on the nature of the variable being measured. If the performance measured is the efficiency of a group of workers in an industrial setting, several months of data may be required. If the type of products being produced changes often or extraneous conditions that may influence performance are changing, the length of period for a reliable baseline must be extended. The performance of a salesperson may require several months of baseline data if a result is being measured. Seasonal fluctuations, product cycles, and supply and demand considerations must all be taken into account before it is determined that the available data represent a valid baseline of performance. The more variables that influence the result the more data are required for establishing a reliable baseline on performance.

Trends in the data should influence the decision of when a program should be initiated. If the trend in the data is one of improvement, the manager should *not* initiate any change procedure. If he does, he cannot take credit for continuation of the trend present during the baseline period. If he initiates a change in the contingencies affecting the behavior and the trend stops or reverses, he must be prepared to consider the worsening data a result of his project. On the other hand, if the data indicate a worsening trend, the frequency of absenteeism steadily increasing, for example, the manager may be justified in collecting a shorter period of baseline data. The necessity of reversing this trend may dictate action as quickly as possible. The trend is unlikely to worsen, and while the change in the trend may not be entirely a result of his project, his efforts are not damned if the data improve. For sound evaluation the best baseline data provide a stable trend in performance. Months of consistent levels of quality, efficiency, attendance, on-time behavior, or other variables are likely to be representative of performance and are not likely to change as a result of uncontrolled or unforeseen influences.

Data collected before the beginning of a behavior change project should *always* be graphed. Graphing enables the behavior manager to observe any trends, the degree of fluctuation or consistency, and any regularly occurring patterns of performance. The data should be graphed according to the interval on which the data are recorded. In other words, if data are recorded once every day, they should be graphed daily. If data are recorded by the hour, week, or month, the graph should be arranged to provide for visualizing the data by those intervals. Any of the graphs representing case studies in this book provide examples of arranging data on graphs to visualize the baseline and program data. You can study these graphs and use them for models when constructing your own graphs.

The units of measure on the graph should be arranged so as to provide maximum visualization of change. If the counts of behavior vary between eighty and ninety occurrences per day, there is no need to arrange the graph from zero to one hundred, or worse yet, from zero to one thousand. These scalings on the graph would provide little visualization of changes in performance. The graph should be scaled from eighty to one hundred, providing greater space for visualizing the fluctuations likely to occur.

The most important consideration in measuring performance is to be certain that *baseline data are collected before* the initiation of any change effort. The manager who understands this need is likely to succeed in his change efforts.

## BEHAVIORAL ANALYSIS

A behavioral analysis is an examination of the causes for the current frequency of performance. This analysis should identify the *current* contingencies of reinforcement controlling performance. An effective behavior change strategy is best developed after an analysis of the current contingencies. A behavior change project implemented in ignorance of the current contingencies attempts to apply preconceived solutions to situations likely to contain unique elements that should influence the selection of the change strategy.

### Is the Deficiency One of Skill or Rate?

The first step in the behavioral analysis is determining whether the performance deficiency is one of skill or rate (motivation) of perform-ance. Entirely different strategies are appropriate in problems of skill or rate. If the problem is one of lack of skill, a training solution is required in which the individual may acquire the necessary behaviors. If the problem is not one of skill but one of low rate (motivation), the solution involves a change in the contingencies of reinforcement. Failure to recognize problems of skill deficiency may result in a situation that may properly be described as "unfair." It is unfair to offer reinforcement contingent upon typing fifty words per minute if the individual involved possesses only the skill to type twenty words per minute. The individual is not able to achieve the stated level of performance, regardless of the incentive to perform.

How do you know whether the performance deficiency is one of skill or rate? With some performances the answer may be fairly obvious. If you wish to increase attendance or arriving to work on time, you can justifiably assume that the problem is not one of skill. The individual has certainly performed these behaviors before and no new skill is required to perform them today. This is one way that you may know whether or not the problem is an absence of skill or a deficiency in rate of performance. *Has the behavior been performed in the past?* If it has, then the problem is one of motivation. If the behavior has never been performed before, then it is most likely that the deficiency is one of skill. The rate of performance may, however, require skill. The individual may have demonstrated that he can assemble an electronics unit in the past. But his rate of assembly is three per hour and the average rate for all workers is five per hour. While he knows how to perform the task, he may still lack the skill required to perform at the desired level. For simple tasks such as arriving to work on time, the problem is virtually certain to be one of motivation. For complex tasks such as performing the assembly on an electronic component the problem may be one of skill or of motivation.

*The more complex the task the greater the probability that the*

*deficiency is the lack of skill.* The salesperson who has difficulty closing sales is very likely to suffer from a lack of skill rather than of
motivation. The behaviors required to close a sale are complex and
are not learned simply because one "wants to." Training is required
to develop the behavioral skill in the repertoire of the individual.

Perhaps the best way to determine whether the behavior of concern requires training or alteration in the contingencies of reinforcement is *to establish the necessary contingencies for performance for
at least a brief period to observe the individual's performance.* The
ability of the salesperson in presenting his product and closing sales
is a good example of where this may be done. When the salesperson makes a presentation to a client in the presence of the manager, that salesperson is very likely to be sufficiently motivated to
perform. The contingencies of reinforcement are present so that the
individual performs (his rate is high) if he possesses the necessary
skill. In observing the salesperson in his presentation the skilled manager is able to determine whether or not the salesperson establishes
the necessary preconditions for a successful close. It can be argued
that the salesperson may be under such pressure in this situation that
he will find it difficult to perform the task while being observed by
his manager. This may be true on a first or second field trip. If, however, field trips are fairly regular events, the salesperson becomes
sufficiently comfortable to reduce this likelihood.

A fourth way to determine whether the performance deficiency
is a skill or motivation problem is to *examine the ongoing contingencies of reinforcement to determine whether sufficient contingencies are present* so that the individual "ought to want to" perform.
One may assume that, if a secretary is applying for a job, and she is
given a typing test but cannot perform it at the required words per
minute rate, the conditions were present under which she "oughta
wanna" perform. The reinforcer for performing was certainly strong
enough. After all, she did make the effort of coming to apply for the
job. She was given the necessary instructions and had all the necessary
instruments. She simply couldn't perform. The manager who fails to
complete his monthly projections and activity report may also be
examined to determine whether or not the performance may result
from inadequate contingencies. Are the necessary antecedent conditions present? Has he received clear instructions regarding the monthly
reports he is supposed to submit? Is he aware of the importance

of having these reports to the home office on time? Does he know the format for writing these reports? If the answers to these questions are all "yes," then the antecedents for this performance are most likely present. How about the consequences to performance? Is there any reinforcer associated with completion of these reports? Does he know that the last manager promoted had an excellent record of completing his reports on time and submitting accurate and informative reports? Has he previously received feedback about his late or incomplete reports? What is the potentially punishing consequence for failing to complete this report? If it is clear from the answer to these questions that there are operating and important consequences to the individual for performing this task and he still fails to perform, it is likely that there is a skill deficiency. If these conditions are not present, then there is a reasonable probability that the deficiency is one of motivation and the solution will be found in the strengthening of the contingencies of reinforcement.

There are, therefore, four tests that you may apply to determine whether the deficiency is one of skill or motivation:

**1.** Has the behavior been performed in the past? If it has never been performed, the deficiency is likely one of skill. If the behavior has been performed, the problem is likely to be one of motivation requiring alteration of the contingencies of reinforcement.

**2.** How complex is the task? The more complex the task the more likely a skill deficiency. The more simple the task the more likely a motivation problem.

**3.** Temporarily establish a set of contingencies that you are certain will be sufficient to evoke the behavior if the individual is able to perform. If the behavior is performed, the problem has been motivation. If it is not performed, the definciency is one of skill.

**4.** Examine the current contingencies of reinforcement. Are contingencies present that are reasonably likely to reinforce performance? If meaningful antecedents and reinforcers are not present, the deficiency is likely to be one of motivation. If reasonable contingencies do exist, the deficiency is more likely to be one of skill.

If the deficiency is one of skill, the only additional behavior analysis required is to determine the current skill level of the individual. This may be accomplished during the first analysis which determined that the problem was a skill deficiency. For example, if you are concerned with the ability of an individual production worker, you may have worked closely with that worker to observe his behavior under conditions which included the contingencies of reinforcement likely to result in performance. You observed his skill deficiency under these conditions, so you now know approximately how he is able to perform. The manager and the training specialist, when one is available, should now define the specific skill deficiency and the preferred method of providing the desired training.

### Identifying Antecedents and Consequences

If the deficiency involves increasing motivation and the rate of performance, the manager should now apply the ABC model, an examination of the antecedent-behavior-consequences. He has already specified the behavior and obtained a measure of the frequency of that behavior. He should now determine which antecedents and consequences are exerting control over the performance. An identification of these influences will provide a basis for determining those antecedents and consequences that may be altered to improve the performance.

### Antecedents

*Which events occur immediately prior to the performance of the target behavior?* While counting the frequency of the target behavior, the manager will also be able to identify the events that may serve to set the occasion for the response. If the target behavior is one that the manager wishes to increase, he will be looking for an antecedent whose occurrence can be increased. For example, an employee may arrive to work on time on mornings following a day on which the manager has discussed the employee's objectives. The setting of objectives may set the occasion for arriving to work on time. The occurrence of this antecedent may be increased. However, if the manager is concerned with reducing the frequency of the target behavior, he will be looking for an antecedent whose occurrence can be reduced. The manager may wish to reduce the behavior of leaving work early. He may observe that employees leave work early on days when a particular manager is not on site or has left early himself. The absence of this manager may serve as a discriminative stimulus for the behavior of leaving work early.

The following questions may help the manager further identify antecedents that may set the occasion for the performance:

1.  *Does the behavior occur in particular physical settings?*

2.  *Does the behavior occur in certain social settings?*

3.  *Does the behavior follow the occurrence of a particular behavior of other persons?*

4.  *Does the target behavior usually occur following some other behavior of the individual himself?*

If the answer to any of these questions is affirmative, the manager has identified an antecedent associated with the performance he wishes to change. The manager, after identifying functional antecedents, must now ask himself the question, *"Can I control or alter the occurrence of these antecedents?"* If the answer is no, then these are obviously not antecedents that the manager may use in his behavior change project. It is often not within the manager's authority or ability to control certain antecedents. For example, some employees may tend to be absent following a payday. The manager is not going to alter this antecedent. The employee certainly must continue to be paid. He may also be unable to alter an antecedent that involves the behavior of another individual, perhaps another manager. There are usually antecedents that the manager does control, and he should focus his efforts on altering these.

### Consequences

Now that the antecedents have been identified, the question should be asked, *"Which events occur immediately following or contingent upon the target behavior?"* Again, if the intent of the behavior change project is to increase the frequency of the target behavior, the manager looks for a consequence that may be increased or added to cause an increase in the rate of performance. If the desire is to decrease the performance, the observation of the behavior and the events that occur immediately following it may identify a reinforcer maintaining the performance. This reinforcer may be terminated to extinguish the performance. The manager must also ask if there is a punishing consequence suppressing the desired performance.

*What are the current social consequences following the target performance?* If the target behavior is to be reduced, then there may be a social reinforcer currently following the undesired performance that is maintaining that performance. For example, many undesired work behaviors, such as taking excessive breaks, talking on the job, distracting other workers, and even causing equipment breakdowns or damage, may be followed by peer social approval. Behavior or results, such as production rates, timeliness of work completion, attainment of quality levels, and creative or innovative contributions, and managerial performances, such as accurate budgeting or following personnel procedures, may be increased by the addition of social reinforcement. Once you have identified the ongoing social consequences, ask the following questions: *May these consequences be strengthened or reduced? May these be delivered more or less frequently? May these be delivered more or less immediately?* If the social reinforcers can be altered in any of these ways, then they may be used as part of your behavior change strategy.

The manager should also ask *what additional social reinforcers, not currently delivered, can be added contingent on the desired performance?* With a little bit of imagination many opportunities for additional social reinforcement can be discovered, for example, letters from the company president or other executives expressing appreciation to the target individual for improved performance; a notice of individuals' achieving significant progress toward goals in a company/plant/organization newsletter; taking the individual out to lunch, perhaps with a higher level manager, following improved performance to the target individual's co-workers so that they will let the target individual know that his improvement is being recognized; or announcements over the plant/facility public address system when individuals have reached significant goals.

Social reinforcers should be used in *every* behavior change project. There are no workers, whether executive vice presidents of

## INDIVIDUAL PROJECT WORKSHEET

Target Individual: _____ Date: _____
Manager: _____ Department: _____

1. Target Performance:

    _____

    _____ (can it be observed & measured?)

    Why is this target important? _____

    _____

    What are the results of current vs. improved performance? _____

    _____

    Is the target a behavior ___ or a result ___?
    Do you wish to increase ___ or decrease ___ the performance?

2. Measurement:

    If the target is a behavior, is the desired change one of frequency, duration, or intensity? _____

    _____ If the target is a result, is the desired change one

    of frequency/quantity or quality/type? _____

    Can the target be measured continuously or is a time sample required? _____

    Describe the period of the continuous measurement or the time sample: _____

    _____

    Was the baseline data recorded without any feedback to the individual? (Is the baseline a true baseline?)

    _____

    What is the length of the period of baseline data? _____

    What is the trend of the measurement during baseline? _____

    If the data is improving or worsening during baseline what is the reason for this trend? _____

    _____

3. Behavioral Analysis:

    Is the deficient performance a deficiency of skill or rate? _____

    Has the target been performed in the past? _____
    Is the performance complex or simple? _____
    Have contingencies been sufficient to evoke the performance? _____

**Figure 27** Individual project worksheet.

<u>Antecedents</u>: Which events occur immediately prior to the performance? _____

_____

Does the performance occur in particular physical settings, social settings, following the behavior of other persons, or other behaviors of the target individual? _____

_____

What objectives, instructions, goals, etc. currently are intended to set the occasion for this performance?

_____

Which of the above antecedents may be altered to change the target performance? _____

_____

<u>Consequences</u>: Which consequences occur following the performance? What are the current social consequences following the target performance? _____

_____

    May these be strengthened? _____
    May these be delivered more frequently? _____
    May these be delivered more immediately? _____
    What additional social consequences could be delivered contingent on performance? _____

_____

What are the current tangible consequences following target performance? _____

_____

    May these consequences be strengthened? _____
    May these be delivered more frequently? _____
    May these be delivered more immediately? _____
    What additional tangible reinforcers could be delivered contingent on performance? _____

_____

Does the individual derive any intrinsic reinforcement from the performance itself? _____

_____

    Can the intrinsic reinforcement be increased through self-measurement of results? _____
    Can the variety of the tasks performed be increased? _____
    Can social/group participation in performance be increased? _____
    Can the status/value/responsibility of the work be increased? _____

What feedback (measurement/evaluation) does the individual currently receive on his performance?

_____

_____

**Figure 27**   *continued.*

Is the feedback a direct, objective measurement of the target performance? _____
What is the frequency of this feedback? _____
Is this feedback made important by pairing with social consequences? _____

Which of the above consequences are most meaningful to the target individual? _____

Given the necessary practical considerations, which consequences may be altered? _____

4. Design and Implementation:

Date of Implementation: _____

Antecedents established for performance (include objectives): _____

_____

_____

Consequences established to follow performance: _____

_____

_____

Changes in feedback: _____

_____

Describe schedule of reinforcement and feedback: _____

_____

_____

If performance is to be shaped, what is the initial criterion level and what is the goal level of target performance? _____

_____

What was the initial reaction to the new contingencies? _____

_____

Was the target individual involved in the planning and design of the project in a participatory manner?

5. Evaluation:

Did performance improve over baseline? _____

Did performance stabilize at a higher level? _____

Describe the data reflecting the change in performance: _____

_____

**Figure 27**  *continued.*

264

Was a return-to-baseline or multiple-baseline used to evaluate the change in performance?  If not, describe why not: _____

_____

Describe or compute the value of the changed performance: _____

_____

What secondary changes occurred as a result of this project? _____

_____

If you were to conduct this project again what would you do differently? _____

_____

6.  Performance Maintenance:

What is your plan for maintaining the new level of performance?

Which antecedents will be used on a continuing basis? _____

_____

Which consequences will be continued or altered? _____

_____

Which sources of feedback will be continued? _____

_____

How will the schedule of reinforcement be altered? _____

_____

Will your maintenance plan avoid satiation? _____

Will the measurement of performance be continued or will a different sampling procedure be utilized?

_____

**Figure 27**  *continued.*

the corporation or the part-time hourly workers, who are not reinforced by well-delivered social approval. Tangible reinforcers used
in the absence of social approval quickly lose their effect. Social
approval proves more effective and meaningful to the individual over
a long period of time.

What are the tangible consequences currently following the
target performance? There is rarely a tangible reinforcer following
undesirable behaviors. Undesirable behavior is usually maintained by
social reinforcement, the intrinsic reinforcing qualities of the behavior,
or consequences external to the work setting. When considering the
tangible reinforcers currently following the desired performance, the
manager almost automatically considers salary as such a reinforcer.
But is salary truly contingent on this performance? Does salary change
as a function of this performance? If salary remains the same regardless of this performance, then it is not a reinforcer for this behavior.
Rarely is salary a true reinforcer because it is rarely contingent on
performance.

Tangible reinforcers for the target performance may exist in the
form of bonus or incentive pay. If tangible reinforcement is present,
ask the following questions to identify possible improvements in its
delivery: May these consequences be strengthened? It is possible
that the present tangible reinforcers are not sufficiently powerful to
exert a controlling influence over the performance. May the tangible
reinforcers be delivered more frequently? The schedule of reinforcement may be made more dense, providing payoff for performance more often or following fewer behaviors. This may be done
while not increasing the total amount of tangible reinforcement for
a given level of performance. The increments may be reduced and
delivered more frequently and thereby increase the density of the
schedule. May these reinforcers be delivered more immediately?
Reducing the time between behavior and receipt of reinforcement
enhances performance.

If no tangible reinforcement is present, are there other tangible
reinforcers that may be delivered contingent on the desired performance? In small nonunion organizations it is often possible to
establish tangible reinforcers for improved performance. Raffles may
be established whereby raffle tickets are earned for criterion levels
of performance during the week and a raffle drawing is held at the

end of the week. Special bonus arrangements may be made with employees for achieving desired levels of performance or completion of projects. Some organizations conduct an employee reinforcer survey to identify items of high reinforcing value to the employee so that these items can be delivered contingent on high performance. One sales organization used this reinforcer survey and each quarter of the year awarded the salesperson who had shown the most improvement in performance an item from his reinforcer survey. (See page 149).

When considering additional tangible reinforcers, one must also consider the possible negative side effects of using tangible reinforcement. Several issues should be considered in planning tangible reinforcers. One involves expectations for future performance. In some cases the use of tangible reinforcers may establish a precedent by which employees expect tangible reinforcers for exceptional performance. The failure to deliver these reinforcers once this expectation has been established results in reduced performance. With individual behavior change projects another risk involves making a reinforcer available for improved performance for one individual while similar improved performance of other individuals does not result in similar reinforcement. This situation may result in discontent and reduced performance among those for whom the reinforcement is not available. Another risk presented by the use of tangible reinforcers is created when the reinforcement is made available for improvement in poor performance. This may establish a chain of behavior whereby the employee is reinforced first for performing poorly, then for making a dramatic improvement in that poor performance.

The best advice in implementing individual behavior change projects is first to arrange social reinforcement, feedback, and make any improvements in intrinsic reinforcement before resorting to tangible reinforcers. Second, improve the use of currently available tangible reinforcement. Whenever possible, do this on an organization-wide or group basis, rather than on an individual basis. Third, use tangibles when the individual is already an isolated case. For example, tangible reinforcers for high-level executives are much easier to administer simply because executives tend to be compensated in a more individualized manner than production employees.

The accepted individualization of reinforcement establishes the expectations that make tangible reinforcement acceptable.

*Does the individual currently derive any intrinsic reinforcement from the performance itself?* What consequences follow as a function of performing the behavior itself? For example, is the individual able to see the completion of a product? Is the target individual able to experience a customer's reaction to the result of good work? Is the individual able to measure his own performance so that he can compete with his own previous performance or the performance of others? Often, intrinsic reinforcers can be identified simply by asking the employee what he enjoys about his work. Employees are very often more conscious of the intrinsic reinforcers for performance than a manager is.

If intrinsic reinforcers can be strengthened or added, this strategy should be employed. Intrinsic reinforcers have the advantage of occurring without management administration. If an individual enjoys experiencing the completion of an assembled product, this occurs every time the individual completes the assembly. Virtually all intrinsic reinforcers occur on a fixed-ratio schedule of reinforcement, a schedule that results in high rates of performance and is resistant to extinction. Intrinic reinforcement is also likely to produce other responses in addition to high-rate performance, such as feelings of self-worth, appreciation for quality performance, and positive feelings toward the company and its management.

The following questions may help identify ways to increase the intrinsic reinforcement for the target performance: *Can the intrinsic reinforcement be increased through self-measurement of results?* By measuring one's own performance, a greater feeling of self-management and responsibility is acquired. The greater the sense of responsibility toward one's performance the greater the probability that desired effort will be extended. Self-measurement of performance also increases the feedback to the individual, also a well-demonstrated factor in high performance.

*Can the variety of the tasks performed be increased?* Novelty and diversity of behavior are, in themselves, reinforcing. This is demonstrated in early childhood and, though often unavailable to adults, novelty and diversity of experience remain reinforcing. Monotony on the job not only results in reduced rate of performance but also may result in increased dissatisfaction toward the employer or manager, and increased probability of turnover. Increasing the diversity of the tasks performed increases the interest level and results in other dimensions of improved performance. Increasing the variety of the tasks performed again presents a challenge to the manager's imagination. Which responsibilities can be shared among employees? Which tasks currently performed by the manager can be delegated? Which tasks of other jobs can be learned by an employee while still performing a current job? These and other questions should be examined by the manager in an effort to increase the variety and novelty of the tasks the target individual is asked to perform.

*Can the social or group participation of the target employee be increased to improve intrinsic reinforcement?* Instrinsic reinforcement is often derived from the social interaction occurring as a normal part of the job itself. If a bank teller were asked to perform transactions with an impersonal machine, rather than with dozens of unique individuals each day, the job would surely prove less interesting. The assembly line worker who works as part of a team derives reinforcement from the social interaction with his fellow team members. This reinforcement helps maintain interest in the job and overcome what would otherwise be a highly repetitive, boring task. The manager has to weigh the advantages and disadvantages of increasing the social interaction of an employee. In some cases the increased social interaction may result in distraction from the work and reduced performance. Only a careful examination of the particular circumstances of the work and experimentation can provide the basis for determining the value of increasing the social/group participation.

*Can the status, value, or responsibility of the work be increased?* The perceived importance of the work is critical to the individual's ability to derive reinforcement from the work. If the target individual feels his work is unimportant, he is unlikely to consider high performance important. The manager can increase the perceived importance of the target individual's work by discussing the relationship of his work to that of others. This should be prompted by a positive occasion. When the individual's work has contributed to the work of another person or group, this should be pointed out by the manager. The manager communicates the importance of a job to the worker daily. A manager often considers a particular job to be of little importance, and his actions convey this feeling to the employees.

The result is a reduction in performance of those employees. The truth is that every job is important; if not, it should be eliminated. It is the manager's job to convey this to his employees.

*What feedback does the individual currently receive following performance?* What methods of measurement or evaluation of performance are currently available and are these measurements fed back to the employee? Numerous research studies from the historic Hawthorne (Parsons, 1974) studies to very recent research (Panyon, Boozer, and Morris, 1970) have demonstrated the effect of feedback on performance. Research and practical experience in establishing performance improvement projects in the organizational setting have consistently demonstrated that more frequent, data-based, and visualized feedback of measurement of performance result in increases in that performance. If the individual is not receiving any measured feedback, a procedure should be established to provide this feedback. If feedback is present, the following questions may point to improvements that can be made in the current feedback delivery.

*Is the feedback a direct, objective measurement of the target performance?* Feedback that is a direct measure of performance is most responsive to changes in the individual's behavior. If feedback is the result of another person's judgment about performance, it is less direct and is less responsive to changes in the individual's behavior. Feedback is most effective when it is a direct measure of behavior and is highly responsive to changes in behavior.

*What is the frequency of feedback?* Generally, the more frequent the feedback the greater the impact on behavior. The ideal system of feedback must be weighed against the costs and other requirements of time and personnel. Feedback systems must be cost effective. Feedback systems should be designed to provide the most frequent possible feedback without additional time and costs beyond that gained from the improved feedback.

*Is the feedback made important by pairing the delivery of the feedback with social reinforcement?* If feedback is ignored, it is useless. The value of feedback is directly related to the attention paid to it. The example of the use of data-based feedback in one major sales organization is not unusual. The data processing center of this major textile firm provided its sales organization with a monthly analysis of all sales. Sales were broken down by customer, by salesperson, and by type of fabric sold. A voluminous computer printout with all the pertinent data on a salesperson's performance was available to each salesperson every month. None of the salespersons were, however, aware of how they were performing relative to their objectives, their previous performance, or the performance of other salespersons. The reports were glanced at, at best. The tens of thousands of dollars spent by this organization to provide its salespersons with pertinent feedback was virtually wasted because the managers did not attend to the data in a manner that would establish the feedback as *important!* The data on results must be made important by the manager's attention to those results. The managers in this organization attended to crisis and ancedotes on performance, rather than to the data that provided a more meaningful measure of the individual's performance. The manager must make the feedback matter by his visible concern about the data and his social approval when the feedback indicates improved performance.

From this series of questions you have identified reinforcing consequences that may be altered to increase performance. Before making your decision to use a consequence in your behavior change project, you should ask two questions that narrow your selection. First, *which of these consequences are most meaningful to the target individual?* And, second, *what are the practical considerations that may restrict the use of a reinforcer and what consequences remain that may be used practically?*

The degree to which a consequence is important to the target individual is the degree to which it functionally reinforces or punishes the target behavior. If the reinforcer survey suggested earlier has been administered, this can provide a basis for selecting reinforcing consequences important to the individual. The daily communication between manager and employee should also provide a basis for selecting reinforcers. Every manager should have a good idea of what is reinforcing to his employees. It is a useful exercise simply to look over a list of employees and attempt to write down one or two things or activities you know to be reinforcers for each individual. The ability to identify reinforcers is a good test of how well the manager knows the employee.

Many practical considerations may dictate the use or nonuse of a reinforcer. For example, if tangible reinforcers have never been used in an organization, it may be unwise to use them once without a commitment to use them in the future. The one-time use of a tangible reinforcer sets the expectation for future tangible reinforcers. Another practical consideration is one of economics. Economics influences your ability to provide reinforcement. Obviously you cannot expend a great deal of money on individual behavior change projects, and there is no need to do so. Most projects are implemented with little or no funds.

The economics of your time and other resources may also play a part in the design of your program. There are limits to the amount of time you have to devote to a project. These economics may dictate use of a VR schedule rather than a continuous schedule of reinforcement. Or your time constraints may dictate that a graph on an individual's performance be based on intervals of days or weeks rather than hours. A greater awareness of the practical considerations in the initiation of a behavior change project results from experience. It is common for the first effort at implementing a behavior change program to result in practical difficulties. The first attempts at applying behavior management strategies begin to develop the balance between theoretical guidelines and the practical limitations and requirements.


### DESIGN AND IMPLEMENTATIONS

The behavioral analysis just completed provides the core input required for the determination of a behavior management strategy. From this analysis you should now select those antecedents and consequences you feel are most likely to result in the desired change in behavior. Your analysis has identified antecedents that are influencing the behavior and that may be withdrawn or increased to effect a change in the performance. You have identified current and potentially reinforcing events that may be arranged to provide consequences that will alter performance.

The use of a change strategy should always be viewed as a dynamic process, rather than a firm and final procedure. The behavior manager is a student of performance and recognizes that the initial implementation is likely to be an approximation to the best possible strategy. He makes his best guess about the most desirable arrangement of contingencies, introduces those contingencies, and then watches the data to assess the procedure. Most behavior management procedures that prove successful go through a period of evolution.

The procedure is begun, the change evaluated, procedures are modified, and the data are monitored to assess the effects of various alterations. This ability to "let the data speak" is the hallmark of the "attitude of science" of which Skinner spoke (Skinner, 1954).

Many behavior change projects succeed or fail at the time of introduction, for the introduction of the strategy is itself an antecedent to the desired change. The manager should try to evoke as much participation as possible by the individual whose behavior he hopes to change. Every manager and employee wants to feel that he has as much control over his work environment as possible. If a procedure is introduced with no participation in its design by the individual who will be affected by that procedure, it has the effect of denying control to the individual. If the manager can involve the employee in the design and establishment of a new set of contingencies, that employee is more likely to cooperate with the change. The introduction of a behavior change procedure usually involves the setting of an objective for performance. It is the manager's job to establish these objectives in such a way that the objectives "belong" to the employee.

This ability to obtain commitment to the objective of a behavior change project and to establish a sense of mutual effort rather than of an imposed requirement demands skilled communication on the part of the manager. Poor performance may have resulted from poor communication at the outset. Over several years of implementing performance improvement projects the author's organization has found training in communication skills to be an essential element of effective application of behavioral principles. One of our first occasions to recognize the need for communication training occurred when a line supervisor planned a project to measure performance in a textile mill and provide each employee with visual and verbal feedback and reinforcement. The consultant had helped the supervisor design the program, and the day arrived for the supervisor to go out on the plant floor, make contact with the employee, and socially reinforce the improved performance. To the consultant's surprise the supervisor appeared nervous and frightened and asked "But what do I say to him?" After twenty years of managing by directives and threats of punishment this is a very difficult change for a manager. Many managers and supervisors literally do not know what to say to reinforce an employee.

This problem has also showed itself in differing interpretations by managers and employees of the manager's own behavior. On several occasions managers reported that their behavior change projects were not working. The data on an individual's performance showed no improvement. When the consultant reviewed the project with the manager, the manager may have reported that he was giving feedback to his employees on their performance twice a day. The consultant, certain that this schedule of feedback would produce a change in performance, went to the employees to ask if the manager was actually providing this feedback. The employees reported that the manager had said nothing to them about their performance. After observing the manager's behavior of providing feedback, the consultant concluded that the problem was the different perception the manager had of his own behavior and the employee's perception of that same behavior. The manager might have said "OK Bob, keep up the good work." The manager may have interpreted this as providing feedback on Bob's performance. Bob did not, however, recognize this as feedback of any sort and certainly didn't recognize this comment as social approval. The tone of the manager's voice, timing of presentation, and other factors affect how the manager's communication is received by the employee.

Both of these cases illustrate the need for many managers to experience workshop training in communication skills that allow the manager to develop the interpersonal skills required for successful management of employees. It is not enough to know that he should reinforce his employees, he must also have the skill to communicate appreciation in a manner that will be "received" as reinforcement.

### EVALUATION

The feature of behavior management that most clearly distinguishes it from other management or performance improvement techniques is evaluation. The behavior manager not only believes in the value of evaluation but also makes evaluation an essential part of his strategy. The importance of evaluation is not to prove to someone else that your procedure worked. Rather, it is learning and refining the techniques of the practitioner. Behavior managers should be more skilled at improving performance than other managers because they are constantly receiving feedback on their efforts from their own evaluation strategies. The understanding of the value of data enables the practitioner to achieve a relative degree of objectivity despite his interest in his effort.

The problem in establishing the validity of a behavior management project or procedure is to establish the functional relationship between the independent and dependent variables. For example, if the behavior we wish to change is arriving to work on time (the dependent variable), and we are going to attempt to cause this increase by posting a feedback graph of the number or percent of employees on time each day (the graph is the independent variable), we must establish beyond any reasonable doubt that a relationship between the posting of the graph and the behavior of arriving to work on time does exist or is, in fact, functional.

The goal of any research technique is (1) to establish this functional relationship: When A changes, it results in a change in B and (2) to eliminate possible alternative explanations for the resulting change. These goals are met by satisfying two criteria: control and replicability. The evaluation designs we discuss below accomplish these goals. Most of the data on behavior management projects in industry present baseline data and postbaseline or intervention data. We may call this an A-B design: there is an A phase, the baseline phase, and a B phase, the intervention phase. The data generally show that performance was at a certain level before the beginning of the procedure and it increased or decreased to another level following the intervention. Unfortunately, these data do not fulfill either of the criteria for acceptable evaluation. We do not know that there is a functional relationship between the independent and dependent variables. Why? The criteria for evaluation here have not been met: control and replicability. We have no reason to believe that this change in the dependent variable (arriving to work on time, for instance) would not have occurred regardless of the change in the independent variable (the posting of a graph of number of employees arriving to work on time). Behavior may change for many reasons. Perhaps the employees were tired of arriving to work late. Maybe the change was caused by a change in seasons and an earlier sunrise. Or it may be approaching the time of year when annual performance reviews are conducted and employees become aware of their own compliance with company policies. Or their performance may have improved simply because someone did something different, the alleged Hawthorne Effect.

The burden of proof always falls on the proponent of a proposition. If you propose a functional relationship between the feedback graph and the behavior of arriving to work on time, the burden of proof is on your shoulders. The independent variable is innocent until proven guilty. The burden of disproof does not lie with the individual who doubts the relationship. The functional relationship should not be accepted until proof for the acceptance of the proposition is offered and evidence presented that the alternative explanations for the change in the dependent variable are not plausible.

There are essentially two dimensions that provide the proof that the functional relationship does exist. These two dimensions are *replicability* and *control*. All experimental procedures attempt to demonstrate this functional relationship. If A changes, then B changes, under the conditions of replicability and control. In the applied setting, particularly in business and industrial settings, control is extremely difficult to establish. If you have two identical pigeons in cages and you implement one procedure with one pigeon and hold the variables constant with the second pigeon, you can maintain a reasonably high degree of control. With small animals, control is much more simple than with large, two-legged, highly mobile animals who have the ability to talk back, form unions, and quit working. We must, therefore, rely heavily on replication to demonstrate a functional relationship.

Replicability more than any other single factor is the criterion by which the validity of a behavior management procedure must be judged. This makes a lot of sense from the most practical standpoint. The very purpose of any evaluation is to develop or demonstrate a procedure that can be reliably implemented again. If a result can be achieved only one time, it is of no value. The value of a procedure is derived from the ability to achieve a result again and again without having to "guess" or make a random selection of procedures. Efficiency is derived from our knowledge of the ability to produce a result repeatedly. Imagine the cost of starting from scratch every time you wanted to achieve a result and trying every possible change in independent variables to see which change produced the desired outcome. Progress would be slow or nonexistent. Progress is related to the degree to which we can have confidence in a procedure, the degree to which we are able to replicate a result.

Replication must also be demonstrated within some control. For example, an *A-B* set of data produced in one plant today that is similar to an *A-B* set produced a year ago in another plant does not demonstrate any replication. There are too many variables that are not controlled. For example, the alternative explanation of seasonal effects, effects of doing "anything," or a hundred other explanations or independent variables remain constant.

Two research designs that are practical in the business and industrial setting and that do meet these conditions for validity are the *ABAB* design and the multiple-baseline design.

### *ABAB* DESIGN

Figure 28 illustrates the *ABAB* design. The first *A* represents the baseline data. The first *B* represents the implementation of the procedure, the change in the independent variable, and the data illustrate the resulting change in the dependent variable. The second *A* period represents a "return to baseline," which is a return to the exact stimulus conditions that existed during the original baseline period. If these exact conditions are not present, then the validity of the experiment is questionable.

The second *B* period is a reimplementation of the procedure, or

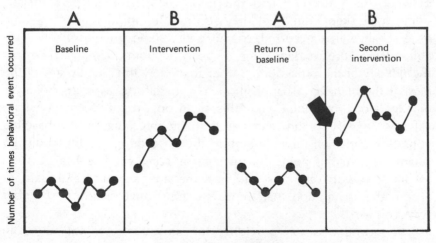

Intervals of time: Hours, days, weeks, months.

**Figure 28**  ABAB design.

change in independent variable, that occurred in the first period *B*. It is at this point, and not until this point, that validity is achieved (arrow on graph). It is at this point that the first evidence of replicability is demonstrated. The return to the baseline period does not present any evidence that the procedure begun in the first intervention phase can ever be repeated. Validity is achieved only when this second intervention phase is introduced (with the assumption that this procedure is identical to that previously implemented).

There are some obvious difficulties in implementing *ABAB* designs in business and industry. The sales manager who has witnessed the institution of behavior management procedures and observed improvement in the data is going to be reluctant to allow a return to the baseline condition. If the return to baseline succeeds in extinguishing the newly achieved performance, the sales manager's performance is going to suffer and the company is going to lose revenues that it otherwise would achieve. In this situation, maintaining performance takes precedence over evaluation.

One occasion that does provide the opportunity to demonstrate validity through the use of an *ABAB* design occurs when skepticism is voiced by managers who are in control of the independent variables. For example, if a procedure has been used and a significant increase in performance has occurred, you may ask the plant manager or other executive if he believes that a functional relationship exists between the procedure and the improved performance. Managers often, voice skepticism. They may attribute the improvement to some other change that occurred concurrently, some uncontrollable variable such as the weather, time of year, economic circumstances, or the novelty of the procedure. Rather than view this skepticism on the part of the manager as opposition to your efforts, as many behavior managers do, you should view this as an opportunity to demonstrate validity. Suggest to the manager that, by returning to the baseline condition and then reimplementing the procedure, validity could be established. At this point the manager is confronted with a decision to allow you to return to the baseline and acquire valid data or accept the assumption that there is a functional relationship. Either way, you win.

A second occasion providing the opportunity to introduce an *ABAB* design is when a supervisor who is conducting a behavior management procedure becomes tired of the effort required or his maintenance of feedback procedures extinguishes. He stops performing the behaviors that constitute the intervention phase. Therefore, perhaps not by design, the condition that existed in the initial baseline phase is returned to. The behavior manager may then wait a few weeks, or however long is required, to accumulate stable "return to baseline" data and then prompt the manager to reinstitute his efforts. If this supervisor is shown a graph illustrating the baseline, intervention, and return to baseline phases, he may be sufficiently impressed with the results to resume the intervention phase. A little prompting, reinforcement, and modeling on the part of the behavior manager should be sufficient to reintroduce the second intervention phase.

## MULTIPLE BASELINES

The multiple-baseline design is probably the most applicable to organizational behavior management. It avoids the problem of having to return to a baseline condition and yet provides the control and replicability required for establishing validity.

Figure 29 presents data as they might appear in a multiple-baseline design. There are three types of multiple baselines that can be used in organizations: (1) multiple baselines across *individuals;* (2) across behaviors, and (3) across settings.

Let's consider a procedure to use a multiple baseline across individuals. If we are initiating a behavior management procedure in an industrial facility, we have many opportunities to use multiple baselines across individuals. Let us assume that we have three assembly lines with workers performing identical assembly tasks on each line. Perhap there are ten individuals on each line for a total of thirty. Each line is considered a group of individuals, and we gather baseline data on the performance of each group. The behavior we wish to increase is the rate of assembly of our product, widgets. This is our dependent variable. We identify as our independent variable the feedback that the assembly workers are receiving.

We begin by recording the rate of assembling widgets for all three groups. We are collecting baselines for each group at the same time. These data would appear on a graph similar to those in Figure 29 during the A phase.

Once we have established a stable baseline, we introduce the procedure, change the independent variable, perhaps showing a graph of the number of widgets assembled during the day to each member of the first assembly line. We do not use this procedure with assembly lines 2 and 3, which serve as control groups while we observe the effect of the procedure on group 1. This is illustrated in Figure 29 during the B phase. Assuming that the feedback has the desired effect, we see an increase in the performance of the workers on assembly line 1.

The procedure should now be continued during the B phase until the data for assembly line 1 begin to stabilize. Up to this point we have met one of the two criteria for validity: *control*. We have demonstrated a change in the dependent variable while showing that two similar groups, with similar baselines, who did not experience the change in the independent variable, the feedback, did not change in performance. This control eliminates the possibility of most alternative explanations, such as a change in the weather. If the change in the performance of assembly line 1 was caused by a change in the weather, why didn't assembly lines 2 and 3 experience the improvement?

We have not yet demonstrated the second criterion for validity: replicability. This is achieved in the C phase, during which *the same procedure* is used with the second group, assembly line 2. The procedure is continued that you began with assembly line 1, and you continue the baseline for group 3. These two groups, 1 and 3, serve as control groups while you change the procedure with group 2.

In Figure 29, phase C, you see that the second assembly line also responds to the feedback procedure, as did assembly line 1 during the previous phase. You have now demonstrated both criteria for validity: *control* and *replication*.

The more baselines you have and the more separate implementations the greater the validity of your data. Every time you can replicate a procedure and obtain the same result, the stronger the argument that a functional relationship does exist between the independent and dependent variables, in this case the feedback and the rate of assembly.

During phase D, illustrated in Figure 29, you see that the third assembly line experienced the beginning of the feedback procedure and also responded to the procedure in the same manner as groups 1 and 2. During this phase groups 1 and 2 serve as the control groups while group 3 experiences the change in independent variables.

This procedure of multiple baselines across individuals could be applied to several individuals in a department of a plant, to different salespersons in a sales organization, to different shifts or departments in a plant, or to different plants. The important factor is to be sure that the baselines are acquired for the same dependent variable, at the same time, and that the same independent variable is changed during the different periods. If the baselines are not recorded for the same periods, there is no validity.

The second type of multiple baseline, across behaviors, is also readily applied to industry. In this procedure you identify two, three, or more behaviors of the same individuals or groups and collect baseline data, at the same time, on all three of the behaviors. You then introduce the behavior change procedure for one behavior while holding conditions constant for the other behaviors and using the data on those behaviors as control data in the same manner as previously described.

A graph for a multiple baseline across behaviors would look identical to that of Figure 29. This time, however, the baselines represented during phase A would be for different behaviors such as (1) arriving to work on time, (2) attendance; and (3) leaving work only after 5:30. You record baseline data for each of these behaviors during the same period of time, period A. You then introduce your change in independent variable, perhaps a consequence such as verbal praise,

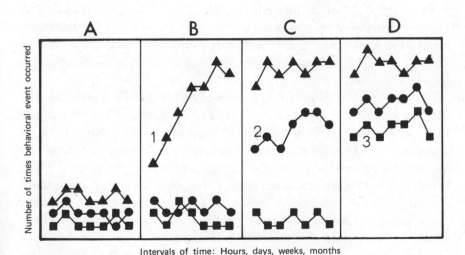

Intervals of time: Hours, days, weeks, months

**Figure 29**   Multiple-baseline design.

for each individual in the group who arrives to work on time. While you initiate this change for your first behavior, you hold the conditions constant for the other two behaviors, providing your control. This would appear as phase *B*. Again you then institute the *same* procedure with the second behavior, and then during the following phase with the third behavior. Each time that the independent variable is changed for one behavior, the data reflecting the constant conditions for the other behaviors serve as your control. Again you establish both control and replicability.

The third type of multiple baseline, multiple baseline *across settings,* must involve the same subjects and behavior, but within different settings. This type of multiple baseline is not as practical in most organizations because people tend to perform one task in one setting and different tasks in other settings. You may, however, have a worker, for example a maintenance worker, who cleans production equipment. He may clean equipment in three different departments, three floors of a building, or three different plants. These may serve as the different settings and provide the opportunity to use three baselines, one for each setting, and implement the procedure in one setting, while holding the other two settings constant. The behavior might be the rate of work or the degree of cleanliness achieved. Verbal praise and feedback might be the independent variable. You could easily establish the baselines for this *one* individual (or a group of individuals, but not a different individual or different groups) and use the procedure in phases with different settings for controls and replication. Again the graph would be similar to that presented in Figure 29, each baseline this time representing the chosen behavior in a specific setting.

There can be powerful consequences for having data that can support your efforts, most of them economic. As the manager responsible for achieving performance improvement, you want to gain support for your efforts. Data that are valid and for which you can explain the validity help you gain support for your efforts from plant managers and corporate executives. This may result in continuing the expenditures required to maintain the existing behavior management program and result in expansion of your program to other facilities. These data also increase your own confidence in the work you have done and provide documentation that is hard to dispute by anyone who may wish to take credit away from the program or assign the results to some other variable.

We know that every behavior management program must be supported by data. If you are going to go to the effort of counting and recording behavior, you can, with just slightly more effort, do so in a way that provides data that cannot be refuted.

## MAINTAINING HIGH PERFORMANCE

Once a behavior change procedure has been begun and has succeeded in producing a higher rate of performance, the problem of maintaining that performance must be addressed. High rates of performance achieved for a short period of time are not likely to remain at that high rate without a planned effort on the part of the manager. Generally, there are two reasons why the rate of performance may revert to its original rate. First the contingent reinforcers that were provided and that resulted in the new rate of performance are withdrawn, resutling in extinction. Second the individual may tire or satiate on the reinforcers that are maintaining the new rate of performance.

The withdrawal of the reinforcers generating the new level of performance is perhaps the most common reason why behavior management efforts, which at first produced desired results, fail to maintain those results. A supervisor in a manufacturing plant may institute a procedure whereby he measures the rate of first-quality units produced. He may measure the rejects and reinforce his employees for the rate of first-quality goods produced, and this should result in a reduction of rejects, or second-quality goods. He may have included in this project a combination of weekly meetings with his employees, at which time the data on their previous weeks' production are presented, and he leads the group in a goal-setting exercise. He asks the employees to set both individual and group goals for numbers of first-quality goods. He then draws a line on a feedback graph indicating the goal level of first-quality goods for the coming week. The supervisor then posts the graph in a prominent position in the plant so that each employee can look at the graph each day and see how they are doing relative to their goals. The supervisor is to post the new data each day on the graph. He also plans to circulate in the production area each day and discuss the levels of production with each individual, maintaining a high level of positive to negative comments. He plans to count the number of positive to negative comments he makes, with a goal of a four-to-one, positive-to-negative ratio. He, in particular, plans to reinforce verbally those employees who are exceeding their goal.

This project, typical of thousands conducted in manufacturing facilities, requires a fair amount of new behavior on the part of the supervisor. His behaviors are the events that serve as reinforcement for his employees. If he stops his behavior, such as the posting of the daily data on the graph, verbally reinforcing his employees, or conducting the group meetings, the reinforcing events terminate for the employees. Because their behavior is no longer being reinforced, their performance extinguishes. This is a common sequence of events. One of the keys to successfully maintaining a behavior management effort is to sustain the behavior of the supervisor in his management of his employees. If the supervisor's behavior of posting the data on the graph, and so forth can be continued, the results continue to be achieved.

The supervisor's behavior must be reinforced if it is to continue to generate the results from the line employees. In many plants in which serious behavior management efforts have been made an individual is trained as a behavior management consultant or coordinator. His functions are to manage the training of supervisors in behavior management and to manage the contingencies of reinforcement so that the supervisor's behavior continues to provide the reinforcement for the line employees. The behavior management consultant both provides the direction and reinforcement to the supervisor directly and prompts the line managers above the supervisor to reinforce that supervisor's efforts. This model of triadic intervention (the triad is made up of consultant–manager–employee) has maintained high levels of performance in manufacturing plants continuously for more than five years.

While efforts to provide reinforcement for high levels of performance must continue if extinction is to be avoided, the nature of the reinforcement may change considerably without suffering extinction. This is often necessary. A program may be initiated that simply requires more time and effort then can be maintained over an extended period. Many efforts are started with a very heavy, perhaps a continuous, schedule of reinforcement. The schedule may be gradually thinned so that extinction is avoided. The previous chapter discussed methods of altering the interval or ratio schedules and gradually thinning the schedules of reinforcement so as to avoid the extinction of the reinforced behavior. One of the keys to successfully thinning a schedule of reinforcement is to monitor the data continually to be certain that the behavior is maintained as the schedules are altered. The gradually thinning of the reinforcement from daily feedback to every other day, to twice a week, and so on, can result in the maintenance of the performance if the change is made gradually and if the individual is not satiating on the reinforcer simultaneously with the thinning of the reinforcement schedule.

The manager or behavior manager must recognize that a plan must be developed to provide for the maintenance of the new performance over time. The worst assumption is that the employee intrinsically desires to continue the high rate of performance simply because of the satisfaction derived from high performance itself. This is very rarely the case. If the consequences for continued performance are not provided, continued performance will not occur.

The extinction effect can be overcome when the reinforcers are withdrawn if the individual has experienced naturally occurring consequences. In the example described above the manufacturing supervisor may stop posting the feedback graphs and providing the daily verbal reinforcement, and the behavior extinguishes unless there has been a gradual fading of the reinforcement or a natural reinforcer has been introduced. Often reinforcers may occur in a work setting that have not previously been experienced by an employee. When an employee achieves a high rate of performance, he may be introduced to these reinforcers for the first time. This occurs in other settings as well. The school child who has never performed well may be placed on a behavior contract to increase homework and studying performance. The student may then begin to do well on quizzes and tests in the classroom. The new performance on the tests in the classroom may result in new social reinforcement. The teacher may begin to speak in a different, more positive tone of voice to the student, other students may make admiring comments, and the student may experience a reinforcing reduction in anxiety that was present as a result of poor performance. These reinforcers are "naturally" occurring. No manager has to set up a special program for these consequences to occur. These are normal events for the student who is performing well. The introduction of these new reinforcers is a result of the behavior contract that may have been structured by parents in the home to reinforce homework behavior. Now that the student is experiencing the natural consequences of high performance the reinforcers provided on the behavior contract may be faded out without any reduction in behavior. The behavior is maintained by the natural reinforcers occurring in the classroom.

What natural reinforcers occur in the work setting for high performance? This important question is one that many managers have difficulty answering. Unfortunately, too often there are very few if any "natural" reinforcers for high performance. If a planned program of behavior change is gradually faded out, there is no alternative reinforcement in the natural environment. Many behavior change programs, such as the one described above in a manufacturing plant, only arrange reinforcers that should occur naturally. For example, verbal praise by the manager should be a naturally occurring reinforcer and should not have to be structured in a deliberate behavior change effort. As in the classroom, social reinforcement should be a naturally occurring consequence of high performance. This is one management practice, while a component of a deliberate change effort, that should not be discontinued. Managers must be educated to develop this as one of their *management habits*. Many of the practices common in structured behavior change programs only formalize those management behaviors that are not currently habitual but that should be habitual if high performance is to be maintained. The providing of social reinforcement and specific, timely feedback are among the most clear examples of management behavior that should be habitual and that generally are not.

When attempting to answer the question "What natural reinforcers occur in the work setting for high performance?" the manager should examine his system of management. The next chapter presents a model for conducting this examination. The systems of objective setting, performance appraisal, compensation, both salary and bonus, and other formal management functions should reinforce high rates of performance on a continuous basis. When the employee's behavior is increased through an individual behavior change project, these systems should begin to deliver "natural" reinforcement. If this is not the case, the systems are deficient.

There are two reasons why high perrformance may revert to a prior level of poor performance: first, the withdrawal of reinforcement and subsequent extinction; second, the individual's satiation on the reinforcers provided. The first cause can be addressed through a gradual alteration and thinning of the schedules of reinforcement, the maintenance of those management behaviors that should occur after high performance and that should become habitual on the part of the manager, and the structuring of the management systems so that natural reinforcement begins to be experienced by the individuals once they have achieved a high rate of performance.

Satiation, the reduction in performance following repeated delivery of a reinforcer, may be avoided by varying the methods of reinforcement and using generalized reinforcers. At the outset of a behavior change effort the potential for satiation should be considered. Depending on the reinforcer being used satiation is likely to occur, sooner or later. Certain reinforcers, such as data feedback graphs, tend to result in satiation fairly quickly. Social approval, on the other hand, does not. The manager should be prepared to alter methods of reinforcement at the earliest sign of satiation. If a feedback graph is posted and the same graph is used for a month, satiation is likely to occur. Some managers make the mistake of posting feedback graphs for three to six months. It is unlikely that this graph will maintain the attention of workers for that length of time. Far better to post a graph with recording space for two weeks to a month and create a new, different graph at the end of that period. There are numerous ways to design graphs, including various designs incorporating themes such as horse racing or other sports. Feedback can even be tied to common home games such as monopoly or checkers. Individuals or teams can win numbers of moves, rolls of dice, or other events associated with the game. A monopoly game with four players, each a production department, with moves of the players earned daily according to the achievement of goals, can maintain great interest and produce a competition for production that results in high levels of performance. Managers should use their creativity to design varied ways of providing feedback and social reinforcement. By continually altering the method of providing feedback, satiation can be avoided entirely or significantly delayed.

Generalized reinforcers, those that are paired with a variety of other reinforcers, may also be used to delay or eliminate satiation. Money is a generalized reinforcer because it is associated with thousands of reinforcing things or events. Money does not satiate easily, because its value is so "general." Similarly, tokens of various sorts may be used to reduce the probability of satiation. The use of raffle tickets as reinforcers in behavior change efforts is effective because the tickets may be associated with many different reinforcers. A raffle may be designed to award tickets to each employee in the plant with perfect attendance for the week, each employee who met a production goal, each employee in a department in which there was no turnover that week. A raffle may then be held in which there may be ten winners, each of whom gets his pick of prizes available. The raffle tickets serve generalized reinforcers both because of the availability of a choice of things that may be won and because of their social value.

When behavior change projects are introduced that rely on a single reinforcing item, the generalized effect of the reinforcer is very narrow. Some businesses have introduced programs in which the salesperson with the greatest single increase in sales for the year wins a trip to Japan. A program such as this is not likely to produce a good return on investment, for several reasons. First, the reinforcer has no generalized effect. Many people do not want to go to Japan. A salesperson might prefer to replace the furniture in his home, build a greenhouse, or purchase a new car. Any of these may be more reinforcing than a trip to Japan. Moreover, such programs are not likely to be effective, because of the schedule of reinforcement. It may be perfectly clear to everyone that the probability of winning is one hundred to one. Against those odds, the individual is not likely to exert a great deal of effort.

The more generalized the reinforcement the more resistant to satiation. Managers can use gift catalogs, green stamps, raffles, and other procedures to increase the generalized effect of the reinforcement procedure with no additional cost and significant improvements in maintained performance.

## A "SHORT FORM" TRAINING MODEL

The 20,000 managers who have been trained to implement behavior management procedures over the past several years have not followed the comprehensive six steps for individual behavior change projects outlined above. This model, while more thorough and more likely to result in success, is significantly more complicated than the form most managers have followed in starting behavior change projects. Most of these managers have been first-line industrial supervisors. The most important factor in training them to behave in ways more likely to produce high performance among their employees is the use of some project through which *they can experience the effects* of reinforcement and feedback. By introducing simple and successful projects they become "believers" in the behavior management approach and are then more interested in learning more details and additional techniques of behavior management.

Training of managers or supervisors in behavior management is generally conducted over several months. During this period the managers generally attend weekly training sessions for one or two hours. In addition they may view self-instructional audiovisual training programs (Miller, 1974) that provide instruction in behavior management principles and assignments for carrying out the concepts. During the weekly sessions the principles are reviewed, and managers discuss individual projects they are initiating in their work area. Each manager is expected to start a behavior change project and obtained improved performance. The weekly training sessions become less training and more feedback and reinforcement sessions. The supervisors present their projects and share their successes with their peers. During these sessions the instructor can help to identify ways in which a project may be improved or modified or a problem solved.

Most of these projects follow the simplified model illustrated in the five cases shown in Figures 30–34. These projects involve the five steps of (1) stating the general problem, (2) pinpointing the behaviors to be changed, (3) counting and recording, (4) changing consequences for performance, and (5) evaluating changes in performance.

This "short form" model for behavior change projects is a recommended form to follow for initial training with line supervisors and managers. Trainers often make the mistake of presenting supervisors with excessively complicated models and theories that have a low probability of producing any change in the supervisor's world. The behavior management model may be highly simplified and produce a very quick change. He will find this reinforcing. A skilled trainer presents material to the trainee in a manner that causes the trainee to feel comfortable and able to succeed at improving his own work situation. Following this simplified model of a behavior change project enables the trainer to initiate action for the supervisor after the first training session. There is no need to wait for weeks of training before starting a performance improvement project. The supervisor can begin during his first training session to describe a general problem with which he

# Performance Improvement
# Project Worksheet

## 1.   General Statement of the Problem

Jim Gilmore, one of my salesmen, is always complaining that he doesn't have enough leads. He keeps making excuses for why he doesn't develop leads himself. His sales are way below average and he doesn't seem to be doing anything about it.

## 2.   Pinpointed Behaviors

I told him to do two things every day. First, ask one current customer for a referral; second, identify one business prospect from a trade publication.

## 3.   Count and Record

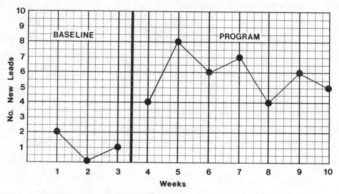

## 4.   Consequences for Behavior Change

I told Jim to do these two things; at the end of each day or the beginning of the next day I would ask him what leads he had identified. If he began to make excuses I just walked away. When he gave me names I talked to him in a friendly manner about these leads and about other things that were happening in the company.

## 5.   What Changes Occurred?

During the three weeks of baseline during which I counted the number of leads he identified he averaged one per week. During the following seven weeks he identified an average of 5.7 leads per week. He also stopped his complaining.

**Figure 30**   Performance Improvement Project Worksheet.

# Performance Improvement
# Project Worksheet

## 1. General Statement of the Problem

The plant manager complained about not having time to follow up on the behavior management programs that were being implemented in his plant and did not review the department manager's objectives as he had been requested. He generally seemed to be hassled and not to have enough time to get things done.

## 2. Pinpointed Behaviors

For 14 days I met with the plant manager, first thing in the morning, and made a list of tasks that he needed to complete that day. I kept the list so that he couldn't see it. I recorded the percentage of tasks completed each day. At the end of the day I went over the list with the manager to check off the tasks that had been completed.

## 3. Count and Record

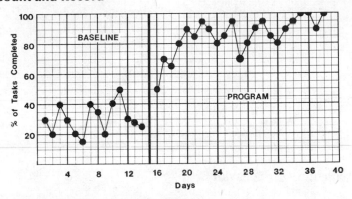

## 4. Consequences for Behavior Change

I continued to meet with him each morning and make a list of tasks to be completed. However, now I placed the list on the wall in front of his desk. I also put up a feedback graph in his office and recorded the percentage of tasks completed. I indicated the baseline count on the graph. At the end of the day I updated the graph with that day's count.

## 5. What Changes Occurred?

During the baseline he completed 30.2% of his tasks. After the program was implemented he completed 85.2% over a period of 23 days. He also seemed to be less harassed and to have more time to get things done.

(This project was completed by a secretary on her boss.)

**Figure 31** Performance Improvement Project Worksheet.

# Performance Improvement
# Project Worksheet

## 1. General Statement of the Problem

I realized that I was not sufficiently reinforcing to my employees. I was making a lot of negative comments and focusing on the negative more than I should have been.

## 2. Pinpointed Behaviors

I had my secretary keep a count of the number of positive and negative comments that she overheard me making. People come in and out of my office all day, and she sits right outside my office so she can count whether I am making positive or negative remarks.

## 3. Count and Record

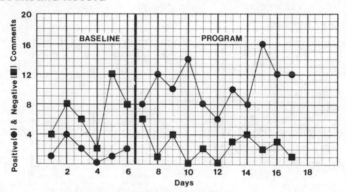

## 4. Consequences for Behavior Change

My secretary showed me the count of my positive and negative remarks and I graphed them. I kept the graph in my desk drawer. I made a mark on a sheet of paper on my desk for each positive or negative remark I made. I graphed them each day. I tried to get to a 4 to 1 ratio of positive to negative remarks.

## 5. What Changes Occurred?

During the baseline period I had an average of 1.66 positive remarks each day and 6.66 negative remarks. After I began counting and graphing I had an average of 10.66 positive and 2.36 negative remarks.

**Figure 32**   Performance Improvement Project Worksheet.

# Performance Improvement
# Project Worksheet

## 1.  General Statement of the Problem

In the #3 blast furnace area the men weren't wearing all the protective clothing they are required to wear by company regulation and OSHA. They are supposed to wear glasses, asbestos gloves, and a smock. The men have been warned about this over and over again. Most of them are usually missing at least one piece of the required clothing.

## 2.  Pinpointed Behaviors

Once each day I went through the furnace area and counted the number of men wearing all of the required clothing. If one piece was missing, I didn't count the man. The behavior I want is wearing all of the required clothing.

## 3.  Count and Record

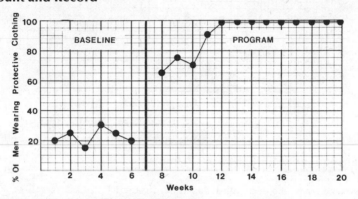

## 4.  Consequences for Behavior Change

I had a meeting with the men on my shift in the furnace area. I showed them my baseline data on a graph. I discussed the safety situation with them and asked them where they thought they should be on the graph. They all agreed to try for 100%. Each day when I counted I made some kind of comment to the men who were wearing their clothing. I posted the graph near the door so they could see it each day. They began to get on each other if someone didn't have all of their protective clothing.

## 5.  What Changes Occurred?

During the 6 weeks of baseline data an average of 22.5% of the men with all of the required clothing. During the 13 weeks that I had the feedback graph up, the average was 92.3%.

**Figure 33**   Performance Improvement Project Worksheet.

# Performance Improvement
# Project Worksheet

## 1.  General Statement of Problem

The accounting department was making too many payroll errors. This increased costs by taking up managers time and accounting time. It also caused a lot of frustration on the part of employees.

## 2.  Pinpointed Behaviors

The accounting department was instructed to count the number of errors reported back to them by department managers.

## 3.  Count and Record

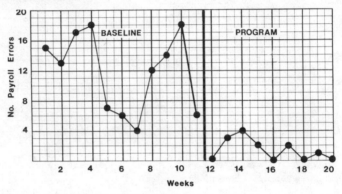

## 4.  Consequences for Behavior Changes

Each bookkeeper in the accounting department started keeping a graph of the number of errors for which they were responsible. The accounting manager discussed each error with them and assigned responsibility. The manager verbally reinforced those bookkeepers who showed improvement on their graphs or who displayed low rates of error to begin with.

## 5.  What Changes Occurred?

The number of errors dropped from an average 11.6 errors per week to 1.17 errors per week.

**Figure 34**   Performance Improvement Project Worksheet.

is concerned, pinpoint the specific behaviors involved, and during the following week, count and record those behaviors. During the next week he can begin to provide feedback and reinforce improved performance. After an initial attempt to change performance the trainer may then provide more instruction in the analysis of behavior and behavior change. The supervisor who has witnessed the effects of his own changes in contingencies on his employees, as well as the reports of his co-workers' projects, develops a sincere interest in the behavior change process. This "short form" project model, can serve as the basis for a supervisory tarining program and an organization-wide performance improvement effort.

## REFERENCES

Bachrach, Arthur J. *Experimental Foundations of Clinical Psychology*. New York: Basic Books, Inc., 1962.

Hamner, W. C., and Hamner, E. P. "Behavior modification and the Bottom Line." *Organizational Dynamics*, Spring 1976.

Kempen, Robert W., and Hall, R. Vance. "Reduction of industrial absenteeism: Results of a behavioral approach." *Journal of Organizational Behavior Management*, **1** (1), 1–21, 1977.

Luthans, Fred, and Kreitner, Robert. *Organizational Behavior Modification*. Glenview, Ill. Scott, Foresman & Company, 1975.

Mager, Robert F. *Analyzing Performance Problems*. Belmont, California: Fearon Publishers, Inc., 1970.

Miller, Lawrence M. *Behavior Management: New Skills for Business and Industry*. Atlanta, Georgia: Behavioral Systems, Inc., 1974.

Panyon, Marion, Boozer, Howard, and Morris, Nancy. "Feedback to attendants as a reinforcer for applying operant techniques." *Journal of Applied Behavior Analysis*, **3**, 1–4, 1970.

Parsons, H. M. "What happened at Hawthorne," *Science*, **183,** March 1974, 922–930.

Skinner, B. F. *Science and Human Behavior*. New York: The Free Press, 1954.

Sundel, Martin, and Sundel, Sandra Stone. *Behavior Modification in the Human Services*. New York: John Wiley & Sons, Inc., 1975.

# CASE STUDY NUMBER TEN

## REDUCING TARDINESS
## IN A FURNITURE PLANT

The behavior of concern in this project is employee tardiness. The specific study group was the K. D. Stock group of an upholstery plant. The basic changes made in the intervention phases included providing feedback (graphs and charts) and increasing the amount of reinforcement available for the desirable behavior. The project showed an increase in the rate of the desired behavior (punctuality) from 73.3 percent to about ninety-four percent.

### BACKGROUND CONDITIONS

The project was conducted in a small upholstery plant employing about 160 people. This plant receives cut fabric, frame parts, and cushion filling and performs basic assembly operations. The operations at this plant might be roughly grouped as frame building; sewing cushions, covers, and other items; filling cushions; and upholstering. The products are sofas, loveseats, chairs, and ottomans. The plant is one of many nonunionized furniture factories in the area. The plant, as well as the industry, has a high turnover rate as employees move from plant to plant. About fifty percent of the employees at the site of this project are on an incentive wage system. Members of the project group were not among the incentive workers and so were limited to earning roughly half as much as the top incentive workers.

The project group consisted of four males and one female, each having been employed for less than one year. The employees had partial or complete high school educations. All the male employees were under 30. The group foreman was also a male under 30.

Appreciation is expressed to Travis Ford for the use of this case study.

The project group was responsible for receiving the wooden frame parts, storing them, and supplying the necessary parts to the frame assemblers as needed.

The employees in the K. D. Stock group were careless about whether they punched in before 7:00 AM. While an individual might occasionally be thirty to forty-five minutes late, more often the tardiness was a matter of fifteen minutes or less and due to no specific reason other than indifference. Although the amount of time lost was not dramatic, the tardiness made quick, smooth startups difficult almost every day. The foreman had to spend the first few minutes trying to determine who was absent and who would be arriving late. The casual behavior of workers toward punctuality seemed to cause a slow start for the entire group, even those who were on time.

## PROCEDURE

The selected target behavior was tardiness among the K. D. Stock group. Tardiness was defined as punching in at the timeclock after 7:00 AM. Any punch-in time at 7:01 or later was considered evidence of tardiness. Tardiness was selected as a target behavior by the group foreman because of its ease in pinpointing and measuring, because of the high level of the problem behavior, and because of the ease in eliminating other variables from consideration. In most other variables such as production and turnover there might be several behaviors within the plant and outside the plant that would have affected the results. With tardiness, only the behavior under consideration had to be looked at.

The antecedents affecting punctuality or tardiness were not available for control, since they occurred before the employee's arrival at the plant.

The consequences during the baseline period had not been defined or controlled. For desired behaviors there were basically neutral responses, nothing being said or done if an employee was on time. For tardiness the consequences were again practically neutral if the problem was infrequent and slight. When an employee seemed to be frequently late or was ten minutes or more late, perhaps the consequence included a comment on the behavior such as, "Where have you been?" or "About time you got here." It is quite possible that some of the employees found these comments reinforcing.

There is evidence that employees were reinforced by the attention received for being tardy. Occasionally a comment such as "Were you afraid I wasn't coming in?" was made to the foreman. Most employees were confident that if they performed their jobs satisfactorily they would never be fired for tardiness, because there was usually enough difficulty replacing employees who left voluntarily.

Tardiness was measured daily for all employees. The measurement was made by simple inspection of timecards to see which had been punched 7:01 or later. For this behavior this daily measurement would also be continuous, since every possible occurrence of the behavior was measured. Although tardiness was the problem behavior measured, the results were recorded as percent on time to emphasize the positive behavior.

The baseline data were graphed for three weeks in December 1976 and January 1977. The baseline data represented a consistent and level pattern of behavior for the group, with a range of twenty percent to one hundred percent on time and a mean of 73.3 percent (see Figure 35). Although the baseline data were graphed for only 15 days, the results of the baseline period were consistent with uncharted observations of the group before the baseline was begun.

The intervention was based on graphic feedback and reinforcement of the desirable behavior. The feedback was, first, a graph of the group performance and later a chart of individual performance. The reinforcement was primarily social.

The first step in the intervention Phase I, was to post a graph of the percent of employees on time out of the employees present on each day. When the employees asked about the graph, explanations were given, and they were encouraged to get the graph above the goal of ninety percent. This goal was chosen so that it could be occasionally exceeded. Of course for this group to meet or exceed the daily goal required one hundred percent on time, since the next lower step was eighty percent with a group of only five employees.

The first social reinforcement was praise given to the individuals who had usually been punctual. In the first few days of the intervention each employee was praised for being on time and contributing favorably to the group's performance. The employees were also praised as

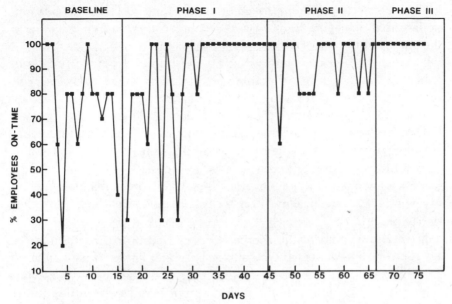

**Figure 35**   Percent of employees on time; Case Study 10.

a group each time they had one hundred percent on time during the first two weeks of the intervention.

The employees began to pay close attention to the graph and were aware of who the guilty party was when one hundred percent on time was not achieved. The employees in the K. D. Stock group would inform the foreman when they had one hundred percent on time. Any delay in marking the graph when all were on time was questioned early in the day. The group was soon encouraging each other to be on time. The one woman employee promised to bake a cake to reward improvement in the percent on time. This cake was brought for morning break on Friday, January 28. A memo from the plant manager was posted on February 1, 1977, to reinforce the group's improvement and particularly the woman's efforts to encourage the rest of the group.

After the first two weeks of intervention, praise was given less often for having one hundred percent on time. The praise, when given, began to cover longer periods of time, "Three days without a tardy, that's great; can you make it a perfect week?" The praise during this period was primarily from the change agent, the group foreman. Other individuals praising the improvement from time to time included the department manager, the personnel manager, the plant manager, and the author of this paper (development manager).

After the first complete week at one hundred percent on time, February 7 through 11, the foreman supplied the employees with donuts for morning break, together with praise.

In the period beginning about February 21 Phase II, the foreman introduced a change in the intervention that was a partial return toward baseline conditions. During intervention phase II the graph was maintained but praise for being on time was essentially discontinued. The foreman felt the graph might alone be sufficient in maintaining the behavior. This would allow him to spend more time shaping other behaviors.

There was a change in the behavior during phase II although the percent on time remained well above baseline. Phase III was initiated March 28 in an attempt to increase the level of the desired behavior. In phase III a chart recording individual performance was added to the feedback program. Now, in addition to having the percentage of the group on time graphed, the chart for each person was colored green for punctuality and left blank for tardiness.

## RESULTS

In the baseline period the data range was from twenty percent to one hundred percent on time. The mean of the baseline data was 73.3 percent. Only twenty percent of the baseline data points were at one hundred percent.

During phase I an upward trend was witnessed until a string of 15 consecutive days at one hundred percent on time was achieved. The range in phase I was from twenty percent to one hundred percent and the mean was 85.4 percent. This period included three days with snow or ice on the roads. On these days only twenty percent (one employee) was on time. By removing these three data points, the mean for the remainder of the period was 93.2 percent. In phase I the data points at one hundred percent on time rose to 64.3 percent.

In phase II the long string of one hundred percent data points was broken. The range for phase II was from sixty percent to one hundred percent with a mean of 91.8 percent. The one hundred percent data points made up 63.6 percent of the days in phase II.

In phase III, with both group and individual charts, there was a return to consistently having one hundred percent. Phase III had been in operation for ten days at this writing with one hundred percent on time every day.

The overall intervention period of sixty working days had a mean of 99.2 percent on time and the 57 days (excluding the three snow days) had a mean of 93.9 percent. The group had one hundred percent on time for 42 of the 60 days (70 percent).

The effect of having the entire group trying to be regularly on time has been to allow them to begin work earlier each day. For an estimate of the effect it was assumed that each of the five employees begins work three minutes earlier each day. This would be equivalent to gaining 62.5 hours of work per year.

## DISCUSSION

This project was done on a small group so that there could be a closer observation of the intervention procedures used and of the effects on the individual employees. Similar feedback and praise programs were used by other foremen and managers participating in the behavior management training series. For the overall plant the 1976 baseline, as obtained by sampling 1976 timecards, was 81.5 percent on time. For the last ten days of observation the average percentage of employees on was about 96 percent.

It was encouraging to see the results of this program, not only in improvement of the target behavior, but also in the general attitude of the employees. They appeared almost eager to have some measurable component of performance that they could attempt to achieve. They did not appear to resent having the individual chart; They seemed to feel that this would help the group get back on top of the graph by pointing out the one who was late on any particular day.

Phase II indicated that group feedback without some form of individualization and reinforcement was not completely effective. If the group had been larger, the effect of having only the group graph would probably have been lessened.

The individual performance chart can be very effective, as was shown in phase III. One big advantage of the individual chart was that it made praise of specific behaviors easier. The foreman was able to look at the chart and say "I see you have been on time every day this month, and I appreciate your effort." The charts were also used to post notices of congratulations. The notices were posted by department and included the names of the individuals who had been present and on time every day during a calendar month.

The major benefit of this project was to illustrate the potential of feedback and praise while using almost no tangible reinforcers.

## QUESTIONS FOR DISCUSSION

1.  The individual who implemented this program initiated several different procedures at different times. Use the specific information in this case to discuss why this staggered implementation is desirable. Refer to the evaluation procedures discussed in this chapter.

2.  Discuss why the target selected in this case was a particularly good one for an initial behavior management project. In terms of each of the six basic steps of the behavior management model described in this chapter, discuss why this case was one with which the manager was likely to experience success.

# CHAPTER ELEVEN

# ORGANIZATIONAL SYSTEMS OF BEHAVIOR MANAGEMENT

**O**rganizational psychologists have long assumed that the structure and practices of the organization influence the behavior of those within it. Numerous theories of organizational behavior have endeavored to provide a basis for performance strategies. If the behavior management approach to individual behavior change is functional, the same principles may be applied to the larger systems by which the organization functions.

## MANAGING MANAGEMENT SYSTEMS

Each system of management (the term *system* is used here as it is commonly used among managers, although this is somewhat of a misnomer) is intended to affect the behavior of individual managers or employees. A compensation system is intended to maintain the behaviors of applying for employment with the organization, retaining those employed, and engaging in the behaviors that may lead to increases in compensation. An objective-setting procedure or system is intended to result in certain types and frequencies of behaviors that are required to fulfill the objectives. A promotion system is intended to identify those individuals who are able to perform, and who are likely to perform, the behaviors required of a position. For each system of management specific behaviors can be identified that the system is intended to influence. The research in operant psychology and the development of principles of behavior management provide a new method of analyzing organizational systems and designing systems that may result in maximum performance.

Very little work has been done applying behavior management principles to the general management system. Most applications and research have focused on single behaviors of the individual, his relationship to his supervisor, and the more immediate tangible and social reinforcers that may be used to improve his performance. While this focus on the individual and immediate relationships is a logical and desirable starting point for the development of any management practice, the greatest gain will ultimately be derived by the application of these principles to the greatest number of people. This can be accomplished only through an analysis of the systems of management that affect large numbers of persons within the organization.

304

This chapter proposes one method of categorizing the management systems and discusses the design of those systems in light of the knowledge we now have regarding behavior and reinforcement.

Applying behavior management to systems and to groups of people necessarily involves some compromises with the rigid discipline of behaviorial analysis that has characterized its application in more controlled settings. In mental health or education behavior management has been characterized by the empirical approach of well-defined dependent and independent variables and precise measurement. Management systems and practices affect many persons and complex behavior of each individual. An alteration of a compensation system, such as that described in Case Study 11, in which the contingency between bonus and behavior became more clearly defined and the frequency of specific feedback was increased, produced a clear change in the reinforcement system. However, contrary to the best practice of behavior management, observing and measuring behavior were next to impossible. The salespersons affected by this point system work across the nation with little supervision. The results are confounded by numerous conditions beyond the control of the practitioner, making well-defined evaluation next to impossible. This is a fairly typical situation when management systems are changed to alter the important contingencies that govern the complex behaviors of members of the organization. Evaluation through the use of multiple-baseline research designs is possible, however, as described in the previous chapter.

What do managers do, how do they behave, to influence the productivity and job satisfaction of those who work under their direction? We know that social reinforcement, tangible reinforcement, and data-based feedback can increase performance. This has been demonstrated hundreds of times, and many of the cases in this volume demonstrate this. There are, however, many other activities that managers perform to influence performance. Why do managers plan? Isn't it to influence some future behavior of their employees? Managers spend much of their time gathering information and making decisions. Surely this process of making decisions and communicating decisions influences the performance of the members of the organization. Managers promote employees and demote others. Surely these behaviors of the manager exert a strong influence on the performance of other members of the organization. Generally, promotions and demotions are based on some system of evaluation or perform- ance appraisal. These systems not only provide the manager with information on which he may make a decision but also influence the behavior of the employee directly by providing feedback. The opera- tion of performance appraisal systems must influence the behavior of members of the organization.

If these systems do influence performance, and most managers would agree they do, the principles of behavior management may be applied to analyze their effectiveness. *Any event that influences behavior is either an antecedent stimulus or a consequence. There is simply no other possibility.* If a procedure, such as planning or objective setting, is an antecedent, coming before the behavior, the principles of stimulus control apply. If the procedure is one that delivers consequences following behavior, then the principles of reinforcement, extinction, and punishment apply. *All management systems that exert any influence on human performance present either antecedents or consequences to the behavior they influence.* Most management systems have been designed and are operated with little or no knowledge of stimulus control, reinforcement, or other behavioral procedures. There is much room for improvement in most management systems, and the application of behavorial analysis to those systems will result in both increased performance and job satisfaction.


## A BEHAVIORALLY BASED MANAGEMENT MODEL

It is helpful to have some method of categorizing the activities of managers as they influence employees. Management functions are often described as planning, leading, delegating, organizing, and controlling. When analyzed according to our present knowledge of behavior, these categories do not provide clear and useful distinc- tions between different types of management behavior. For example, exactly what is the difference between planning and organizing? Don't these overlap? Where does rewarding fall in the traditional description of the manager's activity? Is rewarding part of the con- trolling process or the leading process? Where does the establish- ment of systems of feedback fall? Does that neatly fit within the category of controlling, or might it better be described as organizing?

In view of our new knowledge of managerial and employee behavior, a revised description of the manager's task may be helpful. There appear to be five general categories of fairly unique sets of behaviors in which the manager engages to influence employee performance and job satisfaction. These are direction, performance measurement and feedback, managing consequences, problem solving/decision making, and self-management. The following are definitions of these five general categories:

**Direction.** Direction includes all presentation of stimulus events that occur before a performance and that evoke the desired performance. Managers provide direction by formulating and communicating company policies, formulating and communicating job descriptions, setting and communicating performance objectives, formally and informally communicating all desires and expectations of performance, and modeling the behavior desired.

**Performance measurement and feedback.** Performance measurement is the counting and recording of data on performance of individuals or organizational units in a manner that permits comparison over time and between comparable individuals or organizational units. Feedback is the presentation of performance measurement to the individual or individuals within an organizational unit who have control over the performance measurement data. Performance measurement includes the presence and functioning of all data systems that record performance, systems of performance appraisal or evaluation, and systems or methods by which those measures are fed back to those whose performance is measured.

**Managing consequences.** Consequences include all stimulus events that occur following and contingent on performance. These include both reinforcing and punishing consequences. Included among the common systems of reinforcement are the compensation system, both salary and incentive; social reinforcement from both managers and peers; promotions; intrinsic reinforcement derived from the work itself; and correction or punishment following undesirable performance. These systems of consequences provide the primary source of motivation that result in the maintenance of or increase in performance.

**Problem solving/decision making.** Problem solving and decision making affect performance both as a result of the quality of the decision or problem solution and as a result of the process through which the problem was solved or the decision made. Certain processes result in greater commitment to the decision than others. Both decision making and problem solving may be either individual or group processes and may be analyzed and improved by addressing either or both of these processes. The common behavioral components of problem solving and decision making, whether as individual or group processes, include problem definition, data gathering, brainstorming, decision selection, commitment to the course of action, and follow-up/feedback on the course of action.

**Self-management.** Both manager and employee engage in self-management to some extent. While the four categories of managerial behavior above may influence the type and rate of behavior of other persons, the individual must still initiate control over his own performance. The greater the degree of independence in a job the greater the required degree of self-management. Many of the procedures implemented during the past few years under the label of job enrichment have included some element of increased self-management. There appears to be a correlation between the degree of self-management and the intrinsic reinforcement or job satisfaction the individual derives from his work. The behavorial components of self-management include personal objective setting, self-measurement of performance, stimulus control procedures, self-reinforcement, time utilization assessment, feedback, and the management of stress or emotional responses.

These five categories of managerial behavior include all, or virtually all, of those behaviors by which managers influence the performance of their organizations and the individuals within them. Management occurs at every level of the organization; it is not the sole function of those assigned managerial titles. Everyone in the organization exerts some control over the behavior of others and certainly over his or her own behavior. The corporate-level managers have a responsibility for providing direction, performance measurement, feedback, and so forth, to the division-level managers. The division-level managers, in turn, provide the same management for the plant-level managers, who in turn provide the same function for department-level managers. This relationship continues to the level of the individual line employee. The quality of performance at each level of management exerts an influence on that final relationship between the line supervisor and line employee, who ultimately produce the output of the organization.

A comprehensive, organizational systems approach to behavior management can be applied at one level of the organization or at a series of levels. Obviously, each of the management functions should be performed well at all levels. Any dysfunctioning within the organization contributes to reduced performance.

An organizational system of behavior management may include five components: (1) behavioral definitions of management performance, (2) positive indicators of the performance or results of performance, (3) evaluation/analysis procedures for determining the occurrence or nonoccurrence of the management performance, (4) procedures for the development of the management skills or knowledge so that the individual manager may perform as desired, and (5) procedures of reinforcement to maintain and increase the frequency of the desired performance. Figure 36 provides brief outlines of each of these five elements of a behavior management system for each of the management functions.

The behavioral definitions attempt to define the behaviors in which the managers engage to affect the performance of their employees in the workplace. An effort has been made to define managerial behavior more precisely than previous definitions have. If behavorial technology is to be applied to the management of employee and management behavior, clear and precise definitions of behavior are a necessary starting point. It is virtually impossible to plan effective efforts to analyze, train, or reinforce behavior that is not clearly defined. The behavorial definition begins to define the general types of managerial behavior in a meaningful manner.

The positive indicators further attempt to define the managerial behavior, the behavior of the employee, and the results that will be present if that management function is being performed well. For example, under the major category of *direction, objective setting* is listed. Direction is defined as the *presentation of a stimulus event that evokes the desired behavior.* Objective setting is one set of behaviors the manager may engage in that fulfills the definition of

| Definition | Positive Indicators | Analysis Technique | Training Procedure | Reinforcement Procedure |
|---|---|---|---|---|
| **1. Direction** The presentation of stimulus events prior to a performance which evoke the desired performance. | | | | |
| *Policy Communication* The communication of all policies which are intended to affect employee behavior in a manner that results in the desired behavior. | 1. Employees are familiar with and can state all policies which are intended to affect their performance. 2. Polices are clearly stated and available in writing. 3. Employees and managers feel that company policies are those most likely to result in performance. 4. Employees and managers feel that company policies are those most likely to result in job satisfaction. | 1. Questionnaire: employee knowledge of policies and feeling re: those policies. 2. Observation and examination of policy communication vehicles such as manuals, bulletin boards, etc. 3. Observation and measurement of behavior defined in policies. 4. Management and employee interviews re: knowledge of policies and feeling concerning content of policies. | 1. Consultant to assist in the development of improved communication procedures. | 1. Feedback re: employee knowledge of policies. 2. Verbal reinforcement of managers who engage in procedures designed to effectively communicate company policies. |
| *Job Description* The definition of job functions and the communication of those definitions in a | 1. Managers and employees have written job descriptons. | 1. Examination of written job descriptions and counting of % of employees who | 1. Consultant to assist in the development of job descriptions with managers. | 1. Reinforce managers contingent upon employee's knowledge of job defini- |

| | | | |
|---|---|---|---|
| manner that results in performance consistent with those definitions. | 2. Written job descriptions accurately define the individual's functions and responsibilities.<br>3. The individual is able to state his functions and responsibilities in a manner consistent with his written job description. | have written job descriptions.<br>2. Interviews to determine individual's knowledge of his job definition and contrast between verbal description of job and job description.<br>3. Questionnaire asknig employee and manager if he knows his job functions and responsibilities and if he has a written job description. | 2. Written training materials regarding job definition. | tion and functions.<br>2. Feedback to managers re: employee's knowledge of job description and accuracy of job descriptions. |
| *Planning*<br>The process of defining performance direction and output and establishing long term objectives based on considerations of all input or resource variables. | 1. The organization has long term (2+ years) plan for output type and level.<br>2. The organization has a long term plan for resource (manpower, capital, etc.) utilization.<br>3. The organization has a yearly plan for all major input and output variables.<br>4. The annual plan was formulated with the | 1. Examination of plan to determine completeness, consideration of resources, etc.<br>2. Interviews and questionnaires to managers to determine participation in the planning process and knowledge and use of the plan.<br>3. Simulations to observe decision making process regarding the planning. | 1. Training seminar re: the planning process.<br>2. Literature on the planning process.<br>3. Consultant to assist in the formulation of a long term plan.<br>4. Simulation of planning process. | 1. Social reinforcement of manager's participation in planning process.<br>2. Feedback on completion of planned objectives and activities.<br>3. Data feedback and graphing of each measurable variable in the plan. |

**Figure 36** Organizational systems outline. Copyright Behavioral Systems, Inc., Atlanta, Georgia, 1976. Used by permission.

| Definition | Positive Indicators | Analysis Technique | Training Procedure | Reinforcement Procedure |
|---|---|---|---|---|
| | participation of all managers responsible for its fulfillment. | 4. Data analysis to determine appropriateness of the plan based on prior (before the formulation of the plan) and current data. | | |
| | 5. The annual plan accurately assesses the organization's ability to produce and potential to market production. | | | |
| | 6. The organization has a plan for the development of its human resources. | | | |
| | 7. The organization has a plan for the development of its product/services. | | | |
| | 8. The plan of various units within the organization are linked both horizontally and vertically. | | | |
| | 9. The plan provides for specific measurement of its success and for short term periods of review. | | | |

10. The plan includes contingency courses of action if external factors are altered.
11. The plan is communicated to all responsible for its completion.

*Objective Setting*
The process of determining short term (1 year or less) measurable results, the actions required and the date by which the result is to be achieved.

1. Each manager and employee has specific measurable objectives for which he is responsible.
2. Objectives are considered to be both reasonable and challenging.
3. All objectives indicate results which are directly measurable.
4. All objectives indicate specific dates by which the results are to be achieved.
5. Objectives are set in a participative process that evokes commitment on the part of the indi-

1. Examination of written objectives to determine specificity, measurability, completion date.
2. Interviews with managers and employees to determine their feeling of challenge and achievability.
3. Data Analysis to compare actual performance to objective.
4. Questionnaire to determine employee/manager perception of the objective setting process (participation).
5. Data Analysis to determine relationship between reinforcing consequences and

1. Seminar training in objective setting including practice in writing objectives and rehearsal of negotiation process.
2. Consultation to assist in the design of objective setting procedures/systems, to give feedback to managers on the current process, and assist in implementation of revised systems.
3. Written training materials, case studies, etc.

1. Social and tangible reinforcement of managers contingent upon successful objective setting procedures.
2. Social and tangible reinforcement contingent upon objective completion.
3. Feedback to managers and employees on the performance data versus objectives.
4. Feedback to managers on the employees' perception of the objective setting process.

**Figure 36** *continued.*

313

| Definition | Positive Indicators | Analysis Technique | Training Procedure | Reinforcement Procedure |
|---|---|---|---|---|
| | vidual who must achieve the objective.<br>6. The individual performs in a manner that indicates his committment to achieving the objective.<br>7. Group objectives are set, as well as individual objectives.<br>8. Group objectives are set in a process of consultation which involves all persons responsible for the objective.<br>9. Feedback and reinforcement are delivered contingent on the achievement of all objectives. | objective completion.<br>6. Simulation of objective negotiation between manager and employee. | | |
| *Instruction*<br>The verbal or written direction provided to employees which | 1. Day to day instructions are clear and understandable to the employee. | 1. Behavioral observation of instructions.<br>2. Questionnaire to identify employee | 1. Seminar training including behavior rehearsal of instruction situations. | 1. Feedback to managers on the employee's perception of the instructions |

directs short term activities.

*Communication*
The verbal interaction between the manager and employee through which information regarding job performance is given and received.

feelings re: day-to-day instructions.

2. The employee feels that the instructions he receives are helpful to him in achieving his objectives.
3. Only those instructions which are necessary are provided.
4. Instructions are timely and complete.

1. Employees feel comfortable discussing work related problems, concerns and ideas.
2. When decisions are requested they are made promptly.
3. Day-to-day direction communicated to employees are almost always followed.
4. When an employee presents a suggestion which he feels will improve a work related situation, the manager is eager to

1. Simulations of manager/employee communication situations and group meetings.
2. Observations of manager/employee interaction and group meetings.
3. Interviews and questionnaires to managers and employees to determine their perception of the communication between individuals within the organization.

which he recieves.

1. Social reinforcement, by superior, of managers' demonstration of effective communication.
2. Feedback to managers on their employees' perception of the communication process in the organization.

1. Seminar training to provide rehearsals, modeling, and development of communication and listening skills.
2. Seminar training in conducting group meetings.

**Figure 36** *continued.*

315

| Definition | Positive Indicators | Analysis Technique | Training Procedure | Reinforcement Procedure |
|---|---|---|---|---|
| | listen and consider the suggestion.<br>5. The frequency of communication between manager and employee of all information required in a timely manner.<br>6. Group meetings are held for the purpose of facilitating vertical and horizontal communication. | | | |
| *Modeling*<br>The procedure of observing a behavior or set of behaviors and subsequently imitating those behaviors. | 1. Managers behave in a manner consistent with all company policies and procedures.<br>2. Managers generally behave in a manner consistent with the behavior they desire of their employees.<br>3. Managers will arrange desirable models for individuals whose | 1. Interviews with managers and employees to determine presence of positive indicators.<br>2. Questionnaire to determine employee perception of modeling influence.<br>3. Observation of managerial behavior to compare to stated policies and desired performance. | 1. Seminar training on the principles of modeling and identification of specific behavior to be modeled in working setting. | 1. All reinforcement systems which apply to managers should reinforce those behaviors which they should be modeling.<br>2. When required, the manager should plan modeling to increase specific behavior and this should be socially reinforced by his superior. |

behavior they wish to change.

4. Employees feel that there are individuals in their work setting who exhibit behavior consistent with that which they feel is expected of them.

**2. Performance Measurement and Feedback**  The measurement of behavior or results of behavior of both individuals and groups of individuals and the presentation of that data in a manner that provides for comparison over time and between groups or individuals.

*Data Systems*

Those ongoing systems which record and report the results of performance.

1. There are procedures which regularly record the data on all major performance variables.
2. Those data are up to date. (No data more than 30 days past recording date.)
3. Data are maintained over a period of at least one year for analysis.
4. Statistical procedures are employed to determine trends.
5. The data are available to all managers

1. Examine data to judge completeness, schedule, form, recency.
2. Interview managers to determine relevance, timeliness, and accuracy of data.
3. Interview and questionnaire to determine use of data.

1. Consultant to assist in the formulation of revised data systems.
2. Consultant to assist in formulating data utilization procedures.
3. Seminar training in data utilization and analysis.

1. Feedback to data systems manager on timeliness, accuracy and completeness of data.
2. Contingent social reinforcement for proper maintenance of data systems.

**Figure 36**  *continued.*

317

| Definition | Positive Indicators | Analysis Technique | Training Procedure | Reinforcement Procedure |
|---|---|---|---|---|
| *Feedback Systems*<br><br>Those ongoing systems which provide data on performance to those individuals whose behavior results in the performance. | who are responsible for a data variable.<br><br>1. Each individual receives data-based feedback on each of the major data variables resulting from his performance.<br>2. Reports on major data variables are available to each manager at least monthly.<br>3. Data is provided on a regular and timely basis.<br>4. Managers graph data and analyze the trends in the data.<br>5. Data is graphed and posted to provide visual feedback to the employee.<br>6. Data-based feedback is provided for both individual and group performance. | 1. Examine reports to managers to determine timeliness, recency of data feedback.<br>2. Examine graphs of managers and presence of graphs in the employee work areas.<br>3. Interviews with managers to determine the timeliness, completeness, etc. of feedback.<br>4. Questionnaire to both managers and employees to determine presence of each positive indicator of feedback systems. | 1. Seminar training in feedback procedures, graphing, verbal feedback rehearsals, etc.<br>2. Consultant to assist in the identification of variables requiring feedback, implementation of graphing procedures, and assisting managers in providing verbal feedback to the employees. | 1. Managers should receive feedback and social reinforcement for their maintenance of feedback systems.<br>2. Managerial ability to provide feedback and maintain feedback systems should be incorporated into performance appraisal of managers.<br>3. Feedback systems should be audited to assure timeliness, etc. Feedback on this audit should be provided to managers. |

7. All graphs are up to date.
8. Managers verbally communicate to the employee his interest and concern about the data.
9. If a significant change occurs in the data, this change is communicated to the employee promptly.

*Performance Appraisal*
The evaluation of an individual's performance which is comprehensive in its scope, conducted periodically, and which provides the feedback to the individual required for his professional development.

1. Performance appraisal is based on specific and measurable behavior and results of behavior.
2. Evaluation is based on performance over which the individual has control.
3. Performance appraisals are conducted at least each six months.
4. The appraisal is conducted by someone who has sufficient contact with the individual to enable

1. Examination of written appraisals, appraisal forms, guidelines, etc.
2. Interviews with managers to determine procedures, comfort with appraisal system, and sources of data.
3. Interviews with employees to determine perception of accuracy, helpfulness, etc.
4. Questionnaires to employees and managers to provide data

1. Seminar training in performance appraisal, its techniques, skill development in rating, observation, communication of results.
2. Written material on performance appraisal.
3. Consultation to assist in the development of performance appraisal rating procedures and other behavioral definition, observation, and recording techniques.

1. Feedback to managers on their employees' perception of the appraisal process.
2. Social reinforcement and management evaluation based on the measured quality (accuracy, thoroughness, timeliness, etc.) of performance appraisal.

**Figure 36** *continued.*

319

| Definition | Positive Indicators | Analysis Technique | Training Procedure | Reinforcement Procedure |
|---|---|---|---|---|
| | him to make an accurate evaluation. 5. The appraisal results in specific direction for personal development efforts. 6. The appraisal is balanced in that it points out both the positive and negative aspects of the individual's performance. 7. The appraisal is presented to the individual in a manner so that he fully understands the nature and results of the appraisal. 8. The individual feels that the appraisal is conducted both for the benefit of the organization and his own benefit. | on presence or absence of each positive indicator. 5. Behavioral observation or simulations to observe interaction between manager and employee in performance appraisal situation. | | |
| *Personal Feedback* That informal feedback the manager provides | 1. The manager provides feedback to | 1. Interviews with employees and man- | 1. Seminar training to rehearse feedback | 1. Feedback to managers regarding their |

communication skills.

employees' perception of their feedback.

2. Social feedback from manager's superior for effectively providing feedback to employees.

agers to determine frequency of feedback, positive/negative content, specificity, etc.

2. Behavioral observation and simulations to observe the manager's ability to communicate feedback effectively.

3. Questionnaire to determine employee's and manager's perception of the feedback process.

1. Seminar training to develop uniform salary determination procedures.

2. Consultation to develop uniform and equitable systems of salary determination.

1. Feedback on employee perception of salary changes, reinforcing nature of salary, frequency, etc.

2. Feedback on correlation between salary and data on variables which are intended

---

to his employee on a daily or regular basis regarding performance.

his employee at least once a week.

2. The nature of the feedback is more positive than negative.

3. The manager is able to specify his feedback so that the employee knows exactly what he has done which is either positive or negative.

4. The employee feels that he knows where he stands regarding his managers' perception of his performance.

**3. Management of Consequences** The activities of the manager which result in the presentation or withdrawal of reinforcement or punishment to the individual within the organization.

*Salary Determination*
The procedure of determining an increase or decrease in salary the size, frequency and relationship between salary and performance.

1. Management has determined and clearly stated the basis of salary changes. (They are based either on tenure, performance, or some ratio of each).

2. Managers and em-

1. Examination of written polices re: salary determination.

2. Interviews to determine procedures of awarding salary increases and considerations.

3. Interviews and ques-

**Figure 36**  *continued.*

| Definition | Positive Indicators | Analysis Technique | Training Procedure | Reinforcement Procedure |
|---|---|---|---|---|
| | ployees feel that salaries are a good indication of an individual's value to the organization. | tionnaires to determine employee perception of salary as a reinforcer. | | to be related to salary determination. |
| | 3. Salaries are at least comparable to those salaries the individual could receive elsewhere for similar work and performance. | 4. Data analysis to determine correlation between salaries, tenure, performance appraisal, and other variables. | | |
| | 4. The employee considers his salary to be reasonable compensation. | 5. Analysis of organization's salary data compared to industry, professional or other comparative group data. | | |
| | 5. The frequency of salary increases is sufficient to provide reinforcing value. | | | |
| | 6. The relationship between salary and performance is sufficiently clear to provide reinforcement of desired performance. | | | |

322

*Bonus Determination*

The procedure of determining the size, frequency, and relationship between bonus and performance.

1. Criteria upon which bonuses are based is clearly stated and adhered to.
2. Employees feel that they can earn increased bonuses as a direct result of increased performance on their part.
3. Bonuses are delivered at least semi-annually.
4. Bonuses are delivered on a ratio schedule (contingent on the achievement of a number of responses or results, rather than the passage of time).
5. Criteria for bonuses are objective and measurable and the employee feels that he has control over these measures.
6. The individual considers the bonus to be highly motivating and can report that his behavior is affected by the delivery of a bonus.

1. Examination of written bonus policies and procedures.
2. Interviews with managers and employees to determine perception of the contingency between bonus and behavior and the perception of the effect of the bonus on behavior.
3. Questionnaire to determine employee perception of the effect of the bonus and its relation to performance.
4. Data analysis of bonuses delivered and correlation between bonus and data on performance and performance appraisal.

1. Seminar training to develop uniform bonus determination procedures (this will likely tie into the training re: performance appraisal).
2. Consultation to assist in the design of bonus system (the contingencies to performance, accounting procedures, determination procedures).

1. Feedback to managers re: employee perception of effect of bonus.
2. Feedback based on data analysis of bonus data.
3. Reinforcement, social and tangible, to managers for high performance of employees.

**Figure 36** *continued.*

323

| Definition | Positive Indicators | Analysis Technique | Training Procedure | Reinforcement Procedure |
|---|---|---|---|---|
| *Promotion Determination*<br>The procedure whereby promotions are awarded. | 1. There are procedures whereby promotions are based on measures of an individual's performance and demonstrated ability.<br>2. Employees feel that promotions are given to those who have demonstrated their ability to perform.<br>3. Employees feel that they can earn a promotion through performance. | 1. Interviews with managers and employees to determine their perception of relationship between promotions and performance.<br>2. Examination of any written policies, selection criteria, etc. | 1. Consultation to assist in the development of promotion guidelines and procedures. | 1. Feedback to managers on the success of the individuals whom they have promoted.<br>2. Feedback to managers on the feelings of employees regarding promotions |
| *Social Reinforcement*<br>Those interactions between two individuals in the work setting which result in an increase in a work performance. | 1. Employees feel that their manager does recognize their performance when it is good.<br>2. Employees can recall one recent (within the past week) incident when their managers com- | 1. Interviews and questionnaires to determine employees' perception of the social reinforcement they receive from their managers.<br>2. Behavioral observation of managers to observe their inter- | 1. Seminar training to teach the value and effect of social reinforcement and behavior rehearsal to develop socially reinforcing skill.<br>2. On-site consultation to model and provide feedback to man- | 1. Reinforcement of managers for outcome data changes which are the result of improved social reinforcement.<br>2. Feedback to managers re: employees' perception of the recognition which |

324

mented on their good performance.
3. Managers say that they feel comfortable telling an employee that he is doing a good job.
4. Empolyees feel that the company makes a serious effort to recognize superior performance.
5. Employees feel that their good performance is recognized by their fellow workers.

actior with employees and count the number of reinforcing responses on the part of the manager.

agers on their social reinforcing behavior.

they receive.
3. Social reinforcement of managers by superior following social reinforcement of their employees.

*Intrinsic Reinforcement*
That reinforcement which is received in the course of performing the job and is the function of events directly associated with the job itself.

1. Observation of work tasks to determine variety/repetition factor.
2. Interviews and questionnaires with employees to determine their satisfaction, perception of decision making ability, knowledge of performance level, social interaction, etc.
3. Interviews with

1. Seminar training of managers in theory and practice of behaviorally-based job enrichment.
2. Seminar training in specific procedures designed for their work setting to increase intrinsic reinforcement.
3. Consultant to assist in the design of task alteration to increase

1. Feedback to managers re: their employees' perception of each positive indicator.
2. Reinforcement, both socially and tangibly, of managers for achieving objectives related to increasing intrinsic reinforcement.

**Figure 36** *continued.*

325

| Definition | Positive Indicators | Analysis Technique | Training Procedure | Reinforcement Procedure |
|---|---|---|---|---|
| | performance and generates feedback on his performance. 5. The manager involves the employee in decision making which will affect his work. 6. The employee works with other employees as a team (including group objectives, group problem solving, decision making, and group reinforcement). 7. The frequency of interaction between employees establishes social reinforcement associated with the work. | managers to determine their perception of worker autonomy and decision making ability. | intrinsic reinforcement. | |
| *Correcting* Procedures which reduce the occurrence of undesirable behavior. | 1. Managers and employees feel that when an individual is performing poorly, action is taken promptly to | 1. Interviews with managers and employees to determine perception of probability that poor performance will be | 1. Seminar training in correcting skills, theory, and behavior rehearsal to develop correcting skills. | 1. Feedback to managers re: the employees' perception of correcting skills. 2. Reinforcement of managers by their |

superiors for prompt action re: situations which require correcting.

corrected, promptness and emotional content of correcting, and direction provided for improvement.
2. Questionnaires to determine the above.
3. Behavioral observation of correcting skills of managers.
4. Simulations of situations requiring correcting procedures.

correct the poor performance.
2. When poor performance is corrected, the individual is given clear direction as to how to improve his performance.
3. The actions which are taken to correct poor performance are effective, yet do not create a generally punitive environment.
4. Managers are able to correct poor performance without becoming emotionally upset by the poor performance or the actions required to correct the situation.

**4. Problem Solving/Decision Making** Those behaviors engaged in by either an individual or a group of individuals to arrive at the selection of a problem solution or decision and which has fully considered all relevant inputs, alternatives, and consequences.

*Individual Problem Solving*
The behaviors in which an individual

1. When problems occur the individual responds promptly

1. Simulations of problem solving situations.

1. Seminar training and rehearsal of problem solving.

1. Feedback to managers on the thoroughness and

**Figure 36** *continued.*

327

| Definition | Positive Indicators | Analysis Technique | Training Procedure | Reinforcement Procedure |
|---|---|---|---|---|
| engages to select a problem solution having fully considered the causes of the problem, inputs to a solution, alternatives, and consequences of potential solutions. | by initiating problem solving. 2. Problem solutions are arrived at promptly. 3. Problems are analyzed in specific, pinpointed terms, rather than in generalities. 4. The causes of a problem are analyzed prior to selection of a problem solution. 5. Input is requested and encouraged by all those who may have knowledge of the problem prior to selecting a solution. 6. Alternative courses of action are thoroughly considered and evaluated prior to the selection of a problem solution. 7. Prior to the selection of a solution, the consequences of | 2. Interviews and questionnaires to determine manager and employee perception of past problem solving. 3. Behavioral observation of problem solving situations. | 2. Written and audiovisual materials on problem solving models. | effectiveness of their problem solving by their managers and by trainers following simulations. 2. Feedback from employees and managers on their perception of the current problem solving process. 3. Social reinforcement of prompt and effective problem solving. |

*Individual
Decision Making*
The behaviors in
which an individual
engages to select a
course of action
which will assure
the continued
effective functioning
of the work process.

that solution have
been carefully
considered.

1. Production proc-
   esses are monitored
   in a manner that
   assures decision
   making in a timely
   manner.
2. The decision making
   process anticipates
   and avoids poten-
   tial problems.
3. When decisions are
   made all relevant
   information has
   been considered.
4. The decision maker
   requests the input
   of all persons who
   are likely to have
   input regarding the
   subject of the
   decision.
5. When decisions are
   made, all resources
   required for the
   implementation of
   a course of action
   are fully assessed.
6. Decisions take into
   account prior data
   on similar courses
   of action.
7. Alternative courses

1. Simulation exercise
   to observe decision
   making process.
2. Behavioral observa-
   tion of decision
   making situations.
3. Interviews and ques-
   tionnaires with
   managers and em-
   ployees to determine
   their perception of
   the current decision
   making process.

1. Seminar training in
   decision making.
2. Written and audio-
   visual materials on
   decision making.

1. Feedback to man-
   agers on the quality
   of their decision
   making by their
   managers and by
   trainers following
   decision making
   simulations.
2. Social reinforcement
   and formal reinforce-
   ment through per-
   formance appraisal of
   the manager's deci-
   sion making process.
3. Feedback from em-
   ployees and other
   managers on the
   quality of decision
   making.

**Figure 36** *continued.*

329

| Definition | Positive Indicators | Analysis Technique | Training Procedure | Reinforcement Procedure |
|---|---|---|---|---|
| | of action are thoroughly considered prior to decision selection. | | | |
| | 8. Consequences of decisions are thoroughly analyzed prior to decision selection. | | | |
| | 9. Implementation plans are developed which assure decision implementation. | | | |
| | 10. Responsibility for decision making is clearly established and adhered to. | | | |
| | 11. Following decision making, the actions specified are followed up and feedback given to assure implementation. | | | |
| *Group Problem Solving/ Decision Making* The behaviors engaged in by a group leader and members of a | 1. The problem to be solved or decision to be made is clearly defined | 1. Behavioral observation of group problem solving/decision making. | 1. Seminar training to teach group leadership skills based on group problem | 1. Structured feedback from group members on group process. 2. Consultant/trainer |

group to arrive at a unified consensus as to a course of action.

prior to consideration by members of the group

2. Prior to consideration of courses of action, the group gathers and considers all relevant facts.
3. Principles or outcome criteria are stated prior to consideration of alternatives.
4. All possible alternative courses of action as stated and considered.
5. The group arrives at an agreed upon course of action following statements of preference by all members of the group.
6. All members of the group agree to accept the course of action, although the selected course may not be the preference of all members.

2. Simulations of problem solving/decision making groups.
3. Interviews and questionnaires with managers and employees who engage in group problem solving/decision making.

solving/decision making model.

2. Trainer participation in actual group procedures to provide feedback and modeling of group techniques.
3. Written and audio visual training materials.

observation, feedback, and reinforcement of group leaders and members.

3. Feedback and reinforcement from managers on success of group process with manager/employee problem solving groups.

**Figure 36** *continued.*

| Definition | Positive Indicators | Analysis Technique | Training Procedure | Reinforcement Procedure |
|---|---|---|---|---|
| | 7. Comments made during consultation are relevant to the topic under consideration. | | | |
| | 8. Comments made during consultation are not redundant, but state agreement or present a unique contribution. | | | |
| | 9. Comments follow the general order or process indicated in 2–5 above. | | | |
| | 10. The leader solicits the participation of each member of the group. | | | |
| | 11. Each member of the group considers suggestions made by other members without bias and without punishing comments contrary to one's own stated views. | | | |

**5. Self-Management** Those activities in which an individual may engage to control other behaviors that contribute to productivity.

*Managerial*
*Self-Management*
Those activities in which a manager may engage to control his own behaviors which contribute to his productivity.

1. The manager is able to pinpoint measurable behaviors which contribute to his performance.
2. He is recording or has recently recorded his own behavior.
3. He has specific, measurable objectives toward which he is working.
4. His objectives are to be completed by a specific date.
5. He currently knows the progress he has made toward his objectives and how far he has to go to reach them.
6. The attainment of work related objectives is a reinforcing event to the manager.
7. He provides himself with visualized feedback.

1. Interviews with managers to determine their knowledge of self-management practices and their utilization of self-management.
2. Questionnaires for both managers and employees to obtain their perception of each indicator.
3. Observation of managers' behavior, organization, priorities, and written indicators of self-management.
4. Simulations to observe organizational, objective setting, etc. behaviors.

1. Seminar training on self-management to include knowledge of self-management procedures such as self-measurement, stimulus control, reinforcement, and to include behavior rehearsal, training in relaxation, desensitization techniques.
2. Written and audio-visual training aids.
3. Personal consultation with managers regarding their self-management skills.

1. Feedback and reinforcement of managers by their superior and peers regarding their self-management.
2. Feedback and reinforcement delivered as a natural consequence of self-management procedures.

**Figure 36** *continued.*

333

| Definition | Positive Indicators | Analysis Technique | Training Procedure | Reinforcement Procedure |
|---|---|---|---|---|
| | 8. He prioritizes his work and first accomplishes those tasks of highest priority. | | | |
| | 9. He has recently measured his time utilization. | | | |
| | 10. He arranges his tasks and environment so that he works on one task at a time and avoids distractions. | | | |
| | 11. He plans and initiates a majority of his management activities rather than primarily responding to demands on his time. | | | |
| | 12. He states that he does not feel too pressured or tense due to his work. | | | |
| | 13. He is able to devote time to relaxation despite job pressures. | | | |

14. He is able to respond to high pressure situations in an efficient and comfortable manner.
15. He is aware of his physical state of health and plans his activities to maximize his physical efficiency.

*Employee Self-Management*
Those activities in which the individual employee may engage to manage his own behaviors which contribute to his productivity.

1. The individual employee is able to pinpoint his own behaviors which contribute to his productivity.
2. He records his own performance and he compares that measurement to a goal level of performance.
3. He has specific objectives toward which he is working.
4. The attainment of job related objectives is a reinforcing event to the employee.

1. Observation of employee behavior on the job.
2. Interviews with employees and managers to determine policies regarding employee participation in decision making, etc.
3. Questionnaires of managers and employees to determine presence of indicators.

1. Workshops training for employees in self-management skills such as self-measurement, work scheduling, feedback procedures, etc.
2. Training for managers in managing the self-managed worker.
3. Consultation to assist in the structuring of jobs so that employees may have greater participation, teamwork, and self-management.

1. Reinforcement of employee self-management behavior and of work performance following self-management.
2. Reinforcement and feedback to managers for enabling employee self-management.

**Figure 36** *continued.*

335

| Definition | Positive Indicators | Analysis Technique | Training Procedure | Reinforcement Procedure |
|---|---|---|---|---|
| | 5. He is, to some degree, able to plan and structure the order of the tasks which he must complete. | | | |
| | 6. Upon completion of a required number of tasks he is able to engage in a reinforcing activity such as time off, or he is able to complete more work which will lead to additional reinforcement. | | | |
| | 7. He participates in the decision making process which affects his work assignments. | | | |
| | 8. He participates in group goal/objective setting. | | | |

**Figure 36** *continued.*

336

*direction.* Objective setting is defined as *the process of determining short-term (one year or less) measurable results, the actions required to achieve those results, and the date by which the results are to be achieved.* The positive indicators of objective setting describe those situations that will be present or the behavior that will be present if objective setting is successful. For example, among the positive indicators for objective setting are the following: (1) *Each manager and employee has specific measurable objectives for which he is responsible;* (2) *the individual considers his objectives to be both reasonable and challenging;* (3) *all objectives indicate results or activities that are directly measurable;* (4) *objectives are set in a participative process that evokes commitment to the objectives on the part of the individual who must achieve the objective.* If all of these positive indicators are present, one would conclude that the objective-setting process, this component of direction, was successfully performed in the unit of the organization in question. Generally, these positive indicators may be used as standards against which the management functioning of on organization may be analyzed.

A word of caution is necessary in regard to this entire system of definitions, indicators, and so forth. Numerous other systems of management have been proposed as authoritative statements concerning the functioning of management. The truth is that no system describing desirable management behavior can be offered authoritatively. The research that would demonstrate the validity of each of these definitions and each of the positive indicators has not been conducted, only fragments having been done. These definitions and descriptions represent the author's best guess about desirable managerial behavior. Undoubtedly, as more research is conducted concerning the effect of management behavior on performance, there will be reason to alter these descriptions. Because these descriptions and definitions are derived from the principles of behavior that have been most empirically investigated, as well as general management and organizational behavior research, they are as authoritative as any other definitions and descriptions of desirable managerial performance. Nonetheless, the author's commitment to empiricism and academic honesty demand that this apparently authoritative definition of management behavior be accompanied by the appropriate disclaimers.

## MANAGEMENT PRODUCTIVITY ANALYSIS

Following the presentation of positive indicators, Figure 36 presents potential means of assessing the presence, absence, or quality of those positive indicators. Assessing management performance is a difficult task and one that is usually highly inadequate. Most management audits concern a limited range of management behavior or results. This limiting of scope is usually necessary owing to the complexity of management behavior. Management performance may be assessed for several purposes and the purpose dictates the nature and results of the assessment. Lindberg and Cohn (1972) describe four types of management audits: (1) operations auditing, (2) independent (CPA) auditing, (3) internal auditing, and (4) management consultancy. They describe the objectives of each type of audit as follows:

**Operations auditing.**   To verify fulfillment of plans and sound business requirements; to notify of rising problems or opportunities for improvement.

**Independent auditing.**   To evaluate the integrity of accounting information.

**Internal auditing.**   To measure and evaluate the effectiveness of controls.

**Management consultancy.**   To produce results as directed.

None of these definitions adequately describe the type of management analysis proposed here. Let us label and define our process. We are concerned with a *MANAGEMENT PRODUCTIVITY ANALYSIS*. The purpose of this analysis is *to identify the occurrence or non-occurrence of those management behaviors that contribute to maximum human performance and job satisfaction, to identify the resulting levels of performance and satisfaction, and to define priorities and procedures for improving management behavior and the resulting employee performance and job satisfaction*. Very few such analyses are being conducted, and those that are generally performed by an external consultant. Praxis Corporation, Behavioral Systems, Inc., and Performance Systems Improvement, Inc., conduct audits or assessments for this general purpose. Those conducted by Praxis generally focus on the management practices surrounding a well-defined performance deficiency. Those conducted by Behavioral Systems, Inc., and Performance Systems Improvement, Inc., generally are more broadly based, seeking to identify both management skills and systems in need of improvement. A management productivity analysis could be conducted by an internal consultant, although that consultant would need to have the authority and independence to function with no reporting relationship to the organization he was assessing. Owing to the need for complete independence and objectivity, external consultants are recommended for analysis procedures.

The management training and development function normally performed by a corporate- and/or plant-level department within most firms provides training services designed to influence the performance of the management functions. Most management training is currently provided in the absence of any clear assessment of management skill deficiencies. Training is often prescribed when the deficiency in performance is not a function of a skill or knowledge deficiency but a deficiency in the contingencies of reinforcement. Management training and development specialists could better serve their clients if their service followed an analysis that pinpointed the deficiency, not its cause. It is recommended that in the future management development professionals become management systems analysts and performance improvement specialists.

The functioning of management systems and activities should be monitored by an outside analyst to provide feedback on the degree to which they are performed in the most desirable manner. This feedback should then result in improvement efforts designed to meet the specific deficiencies identified. Figure 37 illustrates a systems approach to management and performance improvement. The results of the organization are determined largely by the behavior of the employees who produce the organization's output. The behavior of

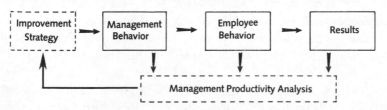

**Figure 37**  Management productivity analysis.

employees is influenced by the behavior of the managers. The managers' behavior includes all the management functions and systems defined in Figure 36. Results may be improved by improving employee performance, which may be improved by improving management performance, which may be improved through a well-designed organizational improvement strategy. This strategy may be the result of a management productivity analysis that monitors, not only the final results of the organization, but also the employee behavior and the management behavior.

Management too often becomes aware of the dysfunctioning of a management system or activity when the results of the entire organization are poor. This may show up in the balance sheet over a period of time. The purpose of feedback systems of any type is to provide management with an "early warning" of the need for change. The management productivity analysis can warn of deficiencies and point out areas of potential improvement before the results shows up in the balance sheet.

It is important that the feedback resulting from the analysis of the management functioning generate reinforcement for those managers whose performance has been analyzed. When management audits are conducted they too often result in punishment. Like financial auditors, the inclination is to look for and point out those things that are not adequate and ignore the things that are adequate. While the ratio of positive to negative performances may be a hundred to one, the hundred will be ignored and the one emphasized. This is unfortunate for many reasons, not the least of which is that this will result in more reduction in performance among those one hundred positive performances than improvement in the one negative performance.

Generating positive reinforcement resulting from a management analysis or audit is a function of the skill of both the auditor and the managers who receive the feedback. The auditor is looking for opportunities to implement improvement strategies. This necessarily results in his identifying weaknesses and attending to them. For this reason the managers being assessed often feel threatened by an audit of their systems and may resist the auditor's efforts. The manager, knowing that the auditor is interested in identifying weaknesses, tends to assume that this identification will be followed by punishment from his superiors. All too often he is right.

Management audits or analyses are usually conducted on a one-time basis. This is unfortunate. Management audits, like the financial audit, would prove far more beneficial if performed periodically. An annual audit of management performance could provide direction to management development and performance improvement efforts for the following year. If conducted periodically, baseline data on management systems could be established and the progress or lack of progress could be tracked. This would serve as extremely valuable feedback to managers. The periodic management assessment is logical for the same reason that the periodic use of any evaluative data is valuable. Data presented for one period of time have a limited value. Only comparison with other organizations, or comparison across groups within the organization, can be used to derive meaning from the data. On the other hand, data presented at some regular interval can be used to compare the change in performance of a single unit against previous data for that same unit. An effective management productivity analysis must reveal some data that are reliable, can be related to specific performance, and can be described in a way that provides for comparison over time.

The management productivity analysis should provide the management of the organization with an identification of areas of management performance that if altered will result in increased or improved output and specific economic benefits. The manager must keep in mind that the management decision makers to whom the analysis will be presented are most concerned with gaining economic benefit. Profit is the universal scorecard to which most business managers respond. Management and organizational development professionals have generally done a poor job of relating their activities to what is reinforcing to the manager. Through an effective management productivity analysis this link can be made. By identifying specific data variables, such as quality, waste, or absenteeism; specifying the management performance deficiencies that contribute to these outcomes; and specifying improvement strategies to alter both the management practice and the related outcome, financial benefits can be demonstrated. If the analysis is conducted yearly, an annual development plan and annual financial benefits can be both predicted and demonstrated.

## IMPLEMENTING ORGANIZATIONAL SYSTEMS

After the management productivity analysis, an improvement strategy for the coming year may be defined. The manner by which this strategy is implemented is critical to its success. Improvement strategies are often well founded in terms of the specific procedures and results that may be expected, but owing to the manner of implementation they may fail. *Management support and consultancy skills are the two most common reasons for failure in the use of organizational behavior management systems.*

*Management support* is gained through effective selling. This is true whether the program is being implemented by an in-house staff member or an outside consulting firm. The commitment and involvement of upper management have proved to be the most common indicators of behavior management success or failure. The key to successfully selling the improvement strategy to upper management is presenting the strategy and the results of the strategy in a way that is reinforcing to those managers.

Identifying what is reinforcing to the upper management of an organization is the first step in selling behavior management efforts. The reinforcers for upper management are surprisingly varied. Whereas economic benefit is certainly the most common and universal reinforcer, the manager often has other reinforcers. It is increasingly common for managers to derive reinforcement from the reinforcement of their employees. Increased job satisfaction is highly desired by a majority of upper managers these days. Often this desire is based on the assumption that happier employees will be more productive and bring economic benefit. However, many recognize a social responsibility to their employees to provide a satisfying work environment. The ability to produce both improved job satisfaction and economic returns through behavior management must be presented to the manager in a way that is believable. In the experience of this consultant nothing sells like success. Satisfied clients who are willing and able to testify to the impact of behavior management have been the major factor in additional management commitment and support.

The importance of upper management commitment and involvement can be well illustrated by two clients with whom the author has worked, both of whom are among the leading firms in the textile industry. I shall refer to them as Firm *A* and Firm *B*. Firm *A* has been active in behavior management for the past five years. Firm A employs fifty full-time behavior managers and has, in addition, spent approximately $2 million for outside consultation and training in behavior management. Firm A considers its return on its investment in behavior management to be approximately ten times its expenditures. Firm B had purchased behavior management consulting and training services on several occasions, but those services and the programs were terminated at the end of a contractural period. Either the consultant or the client failed to initiate behavior management as an ongoing process. Firm B can point to few, if any, economic returns from the behavior management experience.

Both of these firms purchased the behavior management consultancy at the highest levels of the organization. The presidents of both firms believed that this approach would be worthwhile to the organization. In Firm A the consulting firm, in addition to selling the upper management, was required to sell the plant or operational unit manager before the initiation of any project. In Firm B the upper management *directed* the plant or operational management to accept the behavior management project.

Perhaps the most important difference in these organizations was the involvement of the upper managers in the reinforcement process. In Firm A the president and other top managers repeatedly stated that "Behavior management is a way of life in this company." In Firm B the president did not sufficiently understand behavior management to accept it as "a way of life" or an ongoing system of management. Behavior management is recognized as a career path among the managers in Firm A. The president and other top managers confirm this by their actions in reinforcing those who successfully demonstrate improved performance through the use of behavior management. For example, the president of Firm A holds "president's meetings" for all the upper managers of the company. When a middle-level manager has a particularly successful behavior management project, he may be invited to this meeting to present the results. Attendance at, or presenting to, the managers at the president's meeting is a highly reinforcing event for a middle manager. This is a definitive form of recognition, and social reinforcement within this organization and is well used by the president to reinforce those who have demonstrated their ability to improve performance measurably through behavior management.

Behavior management in Firm *B* followed a very different course. One effort in a sales organization of Firm *B* proposed a point system, feedback systems, and training for managers in the measurement and reinforcement of sales performance. A consultant was assigned to the organization for eight months. The program was finally terminated after seven months of futile efforts to institute the proposed procedures. Although they were proposed and accepted after a management assessment and the sales organization's managers were involved in their design, they were never begun. The vice president in charge of this sales division never could find the time to meet with the consultant, even though their offices were next to each other. Recommendations were not followed, and no one could find the time to introduce the specifics of the recommended procedures. It was also decided in the middle of the program that the managers could not take the time for management training once a week. Finally the consultant decided to terminate the effort, even though Firm *B* was willing to continue paying for the nonproductive service.

At the final meeting with the managers of this organization it was pointed out to them that behavior management could not be of value unless they performed their jobs differently, assumed responsibility for the program, and followed the procedures mutually agreed on. Again the managers expressed the time constraints that they felt were of greater priority than the use of the new management procedures. They did not understand that behavior management was a way by which they could achieve *their* objectives. They viewed behavior management as something extra imposed on them.

The real difference between Firm *A* and Firm *B* was the contingencies of reinforcement operating on the line managers. The managers in Firm *A* received powerful reinforcement for using behavior management procedures and demonstrating measurable improvements in performance. The managers in Firm *B* received reinforcement from their upper managers for appearing to be extremely busy, responding to immediate crisis situations, and received no reinforcement for using behavior management and no punishment for failing to use a program for which they had paid approximately $60,000. Firm *A* has returned ten times its investment on $2 million, Firm *B* has lost all of the $60,000 it has expended. The difference, more than any other single factor, was the contingencies of reinforcement acting on the middle level managers.

While the failure of Firm *B* may be viewed as *their problem,* it is also the failure of the consultant. It is the job of the consultant to arrange the contingencies of reinforcement so that the clients do *achieve their objectives.* The consultant should have terminated the effort for Firm *B* upon realizing that the contingencies required for success were not present. A consultant has an ethical responsibility to deliver his services only when, according to his best judgment, those services can result in a reasonable return on the client's investment. One component of the consultant's expertise is to know when his services can be of value to the client and when they cannot. Clearly the value of behavior management practices can be realized only when there is a reasonable probability that the managers who must assume immediate responsibility for the behavior management procedures will be held accountable by their managers. This accountability must include the administration of significant reinforcement for the adoption and success of the behavior management procedures. When this condition is not present, the consultant should withdraw his services, providing the organization with a courteous and sincere explanation of his view of the management situation.

The consultant may gain upper management support for the behavior change effort through his own behavior. The successful consultant is generally one who is able to establish himself and his behavior as reinforcers for the management on whose support he is dependent. If the consultant and the consultant's behavior are punishing to management, he does not gain their support. Experts do not last long in the business setting without establishing mutually reinforcing relationships with their clients.

There are many ways by which a consultant may establish himself as a reinforcer. The consultant must deliver to the managers some ratio of positive reinforcers in the form of "good news." Often the consultant's job is to identify problem areas and correct those areas. The very process of uncovering troublesome areas may be punishing to the management staff. The consultant can offset this by pointing out those things that management is doing well, in addition to pointing out the problem areas. This can be done without any neglect of the consultant's responsibility to "tell it like it is" and by working to improve the organization's functioning. Every manager is doing some things right or he would have experienced total failure before the arrival of the consultant. The consultant's appreciation of the things that the manager is doing right make correcting the problem areas considerably more palatable to the manager.

Consultants also establish themselves as reinforcers by engaging in behaviors with the client manager that the managers find reinforcing. When a consultant goes golfing, plays tennis, or has a drink after work with his client manager, he is not just relaxing. He is pairing himself with established reinforcers of the manager and is thereby establishing himself as a reinforcing stimulus. This pairing is an important part of the behavioral process of creating an environment for change. The change agent, whether an internal or external consultant, must have the ability to reinforce the individual whose behavior he wishes to change. The key managers in the client organization must change their behavior if the entire process of behavior management and performance improvement is to succeed. The social reinforcement that the consultant is able to deliver is a primary means of achieving this change.

The consultant also generates reinforcement for the client managers by the way in which he presents and manages the change procedures. To the degree that the consultant assumes personal credit for the successes achieved during the program he denies opportunity for reinforcement for the managers. The intelligent consultant provides every opportunity for the internal line managers to claim and achieve recognition for the success of the program procedures. Behavioral Systems, Inc., consultants have made a practice of achieving this by turning over the major responsibility for presenting midproject and final project reports to the client managers. A midproject report, for example, is an occasion during which the plant manager, division vice president, and other upper level managers gather to receive a report of the activity and results of a project. The consultant generally gives a broad introduction, outlining the program activities to date. He then recognizes the managers who have contributed to the success of the program and turns the responsibility for reporting the data on the project results over to those managers. These managers, generally department heads or line supervisors, present the projects they have operated in their departments and the graphs of the results they have achieved. The knowledge that they will present such a report to their superiors is generally a significant stimulus for several months before the midproject review and is highly reinforcing. The upper level managers (if they have themselves been trained in behavior management) demonstrate their appreciation for these results and the cost savings achieved and express their enthusiasm and then their hope that these efforts will continue. This reporting process enables the line managers to identify the projects as "theirs" and increases their commitment to the success of the project. Rather than the outside consultant's serving as the expert who has come in and achieved results where the line managers had previously failed, the consultant becomes the individual who "helped" the line managers achieve success and obtain recognition that has great meaning to them. The consultant, rather than being resented for his intervention and assumption of credit, is appreciated for establishing the means for obtaining reinforcement.

The individual consultant, whether internal staff member or external consultant, who is able to induce change in an organization must possess a variety of skills. The ability to obtain management support through effective selling is just one. The consultant must also be technically competent in behavior management. It is the purpose of this book to provide at least the fundamentals of the technical competence required to improve management performance through behavior management.

In addition the change agent must be aware of current management technologies and their relationship to behavior management. When working in the organizational setting these days any change agent is confronted by managers who have been trained in the theories of Herzberg, McGregor, Transactional Analysis, and others. The consultant will have a higher probability of success if he does not challenge the commitment made by managers to these theories. It is far wiser to explain the points of unity and agreement between the various theories. This is a display of tact and wisdom that is appreciated by the manager. Argument against one theory in favor of another produces resentment.

The change agent must also be a model of the behaviors he wishes the managers with whom he is consulting to exhibit. The effect of modeling, particularly by one who is presented as an expert, cannot be overestimated. If the consultant models behaviors at variance with his theories and the practices he wishes managers to adopt he reduces his credibility and his ability to effect change. The consultant must display his ability to reinforce managers, set clear objectives, manage his own behavior, perform at a high rate, and while doing that look as though he is having fun all the while. This last point should be taken seriously. The change agent must enjoy his work and display enthusiasm for the effectiveness of behavior management and satisfaction from both the human and the economic benefits. The emotive model presented by the change agent has as much influence as the more objective behaviors observed.

Perhaps one of the most important and overlooked requirements of the change agent is the ability to learn and adapt. The successful change agent is open to all possibilities. He or she is aware of the limits of his or her knowledge and is prepared and excited about learning from those being taught. It is a successful approach to state "Look I don't know anything about your work or your jobs. You're the expert. I just know a little bit about why people perform the way they do in general. I believe that, if we combine your expertise and my little bit of knowledge, together we can make some improvements that will be a benefit to you!" That type of humility results in support.


## SUMMARY

The principles and techniques of behavior management are only beginning to develop organization-wide applications. Behavior management does provide a technology by which all management systems that affect human performance may be analyzed and improved. The empirical approach of behavior management results in a higher technology of management systems design owing to the respect for measurement and evaluation.

This chapter has presented a model that, it is hoped, will further the conceptual thinking of managers and behaviorists seeking to develop improved management. This model may be a beginning of a much-needed research effort that will apply the techniques of behavior management to the systems in which most of us spend most of our time and energies.

# CASE STUDY NUMBER ELEVEN

## IMPROVING SALES AND FORECAST ACCURACY IN A NATIONWIDE SALES ORGANIZATION

This case reports an effort in a nationwide chemical sales organization to increase sales and to improve the accuracy of monthly sales forecasts submitted by salesmen. An objective-setting and point system was established whereby the salesman and his manager negotiated specific desired behavior, outcome objectives, and the point values for each of those objectives for each forthcoming month, and then computed the achievement of those objectives and the resulting point earnings at the end of each month. The percent of annual bonus available to the individual salesmen was determined by their cumulative point earnings. The procedure was also applied to the district sales managers. This procedure resulted in an increase in sales volume comparatively higher than the industry increase for the three major products, and in the improved accuracy and consistency of monthly sales forecasts by salesmen.

### BACKGROUND CONDITIONS

In 1975 a chemical firm with a sales organization of 17 salesmen and five district managers distributed throughout the continental United States requested that Behavioral Systems, Inc. conduct a Performance Assessment and make recommendations that might result in improved performance. The assessment examined the objective-setting procedure and reinforcement and feedback systems as they were operating prior to an improvement strategy. It was found that objectives were set on a yearly basis and included specific volume goals by product for each salesman as well as goals for new business activity and personal development. Feedback was received monthly on dollar and quantity purchases by product for each salesman. The company had a yearly sales bonus plan intended to reward salesmen for their annual performance. This bonus was determined at the end of the calendar year by examining the objectives set by each salesman and his achievement against those objectives and by then awarding a percentage of his annual salary as bonus. The bonus award was not directly related to his achievement of objectives, but was subjectively considered by the managers during the decision making process. Bonuses were awarded on a calendar year basis, however, checks for the year's performance were not actually received until March of the year following. Because objectives were set in November and December for the upcoming year, a delay of up to 15 months might occur between the establishment of an objctive and the delivery of a bonus. Salesmen voiced dissatisfaction with this delay, and salesmen and managers agreed that a system that increased the frequency of goal setting and reward for goal achievement would be desirable.

This firm faced a problem in the evaluation and reinforcement of salesmen that is faced by many sales organizations. Salesmen function very independently and cannot be closely observed or supervised due to geographical distribution. In addition, sales performance cannot be compared across sales territories because of the market differences in each territory. One territory may have a customer which consumes a huge volume of the firm's chemicals every month and will continue to order a given product regardless of the salesman's performance. A neighboring territory may possess no potential user of the same product. This difference in markets removes any possibility of establishing uniform goals or objectives as a basis of evaluation.

The assessment also indicated that the accuracy of forecasts submitted by each salesman was an area of performance which might be improved. Every month each salesman submitted a forecast of volume by product that he expected his customers to order during the following month. The production at the firm's manufacturing plants was then based on this forecast. The firm produced about seven distinct products but there were significant variations within each product. An order would specify the density, color, and heat resistant properties of a given product. A forecast that was inaccurate on any of these dimensions could result in the production of goods that would go unpurchased for many months. Order volume was in the hundreds of thousands of dollars. Therefore, large amounts of capital could be tied up by inaccurate forecasts.

Prior to the implementation of the improvement strategy, there was no method for providing feedback to the salesmen or division sales manager on the accuracy of their forecasts. No one in the organization had a clear picture of the baseline accuracy of forecasts.

## PROCEDURE

A monthly point system was recommended to increase the frequency of negotiated objective-setting, evaluation of performance, feedback, and delivery of point (token) reinforcement which would directly represent annual bonus earnings. This system was implemented with the assistance of a consultant. Input was received from numerous managers and salesmen in the design of the point system, and all managers and salesmen proved cooperative in its implementation.

The following five categories of point were established: (1) sales volume, (2) new business, (3) forecast accuracy, (4) reporting, and (5) other. It was decided that 90 points per month per salesman would be available. The percent of the total possible points earned at the end of the year would represent the percent of total available bonus earned (available bonus was determined by a formula based on corporate profitability). In this manner each salesman could determine the percent of his annual bonus which he had earned to date at any time during the year.

An objective worksheet was devised to record the monthly objectives and earnings of each salesman (see Figure 38). The district managers were instructed to meet or telephone (this was necessary due to some of the distances involved) each salesman at the beginning of the month and negotiate the specific objectives for each product and the point values to be assigned to each objective. Determining the number of points to be allocated to the general categories (e.g., volume sales, forecasts, etc.) was a corporate level decision. The specific number of points to be awarded to certain volumes of each product and to the specific objectives in each category was negotiated between

NAME: __S. Jones__     TITLE: __Sales Rep.__

DATE: __4/30/76__     FOR THE MONTH OF: __May 1976__

| Objective Category | Objective | | | Point Value | Objective Outcome | Points Earned |
|---|---|---|---|---|---|---|
| 1. Sales Volume: (55 pts) | Total Profit Plan Assignment Divided by 12 | | | | | |
| Prod. A | 4125 | | | 20 | 3471 | 16.83 |
| " " B | 1333 | | | 10 | 1129 | 8.47 |
| " " C | 560 | | | 25 | 460 | 20.5 |
| | | | | | | |
| | | | | | | |
| | | | | | | |
| 2. New Business: (20 pts) | | | | | | |
| A. Behaviors: (8 pts/mo) | Monthly calls: | | | | | |
| | 1) Co. L | | | 2 | ✓ | 2 |
| | 2) Co. M | | | 2 | ✓ | 2 |
| | 3) Co. N | | | 2 | ✓ | 2 |
| | 4) Co. O | | | 2 | ✓ | 2 |
| B. New Orders: (144 pts/yr) | Vol. | Acct. | Prod. | | | |
| | 2.5 | Co. X | A | 4 | 1.9 | 3.04 |
| | 1.8 | Co. Y | A | 4 | 1.1 | 2.44 |
| | 2.3 | Co. Z | B | 4 | 0.8 | 1.4 |
| 3. Forecast Accuracy: (12 pts) | Product | | | | 5% | |
| | A | | | 8 | Improvement | 1.6 |
| | B | | | 2 | 25% | 2 |
| | C | | | 2 | 25% | 2 |
| | | | | | | |
| | | | | | | |
| | | | | | | |
| 4. Reporting: (15 pts) | DUE: | | | | | |
| A. Call Reports | Each Fri. | | | 6 | ✓ | 6 |
| B. Market Summaries | 15th of month | | | 3 | ✗ | 0 |
| C. Monthly Forecast | 7th " | | | 3 | ✓ | 3 |
| D. Objective-setting Procedure | 4th " | | | 3 | ✓ | 3 |
| 5. Other: | | | | | | |
| A. Accident Free Month | | | | 2 | ✓ | 2 |
| B. Telephone | Under $300.00 | | | 2 | ✓ | 2 |

**Figure 38** Bonus Plan Worksheet recording the monthly objectives, point values, and earnings for one salesperson.

the salesman and the manager. The managers were instructed to allocate the points according to the difficulty and priority of objectives. For example, one salesman may have been virtually assured of selling the majority of his objective volume for Product A because a customer in his territory contracted with the corporation on an annual basis. Because the salesman was not the critical determinant of this sales volume, fewer points were assigned to this objective and more points were assigned to another product volume goal. Another goal, although perhaps less in volume than the goal for Product A, may have required much greater effort.

The initial point distribution was established as follows: volume (30 points), new business (20 points), forecast accuracy (20 points), reporting responsibilities (15 points), and other (5 points). The point earnings were on a 90 point basis and the bonus was figured on the percentage of the possible 1080 points that could be earned during the year.

There were a number of considerations taken into account by the district managers in their monthly negotiations of objectives and point values with the salesmen. Some of those considerations for each category are discussed below:

*Volume:* Volume was the most important category because it represented the end product of the salesman's efforts. Volume objectives were established on a corporate level for each product as part of the yearly plan. The volume objectives were then divided among the districts based on the known potential business for that product within each district. The district manager then allocated the sales quotas to the salesmen based on the potential business in their territories. After the annual volume objective by product for each salesman was determined, it was divided by 12 to arrive at a monthly objective.

While the above procedure established an even distribution of volume objectives throughout the year, it did not conform to the buying patterns of the customers in the salesmen's territories. Since a customer might purchase only once every two or three months, a salesman might show no sales for a product during a given month and earn no points that month, and then show sales in excess of his monthly objectives the next month. The problem was handled by allocating points on a proportional basis. If during any month the volume of sales for Product A was twice the objective, the salesman could earn twice the points established for that objective. In this way the point earnings represented the average volume sales over time. Because the salesman earned points in the direct proportion to volume as established in the objective, he had the potential of earning more than the total number of points available for volume on a yearly basis. He could, therefore, earn more than the one hundred percent of his total possible points and annual bonus.

*New Business:* Computing the point earnings for new business presented an additional problem. New business is acquired in this market only after extensive selling has been done. This entails numerous visits to the client, test sampling of the product, technical evaluation of the product's performance, and in some cases, extensive social contact. This process may require six months or longer. The work required to develop new business presented an especially acute problem of delayed reinforcement. It was decided to take this problem into account. The 20 points available in this category were divided between the final attainment of an actual order and the behaviors required to achieve this sale. Twelve points were allocated to the attainment of the order and eight points to the behaviors. The 12 points available each month for the order were assigned on a yearly basis according to the yearly objective for new business. There were 144 points (12 points x 12 months) available for the year.

A salesman, for example, would set an objective of selling to two of three potential new customers for a given product in his territory. The total yearly points available (144) for these orders would be distributed among the two potential customers. The points would be earned upon receipt of an agreed upon order which represented the average order size for that customer. Each month the salesman and district manager set objectives for the behavior category. These objectives included visiting the potential client, obtaining a sample order, entertaining the client, and telephoning the client to set up appointments. The district manager was responsible for determining that these objectives had been achieved and for allocating the points, although he did rely heavily on the self-reports of the salesmen.

*Forecast Accuracy:* Forecast accuracy was computed as a percent error. Percent error would be zero if the salesman submitted a forecast for a product that exactly equaled the subsequent sales in his territory for the month forcast. If the salesman overforecast, forecasting 150,000 lbs. when the subsequent actual sales reported were 100,000 lbs., he would have a 50% error rate. The salesman might underforecast and receive the same percent error. For example, he might have forecast 50,000 while actual sales were 100,000. This would also be recorded as a 50% error. Points were assigned each month on the average forecast accuracy for all products. A uniform objective of a 25% error margin was established as a standard. Points could be earned either by achieving a standard 25% error, or by achieving a 25% improvement over baseline forecast error. If a salesman had a baseline error of 75%, he would earn his assigned points by improving his error to 50%.

*Reporting Responsibilities:* There were a number of regular reporting activities required of the sales staff. These included the completion of call reports, marketing information summaries, monthly activity reports, the monthly forecast, and the objective-setting procedure. The district manager was free to assign the 15 points available in this category as he wished. In this category points were awarded on an all or nothing basis rather than on a proportional basis as was done with volume, forecast accuracy, and new business. The salesman and manager agreed on the points to be awarded for each reporting responsibility and the points for that activity were earned contingent upon its completion by the specified date.

*Other:* This category was included to provide the manager and salesman with points to be awarded for activities that might be specific to a given salesman. Among the activities for which points were allocated were the following: (1) preparing a special market analysis of the salesman's territory, (2) maintaining a good safety record, (3) engaging in self-improvement and self-development efforts, (4) maintaining expenses within acceptable limits, or (5) completing an outstanding number of calls during a month. Alternatively, points from this category could be added to another category (e.g., volume, new business, forecast accuracy, reporting) to add extra weight to the efforts made in that category.

The point bonus plan was implemented with the assistance of a consultant who visited each district and assisted the manager in their initial negotiation of point vales. A workshop was conducted for district managers on the application of behavior management principles in the work place. A series of eight one-hour sessions were conducted with the corporate office management personnel including the Vice President of Marketing and the General Sales Manager.

## RESULTS

The data would suggest that the program influenced performance in the desired direction. There were three major products that comprised the majority of the sales volume of this firm. Product *A* increased 117.1% in sales volume during the program period over the baseline period. Product *B* increased 63% over the baseline period and Product *C* increased by 40.1% over baseline. These increases in sales would generally be considered an amazing achievement. The increase in dollar volume was in the millions of dollars. However, an examination of the industry trends for these same products during the same period indicates a similarly dramatic increase. Product *A* which increased 117.1% for the company increased 47.9% for the industry (see Figure 39). While the company showed an increase of 63% for Product *B*, the industry averaged an increase of 42.5%. Product *C* which increased 40.1% for the company increased 34.3% for the industry as a whole.

The data support the conclusion that the program was effective in influencing performance. There is a greater percentage increase in the

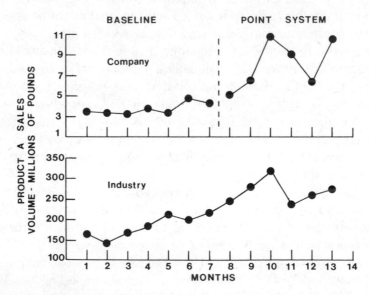

**Figure 39** Comparison of the sales volume increase of the company and the industry before and after the implementation of the point system.

company sales figures for all products than in the comparable industry figures.

The computation of market share data provide a more indicative illustration of the results than the raw volume figures. Figure 40 illustrates the market share data for each of the three major products. Average market share for the seven months prior to the program for Product A was .061. Following the implementation of the points system the average market share for six months was .063. This represents a 4.4% increase in the firm's market share from the preprogram period. Product B average market share during baseline was .052. Following the implementation it was .058 which was a 13.4% increase. Product

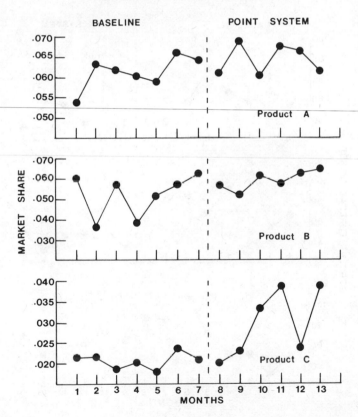

**Figure 40**  Market share data for products *A*, *B*, and *C* before and after the implementation of the point system.

C held .021 market share prior to the program and increased to .029 following the program, a 33.4% increase.

The forecast accuracy for each of these same three products also demonstrated an improvement in performance (see Figure 41). During the baseline period the forecast accuracy for Product *A* averaged 62% error margin and improved to 45% during the program period. Product *B* forecasts improved from an 82% error to an average 43% error during the program. Product *C* forecasts improved from a preprogram average of 95% error to a 90% error during the program period. This 5% improvement for Product *C* does not fully indicate the value of the change in forecasting behavior. The forecasts for Product *C* were very much more consistent during the program period, although only slightly more accurate. This consistency enabled the production

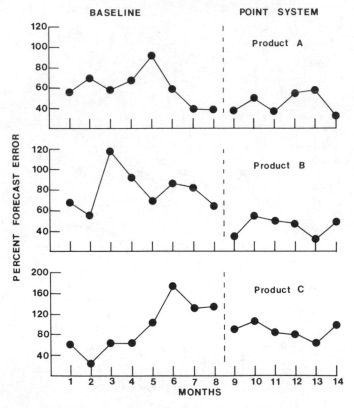

**Figure 41** Forecast error for products *A*, *B*, and *C* before and after the implementation of the point system for all salespersons.

scheduling to be more accurate than when the degree of accuracy of forecasts fluctuated greatly.

The improvement in forecast accuracy may be explained both as a result of the improved feedback and the addition of reinforcing consequences for improving accuracy. Prior to the program there was little or no feedback on the accuracy of forecasts. During the program salesmen and sales managers received graphs each month indicating their level of forecast error. The point also tied the accuracy of forecasts to the annual bonus payment.

Figure 42 lists the point earning for all seventeen salesmen for one month of the program. This distribution of point earnings is representative of other months in the program. This illustrates that the points were being awarded in a selective fashion. It was a concern prior to the implementation of the point system that the managers would establish the objectives and the point values in a manner that would

### EARNINGS OF THE SALES DEPARTMENT
(Month of September, 1975)

| Salesman | Possible Points | Actual Points | Percentage of Possible |
|----------|-----------------|---------------|------------------------|
| 1 | 90 | 92.5 | 102.8 |
| 2 | 90 | 89.3 | 99.2 |
| 3 | 90 | 81.9 | 91.0 |
| 4 | 90 | 80.1 | 89.0 |
| 5 | 90 | 77.6 | 86.2 |
| 6 | 90 | 62.0 | 68.9 |
| 7 | 90 | 58.0 | 64.4 |
| 8 | 90 | 56.4 | 62.7 |
| 9 | 90 | 55.8 | 62.0 |
| 10 | 90 | 52.0 | 57.7 |
| 11 | 90 | 52.2 | 58.0 |
| 12 | 90 | 50.7 | 56.3 |
| 13 | 90 | 34.9 | 38.8 |
| 14 | 90 | 34.7 | 38.5 |
| 15 | 90 | 29.4 | 32.7 |
| 16 | 90 | 20.6 | 22.9 |
| 17 | 90 | 16.3 | 18.1 |

**Figure 42**   Point earnings by salesperson for one month.

fail to deny points to those not meeting objectives and fail to award points to those with extremely high earnings. The actual objectives set by negotiation between the salesmen and managers provided for wide variance in performance evaluation and eventual bonus earnings.

## DISCUSSION

This program did demonstrate that a point system designed to measure performance of salespersons against objectives established by negotiation between salesmen and managers can be successfully implemented in a sales organization. There is good evidence, although open to alternative explanation, that the system did improve sales performance. In addition to the measurable improvements in performance, the managers made numerous comments to the effect that the system gave them a better means of direction and reward. Managers found that the ability to assign points to activities and results which they felt were high priorities. Both salesmen and managers expressed satisfaction that they now "knew where they stood" in relation to their evaluation and bonus compensation.

While improvements in sales volume, market share, and forecast accuracy followed the implementation of the point system, it is possible that these improvements in performance can be explained by other factors. At the time of the program implementation the economy was beginning to recover from a drastic decline. Improvements in the industry sales may have affected this firm's sales more than the average firm in this industry. It is possible that this firm's clients were experiencing a greater increase in sales than other users of this industry's products. It is possible that if this had not been present, this firm might have experienced a more dramatic improvement than the industry as a whole. When asked about this possibility, the firm's managers stated that this was not a plausible explanation based on their knowledge of their client's business conditions. The firm's managers did feel that the program was responsible for the improved performance. The fact that all three major products improved more than the industry also tends to refute this alternative explanation.

This case suggests that more controlled research on the implementation of point earning systems in sales organizations needs to be conducted. The point system augments specified direction as well as evaluation. The frequency of direction and reinforcement is also increased. The separate and combined effects of (1) the alteration in the schedule of reinforcement and (2) the increased specificity of direction and evaluation are subjects of future research.

It would have been helpful if some direct measures of salesmen's behaviors could have been developed and evaluated. Did the point system result in an increase in the activity (e.g., sales calls, etc.) of the salesmen? Was there a change in the nature of the calls made or the clients on whom the salesmen were calling as a result of the increased specificity of direction and reinforcement? Another question which is unanswered by this project is the effect of this system on the satisfaction from the work itself. Did the increase in feedback and the clarification of expectations increase job satisfaction as was reported by a few salesmen?

Point systems are one practical means of improving the schedules of reinforcement and the direction in a sales organization in which manager/employee contact is infrequent. The supervision and reinforcement of salesmen is a constant concern of the business and industrial community and is an area of high income payoff for the organization. Similar point systems may be applicable to other job categories in other types of organizations. This case presents some evidence that further investigation of these systems is warranted by the management community.

### QUESTIONS FOR DISCUSSION

1.  The point system implemented in this case affected more than one aspect of the management system. Using the outline of management systems (Figure 36), discuss which of the systems were altered.

2.  Behavior management is concerned with both the daily interaction among the manager and employee and the formalized system of management. How do you think the system changes made in this case might have affected the daily interaction between employee and manager? Why?

3.  Describe how the following principles of behavior management were applied in this case: (a) immediacy of reinforcement; (b) schedules of reinforcement; (c) shaping; (d) stimulus control.

# CHAPTER TWELVE

# CHALLENGES
# AND RESPONSES

**B**ehavior management raises many questions for the manager. He is asked to view his job in a way that may be very different from the view to which he is accustomed. He is asked to specify behavior, measure performance to obtain baseline data before implementing changes, and evaluate those changes in an objective, data-based manner. He is also asked to use a positive approach, incorporating reinforcement principles into his daily behavior, and this is likely to require a considerable effort and personal change on his part. Any changes of this magnitude are likely to raise questions and challenges. They deserve to be answered.

Similarly the student and expert in organizational behavior or management is presented with a challenge by behavior management, which is another competing approach to organizational and management improvement. Most academicians, consultants, and students of management have made a commitment to some school of thought that attempts to explain human performance and job satisfaction. Behavior management must be rejected, incorporated, or accepted as an alternative explanation.

Both the manager and the student/academician raise a number of questions about behavior management that deserve a direct answer. The following series of questions and responses are those most typically put forth by both groups.

**1.** *Behavior management is manipulative and seeks to impose control on employees, rather than encourage participation and democratic management. Won't this approach eventually result in limited performance and reduced personal satisfaction?"*

Behavior management does provide a basis for a more authoritarian form of management, if one chooses that application of the technology. On the other hand it also provides the foundation for a more democratic, participative, and positive form of management. The most important consideration is that the latter application produces better results for the organization and the employees and is, therefore, the more likely course.

In the record of two hundred organizational applications of behavior management the manager's ability to "control" has been increased. But the job satisfaction, participation, and development of the individual employee have also been increased. In the organizational setting the manager generally recognizes his responsibility for control. To manage and control are essentially snyonymous. The manager must ensure that employees are productive and produce the results that yield the income that enables the employees to be paid. The employee, at least in the business and industrial setting, recognizes the importance of productivity and performance if the organization is to survive and grow, providing personal opportunities for advancement. With this understanding the management or control of productive behavior is to the benefit of all.

In an open, free-enterprise economy, there are self-correcting systems that reduce the likelihood of suppressive, authoritarian use of behavior management. When behavior is controlled through punitive procedures, those procedures result in an avoidance response. In industry this avoidance response is most often expressed in the form of turnover and absenteeism. These are significant cost factors for most industries, and great efforts are made to keep them to a minimum. This reinforces the use of reinforcing rather than punitive procedures. In a closed, authoritarian society, avoidance behavior may not be an option, and the likelihood of punitive application of behavior management is increased.

The emphasis of those applying behavior management in industry is, if anything, overly positive. Most of the training and consulting is directed toward increasing the frequency and amount of positive reinforcement. While this increase results in an improved work environment for the employee it also results in a more satisfying work situation for the manager.

Participation in management by the employee has generally been an integral part of the application of behavior management in industry. It is typical for shift meetings to be initiated by the shift supervisor with his employees. These serve as goal-making meetings. The degree of autonomy and decision ability delegated to the shift employees may vary greatly. But virtually every behavior management program initiated in an industrial plant setting has increased the participation of the line employee.

**2.** *"With all the other management responsibilities I have I don't have time to go around reinforcing everybody!"*

Many managers don't have time to do anything additional because they are not doing the things that can increase their independence and discretionary time. The manager who successfully manages the behavior of his employees is the one with the greatest degree of freedom. If the manager is successful in getting his employee to perform well, to assume responsibility, and to work at a high rate, he has time not only to reinforce those employees but also to use his higher skills, from which he derives most pleasure and which may be of greater benefit to his company.

It is common for managers trained in behavior management to express initially the fear that they will not have the time to follow behavior management procedures. After a few initial successful experiences, however, the manager learns that he is not doing more, he is doing things differently. Where in the past, he spent several hours each day solving problems, those problems are now being avoided because employees are taking more initiative and independent action and being reinforced for those actions. The employees are solving and preventing problems with which the manager previously had to be concerned.

High performance requires no more time than low performance. The manager who applies the principles of behavior management invariably finds his area of responsibility "running more smoothly" and therefore has more discretionary time. It is this time that is often most reinforcing to the manager. It is no fun to spend one's life running from alligators.

**3.** *"If I start posting feedback graphs and reinforcing improved performance, won't my employees think that I am trying to get more work out of them without paying them more?"*

There are a number of routine assumptions in the manager/ employee relationship that are accepted by both parties. One of these is that the manager is concerned with improving performance through the efforts of the employees. Employees rarely react negatively to the desire of management to improve productivity. What does evoke a negative reaction is an effort to increase productivity that is based on pressure, the threat of punishment. Many managers and employees associate all efforts to increase productivity with an aversive procedure. When the manager attempts to increase productivity through the use of behavior management techniques, he does so in a way that increases the satisfaction of the employee. Feedback results in improved performance because it is satisfying to know where you stand, to be able to observe the effect of your efforts on some result. Reinforcement increases productivity because the reinforcer is something desired by the employee and follows performance. Increased productivity through behavior management results in more incidences of those events that produce satisfaction for the employee. Just as an athlete's extra effort that produces a win for his team increases the athlete's satisfaction, so too, increased effort at work can increase job satisfaction, if the feedback and reinforcement are delivered contingent on that performance.

Behavior management programs have been implemented in many unionized plants, as well as nonunion plants. Although union/management agreements may place some restrictions on the types of procedures that may be used, performance has been improved equally in both situations. In fact the reaction in some union plants has been a request by the union representatives that they also receive behavior management training. This has resulted in greater understanding between union and management representatives and improved relationships.

Demands for greater salary are not often made from an analysis of the relationship of productivity to pay. Rather, demands for increased salary are often the result of a general lack of reinforcement. The employee believes that if he is paid more he will feel happier. But increased salary resulting from pressures applied by employees only reinforces the behaviors of applying pressure. It does not reinforce productive behavior and does not result in greater satisfaction. The employee still does not feel satisfied and, since he has just been reinforced for engaging in the behaviors of demanding more salary, he will soon begin to engage in that behavior again. On the other hand, if the employee's work situation provides for high rates of feedback, the satisfaction that may be derived from productivity behavior is increased. If the employee is reinforced for productive, he engages in productive behaviors. Rather than increase the demand for financial reinforcers, feedback and social reinforcement reduce such demands because other sources of reinforcement are provided; productive behavior rather than demanding behavior is increased.

**4.** *"If I start telling my employees that they are doing a good job and start showing them graphs of their performance, they'll just think I'm trying to manipulate them. They won't believe me when I tell them that I appreciate the work they are doing."*

This may be true. Sincerity is an important element of successfully delivering social reinforcement. If you really don't appreciate the work your employees are doing, then you have a hard time trying to fake appreciation. Particularly if your rate of positive comments has been low in the past, a sudden increase in reinforcing comments is likely to result in some suspicion among the recipients of that praise. This is natural and should be expected. If, however, you are sincere, if you truly do appreciate the work your employees are doing, as you should, then the employees are sensitive to this and respond with greater effort.

For many managers the behavior of sincerely telling employees they are doing a good job is novel and difficult. This may be harder for the manager than increasing performance for the employee. Nevertheless, this is an important performance for the manager. Workshop training has been a valuable aid in developing the communication skills that enable the manager to communicate those messages, both of reinforcement and correction. These workshops generally rely heavily on modeling and behavioral rehearsal.

**5.** *"Aren't some of the results that you get from behavior management just the results of the Hawthorne Effect?"*

To answer this question one must have some notion of what the so-called Hawthorne Effect is. In experimental research the Hawthorne Effect is the unwanted effect of the experimental operations themselves. This has sometimes been confused with the idea that any time you make a change in the subject's environment you get some change in behavior. This may be true, but that change is just as likely to be in the downward as the upward direction. Actually the Hawthorne studies have been reexamined thoroughly in recent years (Parsons, 1974) and produce different conclusions in the light of current research than they did forty years ago. The improvements in performance obtained in the Hawthorne studies can be explained as a result of increased feedback and monetary reinforcement. The subjects in the experiments were aware of the measurement of their performance and had access to those data. They were receiving feedback during the experiment that they had not received before. They were also able to increase their income as a function of improved performance in certain components of the Hawthorne experiments. Other explanations for improved performance include increases in social interaction, development of teamwork (also known as group contingencies), and other social relationships.

Regardless of the precise explanation for the various changes in the experimental data produced at Hawthorne, they can all be traced to some change in the discriminative stimuli presented before performance, or the consequences following performance.

With this in mind we can answer the question affirmatively. Yes, the results obtained in many behavior management programs are *just* the result of the Hawthorne Effect. What is important is that we now understand what produces this effect and we can incorporate that into the daily work environment. Those conditions of stimulus-control and reinforcement following behavior that produced increases at Hawthorne have produced increases in performance over and over again in the application of behavior management. And those increases in performance can be maintained over an extended time by applying our knowledge of schedules of reinforcement that did not exist at the time of the Hawthorne studies.

**6.** *"This sounds fine, but how about the people who manage us? Dont' they need to know about these techniques?"*

This is a question that invariably comes up in the course of training managers in behavior management. The only answer is of course they do. It may be very difficult for managers at one level of an organization to increase their rate of feedback and reinforcement to their employees if they do not also receive this increase. The effect of modeling in management can hardly be overemphasized. Managers tend to behave in the way that their managers behave. A major discrepancy between the behavior of upper managers and lower managers is very unlikely to persist. The lower managers tend to adopt the behavior patterns of the upper level managers, who inevitably serve as their models.

An appropriate response to this situation was recently made by the chairman of the board of a major U.S. corporation. After observing the results of a behavior management program in one plant, he noted that this should be spread throughout the sixty-five plants of the corporation. He said "If we are going to do this it should start with me." He arranged a seminar for himself and his closest staff. If he incorporates behavior management practices into his own management behaviors and reinforces similar behavior among those who report to him, his company will be the recipient of a very high return on its investment.

**7.** *"It sounds like you're asking all managers to behave in the same way. Don't managers have different styles that may work well for them but not for someone else?"*

It is true that managers may have styles that work well for them and that could not be easily adopted by another manager. Behavior management does not ask managers to behave in the same way. It asks them to accomplish similar things. Providing high rates of feed-back and reinforcement may be accomplished in many different ways. If, however, the manager is successful at reinforcing his employees, regardless of his style or manner of accomplishing that, he has high performance. The question the manager must ask is "Is my style rein-forcing to my employees?" But the answer to this question is often negative. Many managers have not developed styles of interaction, or patterns of behavior, that employees find reinforcing. In these cases the manager does need to change his style.

Every manager can improve his style or pattern of behavior to provide more reinforcers contingent upon the employees' behavior. Imitating another manager may be a useful means of improving one's own behavior. The only problem that may arise is the attempt to adopt one specific behavior out of the context of a more complex series of behaviors that we identify as someone's style. For example, one man-ager may be a very outgoing, social individual who talks a lot, goes out for drinks, plays sports, and engages in a lot of behavior with his employees. This manager may be very popular with the employees and may be successful at reinforcing high performance, but these are not necessarily related. Another manager may be a very low-key indi-vidual, who is relatively quiet and interacts less often with the employ-ees but is sincere in his concern for them. The first manager may rein-force some specific action of an employee by shouting his approval across the room and taking the employee out for a drink. The second manager would be hard pressed to imitate this behavior. Because it would be incongruent with his normal pattern of behavior, it would not be viewed as reinforcing by the employees. This manager may, however, accomplish the same reinforcing effect by quietly asking the employee to come into his office and quietly and sincerely telling the employee how impressed he was with this same performance. Both of these very different "reinforcers" may produce the exact same effect of reinforcement. What is important is that the manager does some-thing that is "received" as a reinforcer by the individual who has performed.

Managers must work to develop their reinforcing behaviors within the context of their own style. Observing and imitating other man-agers may be helpful if the behaviors one attempts to incorporate as one's own are comfortable within the context of the general patterns of one's behavior.

**8.** *"Won't some individuals respond well to feedback and reinforcement procedures while others won't?"*

Reinforcement, by definition, is the procedure of providing a consequence that results in an increase in the frequency of a behavior. The question is, if I want to increase X behavior of individual A, what consequence will reinforce that behavior? The trick is to identify the things that are actually reinforcers for the individual. It is important that managers recognize the individual preferences and needs of their employees. They must learn to be sensitive to the things their employees find reinforcing.

Sensitivity is the ability to observe the behavior of an individual and respond to that individual in a manner that accomplishes a result based on correct observations. For example, the manager may observe that one employee does not feel comfortable when praised in front of other employees. Another individual may feel especially flattered when praise is provided in the presence of others. By correctly observing the behavior of each of these individuals the manager can respond to them. Even the individual most difficult to reinforce can be reinforced if the manager is sensitive to the things that are reinforcers for that individual.

Feedback is one of the most universally accepted reinforcers. For some unknown reason, knowledge of the results of one's behavior is reinforcing to almost everyone. Perhaps this is one reason why sports are so universally accepted as reinforcing. Sports provide immediate, high-frequency feedback on performance. Very few employees fail to find well-provided feedback reinforcing. When feedback is not a reinforcer, it is probably due to some previous learning experience in which feedback was paired with another, punishing consequence.

**9.** *"Do people of different races, ages, or sexes all respond the same to behavior management?"*

People with different learning histories respond differently to a change in their environment. We have all been conditioned to respond in various ways to our work situations. There is no question that people of different cultural backgrounds have learned different patterns of work behavior. For example, there are many cultures around the world that have been primarily agricultural and only recently have become industrial. In many of these countries the discipline of arriving to work at an industrial factory at a specific hour is culturally foreign. Individuals in that culture have not learned to regard time as important.

Whether it is raining or not is more important than the exact time of day.

Similarly, within the United States or any heterogeneous society there are various subcultures with differing patterns of learning and behavior. To the degree that individuals have these different learning histories they respond differently to a behavior management procedure. It is similarly true that individuals with different learning histories respond differently to the work setting itself. Every work setting includes some arrangement of the contingencies of reinforcement. A weekly paycheck is a reinforcement system to which individuals respond differently.

The question of race, age, or sex is more properly one of learning history. If two individuals have an identical learning history, be they white, black, red, or yellow, they are likely to respond to the work setting or any contingency of reinforcement in a similar manner. If, however, two individuals have a different learning history, even if they are of the same age, race, and sex, they respond differently to a set of contingencies.

Understanding that patterns of behavior are the product of different learning histories, the manager can assist the employee of a minority background to adapt to the work setting. For example, an individual from a predominantly rural, agricultural background who is entering the industrial setting may have a number of difficulties adjusting to the new set of contingencies (this has been a problem in the South for many years). The person who worked on the farm may have been used to exerting a great degree of control over his work activity. He is not likely to have that discretion in the factory. He may also have worked in a group. In the plant he may find himself working very much by himself on a monotonous task. The person from an agricultural background may have been paid daily and in cash. This person is now likely to be paid weekly and by check.

All of these changes require a period of learning. The learning can be increased, and the probability of this individual's quitting and looking for a work setting in which he is more comfortable is reduced by the intelligent use of reinforcement. The manager may plan for social reinforcement at a high frequency if the new employee is used to a high frequency of social contact in his previous setting. If the manager accepts the responsibility of helping to teach employees to feel comfortable in the work setting, the principles of behavior management can be applied with the minority employee and to the advantage of everyone concerned.

**10.** *"My managers have been managing for twenty years. You're not going to come in and tell them to start being nice to people and go around praising their employees! They just won't do it!"*

This warning has been heard in each one of about two hundred industrial locations where behavior management programs have been initiated. It may be true that managers who have been negative and set in a pattern of behavior for many years do not alter that behavior quickly. But virtually all behavior is learned. New behavior can be learned, even by the oldest dog (or manager) given the necessary conditions for learning. The new behavior must be modeled, shaped, and reinforced. Often I have found that some of the older managers have made the most dramatic changes during behavior management programs.

The skill of the trainer is to identify the current level of skill or the current behavior pattern of the trainee and gradually teach new behavior. The trainer who wants the manager to begin to provide social reinforcement, for example, may find it necessary to go out on the plant floor with the manager and go around to his employees and literally help him reinforce improved performance. In this way the trainer can serve as a model for the manager. As the manager witnesses improvements in performance he becomes reinforced by those improvements and the recognition he receives from his peers and superiors. The trainer should accept the responsibility of programming reinforcers for the new behaviors of the manager. If the manager is not reinforced for changes in his behavior, they are not likely to occur and certainly will not be maintained.

Many of the success stories often discussed in plants where behavior management programs have been implemented concern the very manager who was the most negative, hard-nosed taskmaster. Some of the individuals have even broken out in tears during training sessions and announced that behavior management has changed their life. They have reported that they never really enjoyed their work until they changed their behavior and began reinforcing their employees. Managers have on many occassions reported that the lessons they learned during the behavior management training changed their home life. There have been specific reports of managers who have improved the schoolwork of their children, negative behavior of their spouse, and even the ability to control the blood sugar level of a diabetic child who had difficulty holding down sugar intake.

**11.** *"How long will we have to continue this behavior management program?"*

This is a question often asked by managers beginning training in behavior management. The answer is simple: forever. If feedback and reinforcement and other behavioral procedures produce the desired result of high performance, why would you stop? The difficulty that this question raises is the question of a behavior management "program." Behavior management should not be viewed as a program. It should be viewed simply as effective management. If the job is to manage, then those management procedures that produce the best results should be continued until better procedures are identified.

The behavior management methodology is a way of identifiyng what really works in the management of human performance. If the manager is pinpointing behavior, recording baseline data, changing antecedents and consequences, and evaluating performance by measuring the change in the baseline data, the manager learns to identify exactly which changes produce the best result. This should be an ongoing procedure, just as monitoring data on the production process is an ongoing procedure so that changes in input may be made. The changes in the environment of the employees in a work setting are very similar to the changes in material inputs into a production process. If the monitoring systems are working well, changes in performance can be detected quickly, the adjustments in the environment made, and performance maintained at a high level. This is the basic concept of behavior management. Why would any manager consider stopping this procedure if it is working?

**12.** *"It seems that you either ignore or are not concerned with how people feel. You constantly talk about behavior or performance and disregard the employees' inner feelings."*

It is entirely possible that an individual practitioner of behavior management, or any other management, may disregard the individual feelings of the employee. This practitioner is not, however, likely to be very successful. Reinforcement and feedback work because they make the individual feel good. We do what tends to make us feel good. What we do is what is reinforced. Therefore these concepts of reinforcement and improving the feelings of an individual run parallel to each other. You simply cannot reinforce people by making them feel miserable. If you are successful at reinforcing people, you both increase their performance and cause them to feel good.

Behavior management in the work setting, or behavior modification in the clinical setting, deals specifically with the emotions of the individual. Emotions are viewed as internal responses, behavior, and are subject to the same principles of learning and control as overt or external behavior. Feeling depressed, for example, may be reinforced by social attention received contingent on this response. Similarly, dissatisfaction at work can be reinforced if social attention is delivered contingent on this response.

Behavior management does result in an improved emotional climate in a work setting. Every manager who is trying to manage is trying to manage behavior. The difficulty with many managers is that they are using the only means they know to control the behavior of their employees, negative or punishing means. Behavior management gives them the skills by which they can manage in a more positive manner, creating a more positive emotional climate and more satisfied employees.

**13.** *"I understand how behavior management will work on the factory production line, but how about with "knowledge workers"? Creativity and thinking are the behaviors that matter. How can these be reinforced?"*

B. F. Skinner (1974) has discussed thinking and creativity at some length. He explains thinking as verbal behavior. Verbal behavior may go unspoken. The thought is itself a behavior. The process of thinking is one of emitting internal responses. Skinner explains that we present our own internal antecedents, behavior, and consequences. For example, we may be thinking about the upcoming weekend. This thought may serve as an antecedent and set the occasion for the thought that we have nothing planned this weekend. That thought sets the occasion for the thoughts of considering the alternatives that may be available and so forth. We reinforce and punish internal responses. When internally listing the alternative activities for this coming weekend we find some of them more reinforcing and some more punishing. For example, among the alternative thoughts might be (1) working around the house, (2) going to the beach, or (3) coming into the office to work on some special projects.

When the thought of going to the beach is emitted, this thought may set the occasion (antecedent) for the thought "What will the weather be like this weekend?" This sets the occasion for the thought "Oh yes, I heard on the radio that it was going to be cool and rainy." This thought is punishing to the thought of going to the beach. We therefore reduce the occurrence or stop entirely the thought of going to the beach.

As can be seen from this example, thinking and mental or internal problem solving can be behaviorally analyzed in the same manner as any external response.

From this background creativity, emitting novel or unique thoughts can be analyzed and reinforced. Group brainstorming is a situation in which the group of individuals agree not to punish any novel thoughts, no matter how different they may be from previous or conventional thoughts on a topic. In this type of an environment the individual need not be concerned that a "wild idea" will be followed by social punishment. Many work environments include a set of social interactions that include a high probability of punishment for unique ideas. This type of environment is likely to produce little creativity among the member individuals. In a work setting in which creativity is an important factor in success, the managers must work to provide a high rate of reinforcement for unique verbal behavior and a low probability of punishment.

Creativity may also be increased by increasing the reinforcers for the products of creative thinking. This is the course of action most often taken by organizations. Provisions for monetary and social reinforcers contingent on contributing money-saving ideas are common in large corporations such as the 3M Corporation. Reinforcers are also offered for new product applications and other results of creative thinking.

### REFERENCES

Parsons, H. M. "What happend at Hawthorne," *Science*, **183**, March 1974, 922–930.

Skinner, B. F. *About Behaviorism*. New York: Alfred A. Knopf, Inc., 1974.

**GLOSSARY**

**Accountability.** Those conditions that require an individual to account for his behavior or actions. It is present when there is a consequence to an individual's behavior. Accountability in business and industry usually implies prestated goals or objectives and subsequent feedback and consequences. It provides for direction and may allow for high levels of performance if it is sufficiently positive.

**Antecedents.** Those stimulus events presented before the performance of a behavior. A request to "come to the office" is an antecedent to the behavior of "coming to the office." The sight of rain is an antecedent to the behavior of "turning on the windshield wipers."

**Artificial reinforcer.** A reinforcer deliberately planned to be contingent on the completion of a behavior, a reinforcer that does not normally follow the behavior in the natural environment (e.g.: tokens, point systems).

**Assertive behavior.** Behavior by which one stands up for one's position or rights in relation to another person. Maintaining or defending one's position positively and with confidence. Assertive behavior often requires overcoming anxieties and is the subject of assertive training.

**Assertive training.** A training procedure in which an individual learns to engage in assertive behavior. Generally follows the behavior rehearsal procedure. See "Behavioral Rehearsal."

**Aversive stimulus.** A stimulus that is unpleasant. An aversive stimulus that precedes a response result in avoidance behavior or negative reinforcement, an increase in the rate of response to avoid the aversive stimulus. An aversive stimulus that follows a response results in a decrease in the rate of that response, or punishment.

**Backup reinforcers.** A reinforcer for which points or tokens may be exchanged. The points or tokens are used by "buy" the backup reinforcers. A helpful reminder to use when setting up a token economy is that "the tokens are only as effective as the backup reinforcers they buy." To have an effective token economy, therefore, you must have a wide variety of effective backup reinforcers. See "Reinforcer Menu."

**Baseline.** The measurement of a behavior under routine conditions, obtained before implementation of a program to change that behavior. A behavior management program is evaluated by comparing data collected after a program has begun to the data collected during the baseline period. Baseline data should reflect a consistent or predictable pattern.

**Baseline data.**   The data collected during the baseline period. See "Data" and "Baseline."

**Behavior.**   Anything a person says or does, thinks or feels; any response made by a person; any activity. Behavior may be observable (external behavior) or unobservable (internal behavior).

**Behavior contract.**   A written agreement that specifies the pinpointed behavior that one party agrees to perform and the specific consequences that will follow the occurrence of that behavior. A behavior contract is used to formalize the contingent relationship between a behavior and its consequence. It may be used in self-management, supervising, or a behavior management program for children.

**Behavior management.**   The set of principles and procedures that provide for the practical application of those laws of human behavior determined by research and applied to the work setting. Behavior management involves often simple and sometimes complex procedures that are always consistent with the findings of empirical research. Also known as behavior modification, behaviorism, or behavioral psychology.

**Behavior modification.**   Those sets of procedures that rely on the specification, measurement, and control of behavior through the alteration of consequences. Behavior management is the application of behavior modification to the organizational environment.

**Behavior practice.**   See "Behavior Rehearsal."

**Behavior rehearsal.**   A step-by-step procedure for practicing and learning person-to-person skills. When conducting behavior rehearsal, you provide an opportunity to view a model of the skill, identify the specific behaviors that comprise that skill, rehearse each specific behavior, and receive feedback on that performance. Behavior rehearsal is the most effective method for improving person-to-person skills.

**Behaviorist.**   A behaviorist is one who subscribes to the belief that behavior is determined by environmental events. Behaviorists believe that human performance can best be managed by measuring specific behavior, altering conditions in the environment that act on that behavior, and measuring the changes in behavior.

**Bonus.** A reinforcer, in business and industry, that is provided in addition to the regular scheduled reinforcement (salary). Bonuses are effective to the degree that they are delivered contingent upon desirable behavior and to the degree that they are delivered on an effective schedule. See "Schedules of Reinforcement."

**Chaining.** A technique used in teaching complex tasks. Essentially, the large task is broken into many smaller tasks. These smaller tasks are then learned (with consequences contingent upon the completion of each small task) and then linked together in succession, forming the original complex task. A large or major reinforcer follows the completion of the entire chain. Most of our everyday behaviors occur as chains of behavior, for example, starting an automobile (large task) comprises many smaller tasks or behaviors (opening car door, sitting in seat, closing car door, inserting key into ignition, turning key in ignition, releasing key).

**Communication.** The process of giving and receiving information. Communication is composed of specific behaviors on the part of both the giver and receiver of information.

**Concurrent schedules of reinforcement.** A condition in which there is more than one schedule of reinforcement occurring simultaneously in relation to one behavior. Most sales persons operate on a concurrent schedule of reinforcement. One schedule is the monthly or weekly salary. The other schedule is the commission arrangement.

**Consequate.** To provide a consequence following the performance of a behavior.

**Consequence.** A result or event following a behavior. A paycheck is a consequence of work. A traffic ticket is a consequence of speeding. Consequences influence the future occurrence of the behavior they follow. The effect that consequences have on behavior is a central concept in behavior management. Consequences result in the increase, maintenance, or decrease in the frequency of a behavior.

**Contingencies of reinforcement.** The events that may occur before and after a behavior and that influence the performance. The "if–then" relationships between behavior and environmental events. Contingencies of reinforcement include both the antecedents and consequences.

**Contingency (or contingent relationship).** A relationship between two events. Referring to behavior, it is the "if–then" relationship between the behavior and the consequence (if the behavior occurs, then the consequence will follow).

**Contingent.**   Dependent upon, following.

**Continuous reinforcement.**   A schedule of reinforcement in which every occurrence of a behavior is reinforced. Continuous reinforcement is effective in the initial phase of a program to increase the rate of the behavior. Continuous reinforcement may be time consuming or costly and is, therefore, usually used only during an early phase of a behavior procedure.

**Counting.**   Observing a behavior and making some retrievable record of the occurrence of that behavior.

**Covert behavior (internal).**   Behaviors or responses that cannot be observed. Feelings or emotions and thoughts are covert behaviors. Synonymous with internal behavior.

**Data.**   Plural of datum. The measurements of a behavior. The numbers indicating the rate, frequency, magnitude, or duration of a behavior. All behavior management programs should be based on data acquired before the program (baseline data) and program data acquired after the program is implemented.

**Data points.**   A single point on a chart or graph that represents the value, rate, frequency, duration, or other measure of a behavior. Usually represents one observation or measure during a simple interval of time.

**Datum.**   A measurement of a behavior. Singular of "data."

**Dependent variable.**   The variable that is controlled and measured as changes in other variables (independent) are made in an experimental design. In behavior management the dependent variables are the behaviors and results of performance that the manager is seeking to improve.

**Deprivation.**   A condition in which a behavior may be performed with no possibility of receiving reinforcement. The lack of reinforcement.

**Desensitization.**   A procedure of identifying the stimulus that causes anxiety, its gradual presentation, and learning to relax in the presence of that stimulus. Desensitization is usually conducted by first constructing a hierarchy of scenes that successively approximate the most anxiety-producing scene, learning to relax, and then learning to relax while imagining the progressive scenes. In this manner one can gradually and without severe discomfort learn to be relaxed, or not be anxious, in the presence of a given stimulus.

**Differential reinforcement of high rates (DRH).**   A procedure in which a behavior is followed by reinforcement when it is emitted at a high rate. The rate of acceptable performance is defined and ignored when not occurring at this acceptable rate and reinforced when it does occur at this rate.

**Differential reinforcement of low rates (DRL).**   A procedure in which a behavior is followed by a reinforcer when it is emitted at a low rate. The rate of acceptable reinforcement is defined and ignored when it is above this rate and reinforced when below the acceptable rate. Low rates of coffee break behavior may be reinforced to increase the amount of work performed.

**Direct approach.**   The direct approach to changing behavior or performance relies on the direct measurement of specific behavior, alteration of events in the environment, and measurement of altered rates of performance. *Direct* refers to the concern with behavior rather than the concern with internal states, such as attitudes.

**Directive feedback.**   Information about past performance that is presented to the performer and that is neither approving nor disapproving of the performance.

**Discrimination.**   A state of affairs in which a behavior is more likely to occur in one situation, or in the presence of one set of stimuli, than in other situations, or in the presence of other sets of stimuli. A child is discriminating if he shouts on the playground but does not shout while in the classroom.

**Discrimination training procedure.**   Reinforcing a behavior when performed in the presence of one set of stimuli and extinguishing it in other situations. A child's running and screaming behaviors may be reinforced when emitted on the playground, but these same behaviors are extinguished (ignored) when emitted in the classroom.

**Discriminative stimulus.** A stimulus, in whose presence a behavior was previously reinforced, that now serves as a cue evoking that behavior. The behavior is likely to occur in the presence of the discriminative stimulus. Dark clouds are a discriminative stimulus for the behavior of carrying an umbrella. Abberviated as $S^D$.

**Emit.** The occurrence of a behavior. For example, "the behavior is emitted ten times per day" means that the behavior occurs ten times per day.

**Emotional reaction.** A reaction to the environment or to thoughts that is characterized by a change in the feelings or the internal comfort or discomfort of the individual. Changes in emotion are always accompanied by physiological changes such as changes in facial expressions, heart beat, perspiration, and respiration.

**Evaluate.** Continuing the measurement procedure begun before consequating a behavior (baseline) and comparing the new data to the baseline data.

**Expectation.** The internal response of rehearsing the receipt of a reinforcer. Expectation responses are initiated by the presentation of an antecedent stimulus such as a model, by observation of the receipt of reinforcement by someone else performing behavior similar to that performed by the expectant person, or by a comment that a contingency exists between a given behavior and reinforcer.

**External reinforcers.** Reinforcers that occur outside the individual. Any reinforcer other than thoughts or feelings are external reinforcers.

**Extinction.** The procedure of withdrawing reinforcement following a behavior, resulting in the decrease or termination of the rate of that behavior. The extinction may be used to decrease undesirable behavior when one can control the reinforcer maintaining that undesirable behavior. The withdrawal of a reinforcer usually results in an immediate increase in the rate of a behavior. Following this immediate increase, the rate declines. When using extinction, one must be able to continue to withhold reinforcement.

**Extinguish.** The reduction or termination in the rate of a behavior following the withdrawal of a reinforcer. The result of extinction. When a behavior does not "pay off," it extinguishes.

**Extrinsic reinforcer.** A reinforcer that does not occur as a natural by–product of the behavior itself. Intrinsic reinforcers occur as a natural consequence. Not to be confused with external reinforcers. Among the extrinsic reinforcers may be praise, congratulations, smiles, handshakes, money, food, points, and tokens.

**Feedback.**   Feedback is information about past behavior presented to the person who performed that behavior.

**Fixed schedules.**   Schedules of reinforcement that provide for reinforcement after a fixed or constant number of behaviors (ratio) or period of time (interval). Reinforcing every hour on the hour, once a month at the end of the month, or once after every fifteen behaviors are all fixed schedules. Fixed schedules usually produce behavior patterns that are not constant. The rate of behavior generally increases before the time of reinforcement and declines after reinforcement, to increase again before the next reinforcement. See "Interval Schedules" and "Ratio Schedules."

**Frequency.**   The number of times a behavior occurs divided by a unit of time within which the count has been taken. The rate of response. For example, ten responses per hour, six calls made per week. Frequency or rate is the basic unit of behavioral measurement.

**Functional relationship.**   The relationship between an independent and dependent variable or between a behavior and the contingencies of reinforcement. A functional relationship is one in which a change in one event produces a change in another event. A functional relationship is demonstrated if behavior changes in a predictable fashion if a contingency is applied, withdrawn, and reapplied.

**Generalization.**   The tendency for a behavior that has been reinforced in one situation to occur in similar, but different, situations. Generalization is the opposite of discrimination. For example, a young child's saying "Daddy" in presence of father has been reinforced. This response may generalize to other men. That is, the child will have the tendency to say "Daddy" when in the presence of the mailman, milkman, or uncle. The greater the similarity between father and these other men, the greater the likelihood of generalization. This response will eventually be emitted only in the presence of father, owing to the discrimination training procedure. Also see "Discrimination" and "Discrimination Training Procedure."

**Generalized reinforcer.**   A reinforcer that gains its effectiveness by association with a wide variety of other reinforcers. A generalized reinforcer allows access to many other reinforcers. An individual whose behavior is being maintained by a generalized reinforcer cannot become "satiated" with it. Money, tokens, and points are generalized reinforcers. Money by itself is worthless; however, it gains its reinforcing properties by allowing the individual to buy a wide variety of other reinforcers such as food, shelter, cars, and movies. Without these backup reinforcers money would have no value at all. Also see "Backup Reinforcers."

**Graph.** A diagram representing the changes in the value, rate, frequency, or duration of a variable over time—usually a series of intersecting horizontal and vertical lines. Horizontal lines usually represent the number of behaviors. The vertical lines usually represent the time periods during which behaviors occur.

**Incentive systems.** Plans or schedules for delivering rewards or bonuses. If an incentive system does, in fact, produce a measurable effect on behavior, it is a schedule of reinforcement. Many incentive systems do not produce desired results, because they fail to take into account several principles of behavior such as shaping, immediacy of reinforcement, or effects of various schedules.

**Independent variable.** The variable in an experimental design that is altered to affect a change in another variable (dependent). In behavior management the independent variables are all of the antecedents and consequences that may be altered to influence the performance of concern.

**Intangible reinforcers.** Nonmaterial reinforcers; those reinforcers that are not tangible—usually social expressions such as praise, congratulations, smiles, and hugs.

**Intermittent reinforcement.** A schedule of reinforcement in which a behavior is only occasionally followed by reinforcement; noncontinuous reinforcement. Intermittent reinforcement schedules are used to maintain responding, rather than to teach new responses or behaviors. It is desirable to use intermittent reinforcement once the behavior has been strengthened and is occurring at a stable rate. Intermittent schedules result in greater resistance to extinction than continuous reinforcement. The four major types of intermittent reinforcement schedules are fixed ratio, variable ratio, fixed interval, and variable interval.

**Internal behavior.** Behavioral events that occur within the individual.

Thoughts and feelings are behaviorial responses or events that occur within the individual. Internal behavior is learned in a similar manner as external behavior and is subject to most of the same principles of behavior change as external behavior. Sometimes referred to as covert behavior.

**Internal reinforcement.**   The process by which an individual receives reinforcement from responses within the individual. Thoughts and feelings that are pleasant, that follow the occurrence of a behavior and result in an increase in the rate of that behavior are internal reinforcers. Feelings of "self-satisfaction," "pride," and "self-esteem" are examples of internal reinforcers.

**Internal reinforcers.**   Those internal events, thoughts, or feelings that follow the occurrence of a behavior and result in the increased rate or maintenance of that behavior.

**Interval.**   A period of time between two points of time. For example, the ten-minute interval between 5:00 and 5:10. One hour may be divided into six continuous ten-minute intervals. Intervals are often used when counting behavior. You might count during one ten-minute interval each hour.

**Interval recording.**   A technique for recording behavior that involves dividing a time period into equal intervals and recording the number of times the behavior occurs during each interval. This method requires continuous observation during the time interval period.

The behavior recorded was Denise's attending (paying attention) behavior in a classroom.

10 seconds | A | A | N | N | A | N |

A = attending behavior
N = nonattending behavior

**Interval schedules of reinforcement.**   A schedule by which reinforcers are delivered based on the passage of time. There are two major types of interval schedules: fixed-interval (FI) schedules and variable-interval (VI) schedules.

**Fixed-interval schedules.**   A fixed-interval schedule is one by which a behavior is reinforced following a constant passage of time. For example, an FI30 would indicate that the behavior will be reinforced the first time it occurs following the passage of thirty minutes. The FI schedules produce uneven response patterns with an increase in response rate toward the end of the interval and a sudden decline in rate after the reinforcement.

**Variable-interval schedules.** A schedule by which reinforcement is delivered following an average, but varying, passage of time. For example, a VI30 schedule would be one by which the behavior that occurred following a passage of time averaging thirty minutes would be reinforced. For the first interval the behavior might be reinforced aften ten minutes, for the second interval it might be forty minutes. Each interval would be unpredictable but would average thirty minutes. The VI schedules produce relatively even response patterns and a low frequency of response.

**Intrinsic reinforcer.** A reinforcer that occurs as the natural result of a behavior. If you read a book because you enjoy reading and obtaining increased knowledge, then your reading is being maintained by intrinsic reinforcers. Not to be confused with internal reinforcement. Intrinsic reinforcement may be both internal and external, tangible or intangible. Job enrichment is concerned with increasing the intrinsic reinforcers of a job.

**Job enrichment.** Procedures by which the operations of a job are altered to produce an increase in the intrinsic reinforcement derived from that job. Increasing the number of tasks in a job, varying the tasks in a job, and increasing participative decision making are common ways of producing increases in intrinsic reinforcement or job enrichment.

**Learning.** The process whereby new behaviors are acquired. The result of repeated interaction between the learner and his environment. More specifically the result of certain stimulus conditions before and during the emission of a behavior, and the consequences acting on the learner following the emission of the behavior.

**Limited hold.** A requirement on an interval schedule of reinforcement that provides for reinforcement if the behavior occurs within a specified time period following the completion of the prescribed interval.

**Magnitude of reinforcement.** The amount or strength of a reinforcer. Every reinforcer has a magnitude. If reinforcers are competing, as in a multiple schedule of reinforcement, the magnitude of a reinforcer or punisher is likely to determine the response. There may be both a reinforcer and punisher for accepting a new job (higher salary, loss of retirement benefit). That consequence of greater magnitude is likely to control the behavior.

**Measurement.**    The procedure of obtaining data on the occurrence of an event. Usually composed of the two operations of, first, observing and counting the occurrence of a behavior and, second, recording that count in a manner that facilitates its use.

**Modeling.**    The process of learning a behavior by observation and imitation. The procedure of providing a demonstration or example (a model) of a behavior, so that another individual may imitate that behavior. Modeling is used to introduce complex or otherwise unfamiliar behavior.

**Motivation.**    The general condition of relatively high rates of responding produced by reinforcement. In the past, motivation has been considered an internal process or state. It is now understood that motivation is the result of reinforcement and is identified by a relatively high response rate. A high level of motivation cannot be said to exist in the absence of a response rate judged to be high.

**Multiple schedules of reinforcement.**    The presence of more than one schedule of reinforcement for a behavior. A behavior such as arriving to work is followed by several separate reinforcers and may similarly be punished by one or more reinforcers.

**Negative feedback.**    Feedback that states disapproval of past performance. Negative feedback usually results in a decrease in the rate of the disapproved behavior.

**Negative reinforcement.**    The procedure of removing a stimulus contigent on the performance of a behavior; it results in the subsequent increase in the rate of response.

**Negative reinforcer.**    An object or event that, when removed or postponed contingent upon a behavior, results in an increase in the probability of that behavior. The removal or postponement of the negative reinforcer results in the strengthening of the behavior. For example, you are waiting for the bus, and suddenly it begins to rain. You do not like getting wet and don't wish to ruin your clothes, and so you put up your umbrella. This stops the rain from soaking you. Putting up the umbrella was strengthened by negative reinforcement, since it removed or postponed the possibility of your getting wet.

**Neutral consequence.** A consequence that, by itself, is neither reinforcing nor punishing and does not, therefore, maintain the rate of a behavior. When there is only a neutral consequence following a behavior, that behavior extinguishes. In addition to a neutral consequence there may be other consequences occurring at the same time (reinforcers or punishers) that cause the maintenance, increase, or decrease in the rate of a behavior. See "Extinction."

**Objectives.** An objective states an action that is to occur, a measurable result that is to be achieved, and a date by which it is to be achieved. Objectives are generally derived from more general goals and are subsequently broken down into more specific tasks. Objectives are intended to serve as discriminative stimuli for a performance.

**Occasion (to).** To present an antecedent stimulus that evokes a desired response. The presentation of a discriminative stimulus ($S^D$) to increase the likelihood of a response.

**Off Task.** Not engaged in or performing any general task, job, or behavior at a specific moment in time. A condition often counted and recorded to provide a measure of the amount of time spent in productive activity.

**On Task.** Engaged in or performing any given task, job, or behavior at a specific moment in time.

**Operant behavior.** Behavior emitted and controlled by its consequences. Operant behavior "operates" on the environment to produce a contingent event such as a reinforcer.

**Organizational behavior modification.** A term synonymous with behavior management. The application of behavior modification principles and procedures within the organizational setting.

**Overt Behavior (External Behavior).** Behaviors or responses that can be observed, involving body movements. Smiling, coming to work, screaming, blinking the eyes are all overt behaviors. Also referred to as external behavior.

**Personality.** Personality is a set of behaviors. The terms used to describe personality are general descriptions of what are actually a set of very specific behaviors such as smiling, tone of voice, or ex-pressing negative thoughts. Pleasant, cheerful, depressed, sad, dynamic are all terms used to describe personality.

**Pinpoint.**   A specific behavior that can be accurately observed and recorded. When a behavior is properly pinpointed, two persons can observe and record that behavior at the same time and arrive at the same measurement. Working poorly is not a pinpointed behavior, because it cannot be reliably measured. Arriving to work late, produc-ing a specific number of units, and being in a location other than the place of work are pinpointed behaviors.

**Positive feedback.**   Feedback that states approval of past perform-ance. Positive feedback usually results in an increase in the rate of the approved behavior.

**Positive reinforcement.**   The procedure of presenting a reinforcer immediately following a behavior. Positive refers to the act of "pre-senting." Negative reinforcement refers to the "withdrawal" of rein-forcement.

**Positive reinforcer.**   An object or event that, when presented con-tingent on a behavior, results in an increased probability of that behav-ior. A positive reinforcer is roughly the same as a "reward."

**Premack Principle.**   The Premack Principle states that if behavior A is more likely to occur than behavior B, then behavior B may be in-creased by making the performance of behavior A contingent on the performance of B. If watching television has a high likelihood of occurrence (behavior A), it may be made contingent on finishing a report (behavior B) that has a low likelihood of occurrence. This results in the increased performance of behavior B, finishing reports. The Premack Principle is employed whenever there is difficulty in identifying a reinforcer. In applying this principle, there is always a potential reinforcer.

**Primary reinforcers.**   A reinforcer that is unconditional or unlearned. Food, warmth, and sex are among the few primary reinforcers. Sec-ondary reinforcers are conditioned.

**Problem.**   A problem is the discrepancy between a current situation (what is) and a desired situation (what should be). Solving the problem involves removing the discrepancy between what is and what should be. Problems usually involve someone's behavior, someone doing or not doing something. Even when a problem involves equipment, money, time, or other factors, someone must do or not do something to solve the problem.

**Problem-solving skills.** Those skills that enable a person to effectively change a situation from a current unsatisfactory situation (what is) to a satisfactory situation (what should be). These skills involve describing the problem, selecting alternative courses of action, choosing the best course of action, and changing the behavior required to change the situation.

**Programming (behavioral).** Arranging the environment (reinforcement contingencies, schedules of reinforcement, and other conditions) with the intent of increasing or decreasing the probability of a particular behavior.

**Prompt.** A class of antecedent stimuli used to request, suggest, command, question, or comment with the intent of influencing behavior. See "Prompting."

**Prompting.** The procedure in which a suggestion, request, question, or comment is presented and a response is made following that prompt. A "stop sign," a request to "come to dinner," and an order to "perform a job" are all examples of prompting.

**Punishers.** Those stimuli that may be presented or removed following a behavior and result in a decrease in the rate, frequency, or duration of that behavior. Punishers may be either positive (presented) or negative (removed); however, they always result in a decrease in rate of behavior.

**Punishment.** The procedure of presenting or removing a stimulus (a punisher) following a behavior that results in the reduction or termination in the rate of that behavior. The least desirable of the three procedures for decreasing the rate of a behavior.

### Punishment, Effective Rules
1. Punish immediately.
2. Be consistent.
3. Reinforce desirable behavior.
4. Minimize attention.
5. Be fair.
6. Be specific.

7.   Punish behavior, not people.

8.   Remain calm.

9.   Say what you mean and mean what you say.

**Randomly selected.**   Chosen or selected in a manner that does not result in predictability or a consistent pattern. Pulling numbers out of a hat or spinning a wheel may be used to select numbers at random. Random selection procedures may be used to select intervals during which you will count or during which you will reinforce.

**Rate.**   The average number of times an event occurs during a specified time period; the number of events divided by time. For example, the rate of production might be calculated in terms of the average number of units produced per day. The rate of smoking behavior might be calculated in the number of cigarettes smoked per hour.

**Ratio schedule.**   A schedule of reinforcement in which reinforcement is delivered after a number of responses have occurred. There are two major types of ratio schedules:

1.   **Fixed Ratio (FR):** Reinforcement is presented after a fixed or constant number of responses have occurred. On a fixed ratio 3 (FR3) the reinforcer is presented after the behavior has been emitted three times. The behavior is Mark's completing math problems correctly. Mark receives a reinforcer each time he correctly completes three math problems.

2.   **Variable Ratio (VR):** Reinforcement is presented after a variable or unfixed number of responses have occurred. On a variable ratio 3 (VR3), the reinforcer is presented after the behavior has been emitted, on the average of three times. This means that, on the average, every third response is reinforced. When a VR schedule is used, it is impossible for the individual to determine when the reinforcer will be delivered. The VR schedule produces the greatest resistance to extinction.

**Record.**   Arranging counts of a behavior in a manner that visualizes that count. Measuring the frequency of a behavior.

**Recording.**   The procedure of arranging counts of a behavior in a manner that illustrates the change or continuity in the data.

**Reinforcement.**   The process in which a reinforcer is presented (positive) or removed (negative) and there is a resultant increase or maintenance in the frequency, strength or duration of a behavior.

**Reinforcer menu.** A list of reinforcers (activities, things, and people privileges) and their respective values; usually used with a token economy. Tokens may then be "cashed in" to purchase items from the reinforcer menu.

**Reinforcers.** Those objects or events (stimuli) that are presented (positive reinforcers) or removed (negative reinforcers) following a behavior and that result in an increase or maintenance in the frequency, strength, or duration of a behavior. Anything a person will work for is a reinforcer. See Internal, External, Intrinsic, Extrinsic, Tangible, Social, Positive, Negative, Primary, and Secondary Reinforcers.

**Reinforcing incompatible behavior.** The procedure of reinforcing one behavior that is the alternative or opposite behavior of another that you wish to decrease. Increasing the incompatible behavior necessarily means a decrease in the undesirable behavior. Reinforcing an employee for turning in reports on time necessarily results in a decrease in the number of reports turned in late. This is the most desirable procedure for decreasing behavior.

**Relaxation.** A physiological and emotional state characterized by reduced activity, particularly reduced heart beat, perspiration, respiration, and general muscular activity. Relaxation is accompanied by feelings of comfort. Relaxation is generally the opposite of tension and anxiety. Learning to relax, particularly learning to relax in situations that currently cause anxiety, is a cure for unnecessary and bothersome anxiety or tension.

**Respondent behavior.** Behavior elicited and controlled by an antecedent event. Respondents are elicited automatically when the antecedent occurs. Reflexive responses are "respondents."

**Satiation.** The process by which reinforcer effectiveness is decreased with repeated presentations of that reinforcer. For example, every time Mary sat quietly for 15 minutes, her mother gave her an ice cream cone. After 45 minutes Mary no longer sat quietly. She became satiated with ice cream; that is, ice cream was no longer an effective reinforcer. Satiation effects are temporary. Reinforcer effectiveness is regained after a period of deprivation.

**Schedules of reinforcement.** A schedule by which reinforcement is

delivered. A planned ordering of the delivery of reinforcers. Reinforcing one out of every ten behaviors, once every hour, every sixth
behavior, or ten times per day are all schedules of reinforcement. See
"Continuous," "Intermittent," "Interval Schedules," "Ratio Schedules,"
"Fixed Schedules," and "Variable Schedules."

**Scientific.**   Information based on, or in accordance with, the principles and methods of science; systematized knowledge derived from
observations, study, and experimentations. A scientific procedure
would be one in which factors influencing an outcome are held
constant, except that factor being studied. The factor being studied
would be altered and any change in outcome observed. For example:
To determine whether weekly pay or monthly pay results in less absenteeism, you would take two identical groups that had in the past
demonstrated similar absenteeism and place one group on a monthly
pay schedule and one on a weekly pay schedule. All other factors
that might influence absenteeism would have to remain constant
throughout the experiment. The data on absenteeism would be
recorded and compared. Behavior management principles and procedures have been developed by scientific methods. Most other
management techniques have not.

**Secondary reinforcers.**   Reinforcers that have been conditioned or
learned. Money, paychecks, clothes, cars, movies, social approval, and
promotions are all examples of secondary reinforcers. Primary reinforcers are unlearned.

**Selective Reinforcement.**   The procedure of reinforcing certain desired behavior and not reinforcing other behaviors that are in some
ways similar but not identical to the desired behavior. You selectively
reinforce behavior when you are shaping behavior and when you are
communicating with someone. If you nod your head in agreement
following one statement but do not make any response following a
second statement, you are selectively reinforcing the first response.
Selective reinforcement results in the learning of discriminations.

**Self-monitoring.**   Procedures whereby an individual counts and
records his own behavior. This procedure enables the employee to
provide feedback on his own performance. This procedure often
results in increased performance and job satisfaction, because of the
feedback generated by self-monitoring.

**Sensitivity.**   Sensitivity is one's observing and being aware of the

behavior of other persons and appropriately responding to those behaviors. For convenience, sensitivity is divided into observation and
responding. When a supervisor is sensitive to his employees, he is
aware of the employees' normal patterns of behavior, observes changes
from these normal behaviors, and responds to them in a manner
that benefits the employee. Sensitivity results in the ability to socially
reinforce an employee, to communicate effectively, and to create
an atmosphere in which employees feel comfortable and enjoy their
work.

**Shaping.**   The procedure of reinforcing successive approximations to
a terminal or goal behavior. Breaking a large or difficult task down
into "bits and pieces" until the complete task is performed. All difficult
or complex behaviors are shaped. By using the shaping procedure, the
learning of a difficult or complex task may be made easy. The learner
should experience success at each approximation.

**Skill.**   A set of specific behaviors that are normally performed in a
sequence; the ability required to perform a task. Any performance
problem may be analyzed either as a skill problem, the ability to
perform, or as a motivation problem, the desire to perform when the
skill is present.

**Social reinforcer.**   Reinforcers consisting of attention provided by
other individuals. Social reinforcers are among the most powerful
reinforcers in the workplace. Praise, thanks, appreciation, smiles, and
nods are all social reinforcers.

**Stimulation.**   The presentation of antecedent events that arouse
action. The sight of a supervisor in a work area may be a stimulus
or stimulate faster work behavior. The sight of your child may stimulate particular feelings or emotions and overt behavior such as a
smile.

**Stimulus control.**   Procedures whereby the controlling properties of
a stimulus are used to increase or decrease the probability of a
response. A stimulus gains controlling properties by the pairing of
that stimulus with a behavior followed by reinforcement or punishment. If a stimulus is paired with a response and subsequent reinforcement, that stimulus becomes a discriminative stimulus, in the presence
of which the response is more likely to occur in the future. See "Discriminative Stimulus."

**Successive approximations.**   A series of steps or progressions, each in turn, coming closer to a goal performance. Units, ordered in a manner so that each comes closer to a goal than the previous unit. Shaping involves reinforcing successive approximations to a goal behavior.

**System.**   An arrangement of things serving a particular goal so that there is an orderly, consistent, unified, and coordinated relationship between those things. A system provides an orderly or organized form. A system also provides an orderly way of doing something or achieving a goal. A behavorial system involves an analysis and design of the relationships between the behaviors of different persons within an organization.

**Systematic method.**   A method of performing an operation that provides for order, consistency, unity of purpose, direction, and coordinated effort. A systematic method provides a view of a total operation that enables the viewer to see each part of an operation in relation to other parts and the whole.

**Tangible reinforcers.**   Physical or concrete reinforcers. Among these are food, toys, books, and money.

**Tasks.**   Tasks are behaviors required to achieve an objective. After identifying an objective, you must identify the tasks required to achieve that objective. If your objective is to own a home, you might have a specific task of depositing one hundred dollars in a savings account each month.

**Tension.**   A reaction to a stressful situation that is characterized by tightening or tenseness of muscles, increased heart beat, respiration, and perspiration and is often accompanied by headaches and other unpleasant physical conditions. Tension and anxiety are generally one reaction composed of several responses to either specific or generalized stimuli that are unpleasant or aversive. The opposite of relaxation.

**Thin out.**   A schedule of reinforcement is "thinned out" when the frequency or likelihood of reinforcement is reduced. If every other response is currently receiving reinforcement, this schedule may be thinned out to one in which every fourth response is reinforced. A schedule that provides reinforcement once a day may be "thinned out" to one that provides reinforcement twice a week. Behavior management programs are usually begun by using a continuous or nearly continuous schedule, and the reinforcement is gradually "thinned" in a manner so that the new rate is maintained.

**Time out ("time out from reinforcement").**  Removing an individual from a situation where reinforcement is available and placing him in a neutral (neither reinforcing nor punishing) environment. If used to decrease an undesirable behavior, the individual should be removed from the reinforcing situation, contingent upon his engaging in the undesirable behavior, and placed in a neutral situation. If the child's room is used as the "time out room," it could not contain any reinforcers (books, radio, TV, other individuals, etc.). After a short period of time, the individual is brought out of "time out," contigent upon his not engaging in any undesirable behavior.

**Time sampling.**  This recording technique is similar to time interval recording, but it does not require continuous observation. The observation time period is divided into equal intervals, but the behavior is recorded only during the selected segment of each interval. A thirty-minute interval is divided into ten three-minute intervals. The behavior recorded was Denise's attending behavior in a classroom. Behavior was recorded only at the *end* of each three-minute interval. At the end of each three-minute interval, the teacher looked at Denise and recorded whether the behavior was occurring at that instant.

| A | N | N | A | A | A | N | N | A | A |
|---|---|---|---|---|---|---|---|---|---|

30 minutes

A = attending behavior        N = nonattending behavior

The time-sampling techniques of recording allow the observer to engage in other activities while at the same time allowing for an accurate estimate of the prevalence or frequency of a behavior. In the example above, it can be seen that Denise was attending during six of the ten observations; that is, she was attending sixty percent of the time.

**Time utilization.**  The activity, behavior, or task completion that occurs within a given period of time. Time is a resource that is used (rather than managed, as is commonly stated). Time utilization, rate, and frequency as concepts are closely related.

**Time utilization survey.**  A procedure whereby an individual maintains a record of the activities that occur within intervals of time. This record is then compiled, by category, to provide a baseline of data that may be used to set objectives for time utilization and as the basis of a feedback system.

**Token economy system.** A program in which a number of behaviors are assigned point (or token) values, and points (or tokens) are delivered contingent upon the completion of those behaviors. The points or tokens may later be "cashed in" for a variety of reinforcers (items, objects, or activities). A list of these reinforcers and their respective values (called a "reinforcer menu") usually accompanies a token economy.

**Token reinforcer.** A physical reinforcer (such as a poker chip or a point or slip of paper) that may be exchanged at a later date for other reinforcers. Money is an example of a token reinforcer in our society.

**Variable schedules.** An intermittent schedule of reinforcement in which the delivery of reinforcement varies in a random manner, either over time or number of behavior, in a manner so that the person behaving cannot predict when reinforcement will occur. If reinforcement is delivered following a behavior once a day but the time of delivery varies and is unpredictable, this is a variable-interval (VI) schedule. If reinforcement occurs once for each ten or twenty behaviors but varies and is unpredictable, this is a variable-ratio (VR) schedule. All gambling, such as a slot machine, is based on VR schedules. Variable schedules produce constant behavior that are relatively resistant to extinction. See "Interval Schedules" and "Ratio Schedules."

# INDEX

# DATE DUE

| | | |
|---|---|---|
| MAR 2 5 1979 MAR 1 0 1999 | | |
| MAY 1 1979 | | |
| MAY 1 4 1979 APR 2 7 1999 | | |
| NOV 2 1979 | | |
| APR 2 2 '80 | | |
| MAY 9 '80 | | |
| NOV 23 '80 | | |
| AUG 19 '81 | | |
| AUG 27 '81 | | |
| DEC 15 '81 | | |
| NO 1 8 '85 | | |
| AP 6 '90 | | |
| MY 11 '90 | | |
| MY 13 '93 | | |
| MR 2 5 '95 | | |
| NO 6 '95 | | |
| NOV 2 6 1997 | | |